CONSTITUTIONAL RIGH..

South Africa and the United States

The South African Constitutional Court has issued internationally prominent decisions abolishing the death penalty, enforcing socioeconomic rights, allowing gay marriage, and promoting equality. These decisions are striking given the country's apartheid past and the absence of a grand human rights tradition. By contrast, the U.S. Supreme Court has generally ruled more conservatively on similar questions. This book examines the Constitutional Court in detail to determine how it has functioned during South Africa's transition and compares its rulings to those of the U.S. Supreme Court on similar rights issues. The book also analyzes the scholarly debate about the Constitutional Court taking place in South Africa. It furthermore addresses the arguments of those international scholars who have suggested that constitutional courts do not generally bring about social change. In the end, the book highlights a transformative pragmatic method of constitutional interpretation – a method the U.S. Supreme Court could employ.

Mark S. Kende is a Professor of Law, the James Madison Chair in Constitutional Law, and Director of the Drake Constitutional Law Center. Kende earned his BA cum laude with honors in philosophy from Yale University and his JD from the University of Chicago Law School, where he was a member of the Law Review. Before entering academia, he clerked for a federal judge and litigated employment, civil rights, and constitutional cases at a Chicago law firm, where he worked with Barack Obama. He has co-taught constitutional law classes with two current U.S. Supreme Court Justices.

Kende previously taught at Notre Dame Law School, the University of Montana School of Law, the Thomas M. Cooley Law School, and the University of Tennessee Law School. He was Teacher of the Year at Montana in 2002–2003. He has served as a Senior Fulbright Scholar and Visiting Professor of Law at the University of Stellenbosch in South Africa, as a Fulbright Senior Specialist in the former Soviet Republic of Moldova, and as a Visiting Professor at the University of Nantes, France. He has lectured or published scholarship in Canada, China, the Democratic Republic of the Congo (as a rule of law consultant), France (at the University of Paris I – Sorbonne), Germany, Spain, South Africa, the United Kingdom (at Oxford University), and throughout the United States. In 2003, he served as chair of the Association of American Law Schools Section on Africa. In 2008, he served as chair of its Section on Constitutional Law. He also co-directs a Law & Society Research Network on Africa.

Kende's writings have appeared in publications such as *Constitutional Commentary*, the *South African Law Journal*, the *Hastings Law Journal*, and the *Notre Dame Law Journal*. He is also the co-author of a casebook, *Theater Law*, and was one of the authors of *Courting the Yankees: Legal Essays on the Bronx Bombers*.

Constitutional Rights in Two Worlds

SOUTH AFRICA AND THE UNITED STATES

Mark S. Kende

Drake University

CAMBRIDGE UNIVERSITY PRESS

CAMBRIDGE UNIVERSITY PRESS
Cambridge, New York, Melbourne, Madrid, Cape Town, Singapore,
São Paulo, Delhi, Dubai, Tokyo, Mexico City

Cambridge University Press
32 Avenue of the Americas, New York, NY 10013-2473, USA

www.cambridge.org
Information on this title: www.cambridge.org/9780521171762

First published 2009
Reprinted 2009, 2010
First paperback edition 2010

A catalog record for this publication is available from the British Library.

Library of Congress Cataloging in Publication Data

Kende, Mark S., 1960–
Constitutional rights in two worlds : South Africa and the United States / Mark S. Kende.
p.   cm.
Includes bibliographical references and index.
ISBN 978-0-521-87904-0 (hardback)
1. Human rights – South Africa – Cases. 2. Constitutional law – South Africa – Cases.
3. Human rights – United States – Cases. 4. Constitutional law – United States – Cases.
5. South Africa. Constitutional Court. 6. United States. Supreme Court. I. Title.
K3239.53   2009
342.6808'5 – dc22   2008050028

ISBN 978-0-521-87904-0 hardback
ISBN 978-0-521-17176-2 Paperback

This book is dedicated to my father and mother, Andrew and Frances Kende, as well as to the memory of Allard Lowenstein.

Contents

Preface and Acknowledgments

On the vast continent of Africa, South Africa's post-Apartheid Constitutional Court, known for its innovative jurisprudence in the area of rights has emerged as the undisputed favorite of comparative constitutional scholars and social scientists as well as a lodestar for jurists across the globe.[*]

In February 2006, U.S. Supreme Court Justice Ruth Bader Ginsburg told an audience at the South African Constitutional Court in Pretoria that she and Justice Sandra Day O'Connor had received Internet death threats.[1] An Internet posting said they "will not live another week" because they relied on foreign law in their decisions. The American press missed the story initially.[2] Justice Ginsburg used her speech to explain why the U.S. Supreme Court should reference foreign materials. Her speech's title came from the Declaration of Independence: "A Decent Respect to the Opinions of [H]umankind." She had a sympathetic audience.

The South African Constitution requires the Constitutional Court to follow binding international law and specifies that the Court may examine relevant foreign law.[3] The Constitutional Court therefore frequently cites U.S. Supreme Court cases, though usually in disagreement. The U.S.

[*] H. Kwasi Prempeh, Review essay, "African Judges in Their Own Cause: Reconstituting Independent Courts in Contemporary Africa," 4 Int'l J. Con. L. 592–593 (2004).
[1] Justice Ruth Bader Ginsburg, "'A Decent Respect to the Opinions of [Human]kind": The Value of a Comparative Perspective in Constitutional Adjudication, Constitutional Court of South Africa, Feb. 7, 2006, http://www.supremecourtus.gov/publicinfo/speeches/sp_02-07b-06.html (last visited Jan. 25, 2008).
[2] Bill Mears, "Justice Ginsburg Details Death Threat," CNN.com, Mar. 15, 2006 http://www.cnn.com/2006/LAW/03/15/scotus.threat/index.html (last visited June 15, 2008) ("Ginsburg's remarks were made February 7 and posted almost unnoticed on the Supreme Court's Web site March 2. They first gained media attention after a Wednesday report on the Legal Times Web site.").
[3] S. Afr. Const. ch. 2, Sec. 39(1).

Supreme Court also has ties with its South African counterparts. Justice O'Connor authored the foreword to an autobiography by former Constitutional Court Justice Richard Goldstone, *For Humanity, Reflections of a War Crimes Investigator*. Furthermore, Justice Goldstone is friendly with U.S. Supreme Court Justice Anthony Kennedy.[4] Several South African Justices have taken sabbaticals at American law schools and have interacted with American Justices at international judicial conferences. Justice Ginsburg also has been one of America's leading legal advocates for women's rights, so she would have appreciated the South African judiciary's post-apartheid mandate to promote societal transformation.

In 2006, the Constitutional Court invited Justice Ginsburg to speak at its new building, located on the spot of a former prison. This was the only prison in the world to hold both Mahatma Ghandi and Nelson Mandela.[5] The Court's location symbolizes South Africa's new multiracial democracy. Indeed, the acclaimed Constitutional Court architects sought transparency and accessibility, distinguishing it from the impressive U.S. Supreme Court's marble palace to the law. Instead, glass and light predominate; marble and wood were not allowed.

While in South Africa, Justice Ginsburg gave two other speeches. One was titled "*Brown v. Board of Education* in International Context." The other was "Advocating the Elimination of Gender-Based Discrimination: The 1970s New Look at the Equality Principle." This was a more personal account of her efforts to implement gender equality.

The United States, however, is not so open to foreign law discussions, as the Internet threats show. Moreover, American congressional representatives introduced legislation advocating the impeachment of federal judges who employ foreign law.[6] In addition, Justices Stephen Breyer and Antonin Scalia engaged in an extraordinary debate at American University over reliance on foreign law in constitutional cases.[7] Since leaving the

---

[4] Jeffrey Toobin, "Swing Shift, How Anthony Kennedy's Passion for Foreign Law Could Change the Supreme Court," New Yorker, Sep. 12, 2005, http://www.newyorker.com/archive/2005/09/12/050912fa_fact (last visited June 15, 2008).

[5] Constitutional Court of South Africa, About the Court, The Building, http://www.constitutionalcourt.org.za/site/thecourt/the building.htm (last visited Jan. 25, 2008).

[6] The Constitution Restoration Act of 2004, H.R. 3799, 108th Cong. (2004); David J. Seipp, "Our Law, Their Law, History and the Citation of Foreign Law," 86 B.U. L. Rev. 1417, 1423 (2006); Tim Wu, "Foreign Exchange," Slate, April 9, 2004, http://www.slate.com/id/2098559/ (last visited June 15, 2008).

[7] Justices Antonin Scalia & Stephen Breyer, Discussion at the American University Washington College of Law: Constitutional Relevance of Foreign Court Decisions, Jan. 13, 2005, http://www.freerepublic.com/focus/f-news/1352357/posts (last visited June 15, 2008).

Supreme Court, Justice O'Connor has continued to support such reliance, as well as to lobby for the independence of the judiciary. One reason the foreign law issue was less controversial in South Africa is that the nation had little other human rights tradition on which to rely.

The goal of this book is to follow in Justice Ginsburg's internationalist footsteps by discussing the first fifteen years of the South African Constitutional Court's rights jurisprudence. The book compares these cases with U.S. Supreme Court decisions on the same issues. This comparison is overdue as the Supreme Court has not yet cited to a Constitutional Court opinion, despite the South African Court's international acclaim and the commonality of rights issues.

My personal interest in this topic has three sources. First, as a former civil rights attorney, I have been involved with and have focused on issues of racial discrimination and equality. Thus, I have long followed South Africa with its tragic history of apartheid. Second, I did a Fulbright Fellowship in South Africa during the year 2000 – four years into its "final" Constitution's dispensation. I learned about a nation undergoing dramatic legal and political change and discussed these changes with people who drafted the new Constitution, as well as with ordinary South Africans.

Third, after arriving in Cape Town for my fellowship, a driver took me from the airport to the University of Stellenbosch, one of the lovelier and more privileged parts of the country – at least for whites. This is South Africa's wine country – a bit like the Sonoma Valley in California. During the highway drive, however, we passed miles of shanty towns consisting of little more than tin shacks. Stellenbosch itself is surrounded by a poor township. This book therefore describes South Africa's efforts to create a judicial body to help transform the society so that such wide divisions eventually do not exist. I hope this book can do justice to the complexity and inspiration of this relatively new democracy.

I owe thanks to countless people for various forms of assistance regarding this project. The group includes fellow academic travelers, such as Penelope Andrews, Anel Boshoff, David Chambers, Juana Coetzee, Ruth Cowan, David Cruz, Pierre de Vos, Johan de Waal, Lourens du Plessis, John Eastman, Stephen Ellman, Paul Farlam, Melissa Harrison, Lisa Hilbink, Tom Huff, Robert Hunter, Saras Jagwanth, Jonathan Klaaren, Karl Klare, Heinz Klug, Frank Michelman, Keith Miller, Bronwen Morgan, Christina Murray, Andreas O'Shea, Phillip Prygoski, Brian Ray, Kim Lane Scheppele, Danielle Shelton, Geoffrey Stone, Cass Sunstein, André van der Walt, Karin van Marle, and Melissa Weresh – as well as the anonymous peer reviewers for Cambridge University Press, my former assistant, Amy Russell, and my current assistant, Lauren Bartusek. I owe a debt of gratitude to the deans who supported my work financially and otherwise, namely Edwin Eck, James Fourie, Patricia O'Hara, Ben Ullem, and David Walker, as well as numerous library staff, including Amanda Barratt, Phil Cousineau, John Edwards, Brian Fodrey, Stacey Gordon, Susan Lerdal, Shawn Madsen, Fritz Snyder, and Karen Wallace. I conducted research in the libraries at the University of Cape Town, Columbia Law School, Drake Law School, Harvard Law School, the University of Montana Law School, the University of Notre Dame Law School, the University of Stellenbosch, and the Thomas M. Cooley Law School. Commentators from the South Africa Reading Group as well as from the Research Unit for Legal and Constitutional Interpretation also helped shape my thoughts.

In addition, I must thank the busy Constitutional Court Justices – Laurie Ackermann, Edwin Cameron, Richard Goldstone, Kate O'Regan, and Albie Sachs – who responded to my questions. Then there are the law students who provided invaluable research assistance, such as MacKenzie Breitenstein, Karen Carr, David Dance, Deena Flemming, Mary Lindgren, Jennifer McCarville, Kendra Mills, Chase Rosario Naber, Benjamin Patterson, Todd Smith, Molly Spellman, Michelle Warnock, and Andrew Wilcox. I apologize in advance for leaving anyone out. I also could not have embarked on or completed this project without the support of the U.S. Fulbright Program, and the Council for the International Exchange of Scholars. Any mistakes or flaws in the book are mine alone.[8]

Lastly, several law journals have been kind enough to allow me to reprint parts of my earlier writings in original or revised forms. These journals, and their articles, are acknowledged below:

"Stereotypes in South African and American Constitutional Law: Achieving Gender Equality and Transformation," 10 S. Cal. Rev. Law and Women's Studies 3 (2000) (reprinted with permission at 117 S. Afr. L.J. 745 (2000)).

"The Fifth Anniversary of the South African Constitutional Court: In Defense of Judicial Pragmatism," 26 Vermont L. Rev. 753 (2002) (symposium issue).

---

[8] The Internet URL citations included herein are updated, but are obviously subject to change or removal by the Web site publishers themselves.

"The South African Constitutional Court's Embrace of Socio-Economic Rights: A Comparative Perspective," 6 Chapman L. Rev. 137 (2003) (symposium issue).

"The South African Constitutional Court's Construction of Socio-Economic Rights: A Response to Critics," 19 Conn. J. Int'l L. 617 (2004).

"The Constitutionality of the Death Penalty: South Africa as a Model for the United States," 38 G.W. Int'l L. Rev. 209 (2006).

Introduction

It is said in Africa that Western Culture has a 'big mouth and small ears.'

Patrick Glenn, Legal Traditions of the World 84 (2007)

For years, South Africa looked as if it would explode. The oppressed black majority and its allies were battling the powerful, wealthy, and racist apartheid regime on political and military fronts. In turn, apartheid security forces murdered heroic figures like Steven Biko and tried to assassinate Constitutional Court Justice Albie Sachs, blowing off one of his arms with a car bomb in Mozambique. South Africa's relatively peaceful transition to a multiracial democracy during the 1990s was therefore miraculous, especially compared to the civil wars that have broken out in other nations.[1]

Historians, political scientists, and others offer explanations for why this peaceful transition occurred. Nobel Peace Prize winners Nelson Mandela and Desmond Tutu provided crucial leadership. International political and economic pressure played a role as did global developments such as the end of the Cold War.[2] Most important, many South Africans took to the streets at great personal risk.[3] Despite the country's AIDS pandemic,[4] the massive gap between rich and poor that has

---

[1] *See generally* Patti Waldmeir, Anatomy of a Miracle (1997).

[2] Heinz Klug, Constituting Democracy: Law, Globalism, and South Africa's Political Reconstruction 52–61 (2000).

[3] *Id.* at 81.

[4] UNAIDS, 2006 Report on the Global AIDS Epidemic, Annex 2 (5.5 million South Africans have AIDS including 18.8% of those between ages 18–49), http://data.unaids. org/pub/GlobalReport/2006/2006_GR_ANN2_en.pdf (last visited Nov. 19, 2007). In 2007, UNAIDS admitted their statistics had been overstating the problem. Donald G. McNeil Jr., "A Time to Rethink AIDS Grip," N.Y. Times, Week in Review (Nov.

helped produce terrible crime,[5] and political domination by one party,[6] South Africa now has a vibrant economy,[7] a relatively strong infrastructure,[8] and a critical press which enhance the prospects for social stability.[9]

Numerous scholars have chronicled South Africa's constitutional revision process.[10] As of 1983, the country had a bizarre tricameral system with parliamentary chambers for whites, coloured people, and Indians, but not blacks.[11] Moreover, the government had established artificial black homelands in destitute regions.[12] By contrast, South Africa now has a democratically elected bicameral parliament and a new Constitutional Court that authoritatively interprets the Bill of Rights. It also has a rational provincial system.

25, 2007) http://www.nytimes.com/2007/11/25/weekinreview/25mcneil.html?_r=1& ref=weekinreview&oref=slogin (last visited Nov. 27, 2007). There is no doubt, however, that South Africa's situation in this area is dire.

[5] The United Nations and other international organizations use the gini coefficient as a statistical measure of the gap between the rich and poor in a nation. The South African divide is the second largest in the world next to Brazil. Jerome A. Singh, Michelle Govender, Nilam Reddy, "South Africa a Decade after Apartheid: Realizing Health through Human Rights," 12 Geo. J. on Pov. L. & Pol'y 355, 358 (2005). For adiscussion of the South African crime problem and its link to factors such as the wealth gap, *see generally* Diana Gordon, Transformation and Trouble: Crime, Justice, and Democratic Participation in South Africa (2007).

[6] *See generally,* Roger Southall, (Ed)., Opposition and Democracy in South Africa (2001); Michael Wines, "Dark Turns of Party Struggle Enthrall South Africa," N.Y. Times A4 (Oct. 12, 2007).

[7] Sharon LaFraniere, "World Bank Reports Progress in Sub-Saharan Africa," N.Y. Times A3 (Nov. 15, 2007) ("South Africa is ranked among the top third of the best nations in which to do business" in the world, and is part of a region that has a growth rate above many developed countries.).

[8] CIA, The World Fact Book: South Africa, Economy: overview (Nov. 15, 2007) (South Africa has "a modern infrastructure supporting an efficient distribution of goods to major urban centers throughout the region.") http://www.cia.gov/library /publications/the-world-factbook/geos/sf.html (last visited Nov. 19, 2007).

[9] U.S. Department of State, 2006 Country Reports on Human Rights Practices – Africa, South Africa, Sec. 2A., Respect for Civil Liberties, Freedom of Speech and Press (March 6, 2007) ("The constitution and law provide for freedom of speech and of the press, and the government generally respected these rights. Several apartheid era laws that remained in force posed a potential threat to media independence. Individuals criticized the government both publicly and privately without reprisal. The independent media were active and expressed a wide variety of views, although some journalists expressed concern that the government heavily influenced the media.") http://www.state.gov/g/drl/rls/hrrpt/2006/78758.htm (last visited Nov. 19, 2007).

[10] *See e.g.* Lourens du Plessis, Hugh Corder, Understanding South Africa's Transitional Bill of Rights (1994); Hassan Ebrahim, The Soul of a Nation (1998).

[11] Ebrahim, *id.* at 18.   [12] Klug, *supra* n. 2 at 40.

This book examines a crucial aspect of the South African transition: the Constitutional Court's role in social change. The Court has enforced socioeconomic rights,[13] supported gay marriage,[14] and struck down the death penalty.[15] How did the Court address these significant issues without much domestic human rights case law on which to draw?[16]

Certainly, President Nelson Mandela's adherence to the Court's adverse decisions against his government enhanced the Court's authority and the rule of law.[17] Moreover, the Court's Justices have been impressive. They include apartheid opponents, human rights advocates, leading academics, and individuals of different races, genders, and sexual orientations, all with an acute political sensibility. The Court has also gradually become more representative of the population, which is another crucial aspect of transformation.[18] The drafters of the Constitution's judicial selection process deserve credit here. But a comparative perspective can illuminate the Court's rulings.

[13] Republic of South Africa v. Grootboom, 2001 (1) SA 46 (CC)(Court orders national government to develop a policy to help the homeless). *See* Rosalind Dixon, "Creating Dialogue about Socio-Economic Rights: Strong-Form versus Weak-Form Judicial Review Revisited," 5 Int'l J. of Const. L. 391 (2007) (Grootboom "is one of the most important examples of the judicial enforcement of socio-economic rights known to comparative constitutional lawyers.").

[14] Minister of Home Affairs v. Fourie, 2006 (1) SA 524 (CC).

[15] State v. Makwanyane, 1995 (3) SA 391 (CC).

[16] John Dugard wrote that apartheid's "parliamentary sovereignty and . . . primitive positivist outlook have combined to produce a system of law with no constitutional safeguards for individual liberty and a legal profession with neither the power nor, perhaps, the will to resist invasions of the most basic human freedoms." John Dugard, Human Rights and the South African Legal Order xii (1977). *See also* Albie Sachs, "A Bill of Rights for South Africa: Areas of Agrement and Disagreement," 21 Colum. Hum. Rts. L. Rev. 13, 14 (1989) ("South Africa has had anti-slavery agitation and the struggle for a free press as far back as the 1820's, the emerging movement for African rights of the 1880's, the campaigns over the treatment of Boer women and children in concentration camps . . . the feminist movement shortly after that..trade union struggles."); Arthur Chaskalson, "Equality and Dignity," 5 Green Bag 2d 189, 191 (2002) ("There was a continuing tension between what might often have been equitable values of the common law and the grossly inequitable values of the Apartheid laws."). One prominent South African scholar has described the Constitutional Court's job as building a bridge from a culture of authority to a culture of justification. Etienne Mureinik, "A Bridge to Where?: Introducing the Interim Bill of Rights," 10 S. Afr. J. Hum. Rts. 32 (1994).

[17] Klug, *supra* n. 2 at 150 (quoting President Mandela).

[18] Jackie Dugard, Theunis Roux, "The Record of the South African Constitutional Court," in Robert Gargarella, et al., (Eds.), Courts and Social Transformation in New Democracies 108 (2006) ("The racial composition of the Court itself has changed over the last ten years, from the position in 1994 when seven of the judges were white and four black, to the position today in which that ratio has been reversed.").

THE COMPARATIVE ANGLE

To evaluate South Africa's jurisprudence, this book analyzes Constitutional Court rights decisions and compares them with U.S. Supreme Court rulings on similar issues. This comparison should clarify the assumptions underlying the decisions of each Court and its different ways of approaching issues. This comparative approach is consistent with constitutional discourse's increasingly transnational nature, which has been brought about by globalization, democratization, the Internet, and even social networking.[19] The book focuses more on South Africa because the U.S. Supreme Court has been the centerpiece of so much academic attention.

There are other reasons why the juxtaposition of South Africa and the U.S. high courts makes sense. Both nations grew out of revolutions that rejected tyranny, and both high courts are seminal institutions. The U.S. Supreme Court interprets the oldest written constitution in the world – the model for all that followed. Its framers relied on the latest jurisprudential, philosophical, and political thought from both eighteenth-century Europe and the ancients.[20] Though relatively new, the South African charter has been called "the most admirable constitution in the history of the world" by Cass Sunstein, a leading law professor[21] Indeed, the South African Constitution's framers surveyed the world's constitutions for the best ideas.[22]

In addition, the United States and South Africa share a history of institutionalized racism and a struggle "to overcome," and each is now racially diverse.[23] Moreover, the United States is the world's military and

---

[19] *See generally*, Anne Marie Slaughter, A New World Order (2004).

[20] Melvin Urofsky and Paul Finkelman, A March of Liberty, Vol. I, 45 ("Colonial Constitutional Thought") (2002).

[21] Designing Democracy, What Constitutions Do 261 (2001).

[22] Jeremy Sarkin, "The Effect of Constitutional Borrowings on the Drafting of South Africa's Bill of Rights and Interpretation of Human Rights Provisions," 1 U. Pa. J. Const. L. 176, 181 (1998). Sarkin explains that the framers relied heavily on Canadian and German constitutional developments, as well as international human rights principles.

[23] Several distinguished commentators have compared the history of the two legal systems and societies regarding racial and other issues. *See e.g.* A. Leon Higginbotham, Jr., "Racism in American and South African Courts: Similarities and Differences," 65 N.Y.U. L. Rev. 479, 497 (1990); George M. Frederickson, Black Liberation: A Comparative of History of Black Ideologies in the United States and South Africa (1996); George M. Frederickson, White Supremacy: A Comparative Study in American and South African History 136–198 (1981).

economic superpower whereas South Africa is a regional superpower, perhaps only rivaled by Nigeria.[24] The legal systems of both nations are historically tied to England and their judicial opinions are written in English. In addition, both nations had "precursor" constitutions albeit written under different circumstances.[25] Furthermore, some of the key political figures in these nations initially opposed the creation of a Bill of Rights.[26]

There are, of course, major differences between the two countries. A diverse group of elected representatives wrote the South African Constitution during an era of unprecedented globalization and the spreading of democracy. The underlying legal system is a Roman-Dutch-English hybrid of civil code and common law.[27] Moreover, South Africa is a developing country, in the Southern hemisphere, which calls itself the "rainbow nation" to express its adherence to multiculturalism.[28] Blacks have always been a majority of the population but until recently were oppressed and treated like an inferior minority.[29]

The American Constitution was written by unelected and propertied white British men. The nineteenth-century Civil War constitutional amendments were progressive but the Supreme Court restricted their impact almost immediately.[30] The underlying legal system is based on English common law. The United States is an industrialized "first world" nation with a large and diverse middle class. Moreover, multiculturalism is controversial,[31] and African Americans remain a disadvantaged minority though their situation has improved from the days of slavery and Jim Crow.

[24] *Supra* n. 7 ("South Africa and Nigeria, the continent's leading oil producer, accounted for more than half of sub-Saharan Africa's domestic product.").

[25] As discussed in Chapter 2, the Articles of Confederation came before the U.S. Constitution, and the South African Interim Constitution came before the "Final" Constitution.

[26] As discussed in Chapter 2, Alexander Hamilton and James Madison initially opposed a Bill of Rights. Moreover, the African National Congress leadership had to be convinced of its importance as well.

[27] Dugard, *supra* n. 16.

[28] Eric Berger, "The Right to Education under the South African Constitution," 103 Colum. L. Rev. 614, 657 (2003).

[29] Fredrickson, *supra* n. 23, *Black Liberation* at 6.

[30] *See e.g.* The Slaughterhouse Cases, 83 U.S. 36 (1873) (limiting the scope of the Fourteenth Amendment Privileges & Immunities Clause); The Civil Rights Cases, 109 U.S. 3 (1883) (limiting the Civil War Amendments to prohibiting state action, not private action).

[31] *See e.g.* Allan Bloom, The Closing of the American Mind (1987) (deploring the influence of politically correct multiculturalism on our educational system).

These differences in social context do not undermine the project, but must be kept in mind as law does not exist in a vacuum.[32] The prominent former American jurist A. Leon Higginbotham and the American scholar George Fredrickson have written valuable comparisons of the racial histories of these two nations while issuing similar cautions.[33]

TWO CONSTITUTIONS

The U.S. Constitution was revolutionary because it made the people sovereign. It set up a presidential republic with many democratic qualities. The Bill of Rights gave people basic political and civil rights such as freedom of expression and freedom of religion. The Civil War amendments provided for equal protection. These "first-generation" rights are considered "negative" as they typically prohibit the government from interfering with individuals.

More than two hundred years later, South Africa enacted a lengthier and more detailed constitution that is designed to be socially transformative.[34] It has a Bill of Rights that includes not just first-generation rights but also second and third-generation rights. It guarantees human dignity, which is not specifically mentioned in the American Constitution. The South African equality provision goes beyond the American one by prohibiting discrimination based on sexual orientation and authorizing affirmative action. The South African Bill of Rights also protects the right to unionize and diverse rights for children.

The second-generation socioeconomic provisions cover housing, health care, the right to an education, and the like. These "positive" rights require the government to provide resources that enable those rights to be fulfilled. As discussed later, however, the distinction between negative

---

[32] *See* Ran Hirschl, "Constitutionalism, Judicial Review and Progressive Change: A Rejoinder to McClain and Fleming," 84 Tex. L. Rev. 471, 504 (2004) (criticizing the "emerging 'armchair' anthropology style study of comparative constitutional law" where the scholar really is not embedded in studying the comparative society outside of knowing about a few interesting legal cases). Ironically, as discussed later in this book, Hirschl himself may be guilty of this approach in his important book's discussions of South Africa. Ran Hirschl, Towards Juristocracy (2004).

[33] *Supra* n. 23. *See also* Ronald W. Walters, The Price of Reconciliation (2008) (comparing American and South African racial reconciliation and reparations narratives).

[34] Chief Justice Pius Langa, "Transformative Constitutionalism," Prestige Lecture delivered at Stellenbosch University on 9 October 2006, http://law.sun.ac.za/LangaSpeech. pdf (last visited June 15, 2008); Deputy Chief Justice Dikgang Moseneke, "The Fourth Bram Fischer Memorial Lecture: Transformative Adjudication," 18 S. Afr. J. Hum. Rts. 309 (2002).

and positive rights breaks down because the government expends funds for negative rights, and positive rights have negative dimensions. The right to a clean environment and the cultural membership rights are third-generation solidarity rights. The South African Constitution also provides for eleven official languages, though English is the most commonly used for business and other official transactions. In addition, the Bill of Rights outlaws violations by private actors, not just the government.

Another important issue addressed differently by the two Constitutions is property. Because the South African government and whites used apartheid to steal the land of many blacks and others, its Constitution governs land redistribution. In contrast, the U.S. Constitution's property provision authorizes government expropriation in certain instances but not for wealth redistribution.

To assist with its implementation, the South African Constitution established several government agencies including a Human Rights Commission and a Commission on Gender Equality. It also established a Truth & Reconciliation Commission that was supposed to facilitate national healing. There are no similar government agencies to guide the implementation of the U.S. Constitution.

In sum, the South African Constitution looks somewhat like the charter that American liberals thought the U.S. Supreme Court was going to create out of cases like *Brown v. Board of Education*[35] and other decisions in the 1960s and early 1970s favoring civil rights plaintiffs, criminal defendants, and the poor.[36] Scholars such as Frank Michelman were writing about the right to welfare and finding sympathetic ears.[37] The U.S. Supreme Court, however, backtracked for reasons that Cass Sunstein,[38] Gregory Alexander,[39] and Gerald Rosenberg[40] dispute.

---

[35] 347 U.S. 483 (1954).

[36] Goldberg v. Kelly, 397 U.S. 254 (1970) (government cannot terminate welfare benefits without a hearing); Douglas v. California, 372 U.S. 353 (1963) (appellate court must provide counsel to impoverished criminal defendant).

[37] Frank Michelman, "On Protecting the Poor through the Fourteenth Amendment," 83 Harv. L. Rev. 705 (1969).

[38] Cass Sunstein, The Second Bill of Rights: FDR's Unfinished Revolution and Why We Need it More than Ever 163 (2004) (arguing that changes in the Court's membership caused it to backtrack).

[39] Gregory Alexander, "Socio-Economic Rights in American Perspective: The Tradition of Anti-Paternalism in American Constitutional Thought," in A. J. van der Walt, (Ed.), Theories of Economic and Social Justice 6 (2005) (rejecting Sunstein's view and arguing that anti-paternalist traditions explain the Court's unwillingness to find socioeconomic rights).

[40] The Hollow Hope (1991) (arguing the Court will not take any radical actions to alter existing distributions of power and wealth).

THE TWO COURTS

Constitutions are pieces of paper. The judiciary usually gives them life. This book reveals important distinctions between the jurisprudence of the South African Constitutional Court and the U.S. Supreme Court.

First, the U.S. Constitution provides no interpretive directions. This partly explains why the U.S. Supreme Court is divided between "liberals" who suggest they favor a "living constitution" and conservatives who say they believe in "originalism."[41] A living constitution evolves over time to accommodate changes in society, people's values, and other developments.[42] Originalists supposedly interpret the Constitution in accord with its meaning when adopted.[43]

Section 39 of the South African Constitution reads as follows:

(1) When interpreting the Bill of Rights, a court, tribunal or forum –
   (a) must promote the values that underlie an open and democratic society based on human dignity, equality, and freedom;
   (b) must consider international law; and
   (c) may consider foreign law.

The Constitutional Court must therefore follow a progressive agenda, which includes relying on foreign law, unlike the U.S. Supreme Court.[44]

---

[41] Some scholars have argued that there are also divides within the conservative quarters. Mark Tushnet, A Court Divided, The Rehnquist Court and The Future of Constitutional Law (2005).

[42] As former U.S. Supreme Court Justice William Brennan said, "The genius of the Constitution rests not in any static meaning it might have had in a world that is dead and gone, but in the adaptability of its great principles to cope with current problems and current needs." William J. Brennan Jr., "The Constitution of the United States: Contemporary Ratification," in Alpheus Thomas Mason & Donald Grier Stephenson Jr. (Eds.), American Constitutional Law: Introductory Essays and Selected Cases 607, 609 (8th ed. 1987).

[43] Steven G. Calabresi (Ed.), Originalism: A Quarter-Century Debate (2007); Randy Barnett, Restoring the Lost Constitution: The Presumption of Liberty (2005); Dennis Goldford, The American Constitution and the Debate over Originalism (2005).

[44] See e.g. Roper v. Simmons, 543 U.S. 551 (2005) (outlawing death penalty for juveniles); Lawrence v. Texas, 539 U.S. 558 (2003). Justice Scalia dissents from the use of foreign law in these cases as do some scholars. See e.g. Robert DelaHunty, John Yoo, "Against Foreign Law," 29 Harv. J. L. & Pub. Pol'y 291 (2005). See generally Justices Antonin Scalia & Stephen Breyer, Discussion at the American University Washington College of Law: Constitutional Relevance of Foreign Court Decisions (Jan. 13, 2005), http://www.freerepublic.com/focus/f-news/1352357/posts (last visited June 15, 2008).

Second, the Constitutional Court takes a more communitarian and dignity-oriented approach unlike the individualistic and liberty-oriented U.S. Supreme Court. For example, the Constitutional Court recently ruled that a school could not prevent a female student from wearing a nose-stud. Doing so would violate her cultural and religious heritage. In his ruling, Chief Justice Pius Langa wrote,

> The notion that "we are not islands unto ourselves" is central to the understanding of the individual in African thought. It is often expressed in the phrase *umuntu ngumuntu ngabantu* which emphasizes "communality and the inter-dependence of the members of a community" and that every individual is an extention of others.... This thinking emphasizes the importance of community to individual identity and hence to human dignity.[45]

Third, the Constitutional Court embraces "substantive equality" as opposed to the U.S. Supreme Court's "formal equality."[46] Laws that benefit historically disadvantaged groups are generally permitted in South Africa because they facilitate societal transformation. In contrast, the U.S. Supreme Court presumes that all people should be treated the same. There is some tension, though, between substantive equality and the South African ideal of reconciliation, which this book discusses.[47]

Fourth, the Constitutional Court has rejected the American view that fundamental rights trump all other concerns. Instead, the South African

---

[45] Kwa Zulu Natal MEC v. Pillay, Par. 53, CCT 51/06 (Oct. 5, 2007). As referenced in the Preface, even the Constitutional Court's new building embodies this ethos. It was born of a "remarkable and uniquely inclusive process – one that resulted in a public building like no other. This structure, South Africa's first major post-apartheid government building, was designed to embody the openness and transparency called for by the Constitution itself.... The building is noted for its transparency and entrancing volumes. In contrast to most courts, it is welcoming rather than forbidding, filled with sparkle and warmth. It has no marble cladding or wood panelling, but has come to be admired for its graceful proportions. And the principal materials – timber, concrete, steel, glass and black slate – infuse the court with an African feel." http://www.constitutionalcourt.org.za/site/thecourt/thebuilding/htm (last visited Nov. 21, 2007). By contrast, the U.S. Supreme Court has sixteen corinthian marble columns holding up an imposing edifice that approaches four stories in height. National Park Service, The U.S. Constitution, Supreme Court Building, Description, Aug. 30, 2000 http://www.nps.gov/history/history/online_books/butowsky2/constitution9.htm (last visited Nov. 21, 2007).

[46] Ian Currie & Johan de Waal, The Bill of Rights Handbook 232 (2005).

[47] This tension is ironic as the Truth & Reconciliation Commission was supposed to provide reparations to those who were victimized during apartheid, suggesting the compatibility of reconciliation with reparations. Yet. even in the TRC context, there has been little reparations in return for the reconciliation, as discussed in Chapter 2.

Court weighs a variety of factors, including the state's interests, in determining whether a rights infringement can be justified. This context-sensitive approach differs from the U.S. Supreme Court's more categorical analysis.[48]

Fifth, despite its transformative mission, the Constitutional Court has pragmatically refused to decide certain issues. Justice Albie Sachs once told me this approach was "minimalist maximalism." For example, in *Case v. Minister of Safety*,[49] the Court avoided deciding the criteria for obscenity. Moreover, in *Christian Education South Africa v. Minister of Education*,[50] the Court would not address the underlying religious issue in a case about the government restricting a Christian school's ability to use corporal punishment. By contrast, the U.S. Supreme Court has taken varying approaches regarding the scope of its rulings.

What explains the Constitutional Court's general cautiousness? Justice Richard Goldstone told me the following in an interview: "I . . . strongly believe that in the formative years it would be a serious mistake to craft wider opinions than necessary. It is far better to hasten slowly and be more certain of building a coherent jurisdiction. I have no doubt that principles should be clear but that is another matter."[51] This view reveals pragmatic concerns about institutional integrity as well as doctrine.

SOCIAL CHANGE

One of this book's major themes is what role can and should the Constitutional Court play in social change. The comparative dimension is valuable in illuminating that theme as well.

American conservatives have long criticized the U.S. Supreme Court as being activist and undemocratic.[52] Yet, many American progressives also criticize the Court, either for being ineffectual or for creating a backlash against social change. This progressive view is exemplified by

---

[48] One Canadian scholar, active in the South African constitutional deliberations, wrote a book arguing that constitutional law is fundamentally about the weighing of interests. David Beatty, The Ultimate Rule of Law (2005). Several non-American scholars, however, have recently criticized such balancing. *See e.g.* Denise Meyerson, "Why Courts Should Not Balance Rights against the Public Interest," 31 Melbourne L. Rev. 801 (2007).

[49] 1996 (3) SA 617 (CC).   [50] 2002 (2) SA 794 (CC).

[51] Mark S. Kende, "The Fifth Anniversary of the South African Constitutional Court: In Defense of Judicial Pragmatism," 26 Vermont L. Rev. 753, 761 (2002).

[52] Robert H. Bork, Coercing Virtue: The Worldwide Rule of Judges (2003).

Gerald Rosenberg's "hollow hope,"[53] Larry Kramer's judicial review skepticism,[54] Derrick Bell's rejection of desegregation,[55] Mark Tushnet's "thin Constitution,"[56] and Cass Sunstein's minimalism.[57] There are progressive exceptions who are supportive of the Court, such as Ronald Dworkin,[58] Owen Fiss,[59] James Fleming,[60] Sotirios Barber,[61] and the late Charles Black,[62] but they may be a minority.

Ran Hirschl's book *Towards Juristocracy*, which examines the courts of several countries, including South Africa, argues that "hegemonic elites" have designed new constitutional courts to serve their group's political and economic interests.[63] Boaventura de Sousa Santos argues that globalization and the international human rights movement generally bolster the elites.[64]

Yet, South African scholars like Dennis Davis,[65] Alfred Cockrell,[66] Cathy Albertyn,[67] and others write that the Court should be bolder and avoid a hazy minimalist "rainbow jurisprudence"[68] This view is startling

---

[53] Gerald Rosenberg, The Hollow Hope (1991).

[54] Larry Kramer, The People Themselves: Popular Constitutionalism and Judicial Review (2004).

[55] Derrick Bell, Faces at the Bottom of the Well: The Permanence of Racism (1992).

[56] Mark Tushnet, Taking the Constitution Away from the Courts (1999). *But see* Brian Flanagan, "Judicial Rights Talk: Defects in the Liberal Challenge to Judicial Review," 22 S. Afr. J. Hum. Rts. 173 (2006).

[57] Cass Sunstein, One Case at a Time (1999).

[58] Ronald Dworkin, Taking Rights Seriously (1977).

[59] Owen Fiss, The Law as It Could Be (2003).

[60] James Fleming, Securing Constitutional Democracy: The Case of Autonomy (2006).

[61] Sotirios Barber, Welfare and the Constitution (2003).

[62] Charles Black, The New Birth of Freedom (1997).

[63] Ran Hirschl, Towards Juristocracy (2004).

[64] *See generally*, Boaventura de Sousa Santos & Cesar A. Rodriguez Garavito (Eds)., Law and Globalization from Below: Towards a Cosmopolitan Legality (2005).

[65] Dennis Davis, Democracy and Deliberation (1999).

[66] "Rainbow Jurisprudence," 12 S. Afr. J. Hum. Rts. 1 (1996).

[67] "Facing the Challenges of Transformation, "14 S. Afr. J. Hum. Rts. 248 (1998).

[68] *Supra* n. 66. *See e.g.* Patrick Lenta, "Rainbow Rhetoric," in Max du Plessis & Stephen Pate (Eds.), Constitutional Democracy in South Africa 1994–2004, 15 (2004). This criticism is especially intriguing because there is general agreement that the Court's death penalty and gay marriage decisions are opposed by a majority of South Africans. *See e.g.* Dennis Davis, "Has South Africa Become a Juristocracy? Or Who Runs the Country?" Paper, Harold Wolpe Memorial Trust's 54th open dialogue, Oct. 19, 2006, http://www.wolpetrust.org.za/dialogue2006/CT102006davis_paper.pdf (last visited Nov. 3, 2007). ("Listen to any talk radio programme and you will hear complaints about the Constitution, ranging from the unconstitutionality of the death penalty to the recognition of gay marriage. The essence of the complaint is that majority opinion is against these constitutional provisions as interpreted by the Constitutional Court.

given the Court's novel decisions on socioeconomic rights, gay marriage, and the death penalty. Of course, South African progressivism ranges from those with a more individualist sensibility to those with a more African communal approach.[69] But most South African legal academics advocate greater judicial activism – against the view of Hirschl – who advocates less. This book assesses which view about courts and social change is correct, especially for South Africa.

CONTENTS OF THIS BOOK

This section describes the book's contents. Chapter 2 examines South Africa's history and constitution drafting process, as well as the American analogue. The chapter then compares their highest courts in areas such as the selection of Justices, jurisdiction, and the power of judicial review. The chapter further discusses several unique South African Constitution provisions and two Constitutional Court cases for which there is no Supreme Court equivalent.

Chapter 3 compares death penalty decisions made by the two courts. The Constitutional Court found capital punishment to be cruel and inhumane in one of its earliest cases; in contrast, the U.S. Supreme Court has rejected numerous death penalty challenges.[70] Recently, however, American public support for executions has declined, presumably because of exonerations of innocent death row prisoners, grotesque execution methods, and the exorbitant costs of legal representation.[71] Thus, this chapter argues that the U.S. Supreme Court may eventually outlaw capital punishment.

Chapter 4 compares gender discrimination cases. For example, the Constitutional Court upheld President Mandela's selective pardon of nonviolent female prisoners with children under age twelve.[72] The Court

---

Hence it is undemocratic to prevent majority opinion from being implemented."). *See also* Erin Goodsell, Note, "Constitution, Custom, and Creed: Balancing Human Rights Concerns with Cultural and Religious Freedom in South Africa," 21 B.Y.U. J. Pub. L. 109 (2007) (describing public opinion polls on these issues).

[69] Jonathan Klaaren, A Remedial Interpretation of the Treatment Action Campaign Decision, 19 S. Afr. J. Hum. Rts. 455, 456-7 (2003) ("The understandings of the Constitution's transformative potential range from the classically liberal . . . to the social and more radically democratic.")

[70] *See e.g.* Gregg v. Georgia, 428 U.S. 153 (1976).

[71] *See generally,* Stuart Taylor, "The Death Penalty: Slowly Fading?," National Journal, Nov. 19, 2007, http://nationaljournal.com/taylor.htm (last visited Nov. 21, 2007).

[72] President of South Africa v. Hugo, 1997 (4) SA 1 (CC).

decided that the apartheid regime oppressed women and that releasing numerous male prisoners would terrify the public, given the crime rate. This decision reflects the Court's emphasis on substantive equality and pragmatism. A dissent responded that the state needed stronger justifications for treating men differently.

The chapter also examines whether a South African law criminalizing prostitution is biased against women if the law does not make the mostly male clients liable.[73] The American court system would not give such an argument the time of day. Interestingly, Sweden generally prosecutes the patrons, not the prostitute, and has apparently succeeded in reducing prostitution activity compared to nearby countries like Finland.[74]

Chapter 5 looks at the Constitutional Court's rulings favoring gay plaintiffs, including the legalization of gay marriage. The Court has been bolder here than in the racial discrimination area. Perhaps the Court sees gay rights cases as lacking the possible zero-sum qualities of affirmative action or gender cases. Blacks and women are also majorities in South Africa, whereas gay people are an oppressed minority. Admittedly, the U.S. Supreme Court now shows some sensitivity to gay people, though this chapter discusses the confused nature of its decisions, as well as leading lower court decisions on gay marriage.

Chapter 6 focuses on remedies for racial discrimination, especially affirmative action, which is permitted by section 9(2) of the South African Constitution. Nonetheless, South African courts approach such cases with surprising caution despite the nation's history and the textual support for remedying discrimination. Undoubtedly, the Court does not want to undermine reconciliation by treating formerly dominant groups with unnecessary harshness. By contrast, the U.S. Supreme Court has ruled strongly against affirmative action, but has tolerated it in limited circumstances.[75] Interestingly, America's racist history suggests that the U.S. Supreme Court could have embraced affirmative action more eagerly.

Chapter 7 examines freedom of expression, an area in which there are few South African cases. Thus, this chapter focuses on the U.S. Supreme Court. The South African Constitution generally treats dignity as a higher

---

[73] Jordan v. State, 2002 (6) SA 642 (CC).

[74] Emily Bazelon, "Why is Prostitution Illegal," Slate (Mar. 10, 2008), http://www.slate .com/id/2186243 (last visited April 2, 2008); Nikolas D. Kristof, "Do As Spitzer Said", Int'l Herald Tribune (Mar. 13, 2008), http://www.iht.com/articles/2008/03/13 /opinion/edkristof.php (last visited April 2, 2008).

[75] Grutter v. Bollinger, 539 U.S. 306 (2003).

value than free speech.[76] This European and Canadian perspective comes through in hate speech, pornography, and defamation cases.[77]

Chapter 8 addresses freedom of religion. Here, the Constitutional Court has not played a transformative role, as it has usually ruled against religious minorities. The recent case involving a young girl wearing a nose-stud may signal a change.[78] Interestingly, religious values and principles underlie the Constitutional Court and the South African Constitution's emphasis on reconciliation. Archbishop Desmond Tutu, for example, helped originate the Truth & Reconciliation Commission.[79]

Chapter 9 shows how the Constitutional Court has actually enforced socioeconomic rights. For example, it required the national government to aid the homeless in one case, and to distribute a drug that prevents AIDS-infected pregnant women from transmitting the virus to their fetus in another.[80] The Court, however, does not recognize an individual's right to demand immediate benefits from the government, and refuses to submit to recommended international "minimum core" standards.

Many South African academics criticize the Court for not endorsing the minimum core and, therefore, for not giving substance to second-generation rights.[81] Supposedly, this failure to endorse these standards has allowed the government to evade their implementation. Chapter 9 explains why these critics are generally mistaken. The chapter also highlights the U.S. Supreme Court's incorrect assumptions about such rights.

Chapter 10 summarizes what the Constitutional Court has achieved over the last fifteen years and what other courts can learn from it. It concludes that the Court does best when it employs *African transformative pragmatism* as an interpretive approach. Moreover, the chapter argues that Ran Hirschl's contention, that the South African Constitutional Court serves the elite, is largely incorrect. Finally, the chapter responds to some recent scholarly critiques of those courts, that weigh

---

[76] Thus, section 16(2)(c) of the South African Constitution outlaws racist speech designed to incite harm. This would likely be protected by the U.S. Supreme Court. R.A.V. v. City of St. Paul, 505 U.S. 377 (1992).

[77] *See generally,* Kent Greenawalt, Fighting Words (1996).

[78] *Supra* n. 45.

[79] Desmond Tutu, No Future without Forgiveness (1999).

[80] Minister of Health v. Treatment Action Campaign (2) 2002 (5) SA 721 (CC).

[81] David Bilchitz, Poverty and Fundamenal Rights: The Justification and Enforcement of Socio-Economic Rights (2007).

competing interests (government interests vs. the rights of the claimants) to decide cases. This balancing is frequently referred to as proportionality analysis.

This book quotes frequently from South African decisions and scholars so the reader can get a firsthand feeling for the Constitutional Court and the academy there. The book, however, does not discuss many structural issues (such as separation of powers) nor criminal procedure questions, and it devotes limited attention to South African customary law because of the very many fascinating substantive rights topics. One of my conclusions is that the U.S. Supreme Court could have a rights jurisprudence resembling that of the South African Constitutional Court, but for a surprisingly small number of key decisions that went the opposite way.

2

History and Background

I came here because of my deep interest and affection for a land settled by the Dutch in the mid-seventeenth century, then taken over by the British, and at last independent; a land in which the native inhabitants were at first subdued, but relations with whom remain a problem to this day; a land which defined itself on a hostile frontier; a land which has tamed rich natural resources through the energetic application of modern technology; a land which once imported slaves, and now must struggle to wipe out the last traces of that former bondage. I refer of course to the United States of America.[1]

Senator Robert F. Kennedy, University of Cape Town, South Africa, June 6, 1966

During constitutional negotiations in the early 1990's, South African communist party leader Joe Slovo broke the deadlock between the predominantly white National Party and the opposition. The Constitutional Court, however, subsequently rejected the Constitutional Assembly's proposed constitution. Few would have thought that the communist party would supply statesmen-like compromises whereas the Court would appear obstructionist. This is only one example of the twists and turns leading to South Africa's 1996 Constitution.

This chapter focuses on South Africa's transition from apartheid to democracy, and on the birth of the United States – the world's oldest constitutional democracy. Further, this chapter compares the South African Constitutional Court's structure with that of the U.S. Supreme Court. It

---

[1] Speech delivered at the Annual Day of Affirmation for the anti-Apartheid National Union of South African Students, www.rfksa.org (last visited June 25, 2008). This was the introductory part of Senator Kennedy's speech, and the crowd laughed at his unexpected punch line.

also discusses several provisions of the South African Constitution and two Constitutional Court cases with no American parallels. These discussions provide a context for the later chapters.

Let me state one caveat. South African and American history are obviously complex topics about which leading scholars disagree on theory and application. Pierre de Vos describes, for example, neo-Marxist historians who see apartheid as part of capitalist domination, purer Marxists who view racialism as the means to maintain capitalist colonial oppression, transitionists who see the new South Africa as having been achieved at the expense of reducing poverty, and those who believe the new South Africa was designed to maintain oppression under a "smokescreen."[2] Other scholars describe additional South African historical schools.[3] I do not try to resolve these disputes. Instead, I seek to provide a basic historical background of largely undisputed "facts" that can make the legal chapters more comprehensible.

SOUTH AFRICA

South Africa through Apartheid

For thousands of years before the seventeenth century, when Europeans colonized the area, indigenous peoples known as the Khoisan had lived in southern Africa.[4] Some hunted and others were pastoral. Also long before the seventeenth century, Bantu-speaking peoples had entered the northern tip of what is now South Africa.[5]

In 1652, Jan van Riebeck and about ninety white men sailed on Dutch East Indies ships to the Cape of Good Hope.[6] They built a fort and tried to start a vegetable garden for the benefit of Dutch ships on the trade route. Unfortunately, they also brought smallpox, which killed many indigenous

[2] Pierre de Vos, "South Africa's Constitutional Court: Starry-Eyed in the Face of History?," 26 Vt. L. Rev. 837 (2002).

[3] Alan Cobley, "Does Social History Have a Future? The Ending of Apartheid and Recent Trends in South African Historiography," 27 J. S. Afr. Studies No. 3, 613 (2002).

[4] The "classic" work is by Leonard Thompson, A History of South Africa 10 (2000). This chapter relies heavily, however, on a more accessible Web site: "A Short History of South Africa," South Africa Info http://www.southafrica.info/about/history/history.htm (last visited Aug. 30, 2007) (hereinafter "Web"). This chapter has verified this Web site's accuracy by comparing it to the Thompson book at points.

[5] Web, *id.*; Thompson, xii.   [6] Web, *id.*; Thompson, 32.

peoples. More tragedy followed as "the company-government, the senior officials, and the free burgher community all became dependent on slave labor. The Cape had become a slaveholding society."[7] A group of these Europeans then moved north and east, pushing out the Khoisans.

In the late eighteenth century, British mercantilists arrived on the Cape.[8] They fought against the Afrikaaner Dutch descendants and engaged in "ruthless warfare" with indigenous peoples.[9] British missionaries followed in the nineteenth century with progressive ideas about race. These missionaries even freed slaves owned by Afrikaaners. Supposedly, these British actions partly caused the "Great Boer Trek," in which thousands of Afrikaaners moved north and east in an effort to keep their slaves and way of life. Some Afrikaaners today elevate this trek to legendary status because their ancestors overcame many obstacles, such as the 1838 Battle of Blood River against the increasingly powerful Zulu tribes.[10]

Ultimately, the "Voortrekkers" established two states in the mid-nineteenth century: the Orange Free State in approximately 1849 and the South African Republic in approximately 1856 (itself made up of a combination of four states).[11] The Orange Free State occupied the area between the Orange and Vaal Rivers, generally to the east of the British controlled regions. The Republic occupied the area north of the Vaal later known as the Transvaal Province. Interestingly, these states crafted American-style constitutions providing for a democratically chosen legislature and a president, though only whites could vote.[12]

In the 1850s, Britain established a Cape Colony government that actually allowed blacks to vote for representatives but had property qualifications that obviously favored white voters.[13] Diamonds were discovered during the 1860s in a Cape area named Kimberley, which the British quickly annexed to preclude Afrikaaner claims. Cape exports grew from

[7] Thompson, 36.

[8] Web, "Colonial Expansion"; Thompson, 51.

[9] Rita M. Byrnes, ed., South Africa: A Country Study (Library of Congress), "British Colonialism" http://countrystudies.us/south-africa/11.htm (last visited Nov. 1, 2007); Thompson, 54.

[10] Web, *id*; Thompson, 84–85.

[11] Byrnes, *supra* n. 9, "The Voortrekker Republics and British Policies," http://countrystudies.us/south-africa/13.htm (last visited Nov. 1, 2007).

[12] *Id.*

[13] Web, "Diamonds and British Consolidation"; Thompson, 64.

about 2 million pounds sterling in 1870, mainly for wool, to 15 million pounds by 1900 with 4 million from diamonds alone.[14]

A young Cecil John Rhodes came to the area around that time, He gained control of the diamond industry and eventually was named prime minister of the British areas in southern Africa. Rhodes was the prototypical imperialist in that he did not hesitate to use force to protect British financial and political interests. His company, DeBeers, still dominates the South African diamond trade today and his legacy funds the Rhodes scholarships. In 1897, the British incorporated Zululand to the east after more fighting.

The discovery of gold in other parts of the country meant there were more riches to fight over since those areas were largely independent. In 1899, the Anglo-Boer South African war broke out, with a half-million British troops fighting fewer than 100,000 Afrikaaners.[15] The president of the South African Republic, Paul Kruger, declared war preemptively because he knew the British sought the Republic's gold. The Boers began by using guerrilla tactics but the British responded with a scorched-earth policy: "In 1901 and 1902, the British torched more than 30,000 farms in the South African Republic and the Orange Free State and placed Afrikaaner women and children in concentration camps, where, because of overcrowding and unsanitary conditions, more than 25,000 perished."[16] Domestic British politicians such as radical liberal MP David Lloyd George initiated a human rights campaign on behalf of the oppressed Boers that seems ironic today. The British established separate concentration camps for blacks and coloured people as well. 14,000 blacks and coloured people died. The term "coloured" in South Africa means people of mixed race.[17]

Eventually, the British overcame surprisingly strong Boer resistance; a 1902 peace treaty confirmed the Boer defeat. These historical events left the Boers feeling threatened and with a chip on their shoulders. Some scholars blame apartheid's viciousness on this Afrikaaner legacy of defeat.

---

[14] Byrnes, *supra* n. 9, "The Mineral Revolution," http://countrystudies.us/south-africa/14.htm (last visited Nov. 1, 2007); Thompson, 110–32.

[15] Web, "Gold and War"; Thompson 141–43.

[16] Byrnes, *supra* n. 9, "British Imperialism and the Afrikaaners," http://countrystudies.us/south-africa/16.htm (last visited Nov. 1, 2007).

[17] Christina Murray & Richard Simeon, "Recognition without Empowerment," 5 Int'l J. Con. L. 699, 700 n. 6 (2007).

Despite the British victory, the two ex-Boer republics maintained their whites-only voting rules.[18] Blacks also could not serve in the British-run Cape Parliament. Eventually, various Afrikaaner parties merged and became the South African Party. It enacted many racist measures and assumed power over large amounts of indigenous land. In 1910, the British formally recognized that Afrikaaners outnumbered them and established a British dominion known as the Union of South Africa.[19] A dominion has more autonomy than a colony but still ultimately remains in the British empire. The areas known as the Cape, Natal, Transvaal, and the Orange Free State became Union provinces. Under the Union constitution, parliament was sovereign – as in the British Westminster system. Louis Botha became the first Union prime minister, and the Afrikaaner Jan Smuts became the first deputy, only a few years after fighting for the losing Boer forces. They governed a country of "4 million Africans, 500,000 coloureds, 150,000 Indians, and 1,275,000 whites."[20]

In 1912, several black African constituencies that opposed racial discrimination and political disenfranchisement formed the African National Congress (ANC).[21] ANC efforts to block the Afrikaaner land seizures failed but the ANC's founding was key to the growth of the resistance movement. It eventually led numerous black worker strikes in unsuccessful efforts to undermine the white government. In 1918, the organization highlighted its continental connection by temporarily becoming the "Pan African Association." Ironically, the ANC did not allow women to join.

A lawyer named Mohandas Ghandi also led a separate Indian resistance movement before he returned to India in 1914.[22] While in South Africa, Ghandi developed his philosophy of nonviolent resistance, *satyagraha*, in response to various incidents of discrimination.[23] For example, a white magistrate ordered Ghandi to remove his turban in court, he was thrown off a train for being in the white compartment, and he was jailed

---

[18] Web, "Union and the ANC"; Thompson 144.

[19] Byrnes, *supra* n. 9, http://countrystudies.us/south-africa/17.htm (last visited Nov. 1, 2007); Thompson 152–53.

[20] *Id.*

[21] Web, "Union and the ANC"; Thompson 174.

[22] Thompson 113.

[23] "Years of Satyagrahas of Mahatma Ghandi," http://www.gandhi-manibhavan.org /aboutgandhi/chrono_satyagrahas.htm (last visited Nov. 26, 2007).

on numerous occasions.[24] Nelson Mandela has written movingly about the importance of Ghandi's philosophy to the ANC.[25] Ghandi partly explains the South African embrace of reconciliation with one's enemies. Ghandi's nonviolent resistance also had a major impact on Martin Luther King Jr. and the American civil rights movement.[26] That movement in turn influenced South Africans and vice versa.[27]

In 1923, the ANC proposed a short Bill of Rights that included the right to own property, the right to liberty, and the right to equality "irrespective of race, class, creed, or origin."[28] It even referenced "no taxation without representation" – a clear link to the American Revolution.[29]

Ultimately, the Afrikaaner people showed more commitment to governance than the British who recognized the autonomy of the South African Parliament by the Statute of Westminster in 1931. Then in 1934, the South African Parliament adopted The Status of Union Act which asserted South Africa's independence. By 1936, the Afrikaaners had already disenfranchised black Cape voters.[30] In addition, the government passed segregation laws, as well as travel and living restrictions. The Afrikaaner National Party became dominant.

During World War II, the white government officially joined the Allies in fighting the Nazis. Moreover, in 1943, the ANC issued a document called "Africans' Claims in South Africa."[31] A twenty-eight-person

---

[24] Patricia Cronin Marcello, Mohandas K. Ghandi, A Biography 36–39 (2006); "Years of Arrests & Imprisonment of Mahatma Ghandi," http://www.gandhimanibhavan.org/aboutgandhi/chrono_arrestsnimprisonments.htm (last visited Nov. 26, 2007).

[25] Nelson Mandela, "The Sacred Warrior, The Liberator of South Africa Looks at the Seminal Work of the Liberator of India," Time 100: Person of the Century (Jan. 3, 2000), http://www.time.com/time/time100/poc/magazine/the_sacred_warrior13a.html (last visited Nov. 1, 2007). Ghandi told an ANC leader that the way to be as successful as the Indian National Congress was for the ANC's Western-educated elite to become less detached from the masses of ordinary African citizens. George M. Frederickson, Black Liberation: A Comparative History of Black Ideologies in the United States and South Africa 230 (1996).

[26] Fredrickson, *id.* at 226.

[27] *Id.* at 9 ("The fact that there was a degree of mutual awareness and some borrowing of ideas and rhetoric from the other side of the Atlantic and the Equator – especially by the South Africans – adds substance and credibility to the comparison" of South Africa and the United States.) & 13.

[28] Kader Asmal, (Ed.), Legacy of Freedom: The ANC's Human Rights Tradition 47 (2005).

[29] *Id.*

[30] Web, "Union and the ANC"; Thompson 161.

[31] Asmal, *supra* n. 28 at vii.

committee drafted it with an introduction by the legendary Alfred Bitini Xuma.[32] Xuma was a physician who became the ANC's president in 1940. He had studied medicine in the United States at Northwestern University in Chicago and spent additional time in Minneapolis and St. Louis.[33] He was a political moderate who unified the ANC and made it more efficient, despite sometimes clashing with militant members.[34]

The first part of the 1943 document was titled "The Atlantic Charter from the African's Point of View." Nelson Mandela has written that the Atlantic Charter provided hope to South Africans.[35] The Allies issued the Atlantic Charter to highlight the principles of democracy and human rights that were at stake in fighting the Nazis.[36] The ANC, though, believed that whereas American president Franklin Roosevelt sought to apply the Charter everywhere, including Africa, Winston Churchill, the British prime minister, only sought its application to Europe.[37] The ANC document read, "We hope that the mistakes of the past whereby African peoples and their lands were treated as pawns in the political game of European nations will not be repeated."[38]

This statement was a reference to the infamous 1884 Berlin Conference at which European colonial powers greedily carved up African lands on a map with no thought given to the people in Africa or their interests, such as maintaining tribal communities and structures.[39] Europeans assumed Africans to be subhuman. This arbitrary drawing of state boundaries produced many of Africa's later political and human rights tragedies. The second part of the 1943 document was a more specific Bill of Rights than the one proposed by the ANC in 1923. It called for a right to vote for all adults, the right to equal justice, the freedom to live and travel without restriction, the sanctity of the home, equal pay for equal work, and socioeconomic rights such as access to education and medical services.[40] Remarkably, the ANC issued this Bill of Rights five years before the 1948 United Nations Universal Declaration of Human Rights

---

[32] *Id.*

[33] Richard D. Ralston, "American Episodes in the Making of an African Leader: A Case Study of Alfred B. Xuma," Vol. 6, No. 1, Int'l J. of African Historical Studies 72 (1973).

[34] Dr. Alfred Bitini (A.B.) Xuma, http://www.sahistory.org.za/pages/people/bios/xuma-ab.htm (last visited Oct. 31, 2007).

[35] Nelson Mandela, Long Walk to Freedom 96 (1994) (hereinafter "Mandela").

[36] Asmal, *supra* n. 28 at 2.

[37] *Id.* at 8.   [38] *Id.* at 13.

[39] Adam Hochschild, King Leopold's Ghost 84–87 (1998).

[40] Asmal, *supra* n. 28 at 17.

was promulgated. Women could also be full ANC members, a change from the earlier policy.[41]

The ANC may have issued such forceful statements during World War II because of the influence of its newly formed Youth League, made up of individuals like Nelson Mandela, Oliver Tambo, and Walter Sisulu.[42] Mandela had met Tambo at the University of Fort Hare on the soccer field when they were both college students and members of a Christian organization.[43] Mandela met Sisulu after college by which time Sisulu had already started a successful real estate business.[44] These three individuals would change the nation forever because of their willingness to fight injustice.

Mandela was the son of a rural tribal chief. When his father died, the tribal regent became his guardian, and Mandela was therefore destined for royalty. His regal confidence, ease, and warmth with all sorts of people are evident in his dealings with the public. His given name is Rolihlahla, which means "to pull a branch from a tree" or, more loosely, "to be a troublemaker."[45]

In his autobiography Mandela writes of Tambo as being the more logical and analytical of the two, and describes himself as having an emotional nature.[46] They founded one of the few black law firms in South Africa. Tambo was also very religious and considered entering the ministry. He became a long-time president of the ANC and carried out many of his revolutionary activities in exile. He traveled the world on behalf of the movement. Sisulu was not as well educated, but was the kind of person who would remind Mandela that their job was to serve people, not just lead. Sisulu was ANC secretary general from 1949 to 1954.

In 1946, India became the first nation to criticize South African apartheid in the new UN General Assembly.[47] Nonetheless, D. F. Malan and the Afrikaaner National Party won the South African "election" in 1948, and apartheid became institutionalized.[48] The government issued

---

[41] *Id.* at 52. The ANC Women's Charter of 1954 crystallizes this equality even more. *Id.* at 54.

[42] *Id.* at 2.   [43] Mandela at 47.

[44] *Id.* at 68.

[45] Bill Keller, Tree Shaker: The Story of Nelson Mandela, N.Y. Times Upfront, May 5, 2008, http://findarticles.com/p/articles/mi_moBUE/is_14_140/ai_n25400829 (last visited June 16, 2008).

[46] Mandela at 148.   [47] Web, "Union and the ANC."

[48] Richard Spitz, Matthew Chaskalson, The Politics of Transition 4 (2000).

the Group Areas Act and the Population Registration Act in 1950 which reduced greatly the size of areas in which blacks could work and live.[49] Two years later, the government enacted pass laws that restricted black travel. In 1958, Prime Minister H. F. Verwoerd was elected Prime Minister and continued imposing "Grand Apartheid," institutionalizing segregation that was designed to create virtually separate racial nations in which non-whites were subjugated.[50]

In 1955, the ANC gathered en masse in Kliptown, a part of Soweto outside Johannesburg, and issued the famous Freedom Charter, which influenced the 1996 national constitution.[51] Interestingly, the U.S. Supreme Court had just decided *Brown v. Board of Education*,[52] which outlawed racial segregation, and *Brown* lifted black spirits in South Africa.[53] The Freedom Charter specified rights as follows:

> The People Shall Govern!
> All National Groups Shall Have Equal Rights!
> The People Shall Share in the Country's Wealth!
> The Land Shall be Shared among Those Who Work It!
> All Shall be Equal before the Law!
> All Shall Enjoy Human Rights!
> There Shall be Work and Security!
> The Doors of Culture and Learning Shall Be Opened!
> There Shall Be Houses, Security, and Comfort!
> There Shall Be Peace and Friendship!

According to one commentary, the Freedom Charter had a lasting impact because "the Congress of the People itself, which adopted the final draft, was attended by the delegates drawn from all racial groups and from both urban and rural areas. In a real sense, it was the precursor to the democratically elected Parliament, which today, is South Africa's supreme lawmaker."[54] Ivor Chipkin, Chief Research Specialist for Democracy and Governance of the South African Human Sciences

---

[49] *Id.*   [50] *Id.* at 6.

[51] Asmal, *supra* n. 28 at 53. Penelope Andrews makes the same point in an article. *Infra* n. 53.

[52] 347 U.S. 483 (1954).

[53] Penelope E. Andrews, "Perspectives on Brown: The South African Experience," 49 N.Y.L. Sch. L. Rev. 1155 (2005).

[54] Asmal, *supra* n. 28 at 60.

Research Council, however, takes a far more skeptical view of the Freedom Charter's origins.[55]

Interestingly the ANC assumed that political action would result in the protection of human rights, not that the courts would guarantee them.[56] This assumption made sense because the ANC, fought for self-determination and relied on popular mobilization for its legitimacy.[57] Unfortunately, the government brought treason charges against many ANC activists who supported the Freedom Charter, including Nelson Mandela.[58] Miraculous acquittals, however, occurred – acquittals the government would not tolerate again.[59]

As Nelson Mandela stated in his autobiography, *The Long Walk to Freedom*, the pass laws were especially distressing.[60] The South African conflict therefore escalated when police shot and killed black pass law protesters at Sharpeville in 1960.[61] In response to the Sharpeville massacre, there were riots in the black townships, leading the government to declare a state of emergency, detain people without trial, and ban various organizations. Soon after, the government adopted a new constitution aimed at bolstering the regime's legitimacy by retaining the whites-only system of parliamentary supremacy. The opposition went into hiding.

Around the same time, the ANC placed Mandela in charge of its military wing, Spear of the Nation (*Umkhonto we Sizwe*).[62] Albert John Lutuli, the legendary Nobel Peace Prize winner and former Zulu tribal chief, was president of the ANC at the time. Mandela agreed to fight the government, but would not strike at civilians, in compliance with the

---

[55] Ivor Chipkin, Do South Africans Exist? 65–73 (2007) (suggesting that much of the Charter was written unilaterally by an active Communist Party member named Rusty Bernstein).

[56] Heinz Klug, Constituting Democracy 74 (2000): "While the Freedom Charter, with its guarantee of individual and collective rights, was to remain the blueprint of the ANC'svision for a post-Apartheid South Africa, it in no way contradicted the organization's understanding of legislative supremacy. The assertion of both political and socio-economic rights in the Freedom Charter represented the claims of the people against the Apartheid government, not the justiciable rights of individuals or even collectivities."

[57] *Id.* at 81.

[58] Web, "The Gathering Storm." Mandela writes, "The state cited the Freedom Charter as both proof of our Communist intentions and evidence of our plot to overthrow the existing authorities." Mandela at 205.

[59] Mandela at 261.   [60] *Id.* at 220.

[61] Web, "Three Decades of Crisis"; Thompson at 210.

[62] Mandela at 274.

Geneva Conventions.[63] In his autobiography, he humorously recounts that his personality left him ill suited for a military role. In 1962, Lutuli and Martin Luther King Jr. issued a joint statement condemning apartheid.

The 1960s saw growing international pressure on South Africa. The UN became more involved, condemning South Africa both for its apartheid policies and for its actions in southwest Africa, now Namibia.[64] Allard Lowenstein, an American student activist who later became a congressman and Ambassador to the UN, secretly traveled through Namibia and wrote a devastating report, *Brutal Mandate: A Journey to South West Africa.* that influenced the UN to condemn the South African government.[65] The UN, for example, in 1966 withdrew South Africa's mandate over Southwest Africa.[66]

The South African government reacted in various ways to international pressure. Despite losing the large treason trial involving Mandela, previously discussed, the government continued to use Cold War propaganda and label all members of the opposition as communists to delegitimize calls for democracy.[67] This label was plausible because the South African Communist Party had long supported the liberation movement. Moreover, communist nations had provided arms and other assistance to the ANC. The ANC, however, was not a communist front.[68] In his autobiography, Mandela explained that South African communists were among the first whites to support equality.[69] That support, created the alliance between the ANC and the Communist Party.[70]

---

[63] *Id.* at 283.

[64] Jared Genser, "South Africa: Country Should Return the Favour," AllAfrica.Com, Jan. 24, 2007, http://allafrica.com/stories/200701241026.html (last visited Sep. 10, 2007).

[65] William Chafe, Never Stop Running 141–45 (1993).

[66] "South West Africa: United Nations General Assembly," 61 Amer. J. Int'l L. 649 (1967) (contains UN Resolution 2145 of 1966 condemning the South African activities and presence in southwest Africa).

[67] John Dugard, Human Rights and the South African Legal Order 328–29 (1978); Allard Lowenstein, Brutal Mandate 23 (1962). A modern example of this can be found on the Internet even today. The National Alliance, "The Killing of Whites in South Africa . . . and America's Silence," http://www.rense.com/general29/silence.htm (last visited Sep. 10, 2007).

[68] Spitz, *supra* n. 48 at 13. Lowenstein, *id.* at 189.

[69] Mandela at 75.

[70] *Id.* at 176 (The ANC Freedom Charter actually endorsed private property unlike the typical communist position).

The government went beyond labeling opposition leaders as communist; it also hunted them down. Tragically, Nelson Mandela and Walter Sisulu were captured[71] and convicted of sabotage at the 1964 Rivonia trial. The court ordered life imprisonment for the two men. Mandela's closing statement at trial is famous. He looked into the eyes of the judge and said the following:

> During my lifetime I have dedicated myself to this struggle of the African people. I have fought against white domination, and I have fought against black domination. I have cherished the ideal of a democratic and free society in which all persons live together in harmony and with equal opportunities. It is an ideal which I hope to live for and to achieve. But if needs be, it is an ideal for which I am prepared to die.[72]

Mandela and Sisulu spent more than twenty years in prison on Robben Island, off Cape Town's coast. Their prison stay was brutal as the authorities forced Mandela and others to break heavy rocks in a quarry during the hottest part of the day.[73] The government also mixed ordinary violent criminals in with the political prisoners which was frightening at times. One of the criminals repeatedly stole Walter Sisulu's breakfast.[74] Robben Island, though, was filled with ANC and other political prisoners, leading some to call it the "university" because of the political discussions and strategizing that took place there.[75]

During the 1970s, government repression intensified as did international pressure and guerilla resistance against the government.[76] The ANC based its operations in friendly African nations. In 1976, 15,000 schoolchildren marched in Soweto Township to protest a new government policy mandating that half of the secondary school classes be taught in Afrikaans. Without warning, police shot and killed many young marchers, including thirteen-year-old Hector Pieterson, creating an international uproar.[77] Pieterson became the image of the event because Sam Nzima took a photo, seen around the world, showing a dying Hector

---

[71] Web, "Three Decades of Crisis."   [72] Mandela at 368.
[73] Mandela at 405.   [74] Mandela at 407.
[75] Mandela at 429 & 467–68 ("In the struggle, Robben Island was known as the university.... We became our own faculty, with our own professors, our own curriculum, and our own courses. We made a distinction between academic studies, which were official, and political studies, which were not."). Walter Sisulu in particular taught the history of the ANC to new prisoners as part of a politicization effort. The Socratic method was often used, and Mandela even taught a class in political economy.
[76] *Supra* n. 71.   [77] Mandela at 483.

being carried by another person. Despite this international condemnation, the government established black "homelands" in distant parts of the country which actually had governments that were apartheid regime pawns.

In 1977, security forces murdered Steven Biko, a leader of the black consciousness movement. The government insisted that Biko died during a hunger strike but the truth came out eventually.[78] Biko was a charismatic young man who had great influence in urban areas, especially because many ANC leaders had gone underground by that time. Biko is presumed to have helped organize the Soweto student protests. He inspired blacks to be proud. His writings have been compiled in a book appropriately titled *I Write What I Want*.

Interestingly, the ANC was troubled at times by the black consciousness movement's rhetoric, and Mandela's autobiography does not mention Biko. Indeed, Biko criticized the ANC's multiracial appeals and criticized white liberals, though he was quite friendly with journalist Donald Woods. In 1997, however, President Mandela gave a moving speech on the twentieth anniversary of Biko's murder.[79] Based on American political ideology, Mandela resembled Martin Luther King Jr., whereas Biko was more like Malcolm X. King and Malcolm X, however, were religious leaders unlike Mandela and Biko.

In 1983, the government revised the constitution to establish a tricameral parliament giving representation to whites, Indians, and coloreds, but not to blacks.[80] The white chamber retained the real power. The opposition parties, made up of most non-whites and white liberals, rejected this bizarre system and pressured the government through street protests and advocating for international economic sanctions. Activists began lobbying large institutions internationally, such as American universities, to divest their holdings from South African companies.

Others responded that major institutions could better change apartheid through engagement, not withdrawal, as long as the companies complied with the humanitarian Sullivan Principles, named after the

---

[78] Donald Woods, Biko – Cry Freedom (1978). In 1987, Academy Award winning director Richard Attenborough produced a film based on Biko's life and his relationship to Woods. The film starred Hollywood actors Denzel Washington and Kevin Kline.

[79] Address by President Nelson Mandela at the Commemoration of the Twentieth Anniversary of Steve Biko's Death, Sep. 12, 1997, http://www.anc.org.za/ancdocs /history/mandela/1997/sp970912.html (last visited Nov. 2, 2007).

[80] Web, "Three Decades of Crisis."

American Reverend Leon Sullivan.[81] These principles obligated companies doing business in South Africa to require non-segregation in eating, comfort and work facilities; to provide equal pay regardless of race; to increase the number of blacks and non-minorities in management and supervisory positions, and the like. The Sullivan proponents, however, could not hold back the bursting dam of divestment.

Transition

In the 1980s, ANC members engaged in constitution drafting because of the perceived vulnerability of the apartheid government. In October 1987, the ANC released a Statement of Negotiations that endorsed a constitutional Bill of Rights.[82] The ANC, however, apparently did not want the legislature to give up its supremacy.[83] The ANC also issued constitutional guidelines in January 1988.[84]

Later that year, current Constitutional Court Justice Albie Sachs, then an ANC activist and scholar, authored a "Bill of Rights for a Democratic South Africa."[85] This document was groundbreaking because it advocated having a court "on high" decide constitutional matters, rather than the Westminster system. Sachs reassured his allies that judicial enforcement of a Bill of Rights was not a reactionary mechanism to protect white interests. Sachs later helped revise the formal ANC constitutional proposals, though he was joined by many others in this effort.[86] Interestingly, Heinz Klug has shown that Southern Africa's only justiciable bills of rights, at that time, were in the black homelands.[87] This was not the ideal pedigree, but ANC loyalists eventually signed on.

Several international conferences took place regarding a new South African constitution. Ronald Dworkin organized a 1987 Oxford conference,[88] and Jack Greenberg organized a 1989 Columbia University Law School event entitled "Human Rights in the Post-Apartheid South African Constitution."[89] In 1989, the Organization of African Unity issued the

---

[81] http://www.globalsullivanprinciples.org/new_page_4.htm (last visited June 16, 2008).

[82] Klug, *supra* n. 56 at 79.

[83] *Id.* at 82. [84] *Id.* at 80.

[85] *Id.* at 81.

[86] *Id.* at 129. [87] *Id.* at 75.

[88] *Id.* at 83.

[89] Many of the papers can be found in volume 21 of the Columbia Human Rights Law Review including one by the tireless Justice Sachs. Albie Sachs, "A Bill of Rights for South Africa: Areas of Agreement and Disagreement," 21 Colum. Hum. Rts. L. Rev. 13 (1989).

Harare Declaration, which advocated abolishing apartheid and replacing it with a system based on democracy and human rights.[90]

In 1990, the government freed Nelson Mandela from prison, along with other political prisoners, and it lifted the ban on political parties.[91] Shortly after his release, Mandela gave a speech to a joint session of the U.S. Congress acknowledging the following:

> We could not have made an acquaintance through literature with human giants such as George Washington, Abraham Lincoln and Thomas Jefferson and not been moved to act as they were moved to act. We could not have heard of and admired John Brown, Sojourner Truth, Frederick Douglass, W. E. B. DuBois, Marcus Garvey, Martin Luther King Jr. and others – we could not have heard of these and not be moved to act as they were moved to act. We could not have known of your Declaration of Independence and not elected to join in the struggle to guarantee the people's life, liberty, and the pursuit of happiness.[92]

Since 1984, while in prison, Mandela had been engaged in back-channel negotiations with South African officials. He met with President Botha and his successor President de Klerk for the first time in 1989.[93] Negotiations proceeded in earnest for a new South Africa after his release. Eventually, draft constitutions were proposed by each of these groups: the ANC, the South African Law Commission (SALC), the National Party (NP), the Zulu-dominated Inkatha Freedom Party (IFP), and a group of liberal academics.[94]

Moreover, scholars from all over the world descended on the country, by invitation and otherwise, to make their recommendations. Indeed one Canadian constitutional scholar, who was on sabbatical at the University of Cape Town in 1992, may have had quite an influence.[95] Americans

---

[90] Klug at 179.   [91] Spitz, *supra* n. 48 at XI.

[92] Leon Higginbotham, "Racism in American and South African Courts: Similarities and Differences," 65 N.Y.U. L. Rev. 479, 500–01 (1990) (quoting the speech from the Congressional Record). To be fair, Mandela also gave a rousing speech in Havana where he thanked Cuba and Castro for tangibly supporting the ANC.

[93] Max du Preez, "Explaining the Miracle," Chap. 2, Turning Points 4, http://www.sahistory.org.za/pages/chronology/turningpoints/bk6/chapter2.htm (last visited Aug. 22, 2007).

[94] Jeremy Sarkin, "The Effect of Constitutional Borrowings on the Drafting of South Africa's Bill of Rights and Interpretation of Human Rights Provisions," 1 U. Pa. J. Const. 176, 180 (1998) (the one from academics was called "A Charter for Social Justice"). Constitutional Court Justice Kate O'Regan described the document in answer to questions during her judicial interview. The IFP proposals are discussed in the classic book by Hassin Ebrahim, Soul of a Nation 100 (1998).

[95] *See e.g.* David Beatty, The Rule (and Role) of Law in a New South Africa: Some Lessons from Abroad, 109 S. Afr. L. J. 408 (1992). The article discusses at length an important

got involved too,[96] as did Germans and others. Conferences funded by foreign governments and foundations were held in South Africa.[97] South African scholars returning from abroad also came with useful ideas.[98] Indeed, the Final Constitution ended up relying on the German Basic Law, the Canadian Charter of Rights and Freedoms, and international human rights principles.[99]

The ANC supported majoritarianism for the drafting process rather than have elites make the important constitutional decisions.[100] The ANC also did not want a foreign solution "imposed," such as occurred in Zimbabwe when the British government took a leading role regarding negotiations resulting in the Lancaster House Agreement.[101] The National Party by contrast supported the inclusion of minority rights and federalism as a means to protect white interests.[102] The NP therefore endorsed consociational democracy, which emphasized "minority rights, decisions by consensus and autonomy for each group in its own affairs."[103]

Canadian case called Regina v. Oakes. According to South African scholar and jurist Dennis Davis, "The structure of the Charter had been heavily based on the Canadian Charter of Rights and Freedoms, the benefits of which had been documented by a Canadian constitutional lawyer, David Beatty, who had been a visiting professor at the University of Cape Town during 1992." Davis *infra* n. 98 at 186. *See also* Adam M. Dodek, "A Tale of Two Maps: The Limits of Universalism in Judicial Review," 14 & 24 http://ssrn.com/abstract=1067625 (last visited April 4, 2008) (noting Canadian influence on the South African Constitution in part caused by Canada's strong anti-apartheid stance).

[96] For example, Frank Michelman and Cass Sunstein were influential. There was even an American-oriented book written specifically to assist South Africa. *See* Robert A. Licht & Bertrus de Villiers (Eds)., South Africa's Crisis of Constitutional Democracy: Can the U.S. Constitution Help? (1994).

[97] Francois du Bois & Daniel Visser, "The Influence of Foreign Law in South Africa," 13 Transnat'l L. & Contemp. Probs. 593, 628–32 (2003).

[98] D.M. Davis, "Constitutional Borrowing: The Influence of Legal Culture and Local History in the Reconstitution of Comparative Influence: The South African Experience," 1 Int'l J. Const. L. 181, 187 (2003) ("An American influence appeared in the document as well, albeit entering at a later stage. This later borrowing owed much to the intervention of Professor Halton Cheadle, South Africa's most eminent labor lawyer, who had returned to South Africa from a sabbatical year at Harvard Law School. He introduced the concept of scrutiny into the limitation clause by drafting a provision that guaranteed that certain rights could be limited only when the limitation, in addition to being reasonable and justifiable in an open, democratic society based on freedom and equality, was necessary.")

[99] *Supra* n. 95 & 97.

[100] Klug, *supra* n. 56 at 88 & 91.

[101] *Id.* at 78.

[102] *Id.* at 86 & 90.

[103] Siri Gloppen: The Battle over the Constitution 93 (1997). The consociation theory was put forward by a Dutch scholar, Arend Lijharpt.

The various sides participated in 1991 in the Conference for a Democratic South Africa (CODESA) held at Kempton Park near Johannesburg. The negotiations were complex and took place under pressure because fighting was ongoing between the IFP and ANC, as well as between government forces and blacks. CODESA eventually broke down.[104] International pressure and further internal violence, however, resurrected the negotiations.[105]

In early 1993, the ANC supported a "sunset" provision, proposed by Communist Party leader Joe Slovo, that involved five years of power sharing with the NP.[106] The NP, in turn, agreed to hold democratic elections for a Constitutional Assembly that would draft a permanent Constitution. Thus, South Africa had a two-stage drafting process. First, elites from the various groups established a transitional framework that devolved power to democratic institutions. These institutions then made the crucial second-stage decisions.

Slovo's background seemed to make him ill suited to compromise. The son of Jewish immigrants, he was an ardent communist and an ANC military wing member. His first wife, Ruth First, was killed by a parcel bomb in 1982 while they were in Mozambique. She too was a communist activist. However, he was no Stalinist ideologue as his critics asserted. This is shown by his 1989 book, *Has Socialism Failed*. Above all, he was dedicated to South Africa's liberation from apartheid.

The so-called Multi-Party Negotiating Process (MPNP) then began in 1993 at the World Trade Centre in Johannesburg. Its central "Negotiating Council" reported to a "Negotiating Forum."[107] The MPNP also established working groups. The Technical Committee on Constitutional Issues (TCCI) was one such important group, chaired by Arthur Chaskalson. He often provided legal representation for ANC leaders and was the founder of the Legal Resource Center, a civil rights group modeled on the American NAACP Legal Defense Fund (LDF). Chaskalson even

---

[104] Spitz, *supra* n. 48 at 27.

[105] Record of Understanding between ANC and Government, Sep. 26, 1992, http://www .anc.org.za/ancdocs/history/record.html (last visited April 7, 2008). *See also* Spitz, *id.* at 30 ("Indeed in 1992, the NP had adopted a proposal from its constitutional advisor, Francois Venter, to support a two-stage constitution making process, guaranteeing constitutional continuity, an interim executive government, and a justiciable charter of fundamental rights.").

[106] Spitz, *supra* n. 48 at 31; Klug, *supra* n. 56 at 104.

[107] Klug *supra* n. 56 at 105.

worked with LDF leader Jack Greenberg during this time.[108] Chaskalson later became the first president of the Constitutional Court.

Individuals intending to derail the negotiating process then gunned down South African Communist Party leader Chris Hani in 1993. Although he wanted to be a priest as a young adult, Hani trained as a lawyer and became an activist for the working class. At his death, he was probably second in national popularity to Nelson Mandela. After his assassination, the ANC and its allies appealed for calm with relative success.[109] In July 1993, the MPNP adopted 34 Constitutional Principles proposed by the TCCI with which the final constitution had to be consistent.[110]

The Negotiating Council then instructed the TCCI to propose a transitional Constitution.[111] There was much disagreement at this point. The ANC still wanted most issues to be left for the popularly elected Constitutional Assembly.[112] By contrast, the NP wanted to fix detailed principles to protect against the popular will.[113]

The 1993 Interim Constitution became fairly detailed because it had to potentially govern the country from the 1994 elections until enactment of a final Constitution.[114] According to several sources, some of the Bill of Rights drafters, such as Hugh Corder and Lourens du Plessis, decided to incorporate numerous human rights guarantees directly from the interested party submissions so as to ensure that a major transition would indeed take place.[115] Ironically, this decision helped finalize the ANC shift from an emphasis on dramatic wealth redistribution to a focus on rights.

Schedule 4 of the Interim Constitution included the 34 Constitutional Principles. According to provisions of the Interim Constitution, the Constitutional Assembly had two years to write a final constitution which had to pass by a two-thirds majority. The Constitutional Assembly, or Parliament, would be made up of the National Assembly and a Senate

---

[108] George Bizos, No One to Blame 229 (1998).

[109] Ebrahim, *supra* n. 94 at 153.   [110] Klug, *supra* n. 56 at 107.

[111] *Id.* at 108.

[112] Eric Christiansen, "Adjudicating Non-Justiciable Rights: Socio-Economic Rights and the South African Constitution, Socio-Economic Rights and the Constitutional Court," 38 Colum. L. Rev. 321, 326 n. 14 (2007).

[113] Klug, *supra* n. 56 at 108.   [114] *Id.*

[115] Spitz, *supra* n. 48 at 260 ("Corder and DuPlessis on the other hand, appear without political pressures to have pursued a maximalist line. This was their opportunity to draft the founding document of a human rights culture in South Africa, and they took it."); Davis, *supra* n. 98 at 186.

that represented the provinces. Regarding executive power, there would be one president and two deputy presidents, who shared power pursuant to the Slovo compromise . A new Constitutional Court would also have to "certify" that the Constitution fulfilled the 34 Constitutional Principles.

Though many Interim Constitution Bill of Rights provisions ended up in the final Constitution, the ANC prevented the elites from deciding the scope of certain socioeconomic rights provisions.[116] The Interim Constitution also left open the status of customary law, a source of dispute between traditional leaders and women's groups.[117] For example, traditional leaders supported polygamy which was opposed by advocates for women.

The Interim Constitution was revolutionary given where the country had been under apartheid. The Constitutional Court's power to render binding decisions broke with the old legal system.[118] The temporary charter also established governmental institutions to assist with the transition, such as an election commission.

In 1994, South Africa overwhelmingly elected Nelson Mandela as president and the African National Congress won more seats than any other party in Parliament. Eligible voter turnout was 86 percent and people proudly stood in line to have their say.[119]

The population breakdown at the time depends on the source:

> The South African government estimated the total nationwide population at 40.4 million, after all ten homelands had been reincorporated into South Africa. In that year, the United States Bureau of the Census estimated the total population of South Africa at 43.9 million. Relying on the South African government's enumeration and legal categories, the South African Institute of Race Relations estimated that the population was 76.4 percent black, 12.6 percent white, 8.5 percent coloured, and 2.5 percent Asian.[120]

---

[116] Klug, *supra* n. 56 at 115.

[117] Monique Deveaux, "Liberal Constitutions and Traditional Cultures: The South African Customary Law Debate," Vol. 7 Citizenship Studies No. 2 161 (2003).

[118] Spitz, *supra* n. 48 at 191–210.

[119] Albie Sachs, "The Creation of South Africa's Constitution," 41 N.Y.L. Sch. L. Rev. 669, 673 (1997); Vivien Hart, "Democratic Constitution Making: The South African Experience," United States Institute of Peace, http://usinfo.state.gov/journals/itdhr/0304/ijde/hart.htm (last visited Oct. 31, 2007).

[120] Byrnes, *supra* n. 9, "Population," http://countrystudies.us/south-africa/44.htm (last visited Nov. 3, 2007). A summary of some of the most recent statistics on population in terms of race and ethnicity can be found at Christina Murray & Richard Simeon,

The ANC won 63 percent of the votes, the National Party won 20 percent, and the IFP received 11 percent.[121] ANC official Thabo Mbeki and former President de Klerk of the NP became deputy presidents.

The Constitutional Assembly began discussing and drafting the final Constitution in the face of great discord. For example, the IFP refused to participate and its deadly fighting with the ANC continued, especially in Kwa Zulu Natal.[122] Moreover, there seemed to be insurmountable disagreements on labor union lockouts, property rights, language and cultural group rights, provincial powers, and the preamble.[123] Heinz Klug has discussed the property debates at length based on his participation in the discussions.[124] Recent developments in Zimbabwe highlight that issue's importance.

Numerous constitutional experts assisted the drafting process at both the interim and final stages. Several of those involved with the Interim Constitution, particularly the Bill of Rights Technical Committee, have already been mentioned. The experts at the final stage may have actually played a less important role because a presumption existed that the interim language should prevail unless shown otherwise. The final group of experts included the likes of Christina Murray, Gerhard Erasmus, Jeremy Gauntlett, John Dugard, Ig Rautenbach, and Halton Cheadle. Many had extensive foreign training. Moreover, ANC lawyer-politicians such as Albie Sachs, Kader Asmal, and Zola Skweyiya played a major role.[125]

To its credit, the Constitutional Assembly solicited public participation by innovative means and this input resulted in some changes. It put out a newsletter that included cartoons and it distributed posters throughout the country showing Nelson Mandela speaking on a cell phone about drafting the new constitution.[126] Some of the public submissions were quite amusing; for example, "A well known nudist demanded the right not to wear clothes."[127] Other submissions were poignant, expressing desires such as to have shelter from the weather.

"Recognition without Empowerment: Minorities in a Democratic South Africa," 5. Int'l J. Con. L. 699, 703 (2007).

[121] Byrnes, *supra* n. 9, "The Election," http://countrystudies.us/south-africa/37.htm (last visited Nov. 3, 2007).

[122] Ebrahim, *supra* n. 94 at 263.   [123] *Id.* at 198 & 204.

[124] Klug, *supra* n. 56 at 124.   [125] Dubois, *supra* n. 97 at 630 n. 155.

[126] Christina Murray, "Negotiating beyond Deadlock," in Penelope Andrews & Stephen Ellman (Eds.), Post-Apartheid Constitutions 110 (2001).

[127] *Id.* at 108.

One commentator summarized the drafting process as follows:

> The working method of the Assembly consisted of dividing its members into several Theme Committees, each of which was charged with reaching agreement on draft texts dealing with a specific aspect of the constitution, and was assisted by its own appointed Technical Experts, who produced proposals for drafts and answered queries. Issues which could not be resolved in this way were settled by the full Assembly which, in turn, was assisted by an appointed Panel of Constitutional Experts as well as Law Advisors. The Assembly considered numerous drafts for the various Chapters of the Constitution, and adopted a text produced by a Technical Refinement Team consisting of some of the Technical Experts, members of the Panel, and Law Advisors. Consultation consisted of invitations to the public to submit proposals (many of which were received from a wide range of individuals and organizations), public hearings, consultation "roadshows" (especially in rural areas) and more formal events at which particular interest groups were consulted (e.g., the views of the judges of the Constitutional Court on the future of that Court were formally requested, the rest of the judiciary, the Association of Law Societies, General Council of the Bar, National Democratic Lawyers Association, Black Lawyers Association, and Lawyers for Human Rights were specifically invited to submit their views, and a consultation was held on April 3, 1996, with representatives of the legal profession). According to the Constitutional Assembly Annual Report 1995–1996, more than two million submissions were received and more than sixty workshops, meetings, and consultations held with various "outside" stakeholders.[128]

Ultimately, the Constitutional Assembly (CA) reached a compromise just before the two-year limit expired.[129]

The CA chairman was ANC Secretary-General Cyril Ramaphosa, a lawyer and the former general secretary of the National Union of Mineworkers. His negotiating skills were tested but he proved to be firm at the right time while flexible at other times. As Christina Murray notes, "Occasionally, one would encounter Ramaphosa ... settled comfortably with a whisky discussing a way of resolving seemingly intractable problems with his National Party counterpart, Roelf Meyer."[130]

---

[128] DuBois, *supra* n. 97 at n. 150. *See also* Jeremy Sarkin, "The Drafting of South Africa's Final Constitution from a Human-Rights Perspective," 47 Am. J. Comp. L. 67, 70–71 (1999).

[129] Ebrahim, *supra* n. 94 at 205–11.   [130] Murray, *supra* n. 126 at 113.

The Constitutional Court, however, refused to certify the proposed Constitution because it violated some of the 34 Constitutional Principles. The *First Certification Judgment*'s[131] refusal was bold given South Africa's negligible history of judicial review. The Court explained that provincial powers were not adequately defined, that the labor clause was improperly insulated from judicial review, and that certain rights were not sufficiently entrenched to preclude amendment.[132] The Constitutional Assembly enacted the necessary changes and the Court approved them in the *Second Certification Judgment*.[133] Under the final Constitution, a National Council of Provinces replaced the Senate.

In a lecture at the New York Law School in 1996, Justice Sachs discussed the Court's *First Certification Judgment*, which was unanimous and unattributed. The Court had to examine numerous objections in a dramatic context, as he described: "About one month ago, the Constitutional Court of South Africa declared the Constitution of South Africa to be unconstitutional, which I think is a unique jurisprudential and political event in the world."[134] He explained further,

> Our basic decision was to give what we called a continental-type response, and not the full-flowing, sophisticated, precedent-based analysis that an ordinary judgment would have. We wrote more laconically in part because we had to cover everything. We were also very aware of the fact that our decisions would be binding in the future, and that here we were, most unusually, interpreting a Constitution from beginning to end and already establishing perspectives and fundamental interpretations. So we were reluctant to go beyond the absolutely minimum necessary to answer the questions that were asked.[135]

This description reveals the Court's adherence to principle combined with minimalism and pragmatism.

UNITED STATES

The South African constitutional drafting process resembled the American framing process in several ways: Elites played important roles, there were two drafting stages, and both constitutions promoted democracy and human rights. Moreover, British colonialism was still a force during both processes. In comparing the Afrikaaner and American struggles

---

[131] 1996 (4) SA 744 (1996).
[133] 1997 (2) SA 97 (CC).
[135] *Id.* at 677.

[132] Ebrahim, *supra* n. 94 at 158.
[134] *Supra* n. 119 at 669.

against British colonialism, George Frederickson notes that both situations contributed to the development of democratic human rights principles despite horrific racism.[136]

In the seventeenth century, British mercantilists established Virginia and Massachusetts beachheads[137] though some came to escape religious persecution. Specifically, Puritans and the Separatists went to Massachusetts,[138] whereas Quakers and Mennonites settled elsewhere. Eventually, thirteen British colonies arose with various types of government; the British encountered indigenous Indian tribes in many of these locations. Thus, America's founders were both revolutionaries and colonizers at the same time, unlike black South Africans. Some critics, however, assail the South African Constitution as being too Western e.g. they assert it contains remnants of a colonial mentality.[139]

Gradually, the monarchy imposed taxes on the colonies. British soldiers also invaded homes looking for illegally traded goods.[140] Massachusetts colonists protested by holding the "Boston Tea Party" in which they threw British tea shipments into Boston Harbor. The colonists came together for the First Continental Congress in 1774.[141] Later that year, some colonial militias fought British soldiers.[142] In 1776, Thomas Paine authored the famous pamphlet *Common Sense*, which pushed the colonies closer to unity and to war by highlighting the illegitimacy of King George's actions.[143] Thomas Jefferson authored the Declaration of Independence in 1776 explaining why the colonies should become the independent United States of America.[144]

Both *Common Sense* and the Declaration of Independence were propaganda tracts. The Declaration shifted "blame to a wicked king and Parliament, while maintaining that the colonists had done no more than protect their God-given rights.... Drawing heavily on Locke's compact

---

[136] George M. Frederickson, White Supremacy, A Comparative Study in American And South African History 145–46 (1981)(After telling the story of how a pamphlet circulated in Cape Town around 1778 asserting that "the people" had certain rights that the government could not trample, the author writes, "This assertion of the same right of revolution invoked by the American colonists against England may in fact have been influenced by news reaching the Cape about the Declaration of Independence.")

[137] Melvin Urofsky & Paul Finkelman, A March of Liberty, Vol. I 6–8 (2002).

[138] *Id.* at 10.

[139] *See e.g.* Hosea Jaffe, European Colonial Despotism: A History of Oppression and Resistance in South Africa 227–28 (1994).

[140] *Supra* n. 137 at 43.   [141] *Id.* at 54.

[142] *Id.* at 56.   [143] *Id.*

[144] *Id.* at 57–58.

theory of government, [Jefferson] charged the British king with having violated that unwritten agreement."[145] This compact theory was linked to natural law. Many historians, however, argue that King George was not so tyrannical.[146] The ensuing Revolutionary War lasted from 1776 to 1781, and the colonists were almost defeated. George Washington commanded the troops who fought valiantly against the better trained and equipped professional British soldiers. French assistance proved crucial, especially at Yorktown.

The 1955 ANC Freedom Charter resembled Jefferson's Declaration because both contained fundamental statements of values and both were produced by only one group; in contrast, South Africa's 34 Principles grew out of negotiations between two sides. Both the 34 Principles, though, and the Declaration provided a foundation for their respective constitutions and neither is considered binding constitutional law.

Another parallel involves George Washington and Nelson Mandela. Both were revolutionary heroes transcending their era and ordinary politics. They were also both military leaders, but Washington was the true professional soldier, whereas Mandela was an attorney. Of course, the "great man" theory of history is simplistic. It is, however, hard to imagine either nation succeeding without these statesmen who even garnered respect from their political opponents. One can go a step further with Mandela and say that he also resembled Martin Luther King to South Africans in his civil disobedience, imprisonments, racial leadership, and commitment to full equality. The tragedy in this comparison of course is that Washington owned slaves but he was, to that extent, unfortunately, a man of his time.

The U.S. Constitution's drafting process had two stages but was not designed purposely that way, as in South Africa. From 1781 to 1787, the Articles of Confederation governed the new nation. The Articles established a weak national government made up mainly of a legislative branch.[147] Most power resided in the loosely affiliated states. There was no real national executive official or national court[148] because the new nation feared having a strong national government like the British monarchy.[149]

This confederation, not unlike the consociational approach endorsed by some South African whites, proved disastrous. Financial chaos ensued

---

[145] *Id.*
[146] *Id.* at 58.
[147] *Id.* at 63 & 81.
[148] *Id.* at 83.
[149] Carol Berkin, A Brilliant Solution 19 (2002).

because states taxed each other's goods,[150] printed their own monies, and treated debtors so harshly that rebellions broke out.[151] Moreover, the weak national government left the country almost defenseless against hostile foreign forces.[152] It was unclear whether the United States was really one nation or several.

Several states recognized these problems and sent representatives to an Annapolis, Maryland conference that was supposed to reduce state barriers to national commerce.[153] The attendees decided to convene a more substantial constitutional convention in Philadelphia.[154] Thus, economic concerns largely motivated the U.S. Constitution's framers according to controversial historian Charles Beard, not the human rights principles at issue in South Africa.

The Philadelphia Convention's participants, such as the Virginian James Madison, the New Yorker Alexander Hamilton, and the Pennsylvanian James Wilson, are deified as America's founding fathers. That is because the Philadelphia attendees actually drafted a new national charter with Madison often described as its primary author.[155] The Declaration's author, Thomas Jefferson, was not present because he was Ambassador to France. This does not stop Jefferson from remaining an icon.

The delegates debated extensively how to represent the large states and the small states in the national legislature. Eventually, they adopted Roger Sherman's Connecticut Compromise.[156] In the House of Representatives, state population would determine the number of members of Congress, whereas each state would have two U.S. Senators, no matter its population. Many foreign countries, such as South Africa, and almost all states have bicameral arrangements. The Convention further decided that slaves would count as three-fifths of a person for representative purposes.[157] This was not the framer's finest hour. Their concern with the interests of states contrasts with the South African Constitutional Assembly's emphasis on the interests of various civil society groups such as women, traditional leaders, and unions.

The Virginia plan then created three branches of the national government – the legislative, executive, and judicial. Each would have certain powers and there would be checks and balances. The French political

---

[150]*Id.* at 15–16.
[151]*Id.* at 26.
[152]*Id.* at 19–23.
[153]*Id.* at 25.
[154]*Id.*
[155]Madison, rather than Hamilton, has been called the "architect of the Constitution." *Id.* at 31.
[156]*Id.* at 103–04.
[157]*Id.* at 113.

philosopher Montesquieu helped develop this separation of powers conception.[158] The South African parliamentary governmental system is far less separationist.[159] Otherwise, the American framers relied on political conceptions derived from Locke and from the ancients such as Grotius and Puffendorf, as well as republican principles.[160] Like South Africa, the American framers thus relied on foreign sources.

The new Constitution "solved" the state economic barriers problem by giving Congress the power to regulate interstate commerce. It established a U.S. Supreme Court but left Congress the discretion to create inferior federal courts. It vested executive power in a president chosen by an electoral college, made the president Commander in Chief, and gave him the power to enter into treaties. This presidential system differs from South Africa's parliamentary system that is modeled on that of Germany and Britain, though South Africa's leader is called a president, not a chancellor or prime minister. Unlike in the United States, South African parliamentary members who wish to join another party, while in office, may in certain circumstances be removed from office by their former party.

The U.S. Constitution reserved most unenumerated powers to the states but proclaimed the U.S. Constitution, treaties, and federal law to be supreme. The South African Constitution actually specifies which powers are provincial and which are local. Overall, the South African document provides for a more centralized government than the American document. Another difference is that the Constitution approved in Philadelphia in 1787 had few rights provisions.

When the U.S. Constitution was submitted to the states for ratification, many "antifederalists," such as Patrick Henry of Virginia, opposed the national government's increased powers as a threat to liberty.[161] Henry was famous for his statement, "Give me liberty or give me death," justifying his willingness to fight the British. He felt, however, that the U.S. Constitution would create a new monarchy. James Madison and Alexander Hamilton pseudonymously authored the *Federalist Papers* to address these and other concerns. The required number of states ratified the document by 1789.

---

[158] Judith Sklar, Montesquieu (1987).
[159] Anashri Pillay, "South Africa: Access to Land and Housing," 5 Int'l J. of Con. L. 544, 555 (2007).
[160] Urofsky, n. 137 at 45. Blackstone was also influential.
[161] Berkin, *supra* n. 149 at 176.

Moreover, a Bill of Rights was ratified in 1791 to address antifederalist and other concerns about increased national powers.[162] The Bill included rights to free speech, freedom of religion, and freedom from unreasonable search and seizure. The American Bill of Rights may be history's most important human rights document, given its influence on so many other nations and international institutions. It embodied the first generation of rights: political and civil rights.

Interestingly, Hamilton and Madison initially opposed inclusion of a Bill of Rights though Madison championed it through Congress.[163] They believed that listing certain rights might imply that other rights were unprotected. Most scholars argue that Madison drafted the Ninth Amendment to remove this concern.[164] Thus, both the South African and American revolutionary political leaders initially opposed a strong Bill of Rights, as do many progressive scholars today.

Adoption of the U.S. Constitution was likely illegal because the Articles of Confederation only allowed the unanimous acceptance of amendments, yet the U.S. Constitution became effective upon the approval of nine of the thirteen states. Similarly, critics have charged that an unelected elite, through an Interim Constitution, established the procedures for adopting South Africa's Constitution. Moreover, apartheid's illegitimate tricameral Parliament endorsed the Interim Constitution's authority. Transitional justice scholars, such as Ruti Teitel and Jon Elster, have pointed out that constitutional paradigm shifts often have legality gaps.[165]

In addition to the legality question, there were concerns about whether the ratification process was democratic. Forrest MacDonald and Jackson Turner Main each suggest that a majority of contemporaneous eligible American voters would not have supported the Constitution.[166]

---

[162] *Id.* at 179; Urofsky, *supra* n. 137 at 123.

[163] Urofsky, *id.* at 123–24.

[164] *Id.* at 127. *But see* Kurt Lash, "A Textual-Historical Theory of the Ninth Amendment," 60 Stan. L. Rev. 101 (2008).

[165] *Cf.* Christina Murray, "A Constitutional Beginning: Making South Africa's Final Constitution," 23 U. Ark. Little Rock L. Rev. 809, 813 (2001) ("An Unconstitutional Constitution") (discussing how the Constitutional Court's role meant the Constitutional Assembly could adopt an unconstitutional constitution). Ruti Teitel, Transitional Justice (2000); Jon Elster, Closing the Books (2004).

[166] Malla Pollack, "Dampening the Illegitimacy of the United States Government: Reframing the Constitution from Contract to Promise," 42 Idaho L. Rev. 123, 164 n. 156 (2005–2006) (referencing the MacDonald and Main books); Jackson Turner Main, The Anti-Federalists 249 n. 1(1961) ("The Anti-federalists probably had a very small majority – perhaps 52 per cent; but of course it is impossible to be exact.")

These calculations do not even include disenfranchised African Americans, Native Americans, and women. Moreover, the South African Constitution required neither a province by province ratification process nor a referendum. One commentator wrote of South Africa that,

> What these [various study] results indicate is that the debate concerning federalism, power sharing, and the bill of rights was largely an affair for the political elites rather than the ordinary citizen. The surveys conducted to probe for the meanings and understandings of democracy support the contention that many South African citizens, while generally supportive of the transformation the country has undergone, have only vague ideas about what their democracy should entail.[167]

One issue that the American framers left unanswered was the power of the judiciary. In *Marbury v. Madison*,[168] the Supreme Court in 1804 boldly ruled that it had the power of judicial review, meaning that its constitutional decisions bound the other branches. The Court reasoned that the other branches lacked constraints if Supreme Court opinions were merely advisory. Alexander Hamilton's discussion in *The Federalist Papers No.78* supports the Court's view though controversy remains more than 200 years later. *Marbury* resembles the *First Certification Judgment* in their similar demonstrations of the judiciary's power, but Chief Justice Marshall wisely used this power to rule for the Jefferson administration.[169] Otherwise, he might have been impeached.

As is well known, the American North and South fought a tragic war in the 1860s that had many causes including economic rivalries, political differences, and disputes about slavery. The North eventually won, and this victory subsequently led to adoption of the Civil War Amendments – the Thirteenth, Fourteenth, and Fifteenth. They covered rights to equality, due process, and voting, especially for the slaves freed by President Abraham Lincoln's Emancipation Proclamation. These amendments resemble the South African Constitution's concerns with racial equality.

---

[167] Thomas A. Koeble, The Global Economy and Democracy in South Africa 98 (1998).

[168] 5 U.S. 137 (1803).

[169] Heinz Klug has asserted that the true South African analogue to *Marbury* is a Constitutional Court case called Executive Council of the Western Cape Legislature v. President of the Republic of South Africa, 1995 (4) SA 877 (CC) (the Court ruled that a delegation of power to the president was unconstitutional but essentially upheld the national government's ultimate authority to draw local government lines). Klug, *supra* n. 56 at 150–51.

The Reconstruction era followed in the United States, and it looked as if the nation would implement these amendments to promote black equality. Leon Higginbotham compares the American Reconstruction era to the situation South African blacks faced when Mandela was freed and political parties were no longer banned in 1990.[170] However, within a few decades, the U.S. Supreme Court issued several decisions that curtailed these Civil War Amendments, supposedly based on federalism concerns.[171] The vagueness of the amendments facilitated the Court's actions. These decisions are ironic because the North fought the South in part because the Southern states sought too much autonomy. Moreover, the American political situation eventually moved away from the promise of true reconstruction and blacks, though technically free, were still oppressed by Jim Crow, lynchings, denials of the right to vote, and school segregation.[172]

The U.S. Constitution has been amended only twenty-seven times in more than 200 years. However, Bruce Ackerman and other scholars argue that several Supreme Court decisions have effectively amended the Constitution in addition to those formal amendments. Ackerman labels these decisions as "constitutional moments."[173] Perhaps the most notable occurred in 1937, when the Court upheld President Franklin Roosevelt's Depression era New Deal federal assistance programs after striking down similar programs a year earlier.[174] This decision ushered in the modern "administrative state." Of course, politics and changes in Court membership played a role in that ruling, not just sudden enlightenment.

---

[170] Higginbotham, *supra* n. 92 at 494–95 ("The similarities between the countries are most distinct if we compare the plight of free blacks in the United States from the Reconstruction period to the 1970's to the plight of blacks in contemporary South Africa. Of course, these similarities are not limited to the conduct of the courts and the legislatures; rather these institutional differences are indicative of a racism embedded in the political culture of both societies. In both countries, blacks are or were denied voting rights; in South Africa by law, and in the American South by practice.").

[171] *See e.g.*, Civil Rights Cases, 109 U.S. 3 (1883); The Slaughterhouse Cases, 83 U.S. 36 (1872).

[172] Higginbotham, *supra* n. 92 at 487–88 ("The similarity between the institutions of Apartheid and Jim Crow, as interlocking systems of oppressing blacks in both the public and private spheres, allows for the drawing of valid comparisons between South African courts from the 1930's to the present and American courts prior to the 1970's, the point at which the shift in political power produced by the civil rights movement and the Voting Rights Act began to be felt.").

[173] We the People, Vol. 1, Foundations (1991).

[174] *See e.g.* NLRB v. Jones & Laughlin Steel Corp, 301 U.S. 1 (1937).

The Court's 1954 decision in *Brown v. Board of Education* is its most celebrated. Scholars disagree on the relationship between *Brown* and the civil rights movement of the 1960s. As described earlier, however, there were certainly parallels and connections between the South African liberation movement and the American civil rights protests. George Frederickson also writes that the American "black power" movement was linked to the South African "black consciousness" movement led by Biko.[175] Interestingly, U.S. Supreme Court jurisprudence for a brief period, in the late 1960s and early 1970s, came close to resembling the transformative Constitutional Court, particularly in areas like socioeconomic rights.

Perhaps the Supreme Court's most controversial modern case was its 1973 ruling in *Roe v. Wade* that women have a constitutional right to an abortion. Thirty-five years later, the abortion issue still dominates American political discourse and commentary about the Court. No Constitutional Court case has had such an impact in South Africa.

THE JUDICIAL BRANCHES

One difference between the Constitutional Court and the U.S. Supreme Court is that the latter hears federal statutory and administrative law cases, as well as constitutional cases. Why did South Africa create a more specialized judicial body? The general view is that South Africa needed to break from its past including the duplicity of many courts and lawyers under apartheid. The existing South African Supreme Court of Appeal suffered from the apartheid taint. A Constitutional Court meant change.

Austria was one of the first nations to establish such a specialized court on the recommendation of its legal theorist Hans Kelsen. Historically, Germany's Constitutional Court is probably the most influential especially given the nation's economic power.

Eleven Justices who generally serve twelve-year terms sit on the South African Constitutional Court. They can take sabbaticals during their terms unlike their American counterparts.[176] A diverse Judicial Services

---

[175] Fredrickson *supra* n. 25 at 313 & 315 (1996).

[176] For example, Justice Zac Yacoob joined the Court in February 1998, but took a six-month sabbatical during the first half of 2002, spending much time in India. Minu Jose, "Profile, Justice Zakeria Mohammed Yacoob," Combat Law, Vol. 1 No. 1 (2002), http://www.combatlaw.org/information.php?issue_id=1&article_id=39 (last visited May 13, 2008). Several of the Justices have spent sabbaticals as visiting professors at American law schools.

Commission, made up of lawyers, academics, political figures, and others receives nominations, conducts candidate interviews, and proposes a three-person slate to the president, who must then choose one of the three. South Africa modeled its approach on other countries that have judicial commissions.[177] Some American states like Iowa also use variations on the commission model.[178]

By contrast, the U.S. Constitution requires that the U.S. Senate confirm the president's federal judicial appointments by a majority vote. There has been significant debate about whether senators should defer to the president or whether they should be aggressive in their scrutiny given the courts' power.[179] Recently, the Senate battles have been bruising affairs that have even inquired into nominees' personal qualities. The South African judicial commission process appears to reduce some of the acrimony of the American confirmation proceedings, though not completely.[180]

The Constitutional Court is more liberal on justiciability than the U.S. Supreme Court. Plaintiffs "acting in the public interest"[181] can bring constitutional claims, and there is a "direct access" provision.[182] The South African Constitution also provides for numerous other courts though they are not as distinct as the American state courts are separate from the American federal courts. Each province, for example, has a high court. Typically, the Constitutional Court must confirm lower court findings of constitutional invalidity. There also was a rivalry between the Constitutional Court and the South African Supreme Court for a period that has no clear American parallel. Interestingly, most of the South African public's contact with the judiciary occurs in magistrate courts, but the Constitution prohibits magistrates from ruling on constitutional matters. Those matters must be raised in the provincial high courts on appeal.

The plaintiff in the U.S. Supreme Court must typically show a personal injury, causation, and redressability, not a general public interest. The

---

[177] Lisa Hibink, "Assessing the New Constitutionalism," 40 Compar. Politics 227, 229–31 (Jan. 2008); Kate Malleson & Peter H. Russell, Appointing Judges in the Age of Judicial Power 6–7 (2006).

[178] *See e.g.*, Editorial, "Transparency is Key in Selection of Judges," Des Moines Register 16A, June 11, 2008 (discussing Iowa's judicial commission model).

[179] Christopher Eisgruber, The Next Justice (2007).

[180] Penelope Andrews, "The South African Judicial Appointments Process," 44 Osgoode Hall L.J. 565 (2006).

[181] South African Constitution, Sec. 38(d) (1996). Iain Currie, Johan de Waal, The Bill of Rights Handbook, Sec. 4.2 at 89 (2005).

[182] South African Constitution, Sec. 167(6)(a) (1996). Currie, *id.*, Sec. 5.4 at 132.

Court does not issue advisory opinions or allow individuals direct access. It has, however, issued some broad remedies in racial discrimination and other cases, remedies not seen in South Africa.

How do the two courts write their opinions? The Constitutional Court tries to arrive at consensus. According to former Justice Richard Goldstone, the Court will meet as many as a dozen times to discuss a single case when there are disagreements. If no resolution can be reached, the opposing sides will draft opinions. A meeting then takes place in which each side makes arguments designed to strengthen the other side's opinion. The Court's goal is for all opinions to be of the highest quality, regardless of who prevails. The U.S. Supreme Court differs in that it has one meeting after the oral argument, at which each of the Justices voices his or her view, proceeding from most senior in service to junior. The most senior Justice in the majority then assigns the opinion to a member who shares his or her view. Drafts of majority and dissenting opinions are circulated prior to publication so the Justices can address arguments from the other side.

Oral arguments also differ as the Constitutional Court imposes no limitations on their length. In one famous socioeconomic rights case, the arguments went on for two days. By contrast, the Supreme Court has strict time limits. Each side has a half-hour unless the Justices believe more time is needed. There are small lights in the Supreme Court that turn red when an advocate's time has expired. The Supreme Court records all oral arguments and produces transcripts of them. The Constitutional Court generally lacks oral argument records.

What institutional issues face the two high courts? In South Africa, the ANC's political dominance makes judicial independence a concern especially given the Court's youth. Another concern is corruption, particularly in light of the recent finding that a prominent judge was paid for work by a private law firm while on the bench. The Constitutional Court has also recently charged this judge separately with trying to exert undue influence in a case involving a leading ANC figure. The South African judiciary also must continue to undergo racial and gender transformation, as well as professionalization, particularly at the lower levels. Language barriers exist too because the courts act in English, a language many citizens do not speak.

Regarding the U.S. Supreme Court, several Justices have given annual reports bemoaning federal judicial salaries compared to the private sector. The Justices believe these salaries are discouraging talented attorneys from seeking the bench and causing good judges to leave. As previously mentioned, the polarized confirmation process has also created great frustration though the solution is not obvious.

President Franklin Roosevelt's "court packing scheme" in 1937 shows that the Court has always been political. Things may have gotten worse, especially since the U.S. Senate rejected President Reagan's nomination of Robert Bork in 1987. Ironically, President George W. Bush withdrew his second Court nominee, Harriet Miers, because of political opposition in his own party. Both parties have even refused to vote on certain presidential nominees to the lower federal courts. The deeper concern is that this bellicose confirmation process signals a decline in the judiciary's independence. For example, Congress has recently become more involved in the federal judiciary's procedures which had been typically left to the Supreme Court. Justice Sandra Day O'Connor has also objected to threats to judicial independence.

Another issue is length of service. Article III's good behavior clause is generally viewed as providing life tenure to all federal judges absent impeachable malfeasance. Two scholars, however, have recently questioned this view and many scholars argue that life tenure polarizes the confirmation process, permits ideological capture of the Court, and allows Justices in terrible health to continue serving. A term of eighteen years seems to be the new rage.[183] Certainly, almost no foreign courts have life tenure.

WHAT MAKES THE SOUTH AFRICAN CONSTITUTION UNIQUE

This last section describes several unique South African Constitutional provisions, and two Constitutional Court cases that are not presented in later chapters because there are no American parallels.

Provisions

The South African Bill of Rights applies to state and private actors, unlike the American Bill of Rights, which has a state action requirement. Section 8(2) of the South African Constitution specifies, "A provision of the Bill of Rights binds a natural or a juristic person if, and to the extent that, it is applicable taking into account the nature of the right and the nature of any duty imposed by the right." This is an example of

---

[183] *See e.g.,* Steven Calabresi, James Lindgren, "Term Limits for the Supreme Court: Life Tenure Reconsidered," 29 Harv. J. L. & Pub. Pol'y 769 (2006).

direct horizontality and illustrates how far the South African Constitution extends to protect people's dignity. Interestingly, horizontality also means that the Constitution can infringe on the freedom of private individuals to engage in certain actions, such as choosing friends of one race or gender. Thus, it is a tricky area especially because section 8(2) does not set clear standards. Precisely how should the court "take into account"? The leading horizontality case involves freedom of expression as discussed in Chapter 7. One commentary notes that direct horizontality may not be needed because common law remedies are typically adequate.[184]

Moreover, section 39(2) specifies, "When interpreting any legislation, and when developing the common law or customary law, every court, tribunal or forum must promote the spirit, purport, and objects of the Bill of Rights." This is indirect horizontality, and it is also vague. One could imagine American conservatives criticizing this provision as an invitation to judicial mischief.

The South African Constitution's section 37 on state of emergencies also has no parallel. Section 37, however, limits the government's ability to utilize such a potentially dangerous mechanism. Moreover, the Constitution contains "non-derogable rights" that can never be restricted, such as the right to life, the right to dignity, and the right to be free from discrimination on the basis of "race, colour, ethnic or social origin, sex, religion, or language."

The U.S. Constitution does not grant the government state of emergency powers. This is one of its strengths. Congress can, though, suspend the writ of habeas corpus in times of rebellion or invasion. This habeas question has become central in the U.S. Supreme Court because of laws limiting court access for the Guantanamo detainees.

South Africa is also unique because of its eleven official constitutional languages. Significantly, the United States has gone in the opposite direction, with several states making English the official language. These proposals undoubtedly reflect some American anti-immigrant sentiment.

Finally, the South African Constitution protects the rights of cultural and other communities as long as those rights are not exercised "in a manner inconsistent with any provision of the Bill of Rights."[185] Thus, customary law courts are ultimately bound by the Constitution's gender discrimination protections. To put it simply, the women's groups triumphed over the customary law supporters in the constitutional negotiations.

---

[184]Currie, *supra* n. 181 at 51.   [185]Secs. 30 & 31.

Cases

The South African Constitutional Court has decided cases on amnesty
and on the right to public participation in the national legislative process that have no American equivalent. These cases reveal South Africa's
commitment to principles of reconciliation and to democracy.

In *AZAPO v. President of the Republic of South Africa*,[186] the Court
addressed the legality of the internationally famous Truth & Reconciliation Commission (TRC), which was established to allow those who
committed political crimes to be reintegrated into society under certain
conditions. These political crimes were not simply white-collar crimes –
they included murder and attempted assassinations.

Essentially, the perpetrators had to apply for amnesty and testify truth-
fully to a TRC committee about what they did and why they did it.
Amnesty was unavailable for random or private acts of violence. The
theory was that society could only move forward if there was forgiveness
and that the nation needed to learn apartheid's many secrets. The government would then pay reparations to the victims or the families of deceased
victims because the perpetrator would have received legal immunity.

Victim families challenged this last TRC provision as violating the
Constitution's right to access the courts. Moreover, international law
guarantees remedies to those whose rights are violated. Despite acknowledging that the TRC negated court access, the Justices ruled that the
Interim Constitution's "postamble" specifically authorized amnesty and
that some remedy was provided.

The TRC has received international acclaim for facilitating postconflict
social healing yet many in South Africa despair over its operations. Specifically, the government has granted amnesty for some horrific deeds while
making minimal reparations payments. Even Nobel Peace Prize winner
Archbishop Desmond Tutu, head of the TRC, has spoken out against
the government's handling of reparations.[187] And there are occasional
rumors that victim families could again challenge the TRC, as the Constitutional Court found that amnesty was conditioned on reparations, which
the government has not always paid. Despite the South African TRC's
international fame, it is important to note that South Africa adopted the
truth commission idea from Latin America.[188]

---

[186] 1996 (4) SA 671 (CC).

[187] SAPA, "South Africa: TRC Final Report Handed over to Mbeki," Mar. 21, 2003,
http://www.sadocc.at/news/2003-083.shtml (last visited June 16, 2008).

[188] It's also worth mentioning that there is a pending lawsuit in the United States against
American corporations for assisting the apartheid regime. *Khulumani v. Barclay Nat'l*

Another significant case was *Doctors for Life Int'l v. The Speaker of the National Assembly*.[189] The South African Constitution provides for reproductive freedom, so opposing abortion substantively was futile despite the Constitution's right to life section. That is why this book has no comparative chapter on abortion.

A group of pro-life physicians, however, argued that the National Council of Provinces violated the Constitution by failing to hold provincial hearings on two Parliament bills: one delineating when women could get abortions and another that governed traditional healers. The Court agreed, but suspended its ruling for eighteen months to allow Parliament to pass the laws again, this time with adequate public participation. This is an extraordinary procedural due process case writ large, showing democracy's importance to the new nation. There was a dissent in the South African case taking a more American view. The U.S. Supreme Court second-guesses federal agency procedures on occasion but usually treats the legislative process as a political question. These are hints of the fascinating cases to come. The next chapters discuss specific rights.

Bank Ltd., 504 F.3d 254 (2d Cir. 2007), *aff'd w/o judgment*, American Isuzu Motors, Inc. v. Ntsebeza, 76 USLW 3405 (2008). There have also been lawsuits in the United States by African Americans seeking reparations for slavery. It seems the American approach is to litigate these issues, not have truth commissions. By contrast, the American government did pass legislation apologizing to Japanese who were interned during World War II and offering reparations.

[189] (2006) ZACC 11.

3

The Death Penalty

South Africa has disallowed capital punishment for more than a decade, yet violent crime there remains newsworthy even internationally.[1] The crime rate is among the highest in the world.[2] In 2000, a man broke into South African President Thabo Mbeki's house, despite heavy security, and made himself comfortable drinking brandy for several days while

[1] *See, e.g.*, Charles Starmer-Smith, "British Tourists Urged Not to Avoid South Africa," Daily Telegraph (London), July 3, 2004, at Travel 4 ("Concerns about the dangers of travel in South Africa resurfaced following the murder of Darryl Kempster, who was part of Michael Flatley's Lord of the Dance Company.... He was shot trying to run away from a mugger."), available at 2004 WLNR 4152581.

[2] Ted Leggett, senior researcher at the Institute for Security Studies in Pretoria, said, "There is no denying that crime here is still very, very bad. The murder rate of nearly 22,000 a year is higher than that of the United States, a violent country with six-and-a-half times more people." Murder is "the most reliable indicator of the real violent crime situation" as it "is the one form of violent crime that is not heavily underreported." Ted Leggett, "The Facts behind the Figures: Crime Statistics 2002/3," 6 SA Crime Q. 1, (Dec. 2003). Although Columbia has surpassed South Africa to become the "murder capital of the world...with sixty-six murders per 100,000 [people]", the situation in South Africa is still dire with "47 murders per 100,000 citizens (about the same as the most dangerous urban area of the United States, Washington, D.C.)." *Id.* Statistics from 2007 show that South Africa had closed the gap as Columbia had 61 murders per 100,000, whereas South Africa 50. http://www.nationmaster.com/graph/cri_mur_percap-crime-murders-per-capita (last visited Jan. 9, 2008) Additionally, though South Africa "may no longer be the murder capital of the world,... since apartheid ended [in 1994] [t]he number of rapes each year has risen from 44,751 to 54,435 and robberies have doubled." Starmer-Smith, *id.* n. 1. Leggett wrote, in another paper about South Africa, "A country of some 44 million, it experienced nearly 20,000 murders in the fiscal year 2004/2005, which is about 25 percent more than the United States." Ted Leggett, "Just Another Miracle: A Decade of Crime and Justice in Democratic South Africa," Social Research Fall 2005, http://findarticles.com/p/articles/mi_m2267/is_3_72/ai_n15893373 (last visited Jan. 9, 2008).

Mbeki was out of the country.[3] During my year in South Africa as a Fulbright scholar in 2000, I was told about a man who began a walk across the country to bring national media attention to the high crime rate. Robbers supposedly mugged him on the first day.

Despite evidence that many South Africans favored the death penalty,[4] the new South African Constitutional Court in 1995 ruled the death penalty unconstitutional in *State v. Makwanyane & Another*[5] *(Makwanyane)*. The Court's president, Arthur Chaskalson, authored the unanimous opinion, though all of the other Justices wrote separate concurrences.[6] The national government supported the challengers because the government was made up of former apartheid opponents who had risked execution.[7] An attorney general (AG) from one of South Africa's provinces defended the law.[8] The decision contrasts sharply with the U.S. Supreme Court's 1976 landmark ruling in *Gregg v. Georgia*[9] upholding the death penalty's constitutionality.

This chapter examines *Makwanyane* closely because it is one of the first cases to reveal the salient characteristics of South African constitutional interpretation such as an emphasis on values, a willingness to examine

---

[3] *See* "Burglar Guzzles Mbeki's Brandy," Mail & Guardian Online, Sep. 7, 2000, http://www.mg.co.za/articledirect.aspx?articleid=223156&area=%2farchives_online_edition%2f (last visited Jan. 9, 2008).

[4] Ursula Bentele, "Back to an International Perspective on the Death Penalty as a Cruel Punishment: The Example of South Africa," 73 Tul. L. Rev. 251, 271 (1998) ("[The provincial Attorney General] cited public opinion polls [during oral arguments], demonstrating that sixty-three percent of the [South African] general population support capital punishment. Even in the African National Congress, which is officially opposed to the penalty, fifty-six percent of the members were in favor of retention.").

[5] 1995 (3) SA 391 (CC) at 453, ¶ 151 (S. Afr.).

[6] Id. ¶ 152 (Ackermann, J., concurring), 173 (Didcott, J., concurring); 191 (Kentridge, J., conurring), 205 (Kriegler, J., concurring), 215 (Langa, J., concurring), ¶ 235 (Madala, J., concurring), ¶ 261 (Mahomed, J., concurring), ¶ 300 (Mokgoro, J., concurring), ¶ 318 (O'Regan, J., concurring), ¶ 345 (Sachs, J., concurring).

[7] Id. ¶ 11 ("Mr. Bizos, who represented the South African Government at the hearing of this matter, informed us that the Government accepts the death penalty is a cruel, inhuman and degrading punishment and that it should be declared unconstitutional."); Heinz Klug, "The Dignity Clause of the Montana Constitution: May Foreign Jurisprudence Lead the Way to an Expanded Interpretation?," 64 Mont. L. Rev. 133, 139 & n.20 (2003) (describing how former President Mandela faced the death penalty as a possible sentence).

[8] *Makwanyane*, (3) SA 391 at 404, ¶ 11 ("The attorney-general of the Witwatersrand, whose office is independent of the Government, took a different view, and contended that the death penalty is a necessary and acceptable form of punishment.").

[9] 428 U.S. 153, 207 (1976).

international and comparative precedents, and judicial pragmatism. The Court there also developed a test for whether the government could justify limiting a right that was incorporated into the final Constitution. This chapter then compares the Constitutional Court's reasoning with U.S. Supreme Court death penalty cases. Focusing on the potential influence of South Africa's death penalty decision is especially appropriate because it has been almost fifteen years since *Makwanyane* yet the issue still resonates in South Africa and the United States.

The chapter also explores how recent U.S. Supreme Court decisions, which outlaw the death penalty for the mentally retarded[10] and for juveniles,[11] show movement in the South African Court's direction. These recent American opinions even contain foreign law comparisons.[12] Moreover, U.S. juries since 1999 are less willing to recommend death sentences.[13] In addition, Illinois granted clemency to all death row inmates in 2000, and New Jersey recently abolished the death penalty.[14]

In an August 2005 speech to the American Bar Assocation, U.S. Supreme Court Justice John Paul Stevens offered some reasons for this shift. He said that the death penalty generally has "serious flaws" and that DNA evidence has shown that a "substantial number of death sentences were administered erroneously."[15] Though Justice Stevens is only partly right about the impact of DNA evidence, his antideath penalty conversion is emblematic of this shift in thinking.

The first section of this chapter analyzes South Africa's use of capital punishment during the apartheid era and the factors leading to the Constitutional Court's decision to abandon the death penalty. The next section examines the U.S. Supreme Court's death penalty jurisprudence. The final section demonstrates how the U.S. Supreme Court has started to sound somewhat like the South African Constitutional Court.

---

[10] Atkins v. Virginia, 536 U.S. 304, 321 (2002).

[11] Roper v. Simmons, 125 S. Ct. 1183, 1200 (2005).

[12] *See, e.g.,* Roper, 125 S. Ct. at 1198–1200; Lawrence v. Texas, 539 U.S. 558, 573, 576–77 (2003).

[13] *See infra* n. 199 .

[14] Keith B. Richburg, "N.J. Approves Abolition of Death Penalty; Corzine to Sign," Wash. Post A03 (Dec. 14, 2007), http://www.washingtonpost.com/wp-dyn/content/article/2007/12/13/AR2007121301302.html (last visited Jan. 9, 2008).

[15] Associated Press, "Stevens Cites 'Serious Flaws' in Use of the Death Penalty," Wash. Post, Aug. 8, 2005, at A4.

DEATH PENALTY JURISPRUDENCE IN SOUTH AFRICA

History

The apartheid government charged Nelson Mandela with treason in 1956 for his activities leading the African National Congress (ANC).[16] The penalty was death. Yet, Mandela was not the first person to face this threat. Capital punishment in South Africa dates at least to the seventeenth century, with the arrival of the Dutch East Indies Company.[17] By 1910, after a period of English control, the punishment was mainly limited to murder convictions.[18] When the Afrikaaner National Party (National Party) took over in 1948, it used the death penalty for those convicted of aggravated robbery, burglary, sabotage, terrorism, and kidnapping.[19] In theory, judges were mandated to impose a death sentence in certain cases.[20]

The National Party expanded the use of capital punishment to intimidate political resistance.[21] Thus, in 1963 "training or obtaining information that could further an object of communism" meant death, as did "advocating abroad economic or social change in South Africa by violent means through the aid of a foreign government or institution."[22]

According to one commentator,

Capital punishment in South Africa has been viewed as a tool specifically for controlling and punishing opponents of apartheid. These motivations

---

[16] Nelson Mandela, A Long Walk Home 203 (1994).

[17] *See* Peter Norbert Bouckaert, "Shutting Down the Death Factory: The Abolition of Capital Punishment in South Africa," 32 Stan. J. Int'l L. 287, 288 (1996).

[18] *Id.* at 289.   [19] *Id.* at 291.

[20] Ursula Bentele, "The False Promise of Discretionary Imposition of the Death Penalty in South Africa," 9 S. Afr. J. Hum. Rts. 255, 256 (1993). The rate of executions varied, however, according to the granting of clemency, with more than 75 percent of those sentenced to death spared at times. *Id.*

[21] Bouckaert, *supra* n. 17, at 291–92. Apartheid laws required a person to be classified at birth by race, predetermining where a person would live, learn, work, travel, and even the cemetery in which he or she would be buried. "South Africa's Pass Law Embodies Dream for Whites, Burden for Blacks", N.Y. Times, Aug. 16, 1985, at A6, *available at* 1985 WLNR 630243.

[22] *Id.* at 291. The apartheid authorities often tried to denigrate the resistance by accusing it of having communist origins. Emily H. McCarthy, "South Africa's Amnesty Process: A Viable Route toward Truth and Reconciliation?," 3 Mich. J. Race & L. 183, 245–46 (1997–1998); Rafael X. Zahralddin-Aravena, "Development in South African and Venture Capital: The Challenges and Opportunities for the Enterprise Fund for Southern Africa," 15 Berkeley J. Int'l L. 62, 64 & n.6 (1997).

are particularly evident in the state's treatment of accused members of banned liberation movements. In 1983, for instance, the execution of three convicted [African National Congress] combatants was timed to coincide with the seventh anniversary of uprisings in the black township of Soweto.[23]

The government's political repression via the death penalty ultimately elicited international and national protests that weakened the apartheid regime.[24] The protests also influenced government to pardon the "Sharpeville Six."[25]

Another problem was that the South African government still used hanging as its execution method even in the late 1980s. South African Dr. Christian Barnard, who performed the world's first heart transplant,[26] described the gruesome effects of hanging:

> The man's spinal cord will rupture at the point where it enters the skull, electrochemical discharges will send his limbs flailing in a grotesque dance, eyes and tongue will start from the facial apertures under the assault of the rope and his bowels and bladder may simultaneously void themselves to soil the legs and drip on the floor.[27]

[23] Nathan V. Holt, Jr., Note, "Human Rights and Capital Punishment: The Case of South Africa," 30 Va. J. Int'l L. 273, 303 (1989).

[24] Bouckaert, *supra* n. 17, at 292, 296–97 ("The death sentences [in the 'Uppington Twenty-Five' case in 1989, in which twenty-five people were convicted for murder for the death of a policeman after police tear-gassed a peaceful assembly] were handed down at a time of increasing debate in South Africa about the death penalty and sparked mass rallies against capital punishment.").

[25] Five men and one woman, known as the Sharpeville Six, were sentenced to death for the killing of town councilman Jacob Dlamini, who was stoned to death during riots in 1984. John D. Battersby, "6 South Africans Are Denied Retrial," N.Y. Times, June 14, 1988, at A7, *available at* 1988 WLNR 1311017. The defendants had no physical involvement in his murder, but were convicted for having a "common purpose" with the rioters who did kill Dlamini by actively participating in actions that led to his death. *Id.* The harshness of the sentences sparked an international outcry, including appeals from President Reagan, Prime Minister Margaret Thatcher, and Chancellor Helmut Kohl, leading President P. W. Botha to eventually commute the six defendants' sentences from death by hanging to a lengthy prison term. Christopher S. Wren, "Judge Condemns 14 South Africa Blacks," N.Y. Times, May 27, 1989, at 13, *available at* 1989 WLNR 2081884; John D. Battersby, "South Africa Firm on Hanging of Six," N.Y. Times, Mar. 17, 1988, at A10, *available at* 1988 WLNR 1276937.

[26] Daniel S. Greenberg, "The Vanishing Heroes of Science," N.Y. Times, July 4, 1995, at 31, *available at* 1995 WLNR 3794886.

[27] *Makwanyane* (3) SA at ¶ 335 (O'Regan, J., concurring).

In addition, there was evidence of racial inequities in sentencing:

> During a one-year period, forty-seven percent of blacks convicted of mur-
> dering whites were sentenced to death, compared to no death sentences
> for whites convicted of murdering blacks and only two and a half percent
> for blacks convicted of killing blacks. One observer estimates that between
> 1910 and 1975, twenty-seven times as many blacks as whites were exe-
> cuted. A study of rape sentencing between 1947 and 1969 found no whites
> executed for the rape of black women, despite 288 such convictions. Dur-
> ing the same period, 120 black men were executed for raping white women,
> out of 844 convicted for such crimes.[28]

Other studies showed that whether a defendant received the death
penalty depended on which judge heard the case despite the "mandatory" sentencing rules. A Cape Provincial Division survey covering 1986
to 1988 concluded there were "substantial disparities among judges in
handing down death sentences" that "raise serious doubts about the fairness of the system."[29] These disparities were explained in part by "the
differential allocation of trials to judges by the Judge President," as well
as the "personal penal philosophies [that] inform the decision to sentence
a person to death."[30] However, "it can never be accepted in a moral legal
system that whether an accused lives or dies depends on the judge before
whom he or she is tried."[31]

These protests, studies, and other pressures influenced the government's decision to stop executions in 1989,[32] the year before Nelson Mandela was freed and political parties were no longer banned.[33] The government then passed a law giving judges discretion on whether to impose
a death sentence based on new procedural and substantive guidelines.[34]

According to the guidelines, two assessors had to hear the case along
with a judge,[35] and the majority then ruled on guilt or innocence.[36]
Though the judge alone determined the sentence, a defendant could

---

[28] Bouckaert, *supra* n. 17, at 292–93.
[29] Christina Murray et al., "The Death Penalty in the Cape Provincial Division: 1986–
1988," 5 S. Afr. J. Hum. Rts. 154, 170.
[30] *Id.*   [31] *Id.*
[32] *Makwanyane,* (3) SA at 402, ¶ 6.
[33] Bouckaert, *supra* n. 17, at 296–97; Michael Wines, "World Briefing Africa: South Africa:
Mandela Prison Letters," N.Y. Times, Dec. 7, 2004, at A16, *available at* 2004 WLNR
13350637.
[34] Criminal Procedure Act No. 51 of 1977 s. 277 (as amended by Criminal Law Amendment Act No. 107 of 1990 s. 4).
[35] *Makwanyane,* (3) SA at 417, ¶ 45.   [36] *Id.*

automatically appeal.[37] Even if there was no appeal, a reviewing court examined the case and could reverse the decision if it would not have "imposed such sentence itself."[38] The reviewing court also had to consider aggravating and mitigating factors and find beyond a reasonable doubt that the death sentence was justified.[39] Lastly, the reviewing court was obliged to take account of the justice system's goals, namely "deterrence, prevention, reformation, and retribution."[40]

Despite these new protections, the Constitutional Court in *Makwanyane* found the death penalty unconstitutional.[41] When the case was decided, no executions had taken place for more than five years.[42] The following section explores several characteristics of one of the Constitutional Court's most important early opinion.

The Constitutional Court's Analysis

In *Makwanyane*, two defendants were convicted "on four counts of murder, one count of attempted murder and one count of robbery with aggravating circumstances . . . [and] sentenced to death on each of the counts of murder and to long terms of imprisonment on the other counts."[43] The Appellate Division of the Supreme Court dismissed the appeals, concluding that "the circumstances of the murders were such that the accused should receive the heaviest sentence permissible according to law."[44]

The Constitutional Court had to decide whether the death penalty for murder was consistent with the provisions of the 1993 Interim Constitution, which had come into force after the trial.[45] The Constitution did not address the issue though the appellants argued that the punishment conflicted with sections 9 and 11(2) of the Constitution.[46] Section 9 provided that "every person shall have the right to life,"[47] and section 11(2) stated that "no person shall be subject to torture of any kind, whether physical, mental or emotional, nor shall any person be subject to cruel, inhuman or degrading treatment or punishment."[48] The Court faced the question of capital punishment without any significant constitutional rights tradition

---

[37] *Id.* at 417–18, ¶ 45.

[38] *Id.* at 418, ¶ 45.

[39] *Id.* at 418, ¶ 46.

[40] *Id.*

[41] *Id.* at 453, ¶ 151.

[42] *Id.* at 402, ¶ 6.

[43] *Id.* at 401, ¶ 1.

[44] *Id.*

[45] *Id.* at 401–02, ¶¶ 4–5.

[46] *Id.*

[47] S. Afr. (Interim) Const. ch. 3, § 9.

[48] *Id.* ch. 3, § 11(2).

under apartheid. Moreover, the elected Constitutional Assembly was still drafting a final charter.[49]

Several interpretive methodologies were possible. First, the Court could have focused on the original intent of the South African framers. As Michel Rosenfeld illustrates, originalism might have been tempting in European countries given that their constitutions emerged recently.[50] Moreover, several South African Constitutional Court justices were among that country's framers.[51] Though originalism is typically supported by conservatives in the United States, the doctrine could have been progressive in South Africa given that the Interim Constitution's goal was social transformation. This goal was evident from its numerous rights provisions and drafting history.[52] Second, the Court could have corrected procedural deficiencies in the democratic process. American legal scholar John Hart Ely supported this kind of liberal proceduralism.[53] Third, the Court could have endorsed substantive progressive values as advocated by scholars like Ronald Dworkin[54] and Laurence

---

[49] Bentele, *supra* n. 4, at 261. With regard to the issues at stake in this case, however, the relevant constitutional provisions did not change much. *Compare* S. Afr. (Interim) Const. ch. 3, §§ 9, 11(2), with S. Afr. Const. 1996 ch. 2, §§ 11, 12(1)(d–e).

[50] Michel Rosenfeld, "Constitutional Adjudication in Europe and the United States: Paradoxes and Contrasts," 2 Int'l J. Const. L. 633, 656 (2004) (explaining that the "American preoccupation with originalism arises not from a concern over the enduring legitimacy of the Constitution itself, but rather, from a concern over the democratic legitimacy of subjecting majoritarian laws to constitutional review" and that in Europe, unlike America, "constitutions are not regarded as quasi-sacred texts, and statutory interpretation is not seen to be vulnerable to common law judicial lawmaking [,] [resulting in] little need to resort to originalism").

[51] For example, Justice Albie Sachs "returned home [in 1990 from exile] and as a member of the Constitutional Committee and the National Executive of the ANC took an active part in the negotiations which led to South Africa becoming a constitutional democracy." Constitutional Court of South Africa: Justices, http://www.constitutionalcourt.org.za/site/judges/justicealbiesachs/index1.html (last visited Jan. 3, 2006).

[52] For example, the Preamble to the Interim Constitution starts by saying, "Whereas there is a need to create a new order... in which there is equality between men and women and people of all races... "

[53] *See generally* John Hart Ely, Democracy and Distrust (1980) (arguing that judicial review should be used to correct malfunctions in the political process and ensure equal participation for all and "not with the substantive merits of the political choice under attack").

[54] *See generally* Ronald Dworkin, Taking Rights Seriously (1977) (maintaining that judges should rely on rights-based, not majority-based, principles in reaching a decision because constitutionalism dictates "the majority must be restrained to protect individual rights" and the Constitution "is designed to protect individual citizens and groups against

Tribe.[55] Fourth, the Court could have adopted a pragmatic orientation akin to that of Daniel Farber[56] or Richard Posner.[57] In the end, the Court was both transformative and pragmatic.

Values and Socio-Historical Context

The Court's opinion relied on the Interim Constitution's prohibition on "cruel, inhuman or degrading treatment or punishment."[58] The Court, citing a prior South African case, adopted a "generous" and "purposive" hermeneutic approach,[59] bolstered by section 35(1) of the Interim Constitution that provided, "In interpreting the provisions of this Chapter a court of law shall promote the values which underlie an open and democratic society based on freedom and equality."[60] Legal formalism was disfavored.

The concurrences echoed this theme. Justice Ackermann relied on Ronald Dworkin's moral reading of constitutions.[61] Justice Mokgoro wrote, "In interpreting the Bill of Fundamental Rights and Freedoms, . . . an all-inclusive value system, or common values in South Africa, can form a basis upon which to develop a South African human rights jurisprudence."[62] Lastly, Justice Sachs reasoned, "In broad terms, the

certain decisions that a majority of citizens might want to make, even when that majority acts in what it takes to be the general or common interest").

[55] *See generally* Laurence H. Tribe, "The Puzzling Persistence of Process-Based Constitutional Theories," 89 Yale L.J. 1063 (1980) (arguing that the process-perfecting view of constitutional law "determines almost nothing unless its presuppositions are specified, and its content supplemented, by a full theory of substantive rights and values – the very sort of theory the process-perfecters are at such pains to avoid").

[56] *See generally* Daniel A. Farber, "Legal Pragmatism and the Constitution," 72 Minn. L Rev. 1331 (1988) (arguing that legal pragmatism, "which essentially means solving legal problems using every tool that comes to hand, including precedent, tradition, legal text, and social policy[,]" is a sufficient basis for constitutional law and that legal pragmatism "renounces the entire project of providing a theoretical foundation for constitutional law").

[57] *See generally* Richard A. Posner, Law, Pragmatism, and Democracy 85 (2003) (explaining that "the core of pragmatic adjudication [is] . . . a disposition to ground policy judgments on facts and consequences rather than on conceptualisms and generalities").

[58] S. Afr. (Interim) Const. ch. 3, § 11(2).   [59] *Makwanyane* at ¶ 9.

[60] S. Afr. (Interim) Const. ch. 3, § 35(1).

[61] *Makwanyane* (3) SA at 457–58 & n.184, ¶ 165 (Ackermann, J., concurring) (explaining that even a court composed of Professor Dworkin's lawyer of "superhuman skill, learning, patience and acumen" would be incapable of determining whether to impose the death penalty in a case when applying the formulated criteria of Sec. 277(1) of the Criminal Procedure Act).

[62] *Id.* at 500, ¶ 307 (Mokgoro, J., concurring).

function given to this Court by the Constitution is to articulate the fundamental sense of justice and right shared by the whole nation as expressed
in the text of [the] Constitution."[63]

One prerequisite for this approach is the existence of some agreement
among the Court's members on what values the Constitution embodies. In
deriving and applying these values, the Constitutional Court emphasized
that it should examine (1) the text of the Constitution, (2) the "historical
origins" of the right guaranteed by the Constitution, and (3) the relation
between that right and other associated rights within the Constitution.[64]
Justice Chaskalson quoted from the Interim Constitution's Postamble:

> [The Constitution] provides a historic bridge between the past of a deeply
> divided society characterized by strife, conflict, untold suffering and injus-
> tice, and a future founded on the recognition of human rights, democracy
> and peaceful co-existence and development opportunities for all South
> Africans, irrespective of colour, race, class, belief or sex.[65]

This bridge metaphor is ubiquitous in the Constitutional Court's cases.

The Court also took an integrated approach by reasoning that section
11(2)'s cruel punishment clause could only be understood as part of a
Constitution that protected the right to dignity, the right to life, and the
right to equality.[66] The Court, however, did not base its decision on these
other grounds.[67]

Regarding history, the Court concluded that the framers avoided the
death penalty question, delegating it to the Court and not Parliament.[68]
The case therefore bears superficial resemblance to *Marbury v. Madison*[69] in which the U.S. Supreme Court relied in part on foreign law to

---

[63] *Id.* at 514, ¶ 362 (Sachs, J., concurring).

[64] *Id.* at 403, ¶ 9 (internal citations omitted).

[65] *Id.* at 402, ¶ 7. Justice Chaskalson initially seemed skeptical of the usefulness of this
language when Professor Dennis Davis relied on it during oral arguments, "viewing
the postscript [of the Constitution] as essentially a statement of political reconciliation,
rather than a binding constitutional provision." Bentele, *supra* note 4, at 270. Apparently Chaskalson's view changed by the time he authored the opinion, considering the
postscript cited as a relevant part of the Constitution. *Makwanyane* (3) SA at 402, ¶ 7.

[66] *Makwanyane* (3) SA at 403–04, ¶ 10.

[67] *Id.* at 403–04 & n.11, ¶ 10 (explaining that the Court treated the constitutional rights
to dignity, life, and equality together to provide meaning to "cruel, inhuman, [and]
degrading treatment or punishment[,]" not as "separate and independent standards
with which all punishments must comply").

[68] *Id.* at 402 (¶ 5), 409 (¶ 25).

[69] 5 U.S. (1 Cranch) 137 (1803). See also Bouckaert, *supra* n. 17, at 323 ("The [South
African Constitutional Court's decision in *Makwanyane*] was remarkable not only for
the advancement of a human right, but for its validation of the rule of law.... In making

address a monumental issue left open by the U.S. Constitution's framers: judicial review.

Reliance on International and Comparative Law

Section 35(1) of the Interim South African Constitution provided that the Court "shall, where applicable, have regard to public international law applicable to the protection of the rights entrenched in this Chapter, and may have regard to comparable foreign case law."[70] The Court therefore cited cases from Canada,[71] Botswana,[72] the European Court of Human Rights,[73] India,[74] the United States,[75] and other countries. It also relied on the International Covenant on Civil and Political Rights.[76] The Court even justified its references to the South African Constitution's framers' transformative goals by analogizing to the role of *travaux preparatoires* in international law.[77] The Court further explained that, although the global trend favored abolition,[78] international law did not make capital punishment *ultra vires*.[79]

Justice Chaskalson then examined the U.S. Supreme Court's death penalty decisions.[80] The Constitutional Court noted that the Fifth Amendment to the U.S. Constitution "impliedly recognizes [the] validity" of the death penalty.[81] The Court went on to discuss the U.S. Supreme Court's

---

clear that the judiciary would indeed determine what the Constitution means and strike down unconstitutional laws if necessary, the decision resembled the American landmark Marbury v. Madison" [quoting "South Africa Shows the Way," N.Y. Times, June 10, 1995, at 18, *available* at 1995 WLNR 3828855]). *Marbury* also drew on foreign precedent. 5 U.S. (1 Cranch) at 163 ("[F]or it is a settled and invariable principle in the laws of England, that every right, when withheld, must have a remedy, and every injury its proper redress.").

[70] S. Afr. (Interim) Const. ch. 3, § 35(1). Section 39(1) of the 1996 Constitution contains similar language. S. Afr. Const. ch. 2, § 39(1).

[71] *Makwanyane*, (3) SA at 403, ¶ 9.   [72] *Id*. at 428, ¶ 77 n.103.

[73] *Id*. at 425–26, ¶ 68.   [74] *Id*. at 426–30, ¶¶ 71–86.

[75] *Id*. at 415–22, ¶¶ 40–56.   [76] *Id*. at 424–25, ¶¶ 63–67.

[77] *Id*. at 405–07, ¶¶ 16–17. *Travaux preparatoires* are similar to working drafts. Thus, in South Africa there is a close relation between the framer's intent analysis and reliance on comparative sources as the Court's primary purpose is to "promote the values which underlie an open and democratic society based on freedom and equality" by relying on any necessary sources, whether foreign or domestic. *Id*. at 413–14, ¶¶ 34–35. This is not the case for constitutional interpretation in the U.S. Supreme Court. The Court sometimes relies on the framer's intent, but disagrees on the role of comparative law in interpreting U.S. laws.

[78] *Makwanyane*, (3) SA at 412–13, ¶¶ 33–34.

[79] *Id*. at 414, ¶ 36.   [80] *Id*. at 415–17, ¶¶ 40–42.

[81] *Id*. at 415, ¶ 40. The Fifth Amendment to the U.S. Constitution provides: "No person shall be held to answer for *a capital*, or other infamous crime, unless on a presentment

decision upholding the death penalty's constitutionality, *Gregg v. Georgia*,[82] in which – according to the Constitutional Court – the U.S. Supreme Court adopted an approach similar to South Africa's last capital punishment statute.[83]

Unlike the U.S. Supreme Court, the Constitutional Court rejected this approach in light of the death penalty's disparate impact along racial and poverty lines. The Court ruled that:

> Of the thousands of persons put on trial for murder, only a very small percentage are sentenced to death by a trial Court, and of those, a large number escape the ultimate penalty on appeal. At every stage of the process there is an element of chance. The outcome may be dependent upon factors such as the way the case is investigated by the police, the way the case is presented by the prosecutor, how effectively the accused is defended, the personality and particular attitude to capital punishment of the trial Judge and, if the matter goes on appeal, the particular Judges who are selected to hear the case. Race and poverty are also alleged to be factors.[84]

The Court added, "All this is the result of our history, and with the demise of apartheid this will change. Race and class are, however, factors that run deep in our society and cannot simply be brushed aside as no longer being relevant."[85]

The Constitutional Court noted that the poor often are represented by young, inexperienced, appointed attorneys, whereas the wealthy can hire excellent counsel and thereby avoid the death penalty.[86] It added that appellate review cannot make up for gaps in the trial court's factual findings caused by poor counsel.[87] The Court conceded that any criminal

---

or indictment of a Grand Jury, . . . nor shall any person be subject for the same offense to be twice put in jeopardy *of life* or limb; nor shall be compelled in any criminal case to be a witness against himself, nor be deprived *of life*, liberty, or property, without due process of law." U.S. Const. Amend. V (emphasis added).

[82] 428 U.S. 153 (1976).

[83] The Constitutional Court said that guided discretion means that the death sentence cannot be mandatory, but it also cannot be up to the uncontrollable discretion of the trial judge. *Makwanyane*, (3) SA at 416, ¶ 42. There must be specific criteria that can be examined in each case to ensure that the rule of law governs, rather than arbitrariness. *Id.* at 418, Par. 47. The Court's comparison to the "guided discretion" standard in the United States was based on a set of criteria under the Criminal Procedure Act providing consideration of mitigating and aggravating factors, various personal circumstances, the objects of punishment, and any other relevant considerations.

[84] *Id.* at 418–19, Par. 48. [85] *Id.* at 419 n.78, Par. 48.

[86] *Id.* at 419, Par. 49. [87] *Id.* at 421, Par. 54.

justice system is imperfect but quoted a prominent American lawyer that
"death is different."[88] Lastly, the Court noted that U.S. courts allow
prolonged legal appeals that leave the death row defendant in limbo
for many years, a "dragging out of the process" that was "cruel and
degrading."[89]

The Right to Dignity
The Constitutional Court also examined the Constitution's mandate
under section 10 that "every person shall have the right to respect for
and protection of his or her dignity."[90] Though the U.S. Constitution
lacks any dignity clause, the Constitutional Court pointed out that Justice Brennan had invoked the concept while dissenting from the Supreme
Court's death penalty rulings.[91] Relying on constitutional provisions

---

[88] *Id.* Professor Anthony Amsterdam coined this phrase before the U.S. Supreme Court
during oral arguments in Gregg v. Georgia, 428 U.S. 153 (1976). Note, "The Rhetoric
of Difference and the Legitimacy of Capital Punishment," 114 Harv. L. Rev. 1599,
1599 n.1 (2001).

[89] *Makwanyane,* (3) SA at 421, ¶ 55. In contrast, some U.S. Supreme Court Justices have
expressed frustration at the tendency to postpone or delay the enforcement of capital
punishment. *See, e.g.,* Coleman v. Balkom, 451 U.S. 949, 959 (1981) (Rehnquist, J.,
dissenting from the denial of certiorari) ("[The Supreme Court] has made it virtually
impossible for States to enforce with reasonable promptness their constitutionally valid
capital punishment statutes."); Bryan A. Stevenson, "The Politics of Fear and Death:
Successive Problems in Capital Federal Habeas Corpus Cases," 77 N.Y.U. L. Rev. 699,
714–15, 723–25 (2002) (as Chair of the Ad Hoc Committee on Federal Habeas Corpus
in Capital Cases, Justice Powell expressed frustration with the availability of unlimited
federal collateral review because it hinders the state's legitimate interest in deterring
crime). In 1989, Chief Justice Rehnquist expressed this viewpoint to the ABA mid-year
meeting: "To my mind the flaw in the present system is not that capital sentences are set
aside by federal courts, but that litigation ultimately resolved in favor of the state takes
literally years and years and years." Vivian Berger, "Justice Delayed or Justice Denied?
A Comment on Recent Proposals to Reform Death Penalty Habeas Corpus," 90 Colum.
L. Rev. 1665, 1669 (1990). Justice Powell "has consistently advanced positions on the
Court supporting a limited role for habeas [,] . . . stress[ing] the costs habeas imposes by
encroaching on states' interests in enforcing their criminal statutes and creating friction
between the state and federal judiciaries." *Id.* at 1675. The issue was on the legislative
front burner for a period. Henry Weinstein, "Bid to Speed Death Penalty Appeals under
Fire; Conservatives and Former Prosecutors Are among Foes of a Bill, before a Senate
Panel Today, to Curtail 'Endless' Delays in Cases," L.A. Times, July 28, 2005, at A18
(discussing the proposed federal Streamlined Procedures Act that would "dramatically
restrict federal courts' ability to consider habeas corpus petitions from state prisoners
who claim that their constitutional rights have been violated or that they have evidence
they are innocent").

[90] S. Afr. (Interim) Const. ch. 3, § 10.

[91] *Makwanyane,* (3) SA at 422, ¶ 57. The Supreme Court has on several occasions said that
rights are based on the premise of protecting human dignity. *See, e.g.,* Roper v. Simmons,

and cases from Germany, Canada, and India that underscored a concern about the death penalty's objectification of persons,[92] the Court declared that the death penalty "annihilates human dignity, which is protected under [section] 10."[93] The Court, however, refused to base its *ratio decidendi* on dignity and never provided a full definition of this concept.[94]

The Right to Life: Hungarian Case Law

Hungary's decision striking down capital punishment influenced the South African Court's analysis of the guarantee that "every person shall have the right to life" under section 9 of the Interim Constitution.[95] The Constitutional Court noted that the South African Constitution's right-to-life provision lacked conditional language and thus was stronger than Hungary's constitutional provision that provides, "In the Republic of Hungary everyone has the inherent right to life and to human dignity, and no one shall be arbitrarily deprived of these rights."[96] The Hungarian court found that capital punishment negated the essential content of the rights to life and dignity, which together formed the core of all other rights.[97] Nonetheless, the South African Constitutional Court declined to strike down capital punishment based on the right-to-life provision alone.

---

125 S. Ct. 1183, 1190 (2005) ("By protecting even those convicted of heinous crimes, the Eighth Amendment reaffirms the duty of the government to respect the dignity of all persons."); Rice v. Cayetano, 528 U.S. 495, 517 (2000) ("One of the principal reasons race is treated as a forbidden classification is that it demeans the dignity and worth of a person to be judged by ancestry instead of by his or her own merit and essential qualities.").

[92] *Makwanyane*, (3) SA at 423–30, ¶¶ 57–86.

[93] *Id.* at 434, ¶ 95.

[94] By contrast, Justice O'Regan and several other concurrences addressed the concept in more depth, finding dignity to be an independent basis for ruling the death penalty unconstitutional. *See, e.g., id.* at 506–10, ¶ 326–44 (O'Regan, J., concurring).

[95] S. Afr. (Interim) Const. ch. 3, § 9.

[96] *Makwanyane*, (3) SA at 430, ¶ 83 (quoting A Magyar Koztarsasag Alkotmanya [Constitution] art. 54(1) (Hung.)).

[97] *Id.* The Court explained, "Two factors are stressed in the judgment of the [Hungarian] Court. First, the relationship between the rights of life and dignity, and the importance of these rights taken together. Secondly, the absolute nature of these two rights taken together. Together they are the source of all other rights. Other rights may be limited, and may even be withdrawn and then granted again, but their ultimate limit is to be found in the preservation of the twin rights of life and dignity.... These twin rights are the essential content of all rights under the Constitution. Take them away and all other rights cease." *Id.* at 430, ¶ 84.

Rejecting Public Opinion

One of the most vexing constitutional questions is the counter-majoritarian dilemma: Unelected courts act undemocratically when they declare a statute unconstitutional.[98] In South Africa, this problem is less serious because the unrepresentative and racist apartheid regime had passed the laws. Nonetheless, the Constitutional Court worried about public opinion.

As in the United States, South African public opinion has, for many years, supported capital punishment.[99] The AG therefore argued that South African society did not regard the death sentence as a cruel punishment for murder.[100] But the Constitutional Court declared that "there would be no need for constitutional adjudication" if public opinion controlled major constitutional issues.[101] The AG's approach would resemble a "return to parliamentary supremacy" and would allow "a majority view [to] prevail over the wishes of any minority."[102] This is a controversial

---

[98] *See, e.g.,* Barry Friedman, "The Birth of an Academic Obsession: The History of the Counter-Majoritarian Difficulty, Part Five," 112 Yale L.J. 153 (2002) (examining the historical contexts in which critics of judicial review have charged the practice with being counter-majoritarian). Several scholarly works though have recently called into question whether the counter-majoritarian dilemma really is a big problem. *See, e.g.,* Christopher L. Eisgruber, Constitutional Self-Government (2001) (arguing that judges are well equipped to speak on behalf of the people on questions of the moral values of the community and that life tenure enables judges to maintain a disinterested approach unlike elected representatives); Ilya Somin, "Political Ignorance and the Counter-Majoritarian Difficulty: A New Perspective on the Central Obsession of Constitutional Theory," 89 Iowa L. Rev. 1287 (2004) (arguing that the electorates' lack of knowledge of politics and governmental policy minimizes the loss to democracy brought about by judicial review because "legislative output does not represent the will of the majority").

[99] The Court agreed that public opinion supported the death penalty, but declared public opinion to be nondeterminative of whether the death penalty was constitutional. *Makewanyane* (3) SA at 431, ¶ 87–88. Support for the death penalty remained high years after it was outlawed, and advocates, including the press and relatives of crime victims, have sought its reinstatement. A 1997 poll "showed 71 percent favored a return to the practice." Charlayne Hunter-Gault, "South Africans Ponder a Return to the Death Penalty," Cnn.Com, Apr. 24, 1999, http://www.cnn.com/WORLD /africa/9904/24/safrica.death.penalty; *see also* Ilse Fredericks, "They Died for You," Sunday Times, Jan. 20, 2002, at Metro 1 (describing the death of six police officers and the demands of their families for the return of the death penalty for their killers); Diana Mavunduse, "A New Millennium Free from Death Penalty in South Africa?," S. Afr. News Feature, Sept. 30, 1999 ("There is growing public demand to re-endorse the death penalty to curb escalating crime. Early this month a Zimbabwean diplomat was murdered during a carjacking in South Africa, now considered the most dangerous country outside a war zone."), http://www.sardc.net/editorial/sanf/1999/09/30–09-1999-nf2.htm.

[100] *Makwanyane,* (3) SA at 431, ¶ 87.   [101] *Id.* at 431, Par. 88.
[102] *Id.*

equivocation of the legislature with the people. Judicial review, however, should "protect the rights of minorities and others who cannot protect their rights adequately through the democractic process[,] . . .[for] it is only if there is a willingness to protect the worst and weakest amongst us that all of us can be secure that our own rights will be protected."[103]

The Constitutional Court quoted from the U.S. Supreme Court's opinion in *West Virginia State Board of Education v. Barnette*[104]:

> The very purpose of a Bill of Rights was to withdraw certain subjects from the vicissitudes of political controversy, to place them beyond the reach of majorities and officials and to establish them as legal principles to be applied by the courts. One's right to life, liberty, and property, to free speech, a free press, freedom of worship and assembly, and other fundamental rights may not be submitted to vote; they depend on the outcome of no elections.[105]

Yet, Justice Chaskalson at another point wrote that the Court should defer to the legislature,[106] demonstrating how courts walk a counter-majoritarian tightrope. The Constitutional Court also cited California and Massachusetts judicial decisions in striking down the death penalty, as well as the UN Committee on Human Rights,[107] perhaps as a surrogate for international public opinion.

Minimalism and Pragmatism

Chief Justice Chaskalson's opinion was also minimalist and pragmatic even though it reached a bold result. First, Justice Chaskalson stated that the Constitutional Assembly should have decided the question, showing his desire for the Court to stay uninvolved.[108] Second, he reasoned that the Court should not make its ruling based on moral distaste for the death penalty.[109] After all, Justice Chaskalson had plenty of reasons to dislike

---

[103] *Id.*   [104] 319 U.S. 624 (1943).

[105] *Makwanyane*, (3) SA at 432, ¶ 89 (quoting West Virginia State Board of Education v. Barnette, 319 U.S. 624, 638 (1943)).

[106] *Id.* at 436, ¶ 104.   [107] *Id.* at 432, ¶ 90.

[108] *See Makwanyane*, (3) SA at 402, ¶ 5. The Court explained, "It would no doubt have been better if the framers of the Constitution had stated specifically, either that the death sentence is not a competent penalty, or that it is permissible in circumstances sanctioned by law. This, however, was not done and it has been left to this Court to decide whether the penalty is consistent with the provisions of the Constitution." *Id.* Similarly, the U.S. Supreme Court *per curiam* opinion in Bush v. Gore, 531 U.S. 98, 111 (2000) suggested the Supreme Court sought to stay out of the 2000 presidential election dispute. The decision itself belies that assertion.

[109] *See Makwanyane*, (3) SA at 410, ¶ 26.

the death penalty because his former client, Nelson Mandela, could have been sentenced to death[110] and because the apartheid government had tried to assassinate Justice Sachs.[111] Third, Justice Chaskalson's opinion gave "a broad and contextualized definition to the right at issue without being overly concerned about the impact its decision may have on other areas of legal conflict far removed from the case at hand."[112] Fourth, as previously mentioned, Justice Chaskalson focused on the difficulties in administering the death penalty,[113] such as racism, the absence of good lawyers for the poor, and delays in appeals. Admittedly, he rejected the retribution rationale as inconsistent with the new Constitution's values.[114]

The South African academy has criticized the Court's pragmatic minimalist tendencies. Alfred Cockrell wrote that the Court had adopted a "rainbow jurisprudence" issuing opinions that "flit before our eyes like rainbows, beguiling us with their lack of substance."[115] Noted South African scholar and judge, Dennis Davis, has made similar criticisms.[116]

---

[110]Klug, *supra* n. 7, at 139 & n. 20.

[111]Albie Sachs, The Soft Vengeance of a Freedom Fighter 7–18 (2000); *see also* Francis X. Clines, "London Journal; Broken but Unbroken, A Quiet Enemy of Racism," N.Y. Times, May 17, 1988, at A4, *available at* 1988 WLNR 1344132.

[112]Heinz Klug, Constituting Democracy 162 (2000). Klug argues that Chaskalson's opinion differed from the other concurrences along the following lines: "Where they differed was in their reliance on different rights as the basis of their analysis and in whether they treated each of the different rights as a separate basis for striking down capital punishment or as informing the content of a single right, the violation of which was the sole ground upon which the decision was based. This difference, while of little significance to the outcome of the case, reflected a distinction between a case-by-case extrapolation of individual rights and an approach which makes bold declarations as to the extent of all rights implicated in a case and then relies on the limitations analysis to confine the implications of such expansive rights... [T]he first approach [was] adopted by Justice Chaskalson... This judicious strategy enables the Court to give a broad and contextualized definition to the right at issue without being overly concerned about the impact its decision may have on other areas of legal conflict far removed from the case at hand. While the extrapolation of these associated rights does indeed give clues as to the Court's views on the scope and form of those rights, it does not create legal expectations as to the specific content of those rights." *Id.* Some scholars assert that the U.S. Supreme Court has applied a similar minimalist strategy since the early 1990s. See Cass Sunstein, One Case at a Time: Judicial Minimalism on the Supreme Court (1999) (discussing how the Supreme Court decides cases on narrow grounds and avoids issuing clear rules, thereby leaving fundamental issues undecided for the political process to resolve). Minimalism reduces the frequency of judicial errors because the Court's narrow decisions are less likely to have broad unanticipated consequences. *Id.*

[113]*See Makwanyane*, (3) SA at 419–21, ¶ 49–54.

[114]*Id.* at 445–46 (¶¶ 129–31), 448–51 (¶¶ 135–43).

[115]Alfred Cockrell, "Rainbow Jurisprudence," 12 S. Afr. J. Hum. Rts. 1, 10–11 (1996).

[116]*See* Dennis Davis, Democracy and Deliberation 95 (1999).

Yet, striking down the death penalty is dramatic, even if done in a pragmatic way.[117]

The Limitations Issue

Once the Court concluded that the death penalty was "cruel, inhuman and degrading punishment,"[118] it embarked on the second stage of South African rights analysis, namely whether the government could satisfy the Interim Constitution's limitations clause. Section 33(1) provides that rights limitations had to be "reasonable" and "justifiable in an open and democratic society based on freedom and equality."[119]

The Court explained that having two stages of analysis permitted it to interpret the right broadly at the first stage because the right was not absolute.[120] The two-step analysis differs from interpretation of the U.S.

[117] Mark S. Kende, "The Fifth Anniversary of the South African Constitutional Court: In Defense of Judicial Pragmatism," 26 Vt. L. Rev. 753, 761–62 (2002) (recounting interviews with Justices Ackermann, Goldstone, and O'Regan); Iain Currie, "Judicious Avoidance," 15 S. Afr. J. Hum. Rts. 138 (1999) (explaining that the Court avoids making decisions that do not have to be made and that, when a decision must be made, it crafts a decision as "modest as possible in its scope and influence" and "saying no more than necessary to justify an outcome") (internal citations omitted).

[118] *Makwanyane*, (3) SA at 448, ¶ 135.

[119] S. Afr. (Interim) Const. ch. 3, § 33(1). The 1996 final Constitution incorporated much of this language into its limitations clause. S. Afr. Const. 1996 ch. 2, § 36(1) ("The rights in the Bill of Rights may be limited only . . . to the extent that the limitation is reasonable and justifiable in an open and democratic society based on human dignity, equality and freedom.").

[120] *Makwanyane*, (3) SA at 435, ¶ 100. Though the Court stressed interpreting fundamental rights within the Constitution "generous[ly]" and "purposive[ly]" in order to "give expression to the underlying values of the Constitution" *id.* at 403, ¶ 9, the Court may have backed off this approach. As one commentary explains, "The existence of a general limitation clause . . . permits a court to adopt a broad construction of the right in the first (interpretative) stage of the enquiry, then to require the state or the person relying on the validity of the infringement to justify the infringement in the limitation stage of the litigation. Viewed in this light the generous approach dictates that, when confronted with difficult value judgments about the scope of a right, rather than expecting the applicant to persuade the court that a right has been violated, the court should be prepared to assume that there has been a violation and call on the government to justify its laws and actions. However, the indications are that the Constitutional Court is not following this approach. The Court has been unwilling to extend the protection afforded by the rights to an indefinite and unforeseeable number of activities. It seems as if the Court will always choose to demarcate the right in terms of its purpose when confronted with a conflict between generous and purposive interpretation. If this is so, the notion of generous interpretation does not contribute much to constitutional interpretation." Iain Currie, Johan de Waal, The Bill of Rights Handbook 129–30 (2d ed. 1999). The debate over the meaning of the right to freedom best illustrates the Court's struggle with

Constitution, "which does not contain a limitation clause, as a result of which courts in that country have been obliged to find limits to constitutional rights through a narrow interpretation of the rights themselves."[121]

Ultimately, the Constitutional Court employed a "balancing process"[122] by which it measured the harms caused by the rights infringement against the state's justifications. Chief Justice Chaskalson announced the applicable criteria:

> The nature of the right that is limited, and its importance to an open and democratic society based on freedom and equality; the purpose for which the right is limited and the importance of that purpose to such a society; the extent of the limitation, its efficacy, and particularly where the limitation has to be necessary, whether the desired ends could reasonably be achieved through other means less damaging to the right in question.[123]

This is perhaps the Court's most famous language as it was used in the final Constitution and has been quoted by many foreign courts.

Unlike U.S. courts,[124] the Constitutional Court placed the burden on the government at the limitations phase because there was a rights infringement.[125] The Constitutional Court then looked for guidance to

---

this approach. Although some Justices argue the right to freedom provides a right to physical liberty, others believe it grants a broad right not to have obstacles to possible choices placed in your way. *Id.* at 130 n.22.

[121] *Makwanyane*, (3) SA at 435, ¶ 100. However, there is precedent in U.S. Supreme Court cases for use of a proportionality balancing type test in cases where the issue is cruel and unusual punishment. Roper v. Simmons, 125 S. Ct. 1183, 1190 (2005) ("The prohibition against 'cruel and unusual punishments,' like other expansive language in the Constitution, must be interpreted according to its text, by considering history, tradition, and precedent, and with due regard for its purpose and function in the constitutional design.").

[122] *Makwanyane*, (3) SA at 448–51, ¶¶ 135–43.

[123] Par. 104.

[124] American courts typically place the burden of proof on challengers attacking death penalty statutes. *See, e.g.*, McCleskey v. Kemp, 481 U.S. 279 (1987) (finding the defendant's showing that death penalty sentencing in Georgia had a disproportionate racial impact on blacks was insufficient to demonstrate any discriminatory racial effect in the defendant's particular case).

[125] *Makwanyane*, (3) SA at 435–36, ¶¶ 100–02. The Court placed the burden of justifying the infliction of death as a punishment on the state, not the party challenging it. *Id.* But the defendants had the "initial onus" of showing a cruel punishment violation. *Id.* at 410, ¶ 26.

Canada,[126] Germany,[127] the European Convention of Human Rights,[128] and the Tanzanian Court of Appeals.[129] It applied the lessons learned from these countries to the AG's three justifications for capital punishment: deterrence, prevention, and retribution.

Deterrence

The AG pointed out that South Africa's crime rate had skyrocketed since the death penalty moratorium[130] and that any decision abolishing the penalty should be made by Parliament.[131] The Court responded, "It is facile to attribute the increase in violent crime during this period to the moratorium on executions."[132] First, the death penalty was still available as a sentence during this period, although it was not carried out.[133] Second, the Court held that dramatic political changes, including violent disputes between certain political parties,[134] as well as continuing poverty, unemployment, and homelessness, likely caused the upsurge in crime, not the absence of executions.[135] The police and prosecutors "have been unable to cope" with the increased crime.[136] Third, the Court reasoned that the cessation of executions could not have had much impact because the government only carried out a small number of executions before the moratorium.[137] Lastly, life imprisonment remained an effective alternative.[138]

---

[126] *Id.* at 436–37, ¶ 105. Dennis Davis explains that Canadian scholar David Beatty vigorously lobbied for a Canadian-style balancing test regarding rights: "The authors of the Social Charter had been hugely influenced by the work of a Canadian academic, David Beatty, who had been spending part of a sabbatical in Cape Town. With almost evangelical zeal, Beatty had argued in favour of a model of balancing the output of the democratic process with constitutionally entrenched rights as the Canadian courts had interpreted their Charter of Rights and Freedoms." Davis, *supra* n. 116 at 3.

[127] *Makwanyane*, (3) SA at 438, ¶ 108.   [128] *Id.* at 438–39, ¶109.

[129] *Id.* at 440–41, ¶¶ 114–15.   [130] *Id.* at 442, ¶ 118.

[131] *Id.* at 441–42, ¶ 116 ("If in years to come we did so, we could do away with the death penalty. Parliament could decide when that time has come.").

[132] *Id.* at 443, ¶ 119.   [133] *Id.* at 442, ¶ 118.

[134] *Id.* at 442–43, ¶ 119.   [135] *Id.* at 443, ¶ 120.

[136] *Id.*

[137] *Id.* at 443, ¶ 121. This argument is a bit problematic because anti-apartheid leaders had accused the government for years of using executions to effectively stifle political dissent. Bouckaert, *supra* n. 17, at 291–92 ("Capital punishment in South Africa has been viewed as a tool specifically for controlling and punishing opponents of apartheid.").

[138] *Makwanyane*, (3) SA at 443–44, ¶ 123.

Prevention

The Court found the prevention rationale even less persuasive because "imprisonment is regarded as sufficient for the purpose of prevention in the overwhelming number of cases in which there are murder convictions, and there is nothing to suggest that it is necessary for this purpose in the few cases in which death sentences are imposed."[139]

Retribution

The Court stated that South Africa had "long outgrown the literal application of the biblical injunction of 'an eye for an eye, and a tooth for a tooth.'"[140] The Court relied for support on the Interim Constitution's section titled "National Unity and Reconciliation" which referred to the South African concept of *ubuntu*, or harmony in the community.[141] The internationally renowned Truth & Reconciliation Commission, proposed and headed by Archbishop Desmond Tutu, reflected these quasi-religious values.[142] Other Justices focused on the communitarian and uniquely African aspects of the South African Constitution more than Justice Chaskalson.[143]

---

[139] *Id.* at 445, ¶ 128.   [140] *Id.* at 445–46, ¶ 129.

[141] *Id.* at 480–81, ¶ 223. Several concurring Justices authored detailed explanations of how the concept of *ubuntu* supported abolition of the death penalty. Each of the black African Justices discussed *ubuntu*. Justice Langa wrote, "It is a culture which places some emphasis on communality and on the interdependence of the members of a community. It recognises a person's status as a human being, entitled to unconditional respect, dignity, value and acceptance from the members of the community such person happens to be part of. It also entails the converse, however. The person has a corresponding duty to give the same respect, dignity, value and acceptance to each member of the community. More importantly, it regulates the exercise of rights by the emphasis it lays on sharing and co-responsibility and the mutual enjoyment of rights by all." *Id.* at 481, ¶ 224 (Langa, J., concurring). Justice Langa then quoted from a Tanzania Court of Appeal case that referred to "the collective of communitarian rights and duties of society." *Id.* Justice Sachs discussed the importance of using indigenous law and culture in doing the analysis. *Id.* at 513–15 (Sachs, J., concurring).

[142] The Truth & Reconciliation Commission (TRC) assisted in the transition from apartheid to democracy by promoting reconciliation. As Archbishop Desmond Tutu explained, "We contend that there is another kind of justice, restorative justice, which was characteristic of traditional African jurisprudence. Here the central concern is not retribution or punishment. In the spirit of *ubuntu*, the central concern is the healing of branches, the redressing of imbalances, the restoration of broken relationships, a seeking to rehabilitate both the victim and the perpetrator, who should be given the opportunity to be reintegrated into the community that he has injured by his offense." Desmond Mpilo Tutu, No Future without Forgiveness 54–55 (1999).

[143] These other justices were at times more theoretical. For example, Justice O'Regan explained how the Court must utilize the Constitution's values as reflecting the "hermeneutic standard set" and, quoting an aphorism by Ronald Dworkin, stressed

Applying the Limitations Criteria: Balancing and Proportionality

The AG also made this argument:

> If the law recognizes the right to take the life of a wrongdoer in a situation in which self-defense is justified, then, in order to deter others, and to ensure that the wrongdoer does not again kill an innocent person, why should it not recognize the power of the State to take the life of a convicted murderer?[144]

The Court responded that a person uses self-defense to stay alive but a criminal defendant does not threaten the state's existence.[145] The Court further rejected any analogy to the police shooting a fleeing felon.[146] Capital punishment's cruelty outweighed these justifications.[147] The Court concluded, "In the long run more lives may be saved through the inculcation of a rights culture than through the execution of murderers."[148] Thus, after critically assessing the government's justifications, Justice Chaskalson used the limitations criteria mentioned earlier and weighed the justifications against possible alternative punishments, as well as the factors that "taken together, make capital punishment cruel, inhuman and degrading."[149]

DEATH PENALTY JURISPRUDENCE IN THE UNITED STATES

The United States has also applied the death penalty in a racially inequitable manner.[150] Further the U.S. has a horrible history of

that "[b]ecause we honour dignity, we demand democracy." *Makwanyane*, (3) SA at 504 (¶ 322), 507 (¶330) (O'Regan, J., concurring).

[144] *Id.* at 448, ¶ 136.   [145] *See id.* at 448–49, ¶ 138.

[146] *Id.* at 449–50, ¶ 140.

[147] *Id.* at 451, ¶¶ 144–46. Justice Ackermann quoted from a seminal law review article by the famous South African scholar Etienne Mureinik, "If the new Constitution is a bridge away from a culture of authority, it is clear what it must be a bridge to. It must lead to a *culture of justification* – a culture in which every exercise of power is expected to be justified.... If the Constitution is to be a bridge in this direction, it is plain that the Bill of Rights must be its chief strut." *Id.* at 454, ¶ 156 n.171 (Ackermann, J., concurring) (quoting Etienne Mureinik, "A Bridge to Where? Introducing the Interim Bill of Rights," 10 S. Afr. J. Hum. Rts. 31, 32 (1994) (emphasis added)).

[148] *Id.* at 444, ¶ 125. Justice Didcott expanded on this idea, eloquently writing: "South Africa has experienced too much savagery. The wanton killing must stop before it makes a mockery of the civilised, humane and compassionate society to which the nation aspires and has constitutionally pledged itself. And the State must set the example by demonstrating the priceless value it places on the lives of all its subjects, even the worst." *Id.* at 469, ¶ 190 (Didcott, J., concurring).

[149] *Id.* at 448, ¶ 135.

[150] Sheri Lynn Johnson, "Black Innocence and the White Jury," 83 Mich. L. Rev. 1611, 1623 (1985) (explaining that numerous studies have shown that "the victim's race was

lynchings – the vigilante death penalty, though South Africa has seen the use of "necklacing" – the burning of a tire around the neck of traitors to the liberation cause. The U.S. Supreme Court's death penalty jurisprudence, however, has twists and turns unlike the singular South African decision. This section examines the American cases and analyzes the Supreme Court's recent decisions reining in the death penalty for the mentally retarded and juveniles. These decision rely in part on foreign law.[151]

There are at least three relevant textual distinctions between the South African and U.S. Constitutions on capital punishment. First, the Fifth Amendment to the U.S. Constitution seems to authorize capital punishment,[152] making the abolition case difficult. Second, the United

---

an important determinant of sentence, and that black offender/white victim cases were the most likely to result in the death penalty"). The United States also has a horrible history of lynchings, a kind of vigilante mob death penalty. Julian A. Cook, Jr. & Mark S. Kende, "Color-Blindness in the Rehnquist Court: Comparing the Court's Treatment of Discrimination Claims by a Black Death Row Inmate and White Voting Rights Plaintiffs," 13 T.M. Cooley L. Rev. 815, 820–22 (1996) (describing the use of vigilante lynchings by racial hate groups in the late nineteenth century and its replacement by imposition of capital sentences by all-white juries, otherwise known as "legal lynchings"). Southerners by this time had grown accustomed to arbitrarily executing blacks based on perceived wrongs. For example, colonial statutes required the execution of any slave who killed a white person, unless by accident or in defense of his master, and left courts powerless to grant mercy in such cases. Leon Higgninbotham, Jr., In the Matter of Color: Race and the American Legal Process: The Colonial Period 256 (1978). Additionally, whites were required by law to whip slaves who traveled away from the plantation without a pass and were not in the company of "some white person." *Id.* at 171. In fact, the law placed greater restrictions on freeing slaves than on protecting their lives, imposing merely a fine for killing a slave "because the murderer was supposedly justified or excused." *Id.* at 253.

[151] Various similarities between South Africa and the United States show that the Supreme Court should also cite African foreign law, not just European foreign law. Taunya Lovell Banks, "Exploring White Resistance to Racial Reconciliation in the United States," 55 Rutgers L. Rev. 903, 908–09 (2003) ("The Jim Crow era in the United States, when some states mandated and other states permitted race-based discrimination, has been compared to South Africa under apartheid."). To its credit, the U.S. Supreme Court in Roper v. Simmons referred to the African Charter on the Rights and Welfare of the Child, as well as to Nigerian law. *See* 125 S. Ct. 1183, 1199 (2005). For confirmation that the U.S. Supreme Court has generally relied on decisions from Europe, on the apparent theory that our heritage and legal system are more closely connected to that continent than any other, see John Yoo, "Peeking Abroad?: The Supreme Court's Use of Foreign Precedents in Constitutional Cases," 26 U. Haw. L. Rev. 385, 400 n.68 (2004). Yet as mentioned elsewhere in this book, the South African Constitution is considered by some, such as Cass Sunstein, to be the "the most admirable constitution in the history of the world." Cass Sunstein, Designing Democracy, What Constitutions Do 261 (2001).

[152] *See supra* note 81; *see also* Gregg v. Georgia, 428 U.S. 153, 177 (1976) (citing the Fifth Amendment in upholding the death penalty).

States has the jury system. Third, the U.S. Constitution lacks a limitations clause.

Furman v. Georgia

Despite the Fifth Amendment's "capital" crimes reference,[153] the Supreme Court has not treated the U.S. Constitution as frozen in 1791. In the 1972 case of *Furman v. Georgia*,[154] the Supreme Court issued a 5–4 *per curiam* opinion holding that Georgia and Texas administered the death penalty in a cruel and unusual manner, thereby violating the Eighth Amendment.[155] This was a pragmatic objection, however, not one based on fundamental moral principles; it did not disallow capital punishment per se, just how it was administered in this case. Each Justice issued his own opinion as in the South African case.[156] *Furman* resembles the Constitutional Court ruling in another way, in addition to the antideath penalty result. South Africa had not carried out the death penalty for more than five years prior to the *Makwanyane* decision, and the United States had no executions for five years before *Furman*.[157] Interestingly, the U.S. had a de facto moratorium on capital punishment in late 2007 and early 2008 until the Supreme Court decided that lethal injection is allowed as an execution method.

Justices Stewart and White reasoned that whether a criminal defendant received the death penalty was arbitrary.[158] Justice Stewart wrote,

> These death sentences are cruel and unusual in the same way that being struck by lightning is cruel and unusual. For, of all the people convicted of rapes and murders in 1967 and 1968, many just as reprehensible as these, the petitioners are among a capriciously selected random handful upon whom the sentence of death has in fact been imposed. My concurring

---

[153] *See supra* note 81.   [154] 408 U.S. 238 (1972).

[155] *Id.* (explaining that "the asserted public belief that murders and rapists deserve to die is flatly inconsistent with the execution of a random few" and "there is a strong probability that [the death penalty] is inflicted arbitrarily").

[156] The case was described as "not so much a case as a badly orchestrated opera, with nine characters taking turns to offer their own arias." Robert Weisberg, "Deregulating Death," 1983 Sup. Ct. Rev. 305, 315.

[157] During the 1960s, the NAACP Legal Defense and Educational Fund (LDF) had developed a "moratorium strategy [to] create a death-row logjam." Michael Meltsner, Cruel and Unusual: The Supreme Court and Capital Punishment 107 (1973). Largely as a result of LDF efforts in blocking all executions on every conceivable legal ground, when the Court handed down *Furman* in 1972 there had not been a single execution in five years. *Furman*, 408 U.S. at 434 n.18 (Blackmun, J., dissenting).

[158] *Furman*, 408 U.S. at 306–14.

Brothers have demonstrated that, if any basis can be discerned for the selection of these few to be sentenced to die, it is the constitutionally impermissible basis of race. But racial discrimination has not been proved, and I put it to one side. I simply conclude that the Eighth and the Fourteenth Amendments cannot tolerate the inflicting of a sentence of death under legal systems that permit this unique penalty to be so wantonly and so freakishly imposed.[159]

Despite this strong language, Stewart wrote, "The constitutionality of capital punishment in the abstract is not, however, before us in these cases."[160]

Justices Brennan and Marshall doubted that any system of capital punishment could remove arbitrariness.[161] Brennan wrote that it is a "denial of human dignity for the State arbitrarily to subject a person to an unusually severe punishment that society has indicated it does not regard as acceptable, and that cannot be shown to serve any penal purpose more effectively than a significantly less drastic punishment."[162] Justice Marshall wrote,

> The death penalty is no more effective a deterrent than life imprison-ment[because] convicted murderers are rarely executed.... No attempt is made in the sentencing process to ferret out likely recidivists for execution.... [The] punishment is imposed discriminatorily against cer-tain identifiable classes of people.... Innocent people have been executed before their innocence can be proved... [and] [a]ssuming knowledge of all the facts presently available regarding capital punishment, the aver-age citizen would, in my opinion, find it shocking to his conscience and sense of justice. For this reason alone capital punishment cannot stand.[163]

---

[159] *Id.* at 309–10 (Stewart, J., concurring).

[160] *Id.* at 308. One commentator points out the irony that Stewart condemns the death penalty for being carried out too infrequently, when "the truth of the matter is that there *should* be very few death penalty sentences... [since] [o]nly a very few cases warrant this extreme measure. It takes two essential ingredients to obtain a death penalty: (1) overwhelming proof of the defendant's guilt and (2) an extremely aggravated fact situation." Carol S. Vance, "The Death Penalty after Furman," 48 Notre Dame L. Rev. 850, 858 (1973).

[161] Daniel D. Polsby, "The Death of Capital Punishment? Furman v. Georgia," 1972 Sup. Ct. Rev. 1, 15–24 (analyzing Justice Brennan and Marshall's argument that the death penalty is applied arbitrarily to defendants and that "death is an excessive punishment to satisfy the legitimate penal purposes of the legislature").

[162] *Furman*, 408 U.S. at 286 (Brennan, J., concurring).

[163] *Id.* at 362–69 (Marshall, J., concurring).

The four dissenters argued both that the U.S. Constitution's text supported the death penalty and that courts did not implement it arbitrarily.[164] The dissenters raised a host of other objections.

Gregg v. Georgia

After *Furman*, most states revised their death penalty statutes. Georgia bifurcated its criminal trials into a guilt and a sentencing phase, restricted the crimes for which the jury could impose death, and required the jury to find beyond a reasonable doubt the existence of one of ten "aggravating factors."[165] *Furman* also obliged the Georgia Supreme Court to review all death sentences to ensure they were not based on emotion and that the sentence was proportionate to those from other juries.[166] This "guided discretion" resembled the South African statute that was in place before *Makwanyane*.

In 1976 the Court upheld these death penalty revisions in *Gregg v. Georgia*.[167] The Court referenced the Fifth Amendment: "It is apparent from the text of the Constitution itself that the existence of capital punishment was accepted by the Framers."[168] The Court further reasoned that *Furman*'s arbitrariness concerns "are best met by a system [like that of Georgia] that provides for a bifurcated proceeding at which the sentencing authority is apprised of the information relevant to the imposition of sentence and provided with standards to guide its use of the information."[169] The Court found the death penalty did not violate "evolving standards of decency," because most states changed their death penalty laws after *Furman*.

The Court also expressed concerns about undermining federalism and state authority.[170] Moreover, the Court relied on Justice Stewart's *Furman* concurrence:

---

[164] Chief Justice Burger argued that the infrequency of death penalties "attest[ed] to[jurors'] cautious and discriminating reservation of that penalty for the most extreme cases." He also believed that "mandatory sentences of death, without the intervening and ameliorating impact of lay jurors" were more arbitrary than selective imposition by juries on case by case adjudication. *Id.* at 402 (Burger, C.J., dissenting).

[165] Gregg v. Georgia, 428 U.S. 153, 162–68 (1976).

[166] *Id.* at 166–68.　　　[167] 428 U.S. 153, 207 (1976).

[168] *Id.* at 177.　　　[169] *Id.* at 195.

[170] *See id.* at 179–87. The Court explained, "In sum, we cannot say that the judgment of the Georgia Legislature that capital punishment may be necessary in some cases is clearly wrong. Considerations of federalism, as well as respect for the ability of a legislature to evaluate, in terms of its particular State, the moral consensus concerning the death penalty and its social utility as a sanction, require us to conclude, in the absence of

The instinct for retribution is part of the nature of man, and channeling that instinct in the administration of criminal justice serves an important purpose in promoting the stability of a society governed by law. When people begin to believe that organized society is unwilling or unable to impose upon criminal offenders the punishment they "deserve," then there are sown the seeds of anarchy – of self-help, vigilante justice, and lynch law.[171]

This emphasis differs from the South African Court's view that public opinion has no bearing.[172] The U.S. Supreme Court's evolving decency standard, however, and its own proportionality assessment (regarding whether such a severe punishment could be justified for such a crime) actually resemble South African proportionality analysis in the abstract, even though the Courts reached opposite results.

McCleskey v. Kemp: Race Discrimination

In McCleskey v. Kemp,[173] the Supreme Court ruled against a claim that Georgia's death penalty system was racially discriminatory. The 1987 case involved a black man who killed a white police officer during a robbery.[174]

The Court rejected a sophisticated statistical analysis that apparently demonstrated that a black man who killed a white person was far more likely to get death than a black man who killed a black person.[175] Although the Court said it assumed the study's validity, it found that the study did not demonstrate that racial discrimination had an impact on Warren McCleskey's death sentence.[176] Moreover, the Court

---

more convincing evidence, that the infliction of death as a punishment for murder is not without justification and thus is not unconstitutionally severe." *Id.* at 186–87.

[171] *Id.* at 183.   [172] *See supra* n. 101.

[173] 481 U.S. 279, 292 (1987).   [174] *Id.* at 283.

[175] *See id.* at 286–87, 297–98 (finding the Baldus study to be insufficient to support an inference that jurors acted with a discriminatory purpose and insufficient to determine the State of Georgia as a whole acted with discriminatory purpose). In his majority opinion, Justice Powell rejected the proffered statistical evidence, "seem[ingly] ... conced [ing] that a kind of racial discrimination, perhaps a half-conscious kind, probably extends throughout all phases of the criminal justice system ... and fear[ing] that to reverse this particular death sentence would be to effectively declare American criminal justice wholly illegal." Robert Weisberg, "Death Means Never Having to Say 'I'm Sorry'," Slate, July 7, 2004, http://www.slate.com/id/2103517 (last visited Jan. 11, 2008). Years later in retirement, Justice Powell expressed regret for his position and wished he had voted to reverse in *McCleskey. Id.*

[176] *McCleskey,* 481 U.S. at 292–99.

acknowledged that each jury has unique qualities and attitudes, but said this is acceptable because the jury reflects the community conscience.[177] The Court also explained that the Fourteenth Amendment's equal protection clause placed the burden on the defendant to show that a discriminatory purpose tainted his trial.[178] Lastly, the Court raised a "slippery slope" concern that many parts of the criminal justice system could be challenged if a plaintiff only had to show disparate impact.[179]

Justices Brennan and Blackmun responded in dissent that systemic racism in death penalty sentencing should create a presumption that the penalties imposed on black defendants like McCleskey were tainted.[180] The government should therefore show that race was not a factor in such a case.[181] Justice Brennan also said the majority's slippery slope "suggest[s] a fear of too much justice."[182] At a minimum, the dissenters are right that the defendant produced enough evidence to place the onus on the government to show that McCleskey was one of the rare criminal defendants unaffected by the systemic racism.

Summary

The U.S. Supreme Court's decisions upholding the death penalty are quite different from the South African Constitutional Court's pragmatic yet transformative *Makwanyane* decision. The U.S. Supreme Court relied more heavily on constitutional text, the framers' intent, federalism, and concern over the counter-majoritarian dilemma, as opposed to fundamental moral principles, evolving foreign trends, and practical realities. It did not treat American constitutional rights provisions as an integrated whole.[183] Indeed, the cases suggest that the Supreme Court justices are

---

[177] *Id.* at 310 n.32, 311.   [178] *Id.* at 292–93.

[179] *Id.* at 315–18.

[180] *Id.* at 320–45 (Brennan, J., dissenting), 345–66 (Blackmun, J., dissenting).

[181] *Id.* at 359 (Blackmun, J., dissenting).   [182] *Id.* at 339–40 (Brennan, J., dissenting).

[183] The Supreme Court majorities in death penalty cases have almost never discussed how equality protections could be related to the prohibition on "cruel and unusual" punishment in that both seek to ensure the dignity of the individual and the fairness of the procedures. Perhaps the most stark example of the Supreme Court's refusal to view constitutional provisions in an integrated fashion is San Antonio v. Rodriguez, 411 U.S. 1 (1973), where the Court said that the Texas school financing scheme was constitutional. The Court said that there was no fundamental right to education and that the poor were not a suspect class under equal protection. In dissent, Justice Marshall said the Court should have examined the overall picture, which demonstrated arbitrary discrimination regarding a very important right. He treated the constitutional provisions as integrated, unlike the majority.

divided about basic values,[184] unlike their South African counterparts, who are generally progressive.[185] In addition, a majority of the U.S. Supreme Court believed that retribution was permissible.

NEW DEVELOPMENTS IN THE UNITED STATES

In 1974, after *Furman* was decided but before *Gregg*, Charles Black's book, *Capital Punishment: The Inevitability of Caprice and Mistake*, was published. It argues that the American criminal justice system is too rife with human error, arbitrariness, racism, and poverty for capital punishment to be allowed.[186] Nonetheless, *Gregg and McCleskey* seemed to indicate the Supreme Court was immune to change. But there is some evidence that Charles Black's views are experiencing a renaissance as seen in the growing exoneration movement and in several recent Supreme Court decisions.

The Exoneration Movement

Courts and governors have exonerated numerous death row inmates.[187] According to Bryan Stevenson, "in the last several years, dozens of

---

[184] Mark Tushnet, A Court Divided: The Rehnquist Court and the Future of Constitutional Law (2005) (showing in detail that the supposedly conservative Republican appointees on the Court divide frequently into two groups). For an example of the Court's split among not only liberal and conservative justices but also among the conservative justices themselves, *see, e.g.,* Lawrence v. Texas, 539 U.S. 558 (2003).

[185] The generally progressive nature of the South African Constitutional Court is discussed in an interesting article. Jeffrey Toobin, "Swing Shift; How Anthony Kennedy's Passion for Foreign Law Could Change the Supreme Court," The New Yorker, Sept. 12, 2005, at 42, 50 (According to South African Constitutional Court Justice Richard Goldstone, "I think it would be fair to say that the most conservative member of the South African Constitutional Court would be left of the most progressive member of the United States Supreme Court.").

[186] Charles Black, Capital Punishment: The Inevitability of Caprice and Mistake 21 (1974) (arguing that the problems of mistake and caprice are ineradicable in the administration of the death penalty and that "the official choices...that divide those who are to die from those who are to live are on the whole not made, and cannot be made, under standards that are consistently meaningful and clear," but rather are often made "under no standards at all or under pseudo-standards without discoverable meaning").

[187] For an interesting discussion regarding how many death row inmates have been falsely convicted, see Adam Liptak, "Consensus on Counting the Innocent: We Can't," N.Y. Times, Mar. 25, 2008. http://www.nytimes.com/2008/03/25/us/25bar.html (last visited April 10, 2008).

innocent people have been released from death row after narrowly escaping execution. For every eight executions that have occurred in the United States since resumption of capital punishment in the 1970s, one innocent person has been discovered on Death Row and exonerated."[188] The most dramatic development occurred in 2000 when Illinois Governor George Ryan commuted all state death sentences based on a devastating commission report concerning the arbitrariness of the penalty's imposition.[189]

[188] Bryan Stevenson, "Close to Death: Reflections on Race and Capital Punishment in America", *in* Hugo Adam Bedau & Paul G. Cassell, (Eds)., Debating the Death Penalty: Should America Have Capital Punishment? 76, 78 (2004). *See e.g.,* Death Penalty Information Center, "DNA Testing Finds No Connection to Ohio Death Row Inmate – Clemency Granted," http://www.deathpenaltyinfo.org/article/php?did=2587&scid=64 (last visited Jan. 10, 2008).

[189] Governor George Ryan imposed the moratorium on executions on January 31, 2000 after the thirteenth innocent inmate had been released from death row in Illinois. Samuel R. Gross & Phoebe C. Ellsworth, "Second Thoughts: Americans' Views on the Death Penalty at the Turn of the Century," *in* Stephen P. Garvey (Ed.), Beyond Repair? America's Death Penalty 7, 23 (2003). Unfortunately, Governor Ryan himself was eventually convicted of accepting bribes, thus impairing his legacy. Matt O'Connor and Rudolph Bush, "Ryan Convicted in Corruption Trial," Chicago Tribune, April 17, 2006, http://www.chicagotribune.com/news/custom/newsroom/chi-060417ryantrial,0,4525779.story (last visited Jan. 11, 2008). The problem in Illinois was much larger, however, as Rob Warden, executive director of the Center on Wrongful Convictions at Northwestern University School of Law, explained, "Of 289 defendants sentenced to death in Illinois after *Furman v. Georgia*, seventeen had been exonerated and released – an error rate of 5.9%. An eighteenth former death row prisoner . . . would be exonerated in May of 2004, pushing the error rate above six percent. Mistakes in the determination of guilt, however, were only part of the [problem]. . . . As a result of trial errors and omissions, appellate courts had vacated death sentences or ordered new trials for scores of additional death row prisoners. A landmark study found that forty-three percent of Illinois death penalty cases had been reversed on direct appeal or at the post-conviction stage as of 1995. Of the cases that graduated to the federal habeas corpus stage, the study found forty percent had been remanded for retrial or re-sentencing. . . . Stunningly, for each defendant executed in Illinois, 9.5 death sentences had been overturned." Rob Warden, "Illinois Death Penalty Reform: How It Happened, What It Promises," 95 J. Crim. L. & Criminology 381, 381–82 (2005). The Death Penalty Information Center believes the publicity surrounding wrongful convictions to be the main cause of the five-year decline in the use of the death penalty since 1999: "The reasons for the attrition in death penalty use are many, but certainly the number of high profile cases of innocent people freed from death row in recent years has had a profound effect on the system. Last year, 12 people were freed from death row, more than in any other year since the death penalty was reinstated. This year, 5 people have been exonerated." Death Penalty Info. Ctr., "The Death Penalty in 2004: Year End Report 3–4" (2004), http://www.deathpenaltyinfo.org/DPICyer04.pdf (last visited Jan. 11, 2008).

Former federal prosecutor and best-selling novelist, Scott Turow, served on that Illinois commission. He explains in a 2003 book that he became a death penalty opponent as a result of that experience.[190] His book echoes Charles Black's reasoning as well as that of the South African Constitutional Court.[191] Several law schools have established Innocence Projects to assist inmates in securing evidence to support their solid claims to innocence.[192] In Montana, three inmates were mistakenly convicted based on poor forensic testing, and hundreds more cases are currently under appeal in Montana and Washington.[193]

DNA evidence provides support for some exonerations. In 2005, Justice Stevens told the American Bar Association that such evidence has shown "that a substantial number of death sentences have been imposed erroneously.... It indicates that there must be serious flaws in our administration of criminal justice."[194] He said that the accused murderer is often prejudiced by the jury selection process, by the fact that many judges must stand for election, and by the power of victim impact statements.[195] In June 2007, the Death Penalty Information Center reported, "By a wide

---

[190] Scott Turow, Ultimate Punishment: A Lawyer's Reflections on Dealing with the Death Penalty (2003) (describing Turow's struggle with the implementation of the death penalty as a member of the Illinois Governor's Commission on Capital Punishment and his conclusion that, although the death penalty may still be attractive for the most horrific of crimes, constructing a system of justice that would not occasionally condemn the innocent or undeserving is not possible).

[191] *See id.* at 114–15 (discussing how perceived mistakes in the judicial system led the author to change his views of the death penalty); *see also* Black, *supra* n. 186 (discussing how the possibility of mistake and human error makes proper enforcement of the death penalty impossible).

[192] Perhaps the most well known is run by Barry Scheck at Cardozo Law School. The Innocence Project: About the Innocence Project, http:// www.innocenceproject.org/about/ (last visited Jan. 3, 2006).

[193] Maurice Possley, "Lab Errors Cited in Petition on 200 Montana Cases; Retests Reverse Analyst's Findings," Chi. Trib., Aug. 26, 2004, at C12 (discussing appeal of more than 200 cases handled by a crime lab analyst who gave testimony on hair analysts that experts acknowledge as scientifically baseless); Ruch Teichroeb, "They Sit in Prison – But Crime Lab Tests Are Flawed," Seattle Post-Intelligencer, Mar. 13, 2004, at A1, *available at* 2004 WLNR 3192163. Over thirty states have had exonerations. Innocence Project, "Exonerations by State," <http://www.innocenceproject.org/news/StateView.php> (last visited Oct. 10, 2008).

[194] Associated Press, *supra* n. 15. The full Stevens speech is available on the U.S. Supreme Court Web site. Justice John Paul Stevens, Address to the American Bar Association Thurgood Marshall Awards Dinner Honoring Abner Mikva (Aug. 6, 2005), *available at* http://www.supremecourtus.gov/publicinfo/speeches/sp_08–06–05.html (last visited Jan. 11, 2008).

[195] Stevens, *supra* n. 15.

margin, the American public believes that the most significant development in recent years has been the advent of DNA testing and the proof that many who were sentenced to death were innocent."[196] This belief, however, may be incorrect.

As Samuel Gross and Phoebe Ellsworth state:

> Justice Marshall may have been more right than we thought. In the past few years, public support for the death penalty has been undercut by growing experience with one of the problems that Marshall addressed, if not the others – that innocent defendants are convicted and sentenced to death for crimes they did not commit. The power of this issue may reflect the fact that people respond more strongly to concrete cases than to abstract concepts. In the context of the death penalty, this cuts both ways.... It helps that the issue that did it – capital convictions of innocent defendants – is identified in the public mind with DNA evidence. Because DNA identification is new, it is an attractive basis for changing long-held views, and it can provide virtually irrefutable scientific proof of innocence. DNA has not played a role in 90 percent of the cases of death row inmates who have been exonerated, but that goes unnoticed.[197]

Other commentators agree that DNA has not played a large role in exonerations.[198]

The public's belief, that DNA evidence has revealed many erroneous convictions, may partly explain a 57 percent decline in executions since 1999.[199] The number of death sentences also decreased by 60 percent during that period.[200] New Jersey has even banned the death penalty.[201] Moreover, as discussed below, many states have repealed the death penalty for members of groups such as the mentally retarded and juveniles,[202] and the highest courts in several states have found the death penalty to be unconstitutional.[203]

---

[196] http://www.deathpenaltyinfo.org/CoC.pdf (last visited Jan. 11, 2008).

[197] Gross & Ellsworth, *supra* n. 189, at 38–39.

[198] Corrinna Barrett Lain, "Deciding Death", 57 Duke L. J. 1, 47 n. 242 (2007).

[199] Death Penalty Info. Ctr, "2007 Year End Report" (42 executions for the year compared to 98 in 1999), http://www.deathpenaltyinfo.org/2007YearEnd.pdf (last visited June 17, 2008).

[200] There were 110 death sentences in 2007, which is 60% less than in 1999.

[201] *Supra* n. 14.   [202] *See infra* n. 220 & 223.

[203] Death Penalty Info. Ctr., "The Death Penalty in 2005: Year End Report" 2 (2005) (noting that both Kansas and New York courts overturned death penalty laws in 2004), http://www.deathpenaltyinfo.org/YearEndo5.pdf (last visited June 17, 2008). Texas is an exception, as courts there have refused, for example, to overturn death sentences despite evidence that capital defense attorneys fell asleep during trial. Keith

In addition, public support for the death penalty has declined.[204] For years, about 75 percent of the public supported capital punishment, but this figure dropped to about 65 percent from 1996 to 2000.[205] An October 2005 Gallup Poll found that 64 percent of Americans favored the death penalty for murder, the lowest support in twenty-seven years.[206] According to the 2007 Gallup poll, the support bumped up in October 2007 to 69 percent, but still remained below the earlier figure of 75 percent.

This drop from 75 percent may also be due to fewer Americans believing that the death penalty deters murder.[207] In 2004, 62 percent believed the death penalty did not deter, a 21 percent increase since 1991.[208] In June 2006, a poll showed that 64 percent of Americans felt the death penalty was not a deterrent. Moreover, Americans are less sure whether the death penalty is a worse punishment than life imprisonment (without parole) for murder, according to some polls.[209]

These trends make it possible to imagine that one day the U.S. Supreme Court will be less hospitable to the death penalty and more like its South African counterpart. In 2008, for example, the U.S. Supreme Court in *Kennedy v. Louisiana* rejected the death penalty for child rape.[210] The Court's reasoning included concerns over the unreliability of the criminal justice system, particularly given the well-known problems with child

Cunningham-Parmeter, "Dreaming of Effective Assistance: The Awakening of Cronic's Call to Presume Prejudice from Representational Absence," 76 Temp. L. Rev. 827, 828–29 (2003).

[204] One commentator refers to the seismic shift in public opinion. Lain, *supra* n. 198 at 35.

[205] Gross & Ellsworth, *supra* n. 189 at 11.

[206] Lydia Saad, "Support for Death Penalty Steady at 64%, Slightly Lower than in Recent Past," Gallup News Serv., Dec. 8, 2005, *available at* http:// poll.gallup.com/content/default.aspx?ci=20350.

[207] The seemingly never-ending deterrence debate continues with Cass Sunstein taking an unexpected position. Eric Blumenrosen, "Killing in Good Conscience: What's Wrong with Sunstein and Vermeule's Lesser Evil Argument for Capital Punishment and Other Human Rights Violations," 10 New Criminal Rev. 210 (2007).

[208] David W. Moore, "Public Divided between Death Penalty and Life Imprisonment without Parole," Gallup News Serv., June 2, 2004, *available at* http://brain.gallup.com/content/default.aspx?ci=11878.

[209] Death Penalty Info. Ctr., *supra* n. 202, at 3 ("The Gallup Poll of May 2004 reported that 50% of respondents favored the death penalty while 46% favored life without parole, a difference close to the 3-point margin of error in the poll. In 1997, the difference between these two choices was 32 percentage points.").

[210] 2008 Westlaw 2511282 (June 25, 2008). *But see* Baze v. Rees, 128 S.Ct. 1520 (2008) (rejecting the argument that execution by lethal injection amounts to cruel and unusual punishment). Justice Stevens, however, indicated in *Baze* that he no longer could support the death penalty.

witness testimony. The Court even cited an exoneration study by Samuel Gross.[211] The Court also undermined its general rationale for capital punishment by adopting the following Charles Black type of argument:

> As noted above, the resulting imprecision and the tension between evaluating the individual circumstances and consistency of treatment have been tolerated where the victim dies. It should not be introduced into our justice system, though, where death has not occurred.[212]

The Court added, "Evolving standards of decency that mark the progress of a maturing society counsel us to be most hesitant before interpreting the Eighth Amendment to allow the extention of the death penalty,"[213] especially given this risk of error. Several commentators describe the Court as basically establishing a one-way ratchet that only allows restrictions on assessing the death penalty.[214]

Comparative Sources

The U.S. Supreme Court's increased use of comparative constitutional sources also resembles the South African Constitutional Court. The comparative trend was highlighted in *Lawrence v. Texas*,[215] in which the Supreme Court referred to a European Court of Human Rights decision striking down laws prohibiting homosexual sodomy.[216]

A majority of the Justices have supported this use of foreign law in capital punishment cases.[217] Given that most nations do not permit the

---

[211] 2008 Westlaw 2511282 *24.   [212] *Id.* *22.

[213] *Id.* *19.

[214] *See e.g.* Dahlia Lithwick, "Making the Tough Moral Choices, So You Don't Have To...," Slate, The Breakfast Table, June 25, 2008 http://www.slate.com/id /2193813/entry/2194268/ (last visited June 25, 2008) (discussing Eric Posner's blog posting about the one-way ratchet in the case). *See also* Lyle Denniston, "Commentary: Death Penalty Options Narrow," Scotusblog, June 25, 2008, <http:www .scotusblog.com/wp/commentary-death-penalty-options-narrow/#more-7553> (last visited June 25, 2008) ("The trend of its decisions reveals a moral orientation that proponents of the ultimate penalty may have increasing difficulty trying to overcome.")

[215] 539 U.S. 558 (2003).   [216] *Id.* at 573.

[217] According to Yale Law School Dean Harold Koh, "Kennedy and Sandra Day O'Connor have joined Stephen Breyer, John Paul Stephens, Ruth Bader Ginsburg and David Souter in the 'transnationalist' camp of the court, while Scalia, Thomas, and Chief Justice William Rehnquist make up the 'nationalist' bloc, which rejects U.S. interdependence with other countries." Harris Meyer, "Justice Kennedy Wades into International Waters Again," Law.Com, May 17, 2005, http://www.law.com/jsp/article.jsp?id= 1116246912761.

death penalty, this trend encourages abolitionists.[218] Indeed, the Court relied on foreign sources in *Atkins v. Virginia* when it reversed an earlier decision, *Penry v. Lynaugh*,[219] and held that capital punishment for the mentally retarded was cruel and unusual punishment.[220] The Court noted, "Within the world community, the imposition of the death penalty for crimes committed by mentally retarded offenders is overwhelmingly disapproved."[221] Its central rationale, however, was that numerous states had repealed capital punishment for such individuals since *Penry* and that capital punishment was inequitable as such individuals lacked certain mental capacities.[222]

Moreover, in 2005 in *Roper v. Simmons*,[223] the Court consulted international sources to reverse precedent and strike down the death penalty for juveniles.[224] Justice Kennedy, who authored *Lawrence*, reasoned that an emerging consensus among American states supported the decision.[225] However, the dissent rightly questioned this argument because many states have retained the death penalty for minors.[226]

In fact, Justice Kennedy was more accurate when he stated that there was an international consensus against juvenile capital punishment.[227] He wrote that:

---

[218] Many law review articles have been written on this issue as well. *See, e.g.,* Roger P. Alford, "In Search of a Theory of Constitutional Comparativism," 52 UCLA L. Rev. 639 (2005) (analyzing the use of comparative and international material based on a judge's method of constitutional analysis, in particular focusing on four interpretive theories – originalism, natural law, majoritarianism, and pragmatism – and addressing the appropriateness of constitutional compartivism under each theory). Ironically, Justice Scalia has used comparative sources too, especially English law. *See Lawrence*, 539 U.S. at 604 (Scalia, J., dissenting) (citing a Canadian case as evidence of the future harm the majority decision will cause to society); McIntyre v. Ohio Elections Comm'n, 514 U.S. 334, 381 (1995) (Scalia J., dissenting) (citing Australian, Canadian, and English statutory law on elections to support his argument). *See generally* Melissa A. Waters, "Justice Scalia on the Use of Foreign Law in Constitutional Interpretation: Unidirectional Monologue or Co-Constitutive Dialogue?," 12 Tulsa J. Comp. & Int'l L. 149 (2004) (discussing Justice Scalia's disdain for the use of contemporary international materials except when interpreting a treaty to which the United States is a party). And former Chief Justice Rehnquist made some favorable comments about foreign law on at least one occasion. Vicki C. Jackson & Mark Tushnet, Comparative Constitutional Law 183–184 (2006). Rehnquist even cited foreign material in an important case involving the so-called right to die. Washington v. Glucksberg, 521 U.S. 702 (1997) (referring to the Dutch experience).

[219] Penry v. Lynaugh, 492 U.S. 302 (1989).   [220] 536 U.S. 304, 321 (2002).

[221] *Id.* at 316 n.21.   [222] *Id.* at 314–17.

[223] 125 S. Ct. 1183 (2005).   [224] *Id.* at 1198, 1200.

[225] *Id.* at 1192.   [226] *Id.* at 1218.

[227] *Id.* at 1199.

Respondent and his *amici* have submitted, and petitioner does not contest, that only seven countries other than the United States have executed juvenile offenders since 1990: Iran, Pakistan, Saudi Arabia, Yemen, Nigeria, the Democratic Republic of Congo, and China. Since then each of these countries has either abolished capital punishment for juveniles or made public disavowal of the practice.... In sum, it is fair to say that the United States now stands alone in a world that has turned its face against the juvenile death penalty.[228]

Kennedy also reasoned that minors lacked the maturity, well-formed character, and ability to resist peer pressure and thus should not be subjected to such an irredeemable punishment.[229] This certainly sounds like an argument that the South African Constitutional Court would endorse. Kennedy's rejection of retribution for minors also suggests a softening from the Court's position in *Gregg*.[230] In his *Roper* decision, Kennedy wrote:

Whether viewed as an attempt to express the community's moral outrage or as an attempt to right the balance for the wrong to the victim, the case for retribution is not as strong with a minor as with an adult. Retribution is not proportional if the law's most severe penalty is imposed on one whose culpability or blame-worthiness is diminished, to a substantial degree, by reason of youth and immaturity.[231]

There has been much speculation about what has moved the Supreme Court in this comparative law direction. Certainly, globalization and the Internet have facilitated learning about the judicial systems of other countries.[232] In addition, most of the Justices have traveled abroad and interacted with foreign constitutional court jurists and attorneys.[233] Commentator Tony Mauro points out that Justice Kennedy was powerfully

---

[228] *Id.*

[229] *Id.* at 1195. Emily Buss, however, has shown concern regarding courts assuming that children are incapable of making certain judgments. *See e.g.* "The Speech Enhancing Effect of Internet Regulation," 79 Chi.-Kent L. Rev. 103 (2004). That does not mean she supports the juvenile death penalty.

[230] Gregg v. Georgia, 428 U.S. 153, 183 (1976).

[231] Roper, 125 S. Ct. at 1196.

[232] Justice Stephen Breyer, The Supreme Court and the New International Law (Apr. 4, 2003) (discussing the easy accessibility of documents via the Internet and the value of discussions with foreign judges), *available at* http://www.supremecourtus.gov /publicinfo/speeches/sp_04-04-03.html (last visited Jan. 11, 2008).

[233] *Id.*; Melissa A. Waters, "Mediating Norms and Identity: The Role of Transnational Judicial Dialogue in Creating and Enforcing International Law," 93 Geo. L.J. 487, 495–96 (2005).

affected by an American Bar Association meeting held in London at which a British barrister criticized him rather harshly for the Supreme Court's insularity about foreign law.[234] Whatever the reason, the Supreme Court's more recent decisions have distinct connections to the South African Constitutional Court's approach. Given the U.S. legal system's numerous imperfections, this would be a welcome development.[235]

The appointment of new Chief Justice John Roberts does not change this calculus, as former Chief Justice Rehnquist did not support this anti-death penalty trend either.[236] However, Justice Alito's appointment could stem this shift as he is more conservative than O'Connor, whom he replaced. But Justice Alito may not make a big difference as Justice O'Connor was not a crucial fifth vote in the majority of either *Atkins* or *Roper*.[237] Indeed, the Court's recent decision in *Kennedy v. Louisiana* suggests that the addition of Alito and Roberts will not stop the anti-death penalty trend.

---

[234] *See* Tony Mauro, "U.S. Supreme Court v. World.," USA Today, June 20, 2005, at 15A, *available at* 2005 WLNR 9757882.

[235] *See, e.g.*, Andrew Gelman et al., "A Broken System: The Persistent Patterns of Reversals of Death Sentences in the United States," 1 J. Empirical Legal Studies 209, 260 (2004) (analyzing factors predictive of imposition of death penalty sentences and predictive of appellate reversal in light of fact "there is a 68 percent chance that [a death sentence] will be overturned by a state or federal court because of serious error").

[236] During his confirmation hearings, for example, Chief Justice Roberts showed he shares a similar approach with his predecessor, testifying, "If we're relying on a decision from a German judge about what our Constitution means, no President accountable to the people appointed that judge, and no Senate accountable to the people confirmed that judge, and yet he's playing a role in shaping the law that binds the people in this country. I think that's a concern that has to be addressed. The other part of it that would concern me is that, relying on foreign precedent doesn't confine judges. It doesn't limit their discretion the way relying on domestic precedent does.... In foreign law, you can find anything you want. If you don't find it in the decisions of France or Italy, it's in the decisions of Somalia or Japan or Indonesia or wherever. As somebody said in another context, looking at foreign law for support is like looking out over a crowd and picking out your friends. You can find them, they're there. And that actually expands the discretion of the judge. It allows the judge to incorporate his or her own personal preferences, cloak them with the authority of precedent – because they're finding precedent in foreign law, and use that to determine the meaning of the Constitution. I think that's a misuse of precedent, not a correct use of precedent." 151 Cong. Rec. S10,172 (daily ed. Sept. 19, 2005) (statement of Chief Justice Roberts during testimony at his confirmation hearings). Justice Alito expressed similar views in response to questions from Arizona Senator Kyl during his confirmation hearings.

[237] Atkins v. Virginia, 536 U.S. 304 (2002) (decided 6–3 with Chief Justice Rehnquist and Justices Thomas and Scalia dissenting); *Roper*, 125 S.Ct. 1183 (decided 5–4 with Chief Justice Rehnquist and Justices O'Connor, Thomas, and Scalia dissenting).

CONCLUSION

The U.S. Constitution has served as a model for the world's other constitutions, as it is the oldest written national charter. Yet, the South African Constitution's framers rejected many of the U.S. Constitution's provisions, particularly its supposed libertarianism, as being inconsistent with the new South Africa's values.[238] In finding capital punishment to be cruel and unusual, as well as arbitrary and racist (even without a jury), the Constitutional Court cited but rejected the U.S. Supreme Court's death penalty cases.[239]

This chapter argues that it is now plausible that the U.S. Supreme Court could render a death penalty decision that follows in the Constitutional Court's footsteps.[240] Thus, as Justice Marshall said in his *Furman* concurrence, the U.S. Supreme Court could one day rule as follows:

> Punishment for the sake of retribution [is] not permissible under the Eighth Amendment.... At times a cry is heard that morality requires vengeance to evidence society's abhorrence of the act. But the Eighth Amendment is our

[238] *See* Chapter I.

[239] *Makwanyane*, (3) SA at 433–434, ¶¶ 93–95 (citing American judicial opinions opposing the death penalty).

[240] Even death penalty proponents recognize the concerns regarding wrongful death sentences and racial disparity in sentencing, and realize the need, at a minimum, to develop an error-proof death penalty system. Mitt Romney, the former governor of Massachusetts, hoped to reinstate the death penalty in Massachusetts, which was banned there in 1984 and last used in 1947. He sought to implement a fool-proof formula. Governor Romney appointed a state commission on the death penalty that issued multiple recommendations to improve the system, including "raising the bar for a death penalty sentence from the normal legal standard of guilty 'beyond a reasonable doubt' to a finding of 'no doubt about the defendant's guilt[,]'" applying the death penalty only to a narrow list of cases such as torture, murders of police officers, and murders of multiple victims, requiring physical evidence like DNA, fingerprints, or footprints "to strongly corroborate the defendant's guilt [,]" and utilizing a separate jury for trial and sentencing. Pam Belluck, "Massachusetts Offers Plan for Death Penalty," N.Y. Times, May 3, 2004, at A16, *available at* 2004 WLNR 5595662. However, critics argued the plan could establish criteria so narrow that no one will ever be executed. *Id.* Additionally, several Massachusetts district attorneys believed "the troubled state medical examiner's office and State Police crime laboratory can barely carry out current responsibilities, let alone make sure that innocent people don't end up on death row." Jonathan Saltzman, "DA's Rap Governor's Death Penalty Plan," Boston Globe, May 4, 2004, at A1, *available at* 2004 WLNR 3605928. The Massachusetts House of Representatives defeated the proposal in 2007. No Death Penalty in Massachusetts, "The death penalty in Massachusetts, Facts and History," http://www.nodp.org/ma/sl.html (last visited Oct. 10, 2008).

insulation from our baser selves. The "cruel and unusual" [punishment] language limits the avenues through which vengeance can be channeled. Were this not so, the language would be empty and a return to the rack and other tortures would be possible in a given case.[241]

[241] Furman v. Georgia, 408 U.S. 238, 344–45 (1972) (Marshall, J., concurring).

4

Gender Equality

At first glance, the distinction between substantive equality and formal equality looks obvious. Substantive equality requires that the courts favor the historically disadvantaged class. In contrast, formal equality presumes that courts should treat everyone the same. Yet, these distinctions are not always so clear, especially in gender discrimination cases. Do laws that advantage women actually promote equality or demonstrate that women remain second-class citizens who need assistance? Should laws that have a disparate impact on women automatically be illegal even if there is no discriminatory animus?

This chapter addresses these questions by focusing on two important Constitutional Court decisions and their American analogues. The South African cases show that the temptation to treat all people the same, regardless of historical circumstances, remains strong even under South Africa's transformative charter.

The first case involves Nelson Mandela's pardon of women in prison, along with children under age 12, who committed nonviolent offenses. The second case involves the criminalization of prostitution. There is an interesting connection between the two cases as some women may have been imprisoned because of prostitution or other vice-related activities. In addition, both cases touch on the sexual roles that women play – biological mother in one, "temptress" in another. Moreover, the Court in both cases ruled for the government. Yet, the Court applied substantive equality correctly in the first case, but not in the second. This chapter explains how that happened and also addresses privacy issues from the prostitution case.

MANDELA'S PARDON

In April 1994, South Africa elected Nelson Mandela to the presidency in its first democratic election.[1] That June, Mandela released "all mothers in prison on 10 May 1994, with minor children under the age of twelve (12) years" who had not committed violent offenses.[2] The pardon also covered certain minors and disabled prisoners.[3] It celebrated Mandela's May 10th inauguration and the establishment of a new and free South Africa.[4] Fathers in prison who had children under age twelve and who had committed nonviolent offenses were not pardoned.

In December 1991, a South African court had sentenced John Hugo, a white male, to serve more than fifteen years for his crimes.[5] He had been married, but was widowed in 1987; he had a son five years earlier in 1982.[6] In response to Mandela's pardon, Hugo applied for a court order granting his release from prison because he had a child who was then under age twelve.[7] He subsequently amended the application and sought a declaration that the pardon violated the South African Bill of Rights because it constituted unfair gender discrimination against him and because it indirectly discriminated against his son because his son's parent was not female.[8] Thus, a presidential act of mercy, designed to celebrate the nation's new freedom, was challenged as violating one of those freedoms.

The Durban and Coast Local Division of the Supreme Court ruled that the pardon embraced the impermissible stereotype that mothers are the primary caretakers of children.[9] The Constitutional Court, however, reversed this decision in 1997, finding that the pardon was not unfairly discriminatory.[10] The Constitutional Court said that President Mandela acted in good faith to help certain imprisoned mothers and their children.[11] There was a dissent.[12]

Pres. of S. Afr. v. Hugo was one of the Court's first discussions of the Constitution's equality provisions and is frequently cited.[13] Several

---

[1] Hassen Ebrahim, Soul of a Nation 176 (1998).
[2] President of S. Afr. v. Hugo, 1997 (4) SA 1, 5 (CC), Par. 2.
[3] *Id.* n.3   [4] *Id.* at 19, Par. 47.
[5] *Id.* at 5, Par. 1. (according to the Constitutional Court case records, Hugo was convicted of robbery, house breaking, and escaping from custody).
[6] *Id.* at 5, Par. 1.   [7] *Id.* at 6, Par. 2.
[8] *Id.* Par. 3.   [9] *Id.* Par. 48.
[10] *Id.* at 28, Par. 47.   [11] *Id.* at 23, Par. 78.
[12] *Id.* at 31, Par. 62.
[13] The case is cited in virtually every equality decision rendered by the Constitutional Court. *See, e.g.,* Harksen v. Lane NO, 1998 (1) SA 300, 319 (CC); Larbi-Odam v.

scholars, however, have criticized the Court's equality jurisprudence, exemplified in *Hugo*, as being timid.[14] They are incorrect.

My thesis is that the Constitutional Court in *Hugo* and other cases started to develop a coherent transformative equality jurisprudence with three elements: (1) a group-oriented equality norm, (2) an antidominance principle, and (3) a pragmatic interpretive philosophy. To support my thesis, this chapter juxtaposes *Hugo* against the American approach to gender discrimination. The chapter also draws on a number of American constitutional theorists.[15] It further demonstrates that certain international conventions, ignored by the Court, support its ruling.

The *Hugo* discussion has five parts. The first part examines the equality analysis of Justices Goldstone, O'Regan, and Mokgoro. It also briefly discusses whether the pardon raised a nonjusticiable political question. The next section analyzes Justice Kriegler's dissent and discusses how the U.S. Supreme Court would have likely supported his contrary view. The third part discusses several competing constitutional theories, the seeds of which lie under the surface of the Goldstone and O'Regan opinions, as well as the Kriegler dissent. These theories help illuminate the source of the Justices' divergent approaches. The fourth part explains why the differences between the South African and American approaches are understandable given the respective legal systems and cultural milieus. The last part addresses several possible critiques of my thesis.

The Majority Opinions

President Mandela remitted these prison sentences under section 82(1)(k) of the Interim Constitution that said, "The President shall be competent to exercise and perform the following powers and functions, namely . . . to pardon or reprieve offenders, either unconditionally or subject to such conditions as he or she may deem fit, and to remit any fines, penalties or forfeitures."[16] This wording is similar to section 84(2)(j) of the final

---

Member of the Executive Council for Education, 1998 (1) SA 745, 754 (CC); Pretoria City Council v. Walker, 1998 (2) SA 363, 372 (CC).

[14] *See, e.g.,* Dennis Davis, Democracy and Deliberation (1999); Cathi Albertyn & Beth Goldblatt, "Facing the Challenges of Transformation," 14 S. Afr. J. Hum. Rts. 248 (1998); Alfred Cockrell, "Rainbow Jurisprudence," 12 S. Afr. J. Hum. Rts. 1, 10 (1996); Anton Fagan, "Dignity and Unfair Discrimination," 14 S. Afr. J. Hum. Rts. 220 (1998).

[15] *See infra* 106–110.

[16] S. Afr. (Interim) Const. § 82(1)(k). President Mandela's 1994 pardon was based on this provision in South Africa's Interim Constitution because South Africa did not adopt a final Constitution until 1996.

Constitution.[17] The government defended against Mr. Hugo's claims by arguing first that the Court lacked the power to overturn such a discretionary presidential decision.[18] Even if the matter was justiciable, the president did not violate the Bill of Rights.[19]

Justiciability

Justice Richard Goldstone authored the majority opinion, with which six other Justices joined. Justice Goldstone had been one of the "liberal" white judges under the apartheid regime, with an English background, who sought to use the law to assist the disadvantaged. During the transition, he chaired what came to be known as the Goldstone Commission – an important body that investigated the ongoing violence in South Africa between 1991 and 1994. After joining the Constitutional Court, he eventually took a sabbatical and gained international renown as the first war crimes prosecutor at the international tribunals for Yugoslavia and later Rwanda.

Goldstone found the pardon issue justiciable because the Interim Constitution's Preamble obliged the Court to test actions by "any organ of State against the discipline of . . . in particular, the Bill of Rights."[20] Not even the president was above the law. Goldstone acknowledged that certain presidential actions may be practically unreviewable, such as the good faith pardoning of a single prisoner,[21] but he explained that the president's group pardon could be meaningfully reviewed under equality guarantees.[22]

It is not clear whether the U.S. Supreme Court would have followed Goldstone's reasoning if an American president had pardoned a similar group of female prisoners. Article II, section 2 of the U.S. Constitution states that the president "shall have Power to grant Reprieves and Pardons for Offences against the United States, except in Cases of Impeachment."[23] This pardon power lacks qualification, except for the reference to impeachment. Thus, in the 1866 case, *Ex Parte Garland*, the Supreme Court held that the pardon power was unlimited.[24] Under this approach,

---

[17] *Id.* at § 84(2)(j) ("The President is responsible for . . . pardoning or reprieving offenders and remitting any fines, penalties or forfeitures."). There is likewise a pardon provision in the American Constitution. U.S. Const. art. II, § 2(1).

[18] President of S. Afr. v. Hugo, 1997 (4) SA 1,7 n.8. (CC) (hereinafter "*Hugo*"). Pars. 13, 19.

[19] *Id.* Par. 30.   [20] *Id.* at 17, Par. 28.

[21] *Id*, Par. 29.   [22] *Id.* at 18, Par. 29.

[23] U.S. Const. art. II, § 2.

[24] *Ex parte* Garland, 71 U.S. 333, 380 (1866 Wall.).

the Court could refuse to second-guess a presidential pardon by invoking the political question doctrine, which holds that certain matters are constitutionally the sole prerogative of the nonjudicial branches of government.[25]

But in *Schick v. Reed*, the U.S. Supreme Court held that "the pardoning power is an enumerated power of the Constitution and its limitations, if any, must be found in the Constitution itself."[26] Thus, one commentator suggests that the Fourteenth Amendment's equal protection clause might prevent a president from pardoning a group of blacks and not whites in the same situation.[27] Indeed, a federal appeals court struck down a state governor's pardon on equal protection grounds.[28] And *Garland* was decided before the Fourteenth Amendment became effective.[29]

It is therefore unclear how the Supreme Court would rule. Moreover, Justice Goldstone admitted that his equality analysis was deferential because the pardon power in South Africa "is not subject to cabinet concurrence or to legislative control."[30] Thus, the positions of the American and South African Courts may not have differed.

Put another way, even if the American president had unreviewable pardon power, a decision by Congress or a state legislature to remit the sentences of certain mothers in prison would still be reviewable by the U.S. Supreme Court under equal protection principles. Thus, the stereotype question could well arise in the United States.

The Equality Issue

GOLDSTONE'S APPROACH. As discussed in the previous chapter, the South African Interim Bill of Rights required a two-stage analysis. It bears mention that in *Harksen v. Lane NO*, decided a year after *Hugo*, the Constitutional Court adopted a four-stage equality analysis.[31] First, the law must draw a rational differentiation to be minimally

---

[25] *See, e.g.*, Baker v. Carr, 369 U.S. 186, 217 (1962) (referring to those provisions where there is "a textually demonstrable constitutional commitment of the issue to a coordinate political departrnent").

[26] 419 U.S. 256, 267 (1974).

[27] Brian Kalt, Note, "Pardon Me? The Constitutional Case against Presidential Self Pardons," 106 Yale LJ. 779, 791 n. 79 (1996).

[28] *See* Osborne v. Folmar, 735 F.2d 1316 (11th Cir. 1984).

[29] *Garland*, 71 U.S. 333. Garland was decided in 1866, but the Fourteenth Amendment wasn't ratified until 1868.

[30] *Hugo*, 1997 (4) SA at 24. The Constitutional Court rejected an argument that the president's discretionary pardon power violated separation of powers in *Ex parte* Chairperson of the Constitutional Assembly: *In re* Certification of the Constitution of the Republic of South Africa, 1996 (4) SA 744, 812 (CC).

[31] 1998 (1) SA 300, 324–25 (CC).

acceptable.[32] Stage two then looks at whether the law discriminates either on a listed ground (race, sex, gender, etc.) or on a ground that could otherwise impair fundamental human dignity.[33] If it does not discriminate on such grounds, the law is likely permissible.[34] If the law discriminates on either basis, then stage three looks at whether the differentiation amounts to *unfair* discrimination (what *Hugo* looked at).[35] If the answer is no, then the law is upheld. If the answer is yes, then stage four requires the Court to examine whether the government can justify this differentiation under the limitations power.[36] Thus, the normal two-stage South African Bill of Rights analysis is more complex in equality cases.

Justice Goldstone's opinion, however, never progressed to the limitations stage. He referenced section 8(2) of the Interim Constitution's equality provisions which declared that "no person shall be unfairly discriminated against, directly or indirectly . . . on one or more of the following grounds in particular: race, gender, [or] sex."[37] But Section 8(3)(a), specified, "This section shall not preclude measures designed to achieve the adequate protection and advancement of persons or categories of persons disadvantaged by unfair discrimination, in order to enable their full and equal enjoyment of all rights and freedoms."[38]

Section 8(4) in turn stated, "*Prima facie* proof of discrimination on any of the grounds specified in subsection (2) shall be presumed to be sufficient proof of unfair discrimination as contemplated in that subsection, until the contrary is established."[39] In other words, the Constitutional Court should presume that discrimination on a listed ground, whether direct or indirect, is unfair, and the government bears the burden of proving otherwise. Goldstone's analysis would likely have been the same under the final Constitution.

Justice Goldstone then acknowledged that the pardon facially discriminated against certain male prisoners and that the government therefore had to prove that the discrimination was not unfair.[40] Goldstone ruled that the government had met its burden. He relied heavily on an affidavit submitted by President Mandela to which was attached a supporting affidavit from Helen Starke, the national director of the South African National Council for Child and Family Welfare.[41]

---

[32] *Id.* at 324.   [33] *Id.* at 325.
[34] *Id.*   [35] *Id.*
[36] *Id.*
[37] *Hugo*, 1997 (4) SA at 6; S. Afr. (Interim) Const. § 8(2)., Par. 32.
[38] S. Afr. (Interim Const.) § 8(3)(a).   [39] *Id.* at § 8(4).
[40] *Hugo*, 1997 (4) SA at 23, Par. 41.   [41] *Id.* at 20, Par. 42.

President Mandela's affidavit stated that the pardon was motivated by his concern about how young children would be adversely affected by the absence of "the nurturing and care which their mothers would ordinarily have provided. Having spent many years in prison myself, I am well aware of the hardship which flows from incarceration. I am also well aware that imprisonment inevitably has harsh consequences for the family of the prisoner."[42] As to why he selected mothers and not fathers, Mandela stated, "Account was taken of the special role I believe that mothers play in the care and nurturing of younger children. In this regard, I refer to the affidavit of Helen Starke."[43]

Justice Goldstone quoted from Ms. Starke's affidavit in which she wrote:

4. In my opinion, the identification of this special category for remission of sentence is rationally and reasonably explicable as being in the best interests of the children concerned. It is generally accepted that children bond with their mothers at a very early age and that mothers are the primary nurturers and care givers of young children.

5. Although it could be argued that fathers play a more significant role in the lives of older children, the primary bonding with the mother and the role of mothers as the primary nurturers and care givers extend well into childhood.

6. The reasons for this are partly historical and the role of the socialization of women who are socialized to fulfill the role of primary nurturers and care givers of children, especially pre-adolescent children and are perceived by society as such (sic).[44]

Justice Goldstone relied on this affidavit even though it was not based on any sophisticated social science assessments of child rearing.

Justice Goldstone's reasoning can be broken down into five steps. First, he believed in Mandela's good faith and saw "no reason to doubt the assertion that mothers, as a matter of fact, bear more responsibilities for child-rearing in our society than do fathers."[45] Second, Goldstone said that because of the time, money, and emotional energy involved in rearing children it is "difficult for women to compete in the labour market

---

[42] *Id.* Par. 36.

[43] *Id.* President Mandela writes extensively in his autobiography regarding the guilt he felt about the way that his imprisonment hurt his family. Nelson Mandela, Long Walk to Freedom 719 & 749 (1994).

[44] *Hugo*, 1997 (4) SA at 21. Par. 36.   [45] *Id.* Par. 37.

and is one of the causes of the deep inequalities experienced by women in employment."[46] Third, Goldstone noted that section 8(3) of the Interim Constitution authorized measures to alleviate disadvantage caused by prior discrimination.[47] Fourth, Goldstone said that were Mandela "obliged to release fathers on the same terms as mothers, the result may have been that no parents would have been released at all," given the much larger number of male prisoners and the great public concern about the nation's "alarming" crime rate.[48] Fifth, Goldstone said that the pardon did not significantly injure Mr. Hugo because he could still apply individually for a pardon, he had not lost any of his parental rights, and it was his own actions that had landed him in prison.[49]

In his opinion, Justice Goldstone repeatedly showed concern about basing discriminatory treatment on "a particular generalization. Women's responsibilities in the home for housekeeping and child rearing have historically been given as reasons for excluding them from other spheres of life."[50] However, he saw the pardon as assisting these women to be better mothers in circumstances in which their male partners had often failed to meet parental and financial obligations. Thus, although the pardon was facially discriminatory, the government proved it was not unfairly discriminatory. Justice Goldstone concluded that equality principles sometimes demand that those who are not similarly situated be treated differently.[51]

O'REGAN'S APPROACH. Six Justices joined Justice O'Regan's concurring opinion. Like Goldstone, O'Regan argued that mothers actually spend more time raising their children than do fathers and that this contributes to women's inequality in the labor market as they are unable to devote as much time to labor outside the home as men.[52] Before assuming the bench, Justice O'Regan was a young constitutional and administrative law professor with an anti-apartheid liberal bent. She had an English background and had co-authored one of the major proposed drafts of a new constitution with several other prominent academics.

O'Regan's opinion differed from Goldstone's because she proposed specific criteria for determining whether affirmative measures amount to unfair discrimination:

[46] *Id.* at 22, Par. 38.
[48] *Id.* at 25, Par. 46.
[50] *Id.* at 22, Par. 39.
[52] *Id.* at 48, Par. 110.

[47] *Id.* at 23, Par. 41.
[49] *Id.* at 26, Par. 47.
[51] *Id.* at 23 n.63.

The more vulnerable the group adversely affected by the discrimination, the more likely the discrimination will be held to be unfair. Similarly, the more invasive the nature of the discrimination upon the interests of the individuals affected by the discrimination, the more likely it will be held to be unfair.[53]

Her approach responded to Justice Kriegler's dissent, which advocated criteria that would make affirmative measures hard to justify. Justice O'Regan's approach was also "asymmetric" in that historically disadvantaged racial or gender groups could be treated better than others, with some limits.

Justice O'Regan concluded that the pardon was not unfair discrimination because the president was using reasonable means to alleviate social inequality experienced by mothers. She explained that the pardon did not perpetuate female inequality.

MOKGORO'S APPROACH. Justice Yvonne Mokgoro took a third approach. She was a former law professor who had specialized in human rights, customary law, and the impact of law and society on women and children. She was also one of the Court's few black Justices. She was born in Galeshewe Township near Kimberley, the diamond capital. Unlike Goldstone, Mokgoro said that the pardon constituted unfair discrimination against the white male Mr. Hugo, thus failing the first part of the South African Bill of Rights analysis. According to Mokgoro, however, this unfair discrimination was justified under the Interim Constitution's limitations clause. The pardon therefore passed the second stage of the equality analysis that neither Kriegler nor Goldstone reached. Some scholars have argued in favor of Mokgoro's limitations approach.[54]

Justice Mokgoro said the pardon denied "men the opportunity to be released from prison in order to resume rearing their children, entirely on the basis of stereotypical assumptions concerning men's aptitude at child rearing."[55] Moreover, though "mothers may generally be disadvantaged in society, there is no evidence that they are disadvantaged in the penal system in particular."[56]

Nonetheless, Justice Mokgoro thought the pardon was a proportionate response to the problem that young children face when a parent is in prison.[57] Like Goldstone, Mokgoro also found it significant that fathers

[53] *Id.* at 49, Par. 112.
[54] *See* Albertyn & Goldblatt, *supra* note 14, at 248–49.
[55] *Hugo*, 1997 (4) SA at 41, Par. 92.   [56] *Id.* at 42, Par. 94.
[57] *Id.* at 47., Par. 106.

could still apply individually for a pardon and that it would have been politically impossible for the president to release every male.[58]

Justice Mokgoro considered ordering the government to determine on a case-by-case basis whether a prisoner with a child under age twelve was the child's primary caretaker. She rejected that option, however, because verifying that information would be an administrative nightmare for the government.[59]

The Opposing View

Kriegler's Dissent

Justice Johann Kriegler, an Afrikaaner former judge and chairperson of the nation's first Independent Electoral Commission, as well as the founding chairperson of the organization, Lawyers for Human Rights, criticized the majority's statements regarding the impossibility of releasing similarly situated males. He argued that the affidavits provided no hard data so there was no basis "for a finding that the numbers would have caused public disquiet."[60] He elaborated as follows:

> It is, of course, wholly illogical to rely on current [1997] perceptions of the level of crime in drawing inferences about reaction in mid-1994 had substantially more prisoners qualified for release. We also do not know anything about the administrative bother that may or may not have been involved in weighing the family circumstances of individual prisoners, or of applying some other method.[61]

Kriegler then distinguished the South African Constitution from other constitutions in that South Africa's apartheid legacy meant that equality protections were at "its centre."[62] He argued that the equality provisions showed the government had an obligation to make a "persuasive rebuttal" to justify facial discrimination.[63] Doing so could not be accomplished with "relative ease."[64]

Kriegler further wrote that the Court should only allow generalizations about the sexes that are based in reality, that are equalizing, and that satisfy two other criteria. First, the societal advantages of perpetuating the stereotype must strongly outweigh the obvious disadvantage.[65] Second, there must be a clear connection between the discriminatory action and

---

[58] *Id*, Par. 106.
[60] *Id.* at 34, Par. 72.
[62] *Id.* at 34, Par. 74.
[64] *Id.* at 34–35, Par. 75.

[59] *Id*, Par. 106.
[61] *Id*, Par. 72.
[63] *Id.* at 35, Par. 75.
[65] *Id.* at 38, Par. 82.

the benefit to the disadvantaged in the specific context at issue.[66] These criteria resemble the U.S. Supreme Court's restrictive standards for voluntary affirmative action.[67]

Kriegler concluded that the pardon did not meet these requirements because the release of a mere 440 women was far outweighed by the detriment "to all South African women who must continue to labour under the social view that their place is in the home."[68] Kriegler continued,

> In addition, men must continue to accept that they can have only a secondary/surrogate role in the care of their children. [This reinforces]...a view that is a root cause of women's inequality in our society. [A view that is]...foundational to paternalistic attitudes that limit the access of women to the workplace and other sources of opportunity...on the basis of predetermined, albeit time-honoured, gender scripts.[69]

Moreover, Kriegler said that the government provided no evidence showing that women have suffered systematic discrimination in the penal context.[70] He then proposed that facial gender discrimination should only be constitutional if based on an "exceedingly persuasive justification," language he quoted from the U.S. Supreme Court.[71]

The American Approach

Unlike the South African Constitution, the Constitution of the United States does not expressly prohibit gender discrimination. Instead, the Fourteenth Amendment declares, "No State shall...deny to any person within its jurisdiction the equal protection of the laws."[72] It was one of the three Civil War Amendments (along with the Thirteenth and Fifteenth) that Congress passed to help the newly freed slaves.[73] For years, therefore, the Court saw the Fourteenth Amendment as providing no protection for

---

[66] *Id*, Par. 82.

[67] *See* City of Richmond v. J.A. Croson, 488 U.S. 469 (1989) (holding that a city may utilize a narrowly tailored affirmative action plan in contracting to redress its own past discriminatory contracting practices).

[68] *Hugo*, 1997 (4) SA at 38, Par. 82.

[69] *Id*, Par. 83.　　　　　　　　　　[70] *Id*, Par. 84.

[71] *Id*. at 39, Par. 85. (citing United States v. Virginia, 518 U.S. 515,523-24 (1996) (citing Miss. Univ. for Women v. Hogan, 458 U.S. 718, 724 (1982))).

[72] U.S. Const. amend. XIV.

[73] *See, e.g.*, Strauder v. West Virginia, 100 U.S. 303, 305–06 (1900) (declaring that "the true spirit and meaning" of the Civil War Amendments was "securing to a race recently emancipated...[the enjoyment] of all the civil rights that...under the law are enjoyed by [whites].").

women. Indeed, women did not receive the right to vote until almost fifty years after black males.[74]

In the 1970s, the Supreme Court subjected sex discrimination to meaningful scrutiny under the equal protection clause for the first time, although the scrutiny was not as strict as in race cases.[75] Race discrimination receives strict scrutiny, meaning the government must show the law is narrowly tailored to serve a compelling governmental interest.[76] The late Stanford constitutional law expert Gerald Gunther described this standard as "strict in theory, but fatal in fact."[77]

Laws that facially discriminate based on sex receive an intermediate level of scrutiny, meaning the government must show the law is substantially related to promoting an important governmental interest.[78] This standard is less stringent than strict scrutiny although the Supreme Court has said that the government must still have an "exceedingly persuasive justification."[79]

Most laws that discriminate against other groups receive a lenient rational basis review.[80] The plaintiff must prove that the law is *not* rationally related to a legitimate governmental interest.[81] The government generally prevails because it can usually show a legitimate governmental interest behind the discriminatory practice. For example, typical economic legislation advances one industry's interests, even if does not help others.

Why does sex discrimination not receive the same stringent scrutiny as race discrimination? After all, the federal and state governments have often treated both groups as subhuman. Justice Ruth Bader Ginsburg has stated, "'Inherent differences' between men and women, we have come to appreciate, remain cause for celebration, but not for denigration of the members of either sex or for artificial constraints on an individual's

---

[74] The Fifteenth Amendment to the Constitution, prohibiting the denial of the right to vote on account of race, was ratified in 1870. The Nineteenth Amendment, prohibiting the denial of the right to vote on account of sex, was ratified in 1920.

[75] *See, e.g.,* Reed v. Reed, 404 U.S. 71 (1971).

[76] *See, e.g.,* Adarand Constructors, Inc. v. Pena, 515 U.S. 200 (1995).

[77] Gerald Gunther, "Foreword: In Search of Evolving Doctrine on a Changing Court: A Model for a Newer Equal Protection," 86 Harv. L. Rev. 1, 8 (1972).

[78] *See, e.g.,* Craig v. Boren, 429 U.S. 190 (1976).

[79] United States v. Virginia, 518 U.S. 515, 523–24 (1996) (citing Miss. Univ. for Women v. Hogan, 458 U.S. 718, 724 (1982)).

[80] Erwin Chemerinsky, Constitutional Law 533 (1997).

[81] *See* FCC v. Beach Communications, Inc., 508 U.S. 307 (1993) (establishing that economic classifications and laws that burden the elderly generally receive rational basis review).

opportunity."[82] Ginsburg's point was that there are, at a minimum, physical differences between men and women that occasionally justify treating the sexes unequally, whereas there are no such differences between blacks and whites.

Erwin Chemerinsky explains, however, that most unequal treatment is unacceptable:

> The Supreme Court frequently has invalidated laws that benefit women and disadvantage men when the Court perceives the law as being based on stereotypical assumptions about gender roles. Many of these laws were based on the stereotype of women being economically dependent on their husbands, but men being economically independent of their wives.... Other stereotypes also have been rejected as a sufficient basis for gender classifications benefiting women. Some laws are based on stereotypes about women's role in the family and raising children as compared with men.[83]

The Supreme Court illustrated its hostility toward stereotypes in *Caban v. Mohammed*, in which it struck down a law that mandated only a mother's consent, not a father's, before a child born out of wedlock could be put up for adoption.[84] The Court ruled that there is not "a fundamental difference between maternal and paternal relations.... [Such relations are not] invariably different in importance.... The present case demonstrates that an unwed father may have a relationship with his children fully comparable to that of the mother."[85]

The Court rejected Justice John Paul Stevens' dissent, which held:

> There is some sociological and anthropological research indicating that by virtue of the symbiotic relationship between mother and child during pregnancy and the initial contact between mother and child directly after birth a physical and psychological bond immediately develops between the two that is not then present between the infant and the father or any other person.[86]

Stevens' reasoning resembles that of Goldstone and O'Regan in supporting government action based on the social reality of a gender stereotype.

[82] U.S. v. Virginia, 518 U.S. 515, 533 (1996) (referencing Loving v. Virginia, 388 U.S. 1 (1967)).

[83] Chemerinsky *supra* n. 80, at 609–10; *see also* Orr v. Orr, 440 U.S. 268 (1979) (invalidating Alabama law that allows women but not men to receive alimony after divorce).

[84] 441 U.S. 380 (1979). Cf. Fraser v. Children's Court, Pretoria N., 1997 (2) SA 261 (CC) (including facts similar to Caban v. Mohammed, 441 U.S. 380 (1979)).

[85] *Caban*, 441 U.S. at 388–89.   [86] *Id.* at 404–05.

In *Mississippi University for Women v. Hogan,* the U.S. Supreme Court rejected as discriminatory a Mississippi policy banning men from attending an all-women's nursing school.[87] The state explained that the policy helped remedy discrimination against women in the workforce and in higher education.[88] However, Justice Sandra Day O'Connor ruled that the policy impermissibly "perpetuate[s] the stereotyped view of nursing as an exclusively woman's job . . . and makes the assumption that nursing is a field for women a self-fulfilling prophecy."[89] In *Hogan,* the Court said it would use "reasoned analysis" to determine whether laws are based on unacceptable "archaic and overbroad generalizations" about women.[90]

The Supreme Court has even disapproved of accurate stereotypes. In *JEB v. Alabama ex rel. T.B.,* the Court barred lawyers from using peremptory challenges to remove jurors based on their gender, even though Justice Harry Blackmun and Justice O'Connor both acknowledged that women may tend to vote differently from men in certain cases, such as rape and paternity actions.[91]

The Court has also rejected administrative convenience as a justification for sexual stereotypes.[92] By contrast, Justice Mokgoro, in *Hugo,* used administrative convenience to bolster her opinion.[93] The Supreme Court's hostility to stereotypes has also been evident in race and alienage discrimination cases.[94]

The Court, however, has not rejected all sex stereotypes. In *Rostker v. Goldberg,* it upheld a law that required only men to register for the draft, because women were barred from combat.[95] That case, however, involved judicial unwillingness to second-guess military authorities, as

[87] 458 U.S. 718 (1982).　　　　　　[88] *Id.* at 727.
[89] *Id.* at 729.　　　　　　　　　[90] *Id.* at 726,730 n.16.
[91] 511 U.S. 127, 139 n.11; 67; 149 (1994). Professor David Strauss writes that what makes racial generalizations unacceptable is not their factual inaccuracy because "states would [then] be allowed to defend racial generalizations by showing that they are in fact accurate and are not overgeneralizations. . . . It is quite clear, however, that this is not the way the prohibition against discrimination operates." David A. Strauss, "The Myth of Colorblindness," 1986 Sup. Ct. Rev. 99, 119.
[92] *See* Reed v. Reed, 404 U.S. 71,77 (1971) (declaring that state law that arbitrarily treats female estate administrator candidates worse than male estate administrator candidates cannot be justified on administrative convenience grounds).
[93] *Hugo,* 1997 (4) SA at 47, Par. 106.
[94] *See, e.g.,* Palmore v. Sidoti, 466 U.S. 429 (1984) (holding that the child custody decision was improperly based on the racial stereotype that a white child should not be placed in a home with a black stepfather); Sugarman v. Dougall, 413 U.S. 634 (1973) (striking down a New York law that prohibited aliens from holding even low-level state civil service positions).
[95] 453 U.S. 57, 57 (1981).

in *Korematsu v. United States*.[96] Moreover, the Court in *Rostker* noted that the various branches of government had extensively debated the registration issue and had not acted on unreflective stereotypes.[97] This reasoning may not be convincing, but it explains why the Court excused this stereotype.

In *Michael M. v. Superior Court*,[98] the Court upheld a California statutory rape law that permitted prosecution of men, but not women. The Court claimed its ruling did not stereotype men as sexual aggressors, but instead was based on the fact that young women already have a strong disincentive to engage in sex because they can get pregnant.[99]

In summary, the U.S. Supreme Court has generally found that laws based on sexual stereotypes favoring women violate equal protection.[100] Justice Kriegler's dissent in *Hugo* reflects the American approach. Indeed, a female American law school graduate apparently worked for Kriegler during the period he authored the dissent.[101] Determining which approach is superior requires an examination of constitutional theory.[102]

---

[96] 323 U.S. 214 (1944) (upholding the constitutionality of exclusion orders requiring persons of Japanese descent on the West Coast of the United States to leave their homes and live in "Relocation Centers" during World War II).

[97] *Rostker*, 453 U.S. 57, 72.   [98] 450 U.S. 464 (1981).

[99] *Id.* at 475–76.

[100] *See, e.g.*, Califano v. Goldfarb, 430 U.S. 199 (1977) (declaring unconstitutional a law that made it easier for widows to recover survivor benefits than widowers); Stanley v. Illinois, 405 U.S. 645 (1972) (ruling unconstitutional an Illinois statute specifying that an unwed mother could only be deprived of her children on a showing that she is an unfit parent, whereas an unwed father's child could automatically be made a ward of the state upon the death of the child's mother).

[101] Two former Constitutional Court law clerks who prefer not to be identified have independently confirmed this statement.

[102] Scholars have debated the usefulness of comparative analysis. Skeptics contend that it is flawed because one cannot take account of the important cultural and other differences that influence the legal standards. Others like Günter Frankenberg assert that comparative work is valuable but that its limitations must be kept in mind, namely the impossibility of achieving an objective viewpoint because one is always situated in a culturally biased context. *See generally* Günter Frankenburg, "Critical Comparisons: Re-thinking Comparative Law," 26 Harv. Int'l L. 1. 411 (1985). Then there are the relatively unabashed enthusiasts such as Donald Kommers who acknowledge the cultural and political differences in society but who believe that comparative study has great value. *See generally*, Donald Kommers, "The Value of Comparative Constitutional Law," 9 J. Marshall J. Practice & Procedure 685 (1976). It is beyond the scope of this chapter to engage in a detailed assessment of these positions. I generally adhere to the Kommers approach, with a healthy dose of Frankenberg thrown in. I believe that comparative studies are valuable for the reasons Kommers mentions. But I also believe one must not hold on to the illusion that perfect objectivity is possible.

The Underlying Constitutional Theories

The Goldstone/O'Regan approach contains the seeds of three schools of constitutional theory that separate it from Kriegler.

Owen Fiss's Group-Based Approach

Yale Law Professor Owen Fiss argues that the equal protection clause encompasses a group-disadvantaging norm,[103] as opposed to Paul Brest's individualistic antidiscrimination principle.[104] Fiss writes that the Fourteenth Amendment's goal is to protect blacks, a historically disadvantaged group.[105] Accordingly, laws that harm blacks or similarly vulnerable groups are presumptively invalid, even if the law is facially neutral.[106] The law's *effect* is crucial, not the purpose.[107] Courts should therefore generally uphold preferences for blacks and women to make equality a reality.

The Goldstone and O'Regan opinions both have elements of a group-based approach. Goldstone wrote that lawmakers under the Constitution have an affirmative obligation to "avoid discrimination against people who are members of disadvantaged groups."[108] Whether a law is motivated by a discriminatory purpose matters little compared to the effects for Goldstone:

> To determine whether that impact was unfair it is necessary to look not only at the group who has been disadvantaged but at the nature of the power in terms of which the discrimination was effected and, also at the nature of the interests which have been affected by the discrimination.[109]

---

[103] See generally, Owen M. Fiss, "Groups and the Equal Protection Clause," 5 Phil. & Pub. Aff. 107 (1976).

[104] See generally, Paul Brest, "In Defense of the Anti-Discrimination Principle," 90 Harv. L. Rev. 1 (1976).

[105] John Garvey & Alexander Aleinikoff, Modern Constitutional Theory: A Reader, 508 (1999) (excerpting Fiss, *supra* n. 103).

[106] *Id.* at 506 (entitling subsection "The Problem of Facially Innocent Criteria"); *Id.* at 511–12 (recommending that the Equal Protection Clause also cover certain language groups and aliens).

[107] *Id.* at 507 ("It shifts the trigger for strict scrutiny from the *criterion* of selection to the *result* of the selection process.").

[108] *Hugo*, 1997 (4) SA at 22–23. Par. 92.

[109] *Id.* at 23–24, Par. 92. Justice Goldstone did focus on purpose when he wrote that President Mandela acted in good faith in pardoning the women only, not out of prejudice against men. But Goldstone wrote that good faith alone does not prove that the discriminatory effect of the pardon was permissible. *Id.*

O'Regan likewise declared that "it is necessary to look at the group or groups which have suffered discrimination in the particular case and at the effect" on that group.[110] The more harsh the effect and the more vulnerable the group, the greater likelihood the discrimination will be unfair. O'Regan's focus on groups is even clearer in *Brink v. Kitshoff*.[111] Though neither O'Regan or Goldstone expressly rely on Fiss, elements of his theory underlie their approaches.

Admittedly, the Goldstone opinion asserted that equality is about guaranteeing human dignity, which sounds individualistic.[112] But the judiciary cannot employ a group-based equality theory without sometimes discussing its impact on individuals in the groups. Moreover, Judge Dennis Davis has illustrated that the Canadian source of the dignity principle is not individualistic.[113]

By contrast, Paul Brest's antidiscrimination principle assumes that racial considerations generally have "no moral salience."[114] Brest argues that in U.S. Supreme Court decisions, "group membership is always a proxy for the individual's right not to be discriminated against. Similarly, remedies for race-specific harms recognize the sociological consequences of group identification and affiliation only to assure justice for individual members."[115] He rejects Fiss's approach because "if a society can be said to have an underlying political theory, ours has not been a theory of organic groups but of liberalism, focusing on the rights of individuals, including rights of distributive justice."[116]

This individualistic focus is at the core of American equality jurisprudence, and it is especially evident in the Supreme Court's affirmative action cases.[117] Kriegler's concern about how stereotypes injure individuals is in accord.

---

[110] *Id.* at 49, Par. 112.

[111] 1996 (4) SA 197, 217 (CC) (declaring that equality is concerned with "patterns of group disadvantage and harm.... The need to prohibit such patterns of discrimination and remedy them is one of the primary purposes of the equality clause.").

[112] *Hugo*, 1997 (4) SA at 22–23, Par. 41.

[113] Davis, *supra* n. 14, at 77–78 n.26.   [114] Brest, *supra* n. 104, at 48.

[115] *Id.*   [116] *Id.* at 49.

[117] The Court has stated in the affirmative action context that the "Fifth and Fourteenth Amendments protect *persons*, not *groups*." Adarand Constructors, Inc. v. Pena, 515 U.S. 200, 201 (1995) (emphasis added). The problems with this individualistic focus are well set out in the *Adarand* dissents.

Catherine MacKinnon's Dominance Approach

Some American feminist scholars advocate a sameness/difference theory, whereas others, such as Catherine MacKinnon, stress dominance.[118] The sameness/difference view holds that men and women generally have equal abilities and should therefore have equal opportunities, say for jobs or education.[119] It is the opportunity that must be equal, not the end results. Differential treatment can only be justified if there are real and relevant differences between the sexes. This approach generally disfavors gender preferences for women, fearing that the preferences will perpetuate stereotypes.[120] Most U.S. Supreme Court decisions take this approach as does Kriegler.

But the Goldstone and O'Regan opinions seem to have unstated elements of Catherine MacKinnon's dominance approach. MacKinnon virtually invented sexual harassment law.[121] MacKinnon rejects the sameness/difference theory for these reasons:

> It sets up maleness as the standard against which sameness and difference are to be measured, and it supports dominance of women by approving of distinctions based on differences between the sexes. She proposes a "dominance approach" to gender discrimination which would recognize sex inequalities as matters of imposed status, as the subordination of women to men.[122]

MacKinnon believes courts should generally uphold female preferences to remedy women's subordination.[123]

---

[118] Catherine MacKinnon has focused on the ways in which males dominate and subordinate women in numerous books and articles. *See, e.g.*, Catherine MacKinnon, Feminism Unmodified (1987); Catherine MacKinnon, Toward a Feminist Theory of the State (1989). Mary Becker likewise is concerned with the actual subordination that women experience, not the abstract notion of equal opportunity. Mary E. Becker, "Prince Charming: Abstract Equality," 1987 Sup. Ct. Rev. 201. By contrast, the writings of Justice Ginsburg and Wendy Williams take an approach that seems to focus more on equal opportunity above all, as well as an acknowledgment of some real similarities and differences between men and women. *See generally*, Ruth Bader Ginsburg, "Gender and the Constitution," 44 U. Cin. L. Rev. 1 (1975); Wendy Williams, "The Equality Crisis: Some Reflections on Culture, Courts, and Feminism," 7 Women's Rts. L. Rep. 175 (1982).

[119] Leslie Bender, "A Lawyer's Primer on Feminist Theory and Tort," 38 J. Leg. Ed. 3, 5 (1988) ("Some feminists believe that open access to the male world and fair assessment of our accomplishments by its measures will solve the problem.").

[120] *See*, e.g., Williams, *supra* n. 118, at 175.

[121] Catherine MacKinnon, Sexual Harassment of Working Women: A Case Study of Sex Discrimination (1979).

[122] *See* Garvey, *supra* n. 105, at 555.

[123] *Id.* at 588–98 (referencing MacKinnon, Feminism Unmodified: Discourses on Life and Law, ch. 2 (1987)).

Similarly, Mary Becker argues that mothers should generally prevail over fathers in child custody cases because mothers tend to have long suffered as the primary caretakers.[124] Providing concrete benefits to women is far more important than worrying about stereotypes. In another article, Becker argues that the U.S. Supreme Court's gender cases often trivialize sex discrimination concerns and ignore far more fundamental power imbalances between the sexes.[125]

Though Goldstone and O'Regan opinions lack MacKinnon's or Becker's rhetoric, their support of concrete preferences for women is analogous.

Judicial Pragmatism

Judge Richard Posner and Professor Daniel Farber advocate a pragmatic approach to judicial decision making and are skeptical about any unifying theory of law.[126] A judge's goal should be to get the right result. even if it does not conform to arcane precedent.[127] Similarly, Cass Sunstein advocates a pragmatic judicial minimalist approach.[128]

The Goldstone and O'Regan opinions are likewise pragmatic in several ways. First, Goldstone admits that his decision was partly based on the special context of the pardon[129] and acknowledged that the stereotype question might come out differently in another case.[130] Indeed, the Court questioned similar gender stereotypes in the earlier case of

---

[124] Becker, *supra* n. 118 at 201; *see also* Joan Williams, "Do Women Need Special Treatment," 9 J. Contemp. L. Issues 279, 282 (1998).

[125] Mary E. Becker, "Obscuring the Struggle: Sex Discrimination, Social Security, and Stone, Seidman, Sunstein & Tushnet's Constitutional Law," 89 Colum. L. Rev. 264, 271–76 (1989). Professor Becker was involved with the Illinois Clemency Project for Battered Women, which lobbied the Illinois governor successfully to grant clemency to several imprisoned female domestic assault victims who had killed their assaultive partners. *See* Cynthia Grant Bowman & Eden Kusmiersky, "Praxis and Pedagogy: Domestic Violence," 32 Loy. L.A. L. Rev. 719 (1999) (describing the Clemency Project); *see also* DePaul Law School Faculty Web Page Profile of Professor Mary Becker, at http:// www.1aw.depaul.edulbecker.html (describing her as "one of the organizers of the Illinois Clemency Project for Battered Women.") (last visited Oct. 24, 2000). This female-only clemency resembles the Mandela pardon as it was motivated by a desire to help the children of these women.

[126] Richard A. Posner, The Problems of Jurisprudence 454–69 (1990); *see also* Daniel A. Farber, "Legal Pragmatism and the Constitution," 72 Minn. L. Rev. 1331 (1988).

[127] Posner, *id*, at 457.

[128] Cass Sunstein, One Case at a Time: Judicial Minimalism on the Supreme Court (1998); *see also* Neal Devins, "The Courts: The Democracy-Forcing Constitution," 97 Mich. L. Rev. 1971, 1975 (1999) (reviewing Sunstein's book and describing his minimalism as pragmatic).

[129] *Hugo*, 1997 (4) SA at 25, Pars. 29, 44.   [130] *Id*. Par. 41.

Fraser v. Children's Court, Pretoria North.[131] Goldstone does not advocate a single principle for all cases.[132]

Goldstone also said that Mandela probably would not have pardoned anyone if the Court had ordered the release of many male prisoners.[133] Such a broad pardon was implausible because of the high crime rate and nervous populace.[134] Furthermore, Goldstone addressed the feasibility of devising a judicial remedy.[135] The Court's determination that women are the primary caregivers, without scientific studies, shows a common-sense inclination. In fact, Dennis Davis criticized the Goldstone opinion for being overly pragmatic.[136]

By contrast, the Kriegler opinion is more formalistic in finding that gender stereotypes should never be tolerated because they will injure women in the long run, even if they actually benefit women in the particular case.[137] This is the opposite of judicial pragmatism. The U.S. Supreme Court typically has taken the formalist tact.[138]

Given these divergent constitutional theories, the remaining question is whether the South African or American approach is correct or whether they are understandably different.

Analyzing the Approaches

Hugo is correctly decided because the group-based (Fiss) and dominance-oriented (MacKinnon) approaches to gender equality, the seeds of which are in the Goldstone and O'Regan opinions, follow the South African Constitution's promise of substantive, not formal, equality.[139] Substantive equality can only be achieved by allowing governments to give preference to vulnerable groups like mothers in prison.

Numerous scholars and judges acknowledge the transformational purpose of the South African Constitution.[140] By contrast, the U.S. Supreme Court employs a more conservative equality jurisprudence consistent with

---

[131]1997 (2) SA 261,275 (CC) (emphasizing that "blanket rules" are inadequate for the complex area of parental rights and equality).

[132]*Hugo*, 1997 (4) SALR at 23, Par. 41. (arguing that "[a] classification which is unfair in one context *may* not necessarily be unfair in a different context.").

[133]*Id.* at 24–25, Par. 46.   [134]*Id*, Par. 46.

[135]*Id.* at 27, Par. 51. (discussing feasibility of a declaratory order or other relief).

[136]Davis, *supra* n. 14, at 78 ("Sadly, however, from this point in the judgment, principle appears to make way for pragmatism.").

[137]*Hugo*, 1997 (4) SA at 39, Par. 85.

[138]*Supra* n. 91; Caban v. Mohammed, 441 U.S. 380 (1979)(gender stereotype not permitted).

[139]Iain Currie, Johan de Waal, et. al., The Bill of Rights Handbook 184 (1997).

[140]Davis, *supra* n. 14, at 24 (arguing that "the Constitution holds out the hope of transformative constitutional jurisprudence"); Janet Kentridge, "Equality", *in* Mathew

Kriegler's dissent.[141] Thus, the South African Constitution expressly out-laws sex discrimination whereas the American Constitution does not.[142]

The natural response though is that, if the South African Constitution really emphasizes equality, shouldn't that protection benefit John Hugo and not just females? That would, after all, be more equal. Wasn't this pardon unnecessary affirmative action? Kriegler's opinion takes this view, as does a book by South African judge and academic Dennis Davis.[143] There are textual answers to this argument.

Both Goldstone and O'Regan note that the South African equality pro-vision[144] states, "To promote the achievement of equality, legislative and other measures designed to protect or advance persons, or categories of persons, disadvantaged by unfair discrimination may be taken."[145] His-torically, women are disadvantaged, not men. This text therefore man-dates that the Constitutional Court read the South African Constitution asymmetrically and allow acts benefiting certain vulnerable groups.[146] O'Regan makes this asymmetry explicit.[147]

Chaskalson et. al., Constitutional Law of South Africa 14-3 (1998) (discussing the reconstructive goals of attaining substantive, and not mere formal, equality).

[141] Further evidence of how different the Constitutions are is the fact that a textualist approach to the South African Bill of Rights yields progressive interpretations, whereas textualism in the United States has typically been a code word for conservative legal philosophy. Thus, section 12(2) of the South African Constitution says that "[e]veryone has the right to bodily and psychological integrity, which includes the right (a) to make decisions concerning reproduction" S. Afr. Const. ch. II, § 12(2). This language would explicitly seem to support the progressive cause of a woman's right to abortion. However, the U.S. Constitution lacks any such reference to reproductive rights. This textual omission has been used to argue the conservative position that women in the United States have no constitutional right to an abortion. *See, e.g.,* Roe v. Wade, 410 U.S. 113, 171 (1973) (Rehnquist, J. dissenting).

[142] S. Afr. Const. ch. II, § 9(3).   [143] Davis, *supra* n. 14.

[144] *Hugo*, 1997 (4) SA at 22–23, 47–49, Pars. 32, 108.

[145] S. Afr. Const. ch. II, § 9(2).

[146] Titia Loenen, "The Equality Clause in the South African Constitution; Some Remarks from a Comparative Perspective," 13 S. Afr. J. Hum. Rts. 401, 413 (1997) (advocating an asymmetrical approach to South African equality law). The Constitutional Court's decision in Pretoria City Council v. Walker, 1998 (2) SA 363 (CC), does not contra-dict this theory. The Court ruled that the Council unfairly discriminated against those living in wealthier districts, who were predominantly white, by prosecuting individu-als there who were in default on electrical and water payments while not prosecuting people from the predominantly black townships who had been charged a flat rate. This partial victory for a predominantly white area simply shows that there is a limit to what constitutes an acceptable affirmative measure, and that limit excludes arbitrary penalties with a disproportionate racial effect. Unlike the whites who were burdened in *Walker*, Mr. Hugo was made no worse off individually by President Mandela's pardon.

[147] *Hugo*, 1997 (4) SA at 49, Pars. 110–111. *See, also,* City of Richmond v. J.A. Croson Co., 488 U.S. 469, 551–52 (1989) (Marshall, J., dissenting) (writing "[a] profound

The Fiss position, which favors assisting disadvantaged groups, is consistent with such asymmetry and underlies the Goldstone/O'Regan approach. Furthermore, the South African Constitution guarantees language and other rights for numerous groups, unlike the U.S. Constitution, which originally allowed courts to treat slaves and Native Americans as subhuman.[148]

The American Constitution has also been interpreted as being predominantly prohibitive and therefore lacks the South African authorization of affirmative action.[149] Indeed, the South African Constitution created a Commission for Gender Equality and a Human Rights Commission. As discussed in other chapters, the South African Constitution further guarantees socioeconomic and environmental affirmative rights.[150] To quote Karl Klare, "The South African Constitution intends a not fully defined but nonetheless unmistakable departure from liberalism [as in the United States]...toward an 'empowered' model of democracy" with a goal of real substantive equality and redistribution.[151] Preferences are virtually required under this approach.

To put it another way, the U.S. Supreme Court's constitutional jurisprudence assumes a neutral baseline in which government has not caused social inequality.[152] People themselves are responsible for their own situations. Thus, the Court has ruled that the state has no obligation to finance abortions for poor women because the state did not cause their plight.[153]

By comparison, South African equality guarantees are remedial and presume correctly that the apartheid regime oppressed certain

difference separates governmental actions that themselves are racist, and governmental actions that seek to remedy the effects of prior racism").

[148] *See* Kentridge, *supra* n. 140, at 14–18 n.5 (explaining that "many legal distinctions cause individual harm. But not all individual harms track larger patterns of group disadvantage"); Aliaa Abdelrahman, Note, "Affirmative Action in the United States and South Africa: Why South Africa Should Not Follow in Our Footsteps," 19 N.Y.L. Sch. J. Int'l & Comp. L. 195, 206 (1999) (explaining that "the endorsement of affirmative action in South Africa is also supported by the Bill of Rights' emphasis on the protection of group rights as well as individual human rights").

[149] Susan Bandes, "The Negative Constitution: A Critique," 88 Mich. L. Rev. 2271 (1990); Kentridge, *supra* n. 140, at 14-13 (describing the affirmative measures in the South African Constitution).

[150] S. Afr. Const. ch. II, §§ 24, 26-31.

[151] Karl Klare, "Legal Culture and Transformative Constitutionalism," 14 S. Afr. J. Hum. Rts. 146, 152 (1998).

[152] Cass Sunstein, "Lochner's Legacy," 87 Colum. L. Rev. 873, 874–75 (1987) (offering a persuasive critique of the U.S. Supreme Court's neutral baseline).

[153] Harris v. McRae, 448 U.S. 297 (1980).

groups.[154] The societal baseline is presumed to be non-neutral. Affirmative measures are therefore equalizing, not preferential. Catherine MacKinnon and many critical scholars share this unwillingness to accept the idea of a neutral baseline.[155] Janet Kentridge argues that equality is an anti-subjugation doctrine, and Goldstone referenced her writing as support for his opinion in *Hugo*.[156] As Mary Becker states, "In law, inequality is obscured by accepting as discrimination only that which the law prohibits rather than critically examining the law to judge how well it deals with actual discrimination in the real world."[157]

Moreover, to the extent that Dennis Davis made an individualist objection showing concern with the plaintiff, John Hugo, it is at odds with his argument at other points in his book that the Constitutional Court has failed to take a sufficiently communitarian approach to equality.[158] In addition, any pardon designed to help children must have some arbitrary quality, such as an age cutoff. Presidential line drawing cannot therefore invalidate the act. It is impossible to imagine that the South African Constitution could be so different from the American Constitution regarding equality, and yet the American prohibition on virtually all stereotypes could be transmuted to the South African context. That is Kriegler's mistake.[159]

---

[154] S. Afr. Const. pmbl. ("We, the people of South Africa, Recognise the injustices of our past...").

[155] *See* Garvey, *supra* n. 105; Becker, *supra* n. 118.

[156] Kentridge, *supra* n. 140, at 14–5 (stating that "the emphasis there placed on reparation and reconstruction suggests that a fundamental principle underlying the Constitutional commitment to equality is that of anti-subordination or anti-subjugation"); *see also Hugo*, 1997 (4) SA at 49 n.63 (referencing Kentridge, *supra*); Laurence Tribe, American Constitutional Law 1514–15 (1988) (discussing the anti-subordination principle).

[157] Becker, *supra* n. 125, at 265.

[158] The individualistic concern is evident when Davis writes, "It is equally difficult to understand, let alone support, a process of reasoning which concludes that it is not a practice of unfair discrimination to deny to a single parent who happens to be a father benefits which are accorded to a single parent who is a mother." Davis, *supra* n. 14 at 82. Davis later writes that the Constitution's values require "equal distributive concern for each member of the society and that from this *individual* imperative a community can emerge which is welded together by an active commitment to these foundational values. The decision in *Hugo* does little to contribute to a man's dignity and freedom as a father." *Id.* at 83 (emphasis added). At the same time as Davis criticizes the Court for ignoring Hugo's individual interest, he also questions the Court for giving too much of an "individualistic slant to equality of a kind that is incongruent with the need to balance individual and community, concepts which lie at the heart of the South African constitutional idea." *Id.* at 95. Apparently, the Court in this case was guilty of not protecting the individual enough and protecting the individual too much. This will not be easy to solve.

[159] *Hugo*, 1997 (4) SA at 37, Par. 85.

The South African Constitution actually resembles the Canadian Constitution far more than the American, and this resemblance includes Canada's greater receptivity to MacKinnon's theories.[160] As mentioned in Chapter 2, Canadian constitutionalists played an important role in drafting the South African Constitution.[161] Like South Africa, Canada has a two-stage analysis for rights issues. Concerning hate speech, Canada's Supreme Court found MacKinnon's transformative antipornography ordinance not to be in violation of free speech rights because it protects women.[162] South Africa goes even further and constitutionalizes hate speech prohibitions.[163] Meanwhile, the U.S. Supreme Court in *R.A.V. v. City of St. Paul* has struck down such restrictions.[164] Thus, Goldstone and O'Regan are consistent with the South African Constitution's support for the MacKinnon approach.

The South African Constitution also places great value on reconciliation and forgiveness, providing further support for the Mandela pardon. What a stark contrast between the forgiving quality of South Africa's constitutionally required Truth & Reconciliation Commission with the role of the United States in the Nuremburg trials conducted by the Allied powers after World War II.[165] It would have been quite uncharitable and inconsistent with this South African ideal of reconciliation for the Constitutional Court to nullify charity because it is not all-inclusive. As Janet Kentridge writes, the equality protections are supposed to be a "powerful tool of national reconciliation and reconstruction."[166]

Goldstone and O'Regan's pragmatism is also understandable given that it was a single charitable presidential act of discretion. *Hugo* simply opened the door to the dominance-group-oriented approach. In other cases, that approach actually may support striking down legislation based on stereotypes. Thus, *Hugo* did not involve the kind of likely recurring fact pattern that would merit establishment of a powerful binding legal

---

[160] *See infra* n. 162.   [161] Davis, *supra* n. 14, at 65 n 49.

[162] *Compare* Regina v. Butler, [1992] 1 S.C.R. 452 (Can.), and Regina v. Keegstra, [1990] 3 S.C.R. 697 (Can.), *with* American Booksellers Ass'n v. Hudnut, 771 F.2d 323 (7th Cir. 1985) (ruling that the MacKinnon anti-pornography ordinance unconstitutionally violates free speech).

[163] S. Afr. Const. ch. II § 16(2)(c) (The right to freedom of expression "does not extend to...advocacy of hatred that is based on race, ethnicity, gender or religion, and that constitutes incitement to cause harm.").

[164] 505 U.S. 377 (1992).

[165] *See* Ruti G. Teitel, Transitional Justice 33 (discussing "Transitional Dilemmas and the Nuremberg Paradigm Shift"), 51 (discussing "The Dilemma of Peace or Justice") (2000).

[166] Kentridge, *supra* n. 140, at 14–3.

principle that so often characterizes U.S. Supreme Court decisions. How to integrate customary tribal law in South Africa, for example, will require flexibility. Moreover, Mr. Hugo could still apply for an individual pardon, whereas Mandela could not have pardoned all similarly situated males.

Admittedly, Justice Goldstone opinion is imperfect. Despite his international law expertise, he failed to rely on two international conventions. Article 30 of the 1990 African Charter on the Rights and Welfare of the Child entitled "Children of Imprisoned Mothers" specifies, "States Parties to the present Charter shall undertake to provide special treatment to . . . mothers of infants and young children who have been accused or found guilty of infringing the penal law."[167] The special treatment proscribed for the mothers includes noncustodial sentences and alternatives to institutional confinement.[168] The Mandela pardon fulfills these goals. Article 25 of the Universal Declaration of Human Rights likewise declares, "Motherhood and childhood are entitled to special care and assistance."[169] Goldstone's failure to base his opinion on these sources is significant because section 39(1)(b) of the South African Constitution specifies, "When interpreting the Bill of Rights, a court, tribunal or forum . . . must consider international law."[170]

Goldstone also should have explained in more detail why it is not always harmful to permit stereotypes. Cathy Albertyn and Beth Goldblatt, for example, suggest that Goldstone should have argued that the importance of concrete, short-term gains for a disadvantaged group sometimes outweighs establishing a useful, but abstract, legal principle.[171] Furthermore, Goldstone should not have relied so heavily on the Starke affidavit because of its questionable assumptions, which are most apparent from other portions.[172]

---

[167] Afr. Charter on the Rights and Welfare of the Child, art. XXX (1990).
[168] *Id.*
[169] Universal Decl. of Human Rights, art. XXV, cl. 2 (1948).
[170] S. Afr. Const. ch. II, § 39(1)(b).
[171] Albertyn & Goldblatt, *supra* n. 14, at 270–73.
[172] These omitted portions can be found in the Constitutional Court case files or in the Starke Aff., Ex. 6(b), 45–51, Appeal Record Index, President of S. Afr. v. Hugo, 1997 (4) SALR 1 (CC). For example, Ms. Starke quotes approvingly from page 27 of Timmins Guide to Divorce in South Africa (1988) by Gerrit van Wyk & Andre la Cock in which the authors write, "Before the age of one . . . the child will not be affected much by the departure of a father. . . . In fact, it is unlikely that a child under the age of three will really be traumatised by a separation between parents. It is usually only later on that a father will be missed in any important way." *But see* Roger Dobson, "Children Live, Learn Better When Dad is Present," Saturday Argus, May 27–28, 2000, at 7 (arguing that "young children whose fathers are regularly present are better learners, have higher

However, for the reasons already discussed, his cautious tone is understandable.

Critiques

There are three possible criticisms of my thesis, in addition to the viewpoint of the Kriegler dissent. First, was not Mokgoro correct to reach the limitations issue, in contrast to Goldstone and O'Regan? The answer is no. The South African Constitution allows affirmative measures, the pardon was charitably intended to help children, and John Hugo was left no worse off than before. Indeed, the charitable act would have been impossible to do any other way, and Hugo had no entitlement to a pardon. This discrimination was thus fair. Mokgoro's pro-government limitations analysis is also questionable as it is not clear that this pardon amounted to a law of general application.

Second, are Dennis Davis and Anton Fagan correct in their view that the Goldstone and O'Regan opinions overemphasize the connection between equality and dignity?[173] No. The Goldstone and O'Regan opinions correctly assert that inequality is a blow to human dignity. The U.S. Supreme Court in *Brown* similarly held that segregation violated equal protection because it stamped black children as inferior.[174] Moreover, the Goldstone and O'Regan opinions do not suggest that equality is identical to dignity. They are simply cautious about defining the full scope of equality in a unique case.

Third, several criticisms of my characterization of the pardon as affirmative action are possible. For example, Goldstone and O'Regan's reliance on section 8(3) is not without controversy as that provision has generally been viewed as authorizing affirmative action *programs*.[175] President Mandela's pardon does not seem to qualify as a formal program. Moreover, a pardon does not rectify the disadvantage that women have suffered in the labor marketplace if its purpose is to allow these women to go home and take care of their children.

---

self-esteem and fewer symptoms of depression than youngsters who live without their dads, according to a new study"). It is therefore no surprise that Goldstone omitted these affidavit portions from his opinion and that O'Regan did not rely on the Starke affidavit.

[173] Davis, *supra* note 14, at 95; Fagan, *supra* n. 14 at 221.

[174] Brown v. Board of Education, 347 U.S. 483, 494 (1954).

[175] Kentridge, *supra* n. 140, at 14–37.

Additionally, Kriegler and Mokgoro point out that there was no evidence that women were disadvantaged in the prison system.[176] One could go a step further and argue that women are generally treated better in prisons than men. Women often get leniency in both sentencing and release dates if, for example, they are pregnant or because they are not presumed to be as dangerous as men.[177] Women's prison conditions are also generally better and less overcrowded than those of men.[178]

Mandela, however, was not enacting a classic affirmative action program solely to help women. He issued a pardon designed to help young children as well as their mothers. Given the great discretion he must have in issuing pardons, it would be inappropriate to subject his action to the rigors of scrutiny designed for a more traditional affirmative action plan. Indeed, a more rigorous scrutiny of the affirmative aspects of this pardon would be perilously close to the strict scrutiny used by the U.S. Supreme Court for affirmative action plans. And, of course, freeing these women from prison will enable them both to take care of their children and to pursue some employment options, thus improving their position in the labor market. International conventions likewise support this preference.[179]

THE *JORDAN* DECISION

Although the Constitutional Court correctly answered difficult gender discrimination questions in *Hugo*, it strayed from the transformational path in *Jordan v. State*,[180] when it upheld a law prohibiting prostitution despite a powerful equality challenge. *Jordan* involved the final Constitution unlike *Hugo*, which involved the Interim Constitution. In *Jordan*, one of the prostitutes was arrested for giving a "pelvic massage" to a police officer for 250 rand.[181] Plaintiffs argued that the law was discriminatory because it did not permit prosecutors to pursue the largely male clientele that frequented the mostly female prostitutes.[182] Plaintiffs also argued that the state could not interfere with the actions of private consenting

---

[176] *Hugo*, 1997 (4) SA at 38, 42, Pars.84, 94.

[177] Interview with Professor Christina Murray, Director, University of Cape Town Race & Gender Unit in Cape Town, South Africa (Apr. 14, 2000) (on file with author).

[178] Interview with Bronwyn Page-Ship, lawyer at the Centre for Rural Legal Studies in Stellenbosch, South Africa. Ms. Ship used to be a public defender and visited many men's and women's prisons (Mar. 17, 2000) (on file with author).

[179] *Supra* n. 167–169.   [180] 2002 (6) SA 642 (CC).

[181] *Id.* Par. 34.

[182] One commentator reports that the South African advocacy group representing prostitutes informed the South African Law Commission that 95% of prostitutes are women.

adults. This section reveals the Court's surprisingly tradition-based approach to these issues.

Equality

The Court divided on the equality issue, with Justice Sandile Ngcobo,
who wrote the majority for six Justices, finding no violation. Justices
Kate O'Regan and Albie Sachs wrote the dissent for five Justices.

Justice Ngcobo graduated from the University of Zululand with distinction in 1975, received a law degree from the University of Natal,
Durban, and then studied for an LL.M degree at Harvard Law School
where he was a Fulbright Scholarship recipient and the winner of a
Harvard Law School Human Rights Fellowship. From 1986 to 1987,
he was a law clerk to the late Honorable A. Leon Higginbotham
Jr., former Chief Judge of the U.S. Court of Appeals for the Third Circuit.
He worked for some of South Africa's leading civil rights and legal aid
organizations while also spending time at a Philadelphia-based American law firm, Pepper, Hamilton & Scheetz. He later served on the Truth
& Reconciliation Commission Amnesty Committee. From 1976 to July
1977, he was held in detention.

The Majority Opinion

In his opinion, Justice Ngcobo explained that the law is gender neutral
because it covered both female and male prostitutes.[183] Targeting prostitutes also made sense as they would tend to repeat the offense unlike some
of their customers.[184] Many other criminal laws penalize suppliers more
than customers, such as drug distribution laws.[185] He further reasoned
that prostitution breeds crime, the exploitation of women and children,
and the spread of sexually transmitted diseases.[186]

In addition, prosecutors could go after the customers as accom-
plices.[187] Justice Ngcobo acknowledged that society stigmatizes prostitutes, but noted that they caused their own situations.[188] He also argued

---

Rosaan Kruger, "Sex Work from a Feminist Perspective: A Visit to the Jordan Case,"
2004 S. Afr. J. Hum. Rts. 138 n. 4.

[183] *Jordan*, Par. 9.   [184] *Id.* Par. 10.

[185] *Id.*

[186] *Id.* Par. 15 n. 11. He adds that the state's ultimate goal is to protect and improve the
quality of life. Par. 26.

[187] *Id.* Par. 11.

[188] *Id.* Par. 16 ("If the public sees the recipient of reward as being 'more to blame' than the
'client,' and a conviction carries a greater stigma on the prostitute' for that reason, that

that the legislature should decide the nation's approach to prostitution rather than courts.[189] He concluded his opinion as follows:

> A gender neutral provision which differentiates between the dealer and the customer, a distinction that is commonly made by statutes, and which is justifiable having regard to the qualitative difference between the conduct of the dealer and that of the customer, and which operates in the legal framework that punishes both the customer and the dealer and makes them liable to the same punishment, cannot be said to be discriminating on the basis of gender, simply because the majority of those who violate such a statute happen to be women.[190]

The Dissenting Opinion

Justices O'Regan and Sachs dissented on the equality issue for several reasons. First, the law had a hugely disparate impact as an estimated 95 percent of South African prostitutes were women, according to the Sex Worker Education and Advocacy Task Force (SWEAT).[191] The South African Constitution calls this "indirect discrimination."[192] Second, "making the prostitute the primary offender directly reinforces a pattern of sexual stereotyping which is itself in conflict with the principle of gender equality."[193] The woman is the "fallen whore, and the man has simply "given in to temptation, or . . . done the sort of thing men do."[194] He is "at best virile, at worst weak."[195]

Third, they wrote, "In using their bodies as *commodities* in the marketplace, they undermine their status and become vulnerable. On the other hand, we cannot ignore the fact many female prostitutes become involved in prostitution because they have few or no alternatives."[196] Indeed, the customers are often better off financially; else they could not

---

is a social attitude and not the result of the law. The stigma that attaches to prostitutes attaches to them not by virtue of their gender, but by virtue of the conduct they engage in."). This strict division between the law and social attitudes is highly questionable. Par. 72 (O'Regan and Sachs criticize this attempted division).

[189] *Id.* Par. 30.   [190] *Id.* Par. 18.

[191] Jordan Pars. 59–60. There is a similar organization in the U.S. known as COYOTE (Call Off Your Old Tired Ethics).

[192] Iain Currie, Johan de Waal, The Bill of Rights Handbook 262 (2005).

[193] *Jordan* Par. 60. Their opinion also went through certain stages of equality analysis required by other Constitutional Court decisions unlike Justice Ngcobo's opinion.

[194] *Id.* Par. 64.   [195] *Id.* Par. 65.

[196] *Id.* Par. 66 (emphasis added).

pay for sex. O'Regan and Sachs therefore asserted that the law is socio-
logically "upside down" in not going after the customer when "evidence
suggests that many women turn to prostitution because of dire financial
need and they use their earnings to support their families and pay for
their children's food and education."[197]

Justices O'Regan and Sachs then explained that a law that makes both
the prostitute and potential customers liable would deter the activity
more than the South African approach.[198] This argument was made by
the dissenting opinion in the U.S. Supreme Court decision in *Michael M v.
Superior Court*,[199] which argued that gender-neutral statutory rape laws,
making both the underage male and female liable, were stronger than a
California law making only the male liable.[200]

Analysis

The question is whose analysis best implements the principle of substantive equality? The answer is the O'Regan-Sachs opinion. First, however,
it is important to examine the history of these prostitution laws. Next, I
explain the problems with Justice Ngcobo's approach.

HISTORY. The Sexual Offences Act of 1957 prohibited living off the earnings of a prostitute, procuring women as prostitutes, owning a brothel,
and soliciting by prostitutes. These provisions were found mainly in section 20(1)(a) of the act. But it still did not prohibit prostitution.[201]

South African law did not prohibit prostitution until 1988 nor did
it bar sex between two unmarried heterosexuals: "A prostitute was
therefore guilty of a crime only if she had intercourse with a married
man. Both she and the man committed the crime."[202] Thus, the law

---

[197] *Id.* Par. 68.   [198] *Id.* Par. 96.

[199] 450 U.S. 464 (1981).

[200] The majority opinion there was harshly criticized because of the dissent's powerful
reasoning. However, some feminists defended the majority by saying that vulnerable
young women need special protection because they are more likely to be the victims
of rape, and because they might be afraid to report what happened if they also could
be charged. A similar issue has recently arisen in a very controversial South African
Constitutional Court case. Masiya v. Director of Public Prosecutions, CCT 54/06 (2007)
(upholding the constitutionality of a gender-specific law that made it rape to penetrate
a young girl's anus, even though it was not rape if a young boy's anus was penetrated –
that could only be a sexual assault).

[201] South African Law Commission Paper 19 on "Sexual Offenses: Adult Prostitution" Par.
6.5 (July 2002).

[202] Jordan et. al. and State, Case No. A227/99 (High Court of South Africa, Transvaal
Provincial Division, Aug. 2, 2001)(Spoelstra, J.).

assumed that prostitutes were female, but that they could only be guilty of adultery.

For example, in the 1988 case of *S v H*,[203] the Transvaal Provincial Appellate Division of the Supreme Court overturned the conviction of a woman who had undressed and been ready to engage in sexual activity with a police officer. The state charged the woman with living off the earnings of prostitution under the 1957 Sexual Offences Act. But, as summarized by the South African Law Commission,

> On appeal, the Appellate Division... examined the pre-Union enactments in the Transvaal, Cape, Orange, Free State and Natal that preceded the introduction of section 20(1)(a). Significantly, each of these referred to "every male person who knowingly lives wholly or in part on the earnings of prostitution..." (with the exception of the Natal version, which applied to 'every person'). Kumleben J.A. found that the reference to a male person made it clear that these enactments did not have the prostitute in mind, since a prostitute, in terms of the understanding prevailing at the time of promulgation of the Sexual Offences Act was a **woman**.[204]

Thus, South Africa responded to this 1988 decision by making prostitution itself illegal.[205] The gender problem, however, still existed according to John Milton because the 1988 law did not criminalize the client's activity.[206] In 2008, South Africa adopted the Sexual Offences and Related Matters Amendment legislation that contains a provision prohibiting "engaging sexual services of persons 18 years or older"[207] for reward. The National Assembly designed this section to make customers liable and to remedy the inequality discussed in *Jordan*.[208]

---

[203] 1988 (3) SA 545 (AD).   [204] *Id.* Par. 6.95 (emphasis in original).

[205] *Id.* Par. 6.6

[206] John Milton, "Unfair discrimination on the grounds of 'gender, sex... [or] sexual orientation'. How the Sexual Offences Act of 1957 does it all," 10 S. Afr. Crim. Just. 297 (1997).

[207] It can be found at: http://www.info.gov.za/gazette/bills/2003/b50b-03.pdf. Nov. 23, 2006 (last visited June 13, 2007). Section 11 of the bill says: "(1) A person ("A") who unlawfully and intentionally engages the services of a person 18 years or older ("B") , for financial and other reward, favour or compensation to B or to a third person ("C") – for the purpose of engaging in a sexual act with B, irrespective of whether the sexual act is committed or not: or by committing a sexual act with B, is guilty of engaging the sexual services of a person 18 years or older."

[208] "Report of the Portfolio Committee on Justice and Constitutional Development on the Matter of the Tagging of the Criminal Law(Sexual Offences and Related Matters) Amendment Bill," Sec. 4 (discussing how the bill resolves the problem of customer immunity discussed in Jordan), http://www.pmg.org.za/docs/2007/comreports

ARGUMENTS. This discussion shows the gendered history of the *Jordan* prostitution law.[209] This law, however, initially seems more defensible than the one upheld in *Hugo* because the pardon there was facially discriminatory whereas the prostitution law is gender neutral. The 95 percent disparate impact, though, is huge.[210] Justice Ngcobo's opinion unfortunately resembles the U.S. Supreme Court's formalistic rejection in *McCleskey v. Kemp*[211] of sophisticated statistics showing that Georgia's death penalty sentences had a huge racial impact. Perhaps like the U.S. Supreme Court, Justice Ngcobo needed proof of discriminatory intent.[212]

Indeed, given the disparate impact and the goal of substantive equality, the Court should have shifted the burden of proof to the government either to offer proof of a nondiscriminatory intent or to meet the limitations clause. This would have made a difference as O'Regan and Sachs showed that the government failed on the limitations issue.[213] By contrast, in *Hugo*, the government made convincing arguments for why President Mandela could not pardon men.

Justice Ngcobo cleverly asserted that prostitution statutes disproportionately affecting women must not be a problem because robbery statutes disproportionately affect men with no consequence.[214] Justices O'Regan and Sachs, however, pointed out that prostitution requires two people for a crime, unlike robbery,[215] yet the woman alone goes to prison.

/070517pcjustice.htm May 17, 2007 (last visited June 13, 2007). For a sample of commentators who believe that the law will make prostitution clients liable, see Chandra Gould, "Gender Equality and the Sexual Offences Bill in South Africa," ISS Today, Nov. 8, 2006 http://www.iss.co.za/static/templates/tmpl_html.php?node_id= 1821&link_id=26 (The bill criminalizes "any sexual exchange between adults (over the age of 18) for financial or other gain.") (last visited June 12, 2007). *Accord* Pierre de Vos, "Why is it so bad to have sex with a prostitute?," Constitutionallly Speaking (blog), May 25, 2007 (last visited June 12, 2007) ("But until the new Sexual Offences Act comes into operation, it is really only the actions of the sex worker that is [sic] criminalized."); Sex Worker Education and Advocacy Task Force Press Statement, "Sexual Offences Bill altered just days before finalization," Sep. 7, 2006 (last visited June 12, 2007)("Yesterday, the Justice Portfolio Committee added a new provision to the Sexual Offences Bill effectively aimed at criminalizing the clients of sex workers." http://www.sweat.org/za/index2.php?option=com_content &task=view&id=87&Itemid=32 ... Interestingly, the new law rejects the view of some seemingly less progressive countries. For example, in 1959, Britain decriminalized prostitution based on the Wolfenden Report, but banned solicitation.
[209] Par. 69.   [210] *Supra* n. 182.
[211] 481 U.S. 279 (1987)
[212] Washington v. Davis, 426 U.S. 229 (1976).
[213] Jordan Par. 98.   [214] *Id.* Par. 17.
[215] Par. 72–73.

Justice Ngcobo also argued that any disparate impact was caused by the government's nonenforcement of accomplice statutes. Yet, courts typically do not uphold a problematic statute because a related statute exists.

The core dispute, however, is that Justice Ngcobo held the "prostitution as work" view,[216] namely that women freely make this occupational choice, whereas O'Regan and Sachs primarily held the "prostitution as violence" view that women sometimes face desperate circumstances.[217] For example, certain African tribal cultures deny women an education or the chance to work in a more conventional job. Critics of the O'Regan and Sachs opinion, however, have argued that it treats women as frail creatures incapable of making decisions. Both the "prostitution as work" and "prostitution as violence" perspectives, though, oversimplify. South African prostitutes experience a wide variety of personal and financial conditions.[218]

Given that last point, the Sachs and O'Regan analysis makes the most sense as it at least acknowledged that some women face economic constraints while others voluntarily pursue such an occupation.[219] This is a more sophisticated assessment than that presented by Justice Ngcobo. Moreover, Ngcobo's individualist assumptions are inconsistent with the African view that people are molded by their environment and community.[220]

O'Regan and Sachs, however, only did an abbreviated limitations clause analysis. What changes with a full analysis? Section 36 requires the Court to assess the nature of the right, the importance of the purpose of the limitation, the nature and extent of the limitation, the relation between the limitation and its purpose, and less restrictive means to achieve the purpose.

---

[216] Belkys Garcia, "Reimagining the Right to Commercial Sex: The Impact of Lawrence v. Texas on Prostitution Statutes," 9 N.Y. City L. Rev. 161 (2005).

[217] Id. *See also* Elsje Bonthuys, "Sex for Sale: The Prostitute as Businesswoman," 121 S. Afr. L. J. 659, 662 (2004).

[218] SWEAT conducted a 2005 demographic survey of 200 Cape Town prostitutes that highlighted their diversity in terms of whether they worked the streets or worked indoors, education levels, etc. http://www.sweat.org.za/index.php?option=com_content&task=view&id=16&Itemid=18 (last visited Nov. 16, 2007).

[219] *Jordan* Par. 66.

[220] His opinion has a distinctly American resonance. *See e.g.* EEOC v. Sears, Roebuck & Co., 839 F.2d 302 (7th Cir. 1988) (Judge Posner agrees with the lower court that Sears female employees are not discriminated against because they have generally chosen not to take on higher paying opportunities for personal reasons).

The important right to equality is at stake. Moreover, the limitation burdens women greatly as they can go to jail. The purpose behind the discrimination is punishment for the supposedly greater culpability of women. Yet, imposing higher penalties on prostitutes than on their customers could more fairly show culpability, rather than immunizing the customers.

There are, however, two ironies here. First, in reaction to the gender bias concern, Parliament added customers as culpable parties, making more people liable. Yet, I suspect both Justice O'Regan and Justice Sachs would personally be sympathetic to decriminalization.

Second, SWEAT opposed the law as dangerous even though it removed the prosecutorial bulls-eye from their members. For example, it argued, "Clients that feel more vulnerable to prosecution will prefer to interact with the sex worker away from the public and away from the police. So the sex workers move to darker streets and more dangerous areas."[221] Further, NGOs would have difficulty providing valuable health and other services in these locations. Sex workers would also lose their "good guy" clients, who are presumably afraid of being arrested, meaning the workers would have to accept more potentially abusive clients to make the same amount of money. SWEAT added that the law would undermine antitrafficking efforts: "Clients who come across such woman are less likely to come forward with this information if this makes them liable to prosecution."[222] Chandre Gould of the prominent Institute for Security Studies echoed these concerns.[223]

Do these powerful arguments show that the O'Regan-Sachs equality position is wrong? Not really. First, "good guy" clients may not actually be deterred because they know that police are not likely to focus on prostitution in a country with so much violent crime. For example, the 2006–2007 Executive Summary for the South African government's official crime statistics does not list prostitution as one of the crimes being tracked.[224] Second, the NGO impact is unclear. Third, it is strange to think that keeping more good clients solves trafficking because clients

---

[221] SWEAT, "Criminalising the Client: Why It Doesn't Work," http://www.sweat.org.za/index.php?option=com_content&task=view&id=15&Itemid=18 (last visited Nov. 17, 2007).

[222] *Id.*   [223] *Supra* n . 208.

[224] South African Police Service, "2007 Crime Statistics: Report on the Crime Situation in South Africa" http://www.issafrica.org/dynamic/administration/file_manager/file_links /CRIME_SITUATION_EXEC.PDF?link_id=24&slink_id=4706&link_type=12& slink_type=13&tmpl_id=3 (last visited Nov. 26, 2007).

provide the demand for the service. Reducing demand, however, might diminish supply. Evidence from Sweden, in fact, where the police focus on the clients, suggests this is the case.[225] But assuming SWEAT's arguments are correct, they do not demonstrate the constitutionality of a gender discriminatory law. Instead, they suggest that Parliament should decriminalize.

u.s. supreme court. The U.S. Supreme Court would likely agree with the Constitutional Court result despite the differing equality norms. The Supreme Court would decide that prostitutes are not a suspect class and that any law burdening them should undergo rationality review. The law must only be reasonably related to a legitimate governmental purpose. The Supreme Court would find that the law promotes numerous purposes such as protecting public health, ensuring the quality of neighborhoods, and even preserving public morality. This result would occur even though some feminist legal scholars have long argued that American prostitution laws reflect gender discrimination.[226]

In *Beazer v. New York Transit Authority*[227] (NYTA), the Supreme Court ruled that the NYTA could refuse to hire methadone users because the users might relapse on the job. Methadone is a substitute drug to help heroin addicts kick the habit. The Court held that methadone users were not a suspect class, even though many were poor and members of minorities. Thus, the Court used rationality review to uphold the NYTA rule based on safety concerns even though it was both over- and under-inclusive. Similarly, though not all prostitutes are women, the Supreme Court would likely be deferential to the government as in *Beazer*.

Beazer shows one of the major problems with the U.S. Supreme Court's levels of scrutiny approach. It is all or nothing in that one is either a suspect class or not, except for women. Thus, groups that have qualities similar to suspect classes (e.g., a history of discrimination, political weakness, stigma, etc.) may be denied any relief because the Court appears afraid

---

[225] Emily Bazelon, "Why is Prostitution Illegal?," Slate, Mar. 10, 2008, http://www .slate.com/id/2186243 (last visited April 11, 2008) (According to the Women's Justice Center, "in the capital city of Stockholm the number of women in prostitution has been reduced by two thirds, and the number of johns has been reduced by 80%. Trafficking is reportedly down to 200 to 400 girls and women a year compared, with 15,000 to 17,000 in nearby Finland.")

[226] *See e.g.* Catharine A. MacKinnon, "Prostitution and Civil Rights," 1 Mich. J. Gender & L. 13 (1993); Beverly Balos, "Taking Prostitution Seriously," 4 Buff. Crim. L. Rev. 709, 721 n. 46 (2001).

[227] 440 U.S. 568 (1979).

to create too many suspect groups as doing so would endanger a large amount of legislation. By contrast, the South African two-stage proportionality analysis allows for a more nuanced approach and a recognition of such a group's vulnerability.

Privacy

Plaintiffs also argued that the law violated the right to privacy. The provincial court agreed, ruling that a financial transaction did not remove sex from the private realm, analogizing to the Constitutional Court's earlier gay rights cases. The Constitutional Court in separate opinions disagreed with the provincial court. What emerged was a conflict between the provincial court's libertarian view of privacy and the Constitutional Court's more traditionalist view.

Majority Opinion
Justice Ngcobo's majority opinion stated that the transaction's commercial nature nullified any privacy right.[228] He distinguished prostitution from the gay sex cases which involved "the sphere of private intimacy and autonomy which allows us to establish and *nurture* human relationships without interference from the outside community."[229] Moreover, the prostitute must engage with members of the public for her business.[230]

Justice Ngcobo argued, in the alternative, that the law only caused a peripheral privacy intrusion because people could engage in the same sexual activities, just without payment.[231] In addition, the law would reduce the social harms discussed earlier.[232] Justice Ngcobo also removed the decriminalization option from the table by saying that such a potential policy shift was for the legislature to decide upon, not the Court.[233]

Dissenting Opinion
Justices O'Regan and Sachs concurred, but expanded on Justice Ngcobo's reasoning. They wrote that determining where activity falls on the privacy

---

[228] *Jordan* Par. 28.
[229] *Id.* Par. 27 (emphasis added). He says that people's sexuality is "at the core of the area of private intimacy."
[230] *Id.* Par. 28.
[231] *Id.* Par. 29.
[232] *Id.* Par. 24.
[233] *Id.* Par. 25.

continuum depends on the relationship (whether it is meaningful and/or personal) and on the extent of a law's bodily intrusion.[234] Moreover, the right to privacy ultimately fosters human dignity – perhaps the South African Constitution's core value.[235] They argued,

> Moreover, central to the character of prostitution is that it is indiscriminate and *loveless*. It is accordingly not the form of intimate sexual expression that is penalized, nor the fact that the parties possess a certain identity. It is that the sex is both indiscriminate and for reward. The privacy element falls far short of "deep attachment and commitments to the necessarily few other individuals with whom one shares not only a special community of thoughts, experiences and beliefs but also distinctly personal aspects of one's life." By making her sexual services available for hire to strangers in the marketplace, the sex worker empties the sex act of much of its private and intimate character. She is not nurturing relationships or taking *life-affirming decisions* about birth, marriage or family; she is making money.[236]

This surprisingly traditionalist argument, from O'Regan and Sachs, explicitly rejected the plaintiffs' position that "[e]ven if the expression of sexuality is loveless, it is still very personal."[237] Moreover, the concurrence supported the state's argument that prostitution causes eight different harms.[238]

The claimants responded that it is the criminalization of prostitution that causes these harms. The South African Gender Commission wrote as follows:

> The combination of false factual assertions concerning the ills inevitably linked to prostitution and their professed purpose of protecting prostitutes (belied by the form of protection offered) leads to the conclusion that the real purpose of prohibiting prostitution is the one purpose not encompassed within the identified "ills" – the enforcement of the moral views of a section of society.[239]

Justice O'Regan and Sachs replied that it is for the legislature to resolve these conflicting harm theories, especially because no other nation had judicially invalidated laws against prostitution[240] and prostitution was

---

[234] *Id.* Par. 80.   [235] *Id.* Par. 81.
[236] *Id.* Par. 83 (emphasis added).   [237] *Id.* Par. 77.
[238] *Id.* Par. 86 (These harms include the degradation to women, the risk of abuse, the risk of getting sexually transmitted diseases, the connection to drug abuse, etc.)
[239] *Id.* Par. 88.   [240] *Id.* Par. 90.

not "normal business activity."[241] To summarize, the Court should defer to Parliament because the rights limitation was minimal, the law served important purposes, and people could reasonably disagree on whether decriminalization would help or hurt.[242]

Analysis

The O'Regan-Sachs privacy opinion's deference to Parliament seems inconsistent with their equality analysis that second-guessed Parliament. Perhaps they believed that a Constitution designed to overcome apartheid's legacy must be extremely strict when it comes to discrimination. What is most problematic, however, is the argument that privacy only shields nurturing or loving sexual activity, which raises several issues.[243]

First, it is not clear why paying for sex makes it less private.[244] Sex without payment is not obviously different from prostitution in regard to the categories of spatial, bodily, and informational privacy. Indeed, a man's expectation of informational privacy may be greater when seeing a prostitute than when seeing a girlfriend. Perhaps, the focus then should be on what has been called decisional privacy involving intimate choices.[245]

Moreover, African prostitution can be very affectionate and intimate.[246] In addition, some paraplegics or others who cannot easily find sex partners may see prostitution as emotionally invaluable. Further,

---

[241] *Id.* Par. 93.   [242] *Id.* Par. 94.

[243] There are two possible ways to see these statements. One could see them as indicating that any kind of sex that is not commercial is automatically "nurturing" as a matter of law. Or one could see them as meaning that use of the word "nurturing" by Justice Ngcobo, and the words "loving" and "life-affirming" by Justices O'Regan and Sachs really do mean there is a category of noncommercial sex that could lack those qualities. The latter interpretation makes more sense because it gives the words their ordinary meaning.

[244] *See e.g.* Cass Sunstein, "What Did Lawrence Hold? Of Autonomy, Desuetude, Sexuality, and Marriage," 55 Sup. Ct. Rev. 27 n. 158 (2003) (regarding prostitution, "The outcome is easy; but the analysis is not. Why the sharp distinction between commercial and noncommercial sex? Why are sexual relations unprotected, or less protected, if dollars are exchanged? Books, after all, are protected, whether they are given away or sold.")

[245] *See e.g.* Roe v. Wade, 410 U.S. 113 (1973).

[246] Rosaan Kruger, "Sex Work from a Feminist Perspective: A Visit to the Jordan Case," 20 S. Afr. J. Hum. Rts. 138, 143 (2004) ("Dirasse states that prostitution in Ethiopia includes an emotional bond between the prostitute and her regular customers. This idea is supported by Glazer who refers to 'Western style impersonal prostitution' as opposed to traditional African-style prostitution where emotional affection plays a role.") Kruger

although some prostitutes walk the streets, others work indoors and function via a referral network that may facilitate emotional privacy. Lastly, sexually promiscuous people or sex addicts may share far less emotional intimacy with their partners than do prostitutes, even though no payment occurs.

There is, however, an even more fundamental critique of the Court's view offered by Nicole Fritz in a fascinating article, "Crossing *Jordan*: Constitutional Space for (Un)civil Sex"[247]:

> What emerges from the Court's instrumentalist account is a very sanitized, pastoral picture of sex, a "warm, fuzzy, soft-focused cuddling not the hot, steamy, edgy stuff that got us into trouble in the first place. . . , The Court offers up a model that has been bled of all its erotic fraught qualities – its messiness, complexity, its uneasy play with danger, its excess and pleasure for pleasure's sake. In effect, it empties sex of all the quantities that are so constitutive of the erotic that make sex, sexy.[248]

Katherine Franke has critiqued the U.S. Supreme Court's decision protecting gay sex on similar grounds.[249] Ruthann Robson has actually made similar arguments regarding South African gay rights decisions.[250] Nicole Fritz therefore proposes an "emancipatory project of desire"[251] in which courts do not fall into the traditional norms and where we create a "positive sphere of sexuality."[252]

She then argues that prostitution should be legal:

> Recognition of women's power to commodify their sexuality – as done by the *Jordan* minority when it describes prostitutes using their bodies as commodities in the marketplace – and a concomitant acknowledgement that this practice is lawful – as decriminalization must entail – would go some way to compelling an acknowledgement that women have property rights in their sexuality.[253]

---

uses the choice versus constraint feminism distinction. *See also* Fritz, *infra* n. 247 at 246 (describing the continuum of sexual relations in some Caribbean and African nations).

[247] 20 S. Afr. J. Hum. Rts. 230 (2004).   [248]*Id.* at 235.

[249] "The Domesticated Liberty of Lawrence v. Texas," 104 Colum. L. Rev. 1399 (2004).

[250] Ruthann Robson, "Sexual Democracy," 23 S. Afr. J. Hum. Rts. 409 (2007) (The Court must be careful otherwise "a sentimentalized version of sexuality, with certain lesbians and gay men installed as a model minority, threatens to become the democratic standard.")

[251]*Id.* at 236.   [252]*Id.* at 237.

[253]*Id.* at 43. *Accord* Jonathan Barrett, "Dignatio and the Human Body," 21 S. Afr. J. Hum. Rts. 525 (2005).

Are there adequate responses to these arguments? I suspect the Constitutional Court would acknowledge that not all prostitution is heartless, and that consensual sex can be degrading. In general, however, the Court probably believes that sex, with love, deserves more protection than sex for reward because the former serves higher moral values and because there is less risk of exploitation. Pimps and customers abuse prostitutes, and society stigmatizes whores.[254] It's also a bit unfair to expect the Court to characterize sex like a dangerous racy novel as Fritz advocates.

Fritz, however, suggests that the Court is actually being unfair here in turning female sexuality into something instrumental that must benefit society generally. Women should be free to choose these risks. There are two problems with her clever arguments.

First, both she and the Court have unichromatic views of sex. The Court, as discussed, treats sex that has value as involving love or nurturing. Fritz treats sex that has value as involving female autonomy and liberation. Yet, her view may not fit those women who see sex as boring, or as an obligation, or as a chore. She certainly does not focus on the sexual experiences of vulnerable women who are being exploited by traffickers or brothel owners. Perhaps, both Fritz and the Constitutional Court should treat sexual privacy as value neutral yet important, a space in which good and bad experiences await depending on the circumstances.

Second, prostitutes can easily contract AIDS and pass it on, especially because many South African men refuse to wear condoms.[255] Indeed, one can only imagine the international news headlines if South Africa announced it was legalizing prostitution, despite its deadly AIDS epidemic and its need for billions of dollars to fight the problem. Third, Nicholas Kristof nicely summarizes the evidence showing the negative effects that prostitution has on its practitioner's psyche and life expectancy.[256] These

---

[254] *See e.g.* Melissa Farley, et. al., "Prostitution in Five Countries: Violence and Post-Traumatic Stress Disorder," Vol. 8(4) Feminism & Psychology 405–26 (1998) (research study involving interviews, which includes South Africa).

[255] Large Condoms for S. African Men, BBC News, Aug. 16, 2005 http://news.bbc.co.uk/2/hi/africa/4155390.stm (last visited Nov. 17, 2007) (discussing reticence of South African men to wear regular condoms); Arianne Stein, Note, "Should HIV Be Jailed? HIV Exposure Statutes and Their Effects in the United States and South Africa," 3 Wash. U. Global Studies L. Rev. 177, 186 n. 59 (2004).

[256] Nicholas D. Kristof, "Do as Spitzer said," Int'l Herald Tribune, Mar. 13, 2008, http://www.iht.com/articles/2008/03/13/opinion/edkristof.php (last visited April 11, 2008).

are highly pragmatic arguments. Fritz might respond that decriminalization would permit regulation and thus reduce these risks. This causation analysis, however, is at least debatable, which is why O'Regan and Sachs deferred to Parliament. Nonetheless, Fritz's arguments are a powerful reminder that the Court should not view sex in a traditionalist and romanticized manner.

U.S. Supreme Court

How would this privacy argument play out in the U.S. Supreme Court? The Court would likely reject a privacy claim by prostitutes, even though *Lawrence v. Texas*[257] decided that a law prohibiting homosexual sodomy was unconstitutional. The Supreme Court, however, in that decision explicitly refused to rule on commercial sex.[258] Moreover, the Court there did not find a fundamental right despite some flowery language about individual autonomy.[259] Thus, the Court would probably subject a law against prostitution to rationality review, even under a privacy challenge, and the law would be upheld for the harm related reasons mentioned earlier. One state appellate court took this exact route in a prostitution case when the *Lawrence* issue was raised.[260] This American analysis, though, does not take seriously the prostitute's arguments.

CONCLUSION

One last question to be addressed is why the Constitutional Court got the result in one gender discrimination case right (*Hugo*) but not the other (*Jordan*). Perhaps the best explanation is that the pardon ruling was justifiable on both transformational and traditionalist grounds – a rare situation where these approaches do not conflict. The pardon helped women, who had been oppressed, but also "placed" women in the traditional roles of mothers. By contrast, the Court, whether rightly or wrongly, could have been hesitant to rule for a "sexualized" view of women in *Jordan*, especially given the pragmatic concerns about the spread of AIDS.

---

[257] 539 U.S. 558 (2003).   [258] *Id.* at 579.
[259] Sunstein, *supra* n. 244.
[260] People v. Williams, 811 N.E.2d 1197 (3d Dist. Ill. 2004).

One must also acknowledge legal realism. *Jordan* involved a controversial challenge to traditional sexual mores, whereas *Hugo* involved Nobel peace prize recipient Nelson Mandela's act of charity. The *Jordan* decision suggests that the Court still has a ways to go regarding transformation. Even so, it is far more sympathetic to sophisticated gender discrimination arguments than the U.S. Supreme Court.

5

Gay Rights

One of the most important areas of the South African Constitutional Court's jurisprudence is gay rights. The Court has ruled for the plaintiffs in several cases, even invalidating same-sex marriage restrictions. Given the racist legacy of apartheid, it is surprising that these cases are more prominent than the Court's racial discrimination cases. It raises the question of why the South African Court made this area a cause célèbre.

By contrast, perhaps the most prominent U.S. Supreme Court case is *Brown v. Board of Education*,[1] a defeat for American racial apartheid. The Supreme Court has not even heard gay rights cases until recently. Moreover, the plaintiffs in 1986 suffered a big defeat in the first case, *Bowers v. Hardwick*.[2] The Court has since overruled *Bowers* but its gay rights jurisprudence is still muddled.

Indeed, gay marriage rivals abortion as one of the most controversial constitutional issues in the United States even though the U.S. Supreme Court has not decided the question.[3] Only the Supreme Judicial Court of Massachusetts, the California Supreme Court, and the Connecticut Supreme Court have ruled in favor of gay marriage under their state constitutions, though the California decision has been overturned by Proposition 8.[4] New York,[5] Washington,[6] and

---

[1] 347 U.S. 483 (1954).   [2] 478 U.S. 186 (1986).

[3] Jay Lindsay, "Courts a Tough Road to Gay Marriage," Associated Press Sep. 28, 2007, http://miamiherald.typepad.com/gaysouthflorida/2007/09/courts-a-tough-.html (last visited Jan. 3, 2008).

[4] In re. Marriage Cases, S147999 (Cal. May 15, 2008); Goodridge v. Dep't of Public Health, 798 N.E.2d 941 (Mass. 2003); Kerrigan v. Commissioner of Public Health, 2008 Westlaw 4530885 (Conn. 2008). A lawsuit has been filed challenging the constitutionality of Proposition 8.

[5] Hernandez v. Robles, 855 N.E.2d 1 (N.Y. 2006).

[6] Andersen v. King County, 138 P.3d 963 (Wash. 2006).

Maryland[7] disagree. New Jersey,[8] Vermont,[9] and Hawaii[10] have essentially ruled in favor of civil unions but not marriages. Many states have passed laws or constitutional amendments specifying that marriage is between a man and a woman.[11] These states also refuse to recognize same-sex marriages or unions from other states.[12] The federal Defense of Marriage Act passed in 1996 supports this traditional view.[13]

This chapter compares the leading South African and American gay rights cases. The most obvious difference is that the South African Constitution lists sexual orientation discrimination as presumptively unfair.[14] But that does not explain why the South African Constitutional Court has pushed so aggressively in this area. Moreover, a few American states, such as New Jersey, prohibit discrimination against gay people but they still have not embraced gay marriage.

In addition, these cases transcend gay rights, raising issues such as gender equality, the right to privacy, the right to freedom of expression, the right to be a parent, the rights of children, and the right to dignity (especially in the South African context). Several American states, for example, essentially prohibit gay couples from adopting.[15] Moreover, these issues transcend South Africa and the United States, preoccupying other constitutional courts and international tribunals.[16]

The first section examines the major South African gay rights cases. The second section juxtaposes the Court's boldness in these cases with its cautiousness in other areas and examines one interesting line of criticism of the Court's decisions that surprisingly comes from gay rights advocates. The last section briefly surveys the American gay rights cases for comparative purposes.

[7] Conaway v. Deane, 932 A.2d 571 (Md. 2007).
[8] Lewis v. Harris, 908 A.2d 196 (NJ 2006).
[9] Baker v. Vermont, 744 A.2d 864 (Vt 1999).
[10] Baehr v. Lewin, 852 P.2d 44 (Haw 1993).
[11] Jolynn M. Schlichting, Note, "Minnesota's Proposed Same Sex Marriage Amendment," 31 Wm. Mitchell L. Rev. 1649, 1652 n. 15 (2005).
[12] *Id.*
[13] Pub. L. 104–199, 100 Stat. 2419 (Sept. 21, 1996).
[14] Sec. 9(3).
[15] Jeff LeBlanc, Comment, "My Two Moms: An Analysis of Homosexual Adoption and the Challenges to its Acceptance," 27 J. Juv. L. 95, 97 (2006) (listing the approaches of different states). *But see* In the Matter of the Adoption of John Doe, (Miami-Dade Cir. Ct. Nov. 25, 2008) (Court rules Florida ban on gay adoption is unconstitutional).
[16] *See e.g.* Du Toit v. Minister of Welfare, 2003 (2) SA 198 (SA).

SOUTH AFRICAN GAY RIGHTS JURISPRUDENCE

South Africa was the first nation to prohibit sexual orientation discrimination in its Constitution, though it is also now prohibited in some transnational charters such as the European Convention on Human Rights. The conservative white religious Afrikaaner culture that imposed apartheid had a notorious history of sexual Puritanism. Indeed, the state had criminalized gay male sex but not lesbian encounters.[17] This Puritanism produced some odd results as described in a seminal 1993 law review article by the brilliant Oxford-educated South African scholar and Supreme Court of Appeal jurist Edwin Cameron, who is openly gay and has HIV.[18] For example, the apartheid police once raided an event based on a law that a "male person who commits with another male person at a party any act which is calculated to stimulate sexual passion or to give sexual gratification" is guilty of a crime. A judge, however, ruled against the authorities because two men jumped apart when the police arrived, making a "party" impossible.[19]

During the Constitution's drafting, gay advocacy groups played an active and successful role pressing for discrimination protections.[20] One of their leaders was Cameron. It is worth mentioning that Cameron's autobiography, *Witness to AIDS*, has been highly acclaimed. His frank personal revelations almost had the magnitude of Magic Johnson's admission in the United States that he had AIDS.[21] Cameron is to gay rights in South Africa what Ruth Bader Ginsburg is to women's rights or Thurgood Marshall is to the rights of African Americans in the United States.

Since adoption of the South African Constitution, gay rights advocates have promoted their cause through political activism and a strategic litigation campaign waged by the National Coalition for Gay & Lesbian Equality (NCGLE). The NCGLE was organized in 1994 by Cameron, Kevin Botha, and the AIDS activist Zachie Achmat, a former male prostitute whom Pulitzer-Prize-winning journalist Samantha Power calls the

---

[17] Edwin Cameron, "Sexual Orientation and the Constitution: A Test Case for Human Rights," 110 S. Afr L.J. 450, 453 (1993). Judge Cameron has served as an acting member of the Constitutional Court when needed, but lost out to Justice Sandile Ngcobo when a regular opening arose. Richard Calland, Anatomy of South Africa 235 (2006).

[18] Edwin Cameron, Witness to AIDS (2005).

[19] *Supra* n. 17 at 455.

[20] Richard Spitz, Mathew Chaskalson, The Politics of Transition 307 (2000).

[21] Power *infra* n. 22.

"most important dissident in the country since Nelson Mandela."[22] In 1998, Achmat founded the internationally known AIDS activist group, the Treatment Action Campaign. Cameron also founded the AIDS Legal Project to handle the litigation effort.[23]

The NCGLE decided to proceed incrementally by initially challenging anti-sodomy laws and certain other specific provisions.[24] It wanted to establish some favorable decisions and raise public consciousness, using a universalist rhetoric similar to the anti-apartheid movement, before bringing forth the gay marriage issue.[25] This approach resembled that of the NAACP Legal Defense Fund leading up to the U.S. Supreme Court decision in *Brown v. Board of Education*.

The Sodomy Case

The first Constitutional Court decision on gay rights struck down statutory and common law restrictions on homosexual male sodomy. The Court in 1998 in *National Coalition for Gay and Lesbian Equality v. Minister of Justice*[26] ruled that these laws violated principles of equality and dignity, as well as the right to privacy. Justice Laurie Ackermann, an academic expert in human rights law, defined "sexual orientation" as being about erotic attraction,[27] taking this definition from the Cameron article mentioned earlier. The concept must be "given a generous interpretation of which it is linguistically and textually fully capable of bearing. It applies equally to the orientation of persons who are bi-sexual, or trans-sexual and it applies to the orientation of persons who might on a single occasion only be erotically attracted to a member of their own sex."[28]

The Court explained that the Constitution's equality principles precluded any group's "subordination"[29] and that a criminal law prohibiting

---

[22] Samantha Power, "The AIDS Rebel", New Yorker, May 2003, http://www.pbs.org /pov/pov2003/stateofdenial/special_rebel.html (last visited April 16, 2008).

[23] *Id.* The Project brought important cases like Hoffman v. South African Airways, 2001 (1) SA 1 (CC) (ruling that South African Airways should not have discharged a flight attendant who had AIDS).

[24] R. Louw, "A Decade of Gay and Lesbian Equality Litigation" in Max du Plessis & Stephen Pete (Eds.), Constitutional Democracy in South Africa 1994–2004, 65,66 (2004).

[25] *See generally* Pierre de Vos, "The "Inevitability" of Same-Sex Marriage," 23 S. Afr. J. Hum. Rts. 432, 441 & 445 (2007).

[26] 1999 (1) SA 6 (CC).

[27] *National Coalition*, 1999 (1) SA at Par. 20.

[28] Par. 21.   [29] Par. 22.

"sex between men reinforces already existing societal prejudices and severely increases the negative effects of such prejudices on their lives."[30] For example, forcing gay people to "conceal" their identities made them vulnerable to blackmail, police entrapment, and the like.[31] Moreover gay people are relatively powerless and their activities are victimless.[32] Thus, outlawing sodomy was "unfair discrimination" and a dignity violation.[33] The Court relied for support on decisions from the Supreme Court of Canada and from the European Court of Human Rights (ECHR).

Privacy was the only issue on which the Court apparently diverged from Cameron's positions. Cameron argued that gays should not rely on a right to privacy because they should not have to be cloistered or ashamed.[34] Think of the message sent by the U.S. military's "Don't Ask, Don't Tell" policy. The Court, however, explained that Cameron advocated the anti-discrimination justification so that sexual bias prohibitions would be included in the new Constitution. The Court then reasoned that the right to privacy was not about physical space, but rather the opportunity that adults must have to freely choose their relationships.[35] This position is a bit difficult to reconcile with the Court's later ruling upholding anti-prostitution laws in *Jordan v. State*, discussed in Chapter 4.

The Court next analyzed the nature of the right infringed, its importance, the nature and extent of the limitation, and the government purpose. Essentially, the Court balanced these factors as required by the limitations clause.[36] The Court ultimately found that the law caused serious harm to gay men and that prejudices and religious motivations were not legitimate grounds for such a restriction.[37]

The Court added that the ECHR had struck down national laws against gay sex despite using a deferential margin of appreciation in which the ECHR showed great respect for each nation's preferences.[38] The Court also described the international trend against such laws.[39] The Constitutional Court then addressed American exceptionalism: "*Bowers* can really offer us no assistance in the construction and application of our own Constitution. The 1996 Constitution contains express privacy and dignity guarantees as well as the express prohibition of unfair discrimination on the ground of sexual orientation, which the United States

---

[30] Par. 23.
[31] Par. 23–24.
[32] Pars. 25–26.
[33] Par. 28.
[34] Par. 30.
[35] Par. 32.
[36] Par. 35.
[37] Pars. 37–38.
[38] Pars. 40–41.
[39] Par. 47.

Constitution does not."[40] Moreover, the Court pointed out that American scholars had harshly criticized the *Bowers* decision.[41] The Constitutional Court then discussed the appropriate remedy and rejected criticisms from Dennis Davis that it had not developed a strong enough notion of substantive equality.[42]

Justice Albie Sachs concurred by writing, "Only in the most technical sense is this a case about who may penetrate whom where."[43] He explained that the state punished this activity because it was perceived as "deviant," "rather than because of its proven harm."[44] Moreover, the privacy and equality interests of gay people are interrelated.[45] Overall, he advocated a "situation sensitive human rights approach."[46] He relied for support on several American critical race feminist scholars, as well as the important and controversial French philosopher, Michel Foucault. Foucault often wrote about sexuality and is unlikely to be referenced in future U.S.Supreme Court cases.

The Immigrant Same-Sex Partner Case

In 1999, the Court examined whether the government could treat an immigrant spouse better than the immigrant same-sex partner of a South African in *National Coalition for Gay and Lesbian Equality v. Minister of Home Affairs*.[47] Justice Ackermann ruled that this unequal treatment constituted illegal discrimination.

The government made several arguments in support of the law. It argued there was no marital status bias because the law did not prevent gay South Africans from marrying a member of the opposite sex.[48] The Court, however, said that this argument amounted to a "meaningless abstraction"[49] and that the Canadian Supreme Court had rejected the view.

The government also argued that the law was about whether someone had a spouse, not sexual orientation.[50] The Court responded that this law "affords protection only to conjugal relationships between heterosexuals and excludes any protection to a life partnership which entails a conjugal same-sex relationship open to gays and lesbians in harmony with their

---

[40] Par. 55.

[42] Par. 59.

[44] Par. 108.

[46] Par. 126.

[48] Par. 34.

[50] Par. 33.

[41] Par. 54.

[43] Par. 107.

[45] Par. 113.

[47] 2000 (2) SA 1 (CC).

[49] Par. 38.

sexual orientation."[51] The Court added that South African statutes have increasingly recognized same-sex partnerships.[52]

The Court also discussed the broader "transformation" taking place in family relationships,[53] noting that this transformation is particularly fitting for South Africa where there are many different cultures.[54] Justice Ackermann concluded that there was "intersecting discrimination on the grounds of sexual orientation and marital status" that created a presumption of unfair discrimination.[55] The Court's recognition of intersectionality has no U.S. Supreme Court parallel.

Next, the Court analyzed how the law perpetuated insulting stereotypes, such as that gay people are sexual creatures incapable of relationships[56] or that gay people cannot be good parents because they cannot procreate. The Court said that "procreative potential is not a defining characteristic of conjugal relationships."[57] The Court also said that changing this law would not endanger traditional marriage.[58]

At the justification stage, the Court explained, "There is no interest on the other side that enters the balancing process."[59] This shows the Court's boldness in the gay rights cases as there were some state justifications the Court could have addressed, as seen in the later gay marriage case. The decision also includes a complex remedial analysis.

Judges and Their Same Sex-Partners

In July 2002, the Court decided *Satchwell v. Republic of South Africa*,[60] ruling in favor of a judge who claimed that her same-sex partner should receive identical benefits to those received by the spouses of her married colleagues. The Court's reasoning is not surprising given the previously mentioned cases.

One interesting aspect of the decision is the Constitutional Court's emphasis on African culture. Justice Tholakele Madala wrote, "In certain African traditional societies woman-to-woman marriages are not unknown, this being prevalent in families that are childless because the woman is barren or where the woman is in a powerful position in her community, like being a queen or a chieftaness, or where she is very

---

[51] Par. 36.
[53] Pars. 47–48.
[55] Par. 4.
[57] Par. 51.
[59] Par. 59.

[52] Par. 37.
[54] *Id.*
[56] Par. 50.
[58] Pars. 55–56.
[60] 2002 (6) SA 1 (CC).

wealthy."[61] It is worth noting that Justice Madala was a founding member and director of the Prisoners' Welfare Programmes, an association established in 1985 to assist prisoners with their financial, legal, and educational needs. He was also the first black judge in the Eastern Cape and was a former chairperson of the Society of Advocates of Transkei.

Justice Madala's discussion of heterosexual *unmarried* partners was also new:

> Same-sex partners cannot be lumped together with unmarried heterosexual partners without further ado. The latter have chosen to stay as cohabiting partners for a variety of reasons, which are unnecessary to traverse here, without marrying although generally there is no legal obstacle to their doing so. The former cannot enter into a valid marriage. In my view, it is unnecessary to consider the position of heterosexual partners in this case.[62]

This argument reflects a "traditionalist" marriage model and is a rhetorical retreat from the earlier cases.[63] Indeed, Pierre de Vos suggests that the Court's language reflects a "valorization of the mythical nuclear family" as a "'civilizing' Christian institution"[64] and ignores South Africa's embrace of nontraditional pluralism.

The Court's definition of a same-sex partner is also important. The Court stated, "Section 9 generally does not require benefits provided to spouses to be extended to all same sex partners where no reciprocal duties of support have been undertaken. The Constitution cannot impose obligations towards partners where those partners themselves have failed to undertake obligations."[65] Justice Madala elaborated that this support requirement might mandate an evidentiary hearing in certain cases.[66] This part of the opinion is also traditionalist.

Finally, the Court found that the government could not provide any justification for its discrimination. The Court's remedy was to "read into" the law language indicating that the "partner in a permanent same-sex life partnership" should also receive benefits where "[s]uch partners... have undertaken and committed themselves to reciprocal duties of support."[67]

---

[61] Par. 12.   [62] Par. 16.

[63] *See e.g.* Beth Goldblatt, Notes and Comments, "Satchwell v. President of Republic of South Africa 2002," 19 S. Afr. J. Hum. Rts. 118, 123 (2003) (Court displays a "new cautiousness" in gay rights matters).

[64] Pierre de Vos, "Same Sex Sexual Desire and the Re-imagining of the South African Family," 20 S. Afr. J. Hum. Rts., 179, 191 (2004).

[65] *Supra* n. 60 Par. 24.   [66] Par. 25.

[67] Par. 34.

Adoption by Gay Couples

Later in 2002, the Court in *Du Toit v. Minister of Welfare*[68] ruled unconstitutional a statute that banned gay couples from being guardians for
children. This overturned a lower court decision holding that only one
member of a same-sex couple could be a guardian. There has been some
litigation in the United States on this question.[69]

The Constitutional Court opinion was authored by Justice Themba
Skweyiya. He became an advocate in 1970, but his work focused on
human rights and civil liberties from 1981 until he served as a High Court
Judge in the Natal between October 1995 and January 2001. During that
time he served on the ANC's Constitutional Committee. Thus, he is a
relatively new member of the Constitutional Court.

It is revealing to read Justice Skweyiya's description of the plaintiffs:

> The applicants have lived together as life partners since 1989. They for-
> malised their relationship with a commitment ceremony, performed by a
> lay preacher in September 1990. To all intents and purposes they live as
> a couple married in community of property; immovable property is regis-
> tered jointly in both their names; they pool their financial resources; they
> have a joint will in terms of which the surviving partner of the relationship
> will inherit the other's share in the joint community; they are beneficiaries
> of each other's insurance policies; and they take all major life decisions
> jointly and on a consensual basis.[70]

This idyllic description certainly shows how the traditional marriage
model is influential.

The Constitutional Court decision emphasized the importance of
"family life" in South Africa as well as the "child's best interests."[71]
It then argued that the statute "surely defeats the very essence and social
purpose of adoption which is to provide the stability, commitment, affection and support important to a child's development, which can be offered
by suitably qualified persons," including gay couples.[72] It further emphasized "the social reality of the vast number of parentless children in our
country,"[73] caused by the AIDS epidemic, poverty, and other apartheid
legacies that separated families.

---

[68] 2003 (2) SA 198 (CC).

[69] *See e.g.* Lofton v. Secretary of the Dept. of Children and Family Services, 358 F.3d 804
(11th Cir. 2004).

[70] *Du Toit*, 2003 (2) SA Par. 4.   [71] Par. 19.

[72] Par. 21.   [73] Par. 22.

The Court ultimately found discrimination on the basis of sexual orientation and marital status, as well as an infringement on human dignity.[74] The law's "non-recognition of the first applicant as a parent, in the context of her relationship with the second applicant and their relationship with the siblings, perpetuates the fiction or myth of family homogeneity based on the one mother/one father model. It ignores developments that have taken place in the country, including the adoption of the Constitution."[75] The Court pointed out that the law did not even prevent gay people from adopting children. Moreover, the Court reiterated that "legislative and jurisprudential developments indicate the growing recognition afforded to same-sex relationships."[76]

The Court also addressed the absence of a regulatory mechanism to protect these children if the same-sex partnership were to break up. The Court decided that the benefits to children of more adoption opportunities outweighed this concern.[77] Moreover, the courts could look after the child's best interests in such situations.

Gay Marriage

The Constitutional Court's 2005 endorsement of gay marriage in *Minister of Home Affairs v. Fourie*[78] may be its most internationally prominent ruling. Justice Albie Sachs, perhaps the most progressive judge on one of the world's most progressive courts, wrote the opinion. Yet, the decision was a foregone conclusion given the precedents. Indeed, the immigrant case had addressed similar issues.

There were two issues in *Fourie*. First, the common law defined marriage as the "union of one man with one woman, to the exclusion, while it lasts, of all others."[79] Second, the Marriage Act 25 of 1961 ("Marriage Act") required that marriage officers ask the marrying parties a question that was worded in a way that excluded same-sex couples (e.g. the question assumed a man was marrying a woman).

One of the most interesting aspects of *Fourie* was the division that occurred in the South African Supreme Court of Appeal[80] between two distinguished jurists, the previously mentioned Edwin Cameron and I. G. Farlam. They agreed that the common law discriminated on the

---

[74]Pars. 26–27.   [75]Par. 28.
[76]Par. 32.   [77]Par. 34.
[78]2006 (1) SA 524 (CC).   [79]*Id.*Par. 2.
[80]2005 (3) SA 429 (SCA).

basis of sexual orientation but they disagreed on what to do with the Marriage Act.

Cameron said that the plaintiff's lawyers failed to raise the Marriage Act issue in their pleadings. However, *religious* but not secular officials were allowed to modify language in the ceremony.[81] Thus, Cameron reasoned that the Court could not resolve the Marriage Act language problem as applied to gay couples seeking *secular* weddings. That would have to be resolved by a Johannesburg case working its way through the courts.[82]

It was ironic to see South Africa's leading public advocate for same-sex marriage take such a legalistic approach, especially given the powerful language in his opinion regarding the dignity injury to members of his community. On the other hand, perhaps this was Judge Cameron's most brilliant moment because he showed that legal principles transcend personal opinion. His seminal 1993 law review article, mentioned earlier, had perhaps foreshadowed this approach by suggesting that gay people should initially aim for domestic partnership recognition and that marriage could remain the paradigm for heterosexuals.[83]

In contrast, Judge Farlam, giving a history of marriage going back to ancient Rome, argued that the court could address the Marriage Act question because it was inseparable from the common law issue. Moreover, nothing in the Marriage Act endorsed the common law definition of marriage.[84] Farlam advocated a two-year suspension of his ruling's effect to permit Parliament to enact necessary changes in the law. Sachs summarized Judge Farlam's argument as follows:

> Farlam... held both that the common law should be developed and that the Marriage Act could and should be read there and then in updated form so as to permit same-sex couples to pronounce the vows. In his view, however, the development of the common law to bring it into line with the Constitution should be suspended to enable Parliament to enact appropriate legislation. In support of an order of suspension he pointed out that the SALRC (South African Law Reform Comission) had indicated that there were three possible legislative responses to the unconstitutionality, and, in his view, it should be Parliament and not the judiciary that should choose.[85]

All sides therefore ended up dissatisfied. The government objected to allowing gay marriage. The plaintiffs objected to Cameron precluding

---

[81] 2006 (1) SA 524 (CC) Par. 19.
[82] Par. 21.
[83] *Supra* n. 17 at 467.
[84] 2006 (1) SA 524 (CC) Par. 30.
[85] Par. 32.

a secular same-sex ceremony and to Farlam's two-year suspension to allow the common law to be updated.[86]

In *Fourie*, the Constitutional Court decided that it should address both the common law and the Marriage Act issues because they were so intertwined.[87] Justice Sachs then rejected the government's argument that the Constitution did not protect a fundamental right to marry. Relying on *The First Certification Judgment*, he reasoned,

> Families are constituted, function and are dissolved in such a variety of ways, and the possible outcomes of constitutionalising family rights are so uncertain, that constitution-makers appear frequently to prefer not to regard the right to marry or to pursue family life as a fundamental right that is appropriate for definition in constitutionalised terms. This avoids questions that relate to the history, culture and special circumstances of each society. At the same time, the provisions of constitutional text would clearly prohibit any arbitrary state interference with the right to marry or to establish and raise a family.[88]

He added that the Court should reject "references made in argument [by the government] to North American polemical literature or to religious texts."[89]

Sachs then explained "that over the past decades an accelerating process of transformation has taken place in family relationships, as well as in societal and legal concepts regarding the family and what it comprises."[90] Moreover, the Constitution is a "radical rupture" with an intolerant past in which "small gestures in favour of equality, however meaningful, are not enough."[91]

Next, he explained that marriage provides security, and its unavailability forces gay couples to "live in a state of legal blankness."[92] He acknowledged that many homosexuals might not follow the heterosexual marriage model but reasoned that gay couples should have the choice to do so.

He then rejected several arguments against same-sex marriage, many of which were made in the same-sex immigration case. First, marriage is not about procreation as many heterosexual couples do not have children. Indeed, that argument demeans older married heterosexual couples and

[86] Par. 33.   [87] Par. 44.
[88] Par. 47.   [89] Par. 48.
[90] Par. 52.   [91] Par. 59.
[92] Par. 72.

those with physical limitations.[93] Second, any religious objection to gay marriage cannot undermine secular government policy.[94]

Another argument against same-sex marriage is that the South African Constitution must follow international law and gay marriage lacked such acceptance. Indeed, after the case was decided, Roger Alford said that the Court's treatment of international and comparative law was inconsistent with that taken in its death penalty case.[95] The Court therefore turned international law into an unprincipled one-way ratchet that could only create new rights.

Brian Ray responded to Alford by reasoning that gay marriage differs from the death penalty because of the Constitution's ban on sexual orientation discrimination.[96] Since the framers left open the death penalty issue, foreign law reliance was crucial. Alford, however, is correct that the Constitutional Court adheres to foreign law somewhat selectively. In the *Fourie* opinion, Sachs noted that any international conventions regarding marriage were descriptive of their times, not normative.[97]

Sachs also rejected the argument that the Constitution's provision for pluralism in family relations justified the exclusion of gay people from marriage. He responded that this "provision is manifestly designed to allow Parliament to adopt legislation, if it so wishes, recognizing, say, African traditional marriages, or Islamic or Hindu marriages."[98] It therefore supports "diversity" in marriages.[99] After finding unfair discrimination, Sachs rejected the government's limitations clause argument that gay marriage threatens traditional marriage, because that view was based on prejudice.[100]

Justice Sachs, however, surprised many by suspending the implementation of gay marriage for one year to allow Parliament to establish a regulatory scheme. Sachs cited separation of powers concerns and the goal of preventing legal chaos.[101] This suspension is ironic because he

---

[93] Par. 86.   [94] Par. 97.

[95] Roger Alford, "International Law in the Gay Marriage Case," Opinio Juris (Blog), Dec. 2, 2005, http://lawofnations.blogspot.com/2005/12/international-law-in-south-africa-gay_02.html (last visited Jan. 3, 2008).

[96] *Id.* Brian Ray's comments follow the Alford post.

[97] 2006 (1) SA 524 (CC) Pars. 46 & 100.   [98] *Id.*at Par. 108.

[99] Par. 109.   [100] Par. 113.

[101] Par. 136–140, 154. Such chaos broke out when an Iowa District Court judge struck down a law limiting marriage to a man and a woman. Varnum, et al. v Brien, Case No. CV5965 (Polk Cty. Dist. Ct.)(Aug. 30, 2007). The case is pending in the Iowa Supreme Court. Before the state could obtain a stay, one Iowa male couple was able to obtain marriage documents. Monica Davey, "Iowa Permits Same Sex Marriage, for

had earlier rejected "small gestures" toward transformation. Interestingly, in 2004 Kerry Williams published an important scholarly article on gay marriage in South Africa that advocated giving Parliament a two-year implementation period in an effort to promote "dialogue" between the branches.[102] This dialogue theory has become popular among many scholars but it has also engendered criticism.[103]

Justice Kate O'Regan, a former academic like Sachs, concurred generally with Sachs's opinion but disagreed on the one-year delay because that perpetuated an unconstitutional framework. She said the Court's role in the balance of powers is to vindicate constitutional rights.[104] She also did not believe that chaos would occur by legalizing gay marriage and said that any risks were outweighed by a continuing rights violation.[105] Her concurrence took the same position as those who criticized the U.S. Supreme Court's timid "all deliberate speed" remedial approach in *Brown II*.

Justice O'Regan's concurrence is correct in arguing that courts should not lightly delay rights remedies. Justice Sachs's opinion, however, did set a deadline for legalization. Moreover, the Court's ruling conflicted with public opinion. Thus, Sachs was likely trying to provide institutional protection to the unelected Court by requiring Parliament to do the implementation dirty work. In addition, Sachs knew that altering an important institution like marriage, with all of its bureaucratic, governmental, and religious dimensions, would require changes in paperwork, procedures, social expectations, and more. He was trying to provide time for those changes to occur.

The Civil Union Act

With the *Fourie* decision, it looked as if South Africa would join Belgium, Canada, the Netherlands, Spain, and Massachusetts as the only governments in the world legalizing gay marriage. Things did not go as gay marriage advocates planned.

Four Hours, Anyway," N.Y. Times, Sep. 1, 2007, http://www.nytimes.com/2007/09/01/us/01iowa.html?_r=1&oref=slogin (last visited June 19, 2008).

[102] Kerry Williams, "I Do or We Won't: Legalising Same-Sex Marriage in South Africa," 20 S. Afr. J. Hum. Rts. 32, 63 (2004).

[103] Grant Huscroft, "Rationalizing Judicial Power: The Mischief of Dialogue Theory," *available at* SSRN: http://ssrn.com/abstract=1083685 (last visited January 16, 2008) (dialogue theory makes the courts into the constitution's guardian and limits the legislature to act within court directives).

[104] *Fourie*, 2006 (1) SA Par. 171.   [105] Par. 169.

Parliament's initial civil union bill only authorized civil partnerships for same-sex couples, not marriage. This legislation created an uproar as it appeared that the ANC was endorsing the equivalent of "separate but equal."[106] Gay marriage advocates and the South African Human Rights Commission said that allowing only civil unions would perpetuate their status as second-class citizens.[107] Christian groups also opposed the bill urging Parliament to amend the Constitution and define marriage as between a man and woman.[108]

In his criticism of the civil union bill, same-sex marriage advocate Jaco Barnard went the farthest by stating that the legislative process contained "totalitarian moments."[109] He asserted that democracies typically have three qualities: separation of church and state, plurality, and common citizenship. He explained that fundamentalist religious groups and a dominant political party initially acted to subvert *Fourie*. He said that "democratic activism coupled with the strength of and commitment to the South African Constitution and to the decisions of the Constitutional Court ensured the successful evasion of these totalitarian moments while emphasizing that the struggle against totalitarianism in South Africa is far from over." One could certainly take issue with the idea that fervent opposition to a pro gay marriage ruling is the equivalent of totalitarianism.

Ultimately, the bill was amended to allow adult couples of any type to marry or enter into civil partnerships. Yet, there were problems with implementing the legislation. Nearly six months after the law was enacted, "some Home Affairs officers were still using marriage certificate forms that said 'husband' and 'wife.'"[110] Indeed, in a public hearing on the act, Pierre de Vos described an earlier interaction with an African

---

[106] Pierre de Vos, "Gays and Lesbians Now 'Separate But Equal,'" Mail & Guardian online, Sep. 17, 2006, http://www.mg.co.za/articlePage.aspx?artoc;eod=284218& area=/insight/insight_comment_and_analysis (last visited April 17, 2008).

[107] Judith Cohen, South African Human Rights Commission, "Submission to Home Affairs Portfolio Committee, National Assembly on Civil Unions Bill [B26-2006]," Oct. 2006 www.pmg.org.za/docs/2006/061010sahrc.doc

[108] ChristianViewNetwork, "Defend Marriage," Oct. 6, 2006, http://defendmarriage. blogspot.com/2006/10/christianview-network-submission-on.html (last visited April 17, 2008).

[109] Jaco Barnard, "Totalitarianism, (Same-Sex) Marriage and Democratic Politics in Post-Apartheid South Africa," 23 S. Afr. J. Hum. Rts. 500 (2007).

[110] Helen Bamford, "Red Tape 'Strangling' Gay Marriage," Cape Argus, May 28, 2007, http://allafrica.com/stories/200705280404.html (last visited April 17, 2008).

National Congress representative that perhaps revealed the underlying problem:

> Professor Pierre de Vos... said that during the public hearings on the Civil Union Act Patrick Chauke, chairman of the National Assembly's home affairs portfolio committee, asked him why gays even wanted to get married. "I told him it was for those little pictures on the mantelpiece. They are deeply symbolic and make you feel like you belong to society." He said the first draft of the bill only provided for "civil unions" not "marriage." "We argued that that was not good enough. It doesn't have the same ring and you probably wouldn't get the same amount of presents."[111]

ANALYSIS OF SOUTH AFRICAN GAY RIGHTS JURISPRUDENCE

The Court's boldness in these gay rights cases is striking. For example, gay couples can receive more constitutional protection than unmarried heterosexual couples.[112] This section explains the Court's assertiveness in this area compared to others and also addresses some criticisms of its approach.

Why Has the Court Been So Assertive?

There are several explanations for the assertiveness of the Court on gay rights. First, gay marriage and gay adoption are not zero-sum issues. Gay marriage does not preclude heterosexual marriage and gay adoption does not prevent traditional adoption. Moreover, in South Africa there are not enough heterosexual married couples available to adopt every orphan.[113] The Court's boldness is therefore highly pragmatic.

By contrast, some of the Court's race discrimination cases involve affirmative action in which a victory for blacks may mean a loss for whites.[114] Moreover, gender discrimination cases can turn on whether a

---

[111] *Id.*

[112] Pierre de Vos, "A Judicial Revolution? The Court-Led Achievement of Same-Sex Marriage in South Africa," 4 Utrecht L. Rev. 162, 173 (2008).

[113] *Id.* ("It is ironic that with the adoption of the Civil Union Act, same-sex couples will in effect now have more legal rights than different sex couples.").

[114] *Walker v. City of Pretoria*, 1998 (2) SA 363 (CC) (whites complain that black neighborhoods pay lower water rates).

law is based on stereotypes or seeks to remedy gender bias.[115] These cases can therefore be zero-sum situations.

Second, gay people may be the prototypical vulnerable minority group in South Africa. According to Edwin Cameron,

> Traditionally disadvantaged groups such as women and blacks both constitute a majority of the South African population. Gays and lesbians, by contrast, are by definition a minority. Paradoxically, their perpetuation as a social category is dependent on the survival of the procreative heterosexual majority. Their seclusion from political power is in a sense thus ordained, and they will never on their own be able to use political power to secure legislation in their favour.[116]

Cameron's political powerless argument resembles footnote 4 of the U.S. Supreme Court's decision in *United States v. Carolene Products*,[117] which stated that discrete and insular minorities deserve special protection because they are politically vulnerable.[118] The paradigm American group was African Americans, though it will be interesting to see what happens to the theory now that Barack Obama is president. Bruce Ackermann, in his famous 1985 law review article, "Beyond *Carolene Products*,"[119] suggests that gay people form constituencies with others and that they are often invisible (not discrete) as well as diffuse (not insular). Indeed, Kenji Yoshino has written a book on the invisibility point called *Covering*.[120] Thus, although gay people certainly suffer from discrimination and violence, it is not clear they lack political clout either in South Africa or the United States.

Third, the Court has responded to gay rights concerns because some gay people are influential, and because of advocates like Cameron. Justices Ackermann and Sachs have also made gay rights a calling card. Further, it is difficult to criticize laws helping gay people because they were at ground zero of the early AIDS epidemic. *Hoffman v. South African Airways*[121] shows the Court's empathy for HIV-infected South Africans. Ronald Louw and Pierre de Vos demonstrate that gay rights

---

[115] President of the Republic of S. Africa v. Hugo, 1997 (4) SA 1 (CC) (President Mandela pardons only nonviolent female prisoners with children under age twelve, not males).

[116] *Nat'l Coalition, supra* n. 26 Par. 25 n. 32, *citing* Cameron, *supra* n. 17.

[117] 304 U.S. 144, 153 n. 4 (1938).

[118] United States v. Carolene Products Co., 304 U.S. 144 n. 4 (1938).

[119] Bruce Ackerman, "Beyond *Carolene Products*," 98 Harv. L. Rev. 713 (1985).

[120] Kenji Yoshino, Covering, The Hidden Assault on Our Civil Rights (2006).

[121] 2001 (1) SA 1 (CC).

advocates, rather than highlighting their uniqueness, were able to link successfully their equality struggle to the anti-apartheid equality movement.[122] Fourth, there is so much diversity in South African families, including polygamy, that banning gay families would be hypocritical.

Another reason for the Court's assertiveness is that perhaps the Court is reacting to the post-apartheid era just as America jettisoned 1950s Eisenhower morality in the 1960s. During the '60s, there was a sexual awakening championed by the feminist movement and captured by the saying "make love, not war." In 1971, the Supreme Court finally recognized that women deserve some protection under the equal protection clause. Given the sexual orientation language in the new South African Constitution, perhaps the Constitutional Court felt open to recognizing new freedoms in an area in which the apartheid laws had been repressive and used for political purposes.

Criticisms of the Court's Approach

Several criticisms can be levied against the Court's decisions. First, the idea that the institution of marriage evolves raises the question of whether groups can claim a right to enter "communal" marriages if they become fashionable. The evolution argument also has a circular element. Human rights evolve in part due to court rulings but the question is whether courts should issue such rulings. And did not the absence of a textual constitutional right to marry make plausible the government's position? Perhaps the simplest response is that *Fourie* remains a narrow and easy decision given the Constitution's express prohibition on sexual orientation discrimination. These other issues about the evolution of marriage and family are simply not essential to this particular decision.

A second criticism is that the court knows little about how children are affected by having gay parents as compared to heterosexual parents. Studies regarding these newer family arrangements are inconclusive.[123] According to controversial language from New York's highest court, common sense suggests that a child is better off having both a male and female role model in the house.[124] Thus, courts should defer to legislatures on such disputed policy issues. Sachs never discussed this position, though

---

[122] *Supra* notes 24 & 25.

[123] *Hernandez*, 855 N.E.2d at 8, *Goodridge*, 798 N.E.2d at 980.

[124] *Hernandez*, 855 N.E.2d at 7 ("Intuition and experience suggest that a child benefits from having before his or her eyes, every day, living models of what both a man and a woman are like.")

perhaps that is because the same-sex partner immigration case made the gay marriage case a foregone conclusion.

In South Africa, however, this American argument ignores the huge number of orphans, previously mentioned in the *Du Toit* adoption case, caused by AIDS, poverty, and violence.[125] There are not enough available heterosexual adoptive parents, and "common sense" dictates that children are obviously better off with gay parents than as orphans. The argument in favor of heterosexual parents is a First World argument that does not fit the Third World. Moreover, deferring to a social tradition because it is tradition is circular and inherently conservative. Furthermore it ignores the disintegration of the Ozzie and Harriet family model. One judge's "intuition and experience" can be another's idiocy.

A third criticism is that the Court is too progressive for the public. Most South Africans apparently disapprove of gay marriage and support the death penalty.[126] In a related vein, most of the conservative Anglican communion members who oppose gay ministers are from Africa.

However, Justice Sachs did reference the public's extensive participation in the South African Law Reform Commission's study on what kinds of relationships should receive state recognition. Moreover, his cautious remedy reflected a desire to see parliamentary involvement. The Court, however, has taken institutional risks in the gay rights area. Indeed, James Gibson's polling shows the Court's divergence from popular opinion.[127]

---

[125] *Du Toit, supra* n. 70 Par. 22. "South Africa has one of the highest incidences of HIV/AIDS – 21.5% of the adult population. In addition, it is estimated that there are over 1 million AIDS orphans which is half of all orphans." SOS Children's Villages, South Africa, http://www.soschildrensvillages.org.uk/aids-africa/projects-by-country/aids-south-africa.htm (last visited Jan. 3, 2008).

[126] Dennis Davis, "Has South Africa Become a Juristocracy? Or Who Runs the Country?" at 1, Oct. 19, 2006, http://www.wolpetrust.org.za/dialogue2006 /CT102006davis_paper.pdf (last visited Jan. 3, 2008) ("Listen to any talk radio programme and you will hear complaints about the constitution, ranging from the unconstitutionality of the death penalty to the recognition of gay marriage.").

[127] James L. Gibson & Gregory Caldeira, "Defenders of Democracy? Legitimacy, Popular Acceptance and the South African Constitutional Court," 65 J. Pol. 1 (2003). But it has been argued that Gibson's questions and analysis make American definitional assumptions that may be problematic in assessing foreign cultures and institutions. *See e.g.* Ineke van Kessel, "Review of James L. Gibson and Amanda Gouws, Overcoming Intolerance in South Africa: Experiments in Democratic Persuasion, H-SAfrica, H-Net Reviews, June 2004, http://www.h-net/msu.edu/reviews/showrev.cgi?path=49031093440079 (last visited April 16, 2008) (critiquing another study by Gibson as lacking an understanding of the different cultural meanings of words being used in the polling questions).

Max Du Plessis, however, writes that the Court must correctly decide constitutional issues even if the result is unpopular. One function of such a Court is to educate and persuade the public.[128] He invokes the concept of "critical morality" to explain why the Court cannot simply follow public opinion.[129]

Moreover, American decisions like *Brown* or *Loving v. Virginia*[130] were catalysts for public opinion in a manner similar to what Max Du Plessis has asserted.[131] Indeed, it may be even more important in South Africa that the Constitutional Court act as a beacon for the rule of law, regardless of public opinion, given the nation's history of official lawlessness. In addition, the likelihood of backlash regarding the gay rights decisions may be limited in South Africa because the nation has so many economic, health, and crime issues to worry about.

Pierre de Vos, by contrast, maintains in a 2007 article that the Court's gay rights decisions do not go far enough. *Fourie* and the subsequent Civil Union law are nothing more than "small victories" in an "ongoing struggle."[132] He elaborates, "The battle for full marriage rights was a well directed, elite-based legal battle . . . [but] it failed to build a sustainable, vibrant, grassroots movement to take on this task."[133] Is he right that this was a small victory for the elite?

De Vos explains that the Court and the Civil Union Act still rely on the heterosexual marriage tradition as their model for gay equality, rather than fully embracing the differences between that and gay marriage.[134] In an earlier article, he discusses the Christian ethos underlying

---

[128] Max du Plessis, "Between Apology and Utopia – The Constitutional Court and Public Opinion," 18 S. Afr. J. Hum. Rts. 1 (2002).

[129] *But see* Nelson Tebbe, "Witchcraft and Statecraft: Liberal Democracy in Africa," 96 Geo. L. J. 183, 202 (2006) (arguing that Rawls can provide theoretical underpinnings for African liberalism but only if flexibly interpreted and applied).

[130] 388 U.S. 1 (1967) (finding unconstitutional laws that prohibit whites from marrying people of other races).

[131] Louis Trager, "*Brown v. Board of Education*," Stanford Lawyer 20, 22 (Spring 2004) (in a discussion of the case, Jack Greenberg said, "The metaphor I use is that *Brown* was like an icebreaker. It broke all that up. In retrospect, *Brown* wasn't a school case; it was a case that transformed the politics of America."), http://www.law.stanford.edu/publications/stanford_lawyer/issues/68/Brown50.pdf (last visited Jan. 7, 2007).

[132] *Supra* n. 25 at 465 (2007).   [133] *Id.* at 432.

[134] *Id.* at 457 ("It is striking to note the degree to which this judgment valorizes the institution of marriage and endorses the view that legal marriage remains the only comprehensive and valid way in which two people can (and perhaps should) bestow full legal and societal recognition on their relationship.")

the traditional conception of marriage.[135] The traditional conception excludes gay people, bisexuals, transsexuals, polygamists, or others who have truly alternative lifestyles. This exclusion is inconsistent with the diversity embraced by the transformative South African Constitution. Moreover, he notes that, under the Civil Union Act, same-sex couples ended up with more rights than opposite-sex unmarried couples, which further highlights traditional marriage's import.[136]

This latest De Vos article provides an in-depth examination of the South African gay rights movement's political, rhetorical, and legal strategies. He is correct that the Court has not abandoned the traditional marriage model fully and that judicial success did not reflect a full-fledged grassroots movement. But he is incorrect in stating that the gay marriage victory is a "small" one.

The Court's decision was the first national ruling of its kind in the world. It does not remove all the discrimination, violence, and intolerance that gay people face in South Africa, but it moves in that direction. Moreover, as de Vos acknowledges, the decision opens up space for greater activity by gay and lesbian advocates. This is the most one can expect from a court.

AMERICAN GAY RIGHTS DECISIONS

American courts have split on gay marriage while increasingly upholding other rights for gay people. American cases focus more on privacy because the equal protection clause provides no special protection for gay people. Indeed, the U.S. Supreme Court's greatest victory for gay people was the substantive due process case, *Lawrence v. Texas*.[137]

This section discusses relevant U.S. Supreme Court cases and the three categories of state supreme court rulings. It then analyzes the strengths and weaknesses of the state court rulings and compares them to those of the Constitutional Court.

U.S. Supreme Court Cases

In 1986, the Supreme Court in *Bowers v. Hardwick*[138] ruled that there was no fundamental right to engage in homosexual sodomy. In a

---

[135] Pierre de Vos, "Same-Sex Desire and the Re-Imagining of the South African Family," 20 S. Afr. J. Hum. Rts. 179, 192 (2004).

[136] *Supra* n. 25 at 462.   [137] 539 U.S. 558 (2003).

[138] 478 U.S. 186 (1986).

controversial concurrence, Chief Justice Burger said that such activity has long been considered offensive to the Judeo-Christian tradition. The decision was hard to reconcile with the Court's *Roe v. Wade* decision. How could the right to privacy cover aborting a fetus but not extend to seemingly victimless sexual activity?

In *Hurley v. Irish-American Gay, Lesbian and Bisexual Group of Boston, Inc.*,[139] the Court in 1995 found that the Boston St. Patrick's Day parade organizers could refuse to allow a gay Irish American group to march. A contrary decision would violate the organizer's First Amendment rights. In 2000, the Court in *Boy Scouts of America v. Dale*[140] held that the Boy Scouts could discharge an openly gay scoutmaster given its First Amendment right to send a message of moral wholesomeness. *Dale* is troubling as there was no real evidence that the Boy Scouts existed to send any messages about sexuality. By contrast, there can be little dispute that parades are designed to send messages, though *Hurley* can be criticized on other grounds.

In 1996, the Court in *Romer v. Evans*[141] struck down a Colorado constitutional referendum nullifying state or local laws protecting gay people. Justice Anthony Kennedy said the referendum reflected animosity toward gay people, depriving them alone of discrimination protections received by others, and thus amounting to a *per se* violation of the Constitution. Kennedy's argument closely paralleled a brief filed by a group of prominent constitutional scholars.[142] Kennedy's opinion, however, had problems. First, he claimed to be using rationality review but his lack of deference was more like intermediate scrutiny. Second, he never mentioned *Bowers*.

In dissent, Justice Antonin Scalia reasoned that if homosexual sodomy could be barred, removing legal protections from the group that engages in that activity was rational. Moreover, laws against polygamy were hard to justify if other sexual minorities must be protected. Lastly, Scalia accused Kennedy of joining the intellectual elites in the culture wars versus the ordinary public.

In 2003, Kennedy authored *Lawrence*, which overruled *Bowers*. Kennedy reasoned that *Bowers* mischaracterized the issue as whether

---

[139] 515 U.S. 557 (1995).   [140] 530 U.S. 640 (2000).
[141] 517 U.S. 620 (1996).
[142] Akhil Reed Amar, "Attainder and Amendment 2: Romer's Rightness," 95 Mich. L. Rev. 203, 204 (1996), *citing*, Brief of Laurence H. Tribe, John Hart Ely, Gerald Gunther, Philip B. Kurland, Kathleen M. Sullivan as Amici Curiae in Support of Respondents Romer v. Evans.

gay people could engage in sodomy. The question was more general, namely whether gay people can make intimate personal choices without state interference. In describing how such laws infringed on gay people's human dignity, his opinion sounded South African at times. Interestingly, he emphasized the Fourteenth Amendment's liberty provision more than the right to privacy. Kennedy found support for his *Lawrence* opinion in the post-*Bowers* trend of state repeal of anti-sodomy laws. Kennedy also relied on international institutions, such as the European Court of Human Rights, which said that laws against sodomy violate evolving notions of personal freedom.[143]

Kennedy's opinion, however, never declared a level of scrutiny or whether a fundamental right was involved.[144] These omissions may have been necessary to retain the votes of other Justices, but they left doctrinal puzzles. Several American federal appellate courts have divided over the fundamental rights question.[145] Moreover, Kennedy said the decision did not forecast the Court's view on gay marriage.

State Court Decisions

State supreme courts in Massachusetts, California, and Connecticut have ruled for gay marriage but other courts have not. New York is typical. New Jersey is one of a few states in the middle.

New York

The New York Court of Appeals in *Hernandez v. Robles*[146] did not dispute marriage's benefits but said that disallowing same-sex matrimony was rational. First, the legislature could find it more important to promote stability in heterosexual than in homosexual relationships because heterosexual intercourse can lead to children. The court also said of homosexual relationships that "the Legislature could...find that such relationships are all too often casual or temporary."[147]

Second, the court held that, "The Legislature could rationally believe that it is better, other things being equal, for children to grow up with both

---

[143] Eur. Court H.R., Dudgeon Case, Series A no. 45 (1981).

[144] Cass Sunstein, "What Did Lawrence Hold? Of Autonomy, Desuetude, Sexuality, and Marriage," 55 Sup. Ct. Rev. 27 (2003).

[145] *Compare* Reliable Consultants, Inc. v. Earle, 517 F.3d 738, 745 n. 32 (5th Cir. 2008) (no fundamental right), *with* Cook v. Gates, Nos. 6-02313 (1st Cir. 2008) (*Lawrence* recognized liberty interest that requires court to balance interests).

[146] 855 N.E. 2d 1 (2006).   [147] *Id.* at 7.

a mother and a father. Intuition and experience suggest that a child benefits from having before his or her eyes, every day, living models of what both a man and a woman are like."[148] The court added that social science studies had not resolved how having gay parents affects children.[149]

The New York court characterized *Loving v. Virginia* as a racial prejudice situation in contrast to New York's longstanding heterosexual marriage rule. *Lawrence* was also distinguishable because plaintiffs there sought "protection against state intrusion on intimate, private activity. They seek [here] from the courts access to a state conferred benefit that the Legislature has rationally limited to opposite sex couples."[150] Moreover, the law's over- and underinclusiveness did not matter under rationality review. New York's prohibition was valid under either equal protection or substantive due process.

Massachusetts and California: Rulings for Same-Sex Marriage

MASSACHUSETTS. The 2003 Supreme Judicial Court of Massachusetts ruling in *Goodridge v. Department of Public Health*[151] that gay marriage could not be banned under the state's constitution was a shot heard around the world. Indeed, the South African Court in *Fourie* referenced the opinion.[152] Interestingly, the opinion's author, Massachusetts Chief Justice Margaret Marshall, was born and raised in South Africa and attended the University of Witswatersrand. While a student there, she was elected president of the National Union of Democratic Students, an anti-apartheid organization dedicated to the struggle for equality within the country. She is therefore personally familiar with the South African context. She subsequently attended Harvard and then Yale Law School and is married to Anthony Lewis, the politically liberal Pulitzer Prize-winning former columnist for the *New York Times*.

Marshall interpreted the U.S. Supreme Court's *Loving* decision as being about an individual's right to marry the person of his or her choice.[153] The government responded that most states had already withdrawn their anti-miscegenation laws before *Loving* was decided. Marshall, however, then argued that state courts led the way such as in California.[154]

---

[148] *Id.*
[150] *Id.* at 10.
[152] *Fourie*, Par. 18 n. 18.
[154] *Id.* at n. 16.

[149] *Id.* at 8.
[151] 798 N.E.2d 941.
[153] 798 N.E.2d at 958.

Marshall further explained that marriage restrictions must not be arbitrary, capricious, or irrational.[155] She added, "Whether and whom to marry, how to express sexual intimacy, and whether and how to establish a family – these are among the most basic of every individual's liberty and due process rights.... We conclude that the marriage ban does not meet the rational basis test for either due process or equal protection."[156] She rejected the procreation argument, as well as the optimal child-rearing argument, in part because of the state's willingness to allow gay couples to adopt.[157] Several dissenters made arguments that have been previously discussed.

CALIFORNIA. The California Supreme Court also ruled for gay marriage, but used different reasoning than the Massachusetts court.[158] The California court said that same-sex marriage restrictions deserve strict scrutiny under the state constitution for two reasons. First, they violate the fundamental right to marry. Second, they discriminate based on a suspect class, sexual orientation.

In determining that a fundamental right was involved, the court acknowledged that marriage had historically been between a man and a woman. However, the court explained that tradition could not govern such important questions of morality or we would be stuck in the nineteenth century. The court also argued that the right should be defined at a relatively high level of generality because it is usually referred to as the "right to marry," not the "right to heterosexual marriage."

Regarding the suspect classification, the court acknowledged that being gay has not been definitively shown to be immutable,[159] and the court neither accepted nor rejected the government's argument that California gay people have political sway. The court, however, reasoned that gay people have suffered a history of discrimination and that sexual orientation is generally irrelevant for government action. Applying strict scrutiny, the court then found that the state could not show that the prohibition was narrowly tailored to promote a compelling interest. It rejected the state's procreation arguments as well as the state's concerns about sending messages to society.

---

[155] *Id.* at 959.　　　[156] *Id.* at 961.

[157] *Id.* at 963.

[158] In re. Marriage Cases, S147999 (Cal. May 15, 2008). Proposition 8 overturned this court decision in November, 2008.

[159] *See e.g.* William Saletan, "Sexual Antagonism, A Genetic Theory of Homosexuality," Slate, June 25, 2008, http://www.slate.com/id/2194232/ (last visited June 25, 2008).

The California ruling was thought to be of monumental significance nationally because it permitted gay couples from all over the country to marry there whereas the Massachusetts ruling initially only applied to that state's residents. Proposition 8, however, overturned the California decision. Moreover, even if Proposition 8 is invalidated, many other states may not recognize California same-sex marriages when the couple returns home, creating the potential for much litigation. Connecticut has also now ruled in favour of gay marriage.

New Jersey

New Jersey's Supreme Court ended up displeasing everyone in *Lewis v. Harris*.[160] Contrary to the state's position, the court ruled that New Jersey's domestic partnership law violated the state constitution by discriminating against same-sex partners in terms of benefits. Interestingly, the court refused to follow federal equal protection rationality review. It instead held, "The test that we have applied to such equal protection claims involves the weighing of three factors: the nature of the right at stake, the extent to which the challenged statutory scheme restricts that right, and the public need or the statutory restriction."[161] The court thus adopted South-African-style weighing of interests.

The court then explained that New Jersey outlawed sexual orientation discrimination and that the domestic partnership act had not "bridge[d] the inequality gap between committed same-sex couples and married opposite-sex couples."[162] The state had "not articulated any legitimate public need for depriving same-sex couples of the host of benefits and privileges" going to married couples.[163] The court therefore found that the statutory discrimination "bears no substantial relationship to a legitimate governmental purpose,"[164] especially because it actually harmed the children raised by same-sex couples.[165]

Surprisingly, however, the court refused to mandate gay marriage, ruling only that the legislature must set up a scheme that equalized benefits:

> To be clear, it is not our role to suggest whether the Legislature should either amend the marriage statutes to include same-sex couples or enact a civil union scheme. Our role is limited to constitutional adjudication, and

---

[160] 908 A.2d 196 (2006).   [161] *Id.* at 212.

[162] *Id.* at 215. This prohibition did not lead to a victory for the New Jersey plaintiff in *Dale* because it was trumped by the supposed constitutional First Amendment rights of the Boy Scouts.

[163] *Id.* at 217.   [164] *Id.* at 220.

[165] *Id.* at 218.

therefore we must steer clear of the swift and treacherous currents of social policy when we have no constitutional compass with which to navigate.[166]

This decision resembles Justice Sachs's deferring to Parliament in *Fourie*. In response, the dissenters held that gay marriage was the only logical remedy.

The court also said the law did not violate a fundamental right because same-sex marriage was not deeply rooted in the state's traditions: "The framers of the 1947 [New Jersey] Constitution, much less the drafters of our marriage statutes, could not have imagined that the liberty right . . . embraced the right of a person to marry someone of his or her own sex."[167] Moreover, neither *Romer* nor *Lawrence* went so far, and *Loving* was factually distinct.

The New Jersey legislature followed up by enacting a civil union law that improved on its former domestic partnership act by supposedly equalizing benefits of heterosexual marriage and same-sex partnerships. This result may most accurately reflect the current state of American public opinion.

Analysis

These state cases are highly flawed. The New York court's emphasis on tradition and intuition can perpetuate stereotypes, such as the court's generalization that gay relationships are temporary. This stereotype portrays gay people as promiscuous sexual actors, not as individuals capable of meaningful family relationships. Max du Plessis would likely call this view "uncritical morality." Such an approach would never be accepted in the South African Constitutional Court. It is interesting to note, however, that some gay advocates and some studies agree with this proposition in certain respects though it is quite debatable.[168]

Moreover, the New York court resurrected the discredited rights/ privilege distinction by saying that *Lawrence* was about the right to privacy whereas marriage was a government benefit. The Supreme Court

---

[166] *Id.* at 222.   [167] *Id.* at 209.

[168] *See e.g.* Letitia Anne Peplau and Adam W. Fingerhut, "The Close Relationships of Lesbians and Gay Men," 58 Ann. Rev. Psychol. 405, 410–411 (2007) ("In the American Couples Study, only 36% of gay men indicated that it was important to be sexually monogamous compared with 71% of lesbians, 84% of heterosexual wives, and 75% of husbands.") Mickey Kaus, Kausfiles (blog) http://www.slate.com/id/2146861, Aug. 3, 2006 (discussing debate between Andrew Sullivan, Ann Coulter, and Peter Beinart on topic) (last visited April 18, 2008); Eugene Volokh, "Number of Sexual Partners or Don't Believe Everything You Read in College," Volokh Conspiracy, May 16, 2003, http://volokh.com/2003_5_11_volokh_archive.html (last visited April 18, 2008).

rejected this dichotomy in its procedural due process rulings involving licenses and welfare benefits, relying on Charles Reich's notion of the "new property."[169]

In addition, the argument that heterosexual couples deserve more protection because they may have children is both wrong and circular. It is wrong because new technologies and adoption allow same-sex couples to have children. It is circular because, if same-sex couples were equal, the court would see how important it is to protect them.

The Massachusetts decision also has problems. First, the level of scrutiny is not clear. Second, whether the court decided the case on equality or fundamental rights grounds is ambiguous. Third, the argument that the state must allow gay marriage if it allows gay adoption sounds strong, but misses the point. The state's belief that gay couples can be acceptable parents does not speak to whether their parenting is generally as good as married heterosexual couples. Thus, we end up with a revolutionary decision, based on ambiguous foundations, that some argue amounts to the kind of judicial legislating that led to a backlash, bringing more conservatives to the polls.[170] Others disagree with the backlash thesis.

The California decision was stronger because it did not waffle on the scrutiny level.[171] Yet, the ruling still had problems. For example, the fundamental rights section leaves open whether the state can ban adult consensual polygamy or incest because these activities involve the kind of autonomy concerns emphasized by the California court.[172] Although there is no flood of people seeking to engage in such activities nationally, it is troubling that there is no unambiguously principled basis for distinguishing the cases. Interestingly, in South Africa, the existence of polygamy among some tribal members (including Jacob Zuma, the likely future president) probably helped the gay marriage cause, whereas polygamy is a bogey man in the American gay marriage debate.

Second, on equality, the court's acknowledgment that gay people are not politically powerless raises the question of why the court should get involved, rather than being more deferential to the legislative or initiative process. Proposition 8's passage, however, could be viewed as showing that gay people only have limited political sway. A gay couple also does

---

[169] Charles Reich, "The New Property," 73 Yale L. J. 967 (1963).
[170] Gerald Rosenberg, "Courting Disaster: Looking for Change in All the Wrong Places," 54 Drake L. Rev. 795, 813 (2006).
[171] Kenji Yoshino, "Magisterial Conviction," Slate, May 15, 2008, http://www.slate.com /id/2191530/ (last visited May 16, 2008).
[172] William Saletan, "Free to be You and Me," Slate, May 16, 2008, http://www.slate.com /id/2191504/ (last visited May 16, 2008).

have some biological limitations compared to a straight couple, which suggests that being gay is not always irrelevant. For example, Justice Ginsburg used the physical distinctions between men and women to say that laws that discriminate on the basis of sex should only receive intermediate scrutiny, not the strict scrutiny of racial classifications.

The New Jersey decision is schizophrenic as its conservative substantive due process reasoning contrasts with its progressive equal protection approach. The court, however, deserves credit for openly admitting its balancing approach. It had little reason, though, for ignoring the logic of its equal protection analysis and not mandating gay marriage.

CONCLUSION

The South African Constitutional Court went somewhere the U.S. Supreme Court is not likely to go any time soon: legalizing gay marriage. The inclusion of sexual orientation as a protected category in the South African Constitution was key to its decision. Ironically, popular opinion in the United States favors gay people more than in South Africa. In the United States, there has been movement in the area of gay rights in several states, though California Proposition 8 may reflect some backlash. The quintessential American brand, Walt Disney, offers its employees same-sex partner benefits. The U.S. Supreme Court, however, remains very traditional.

6

Affirmative Action

Affirmative action based on race is highly controversial both in South Africa and the United States.[1] Moreover the South African Constitutional Court, as shown by its ruling in *Hugo* (see Chapter 4), analyzes affirmative action differently than does the U.S. Supreme Court. This chapter compares leading racial affirmative action cases from these countries to learn more about their approaches and to assess whether the decisions facilitate social progress.

There are important national differences. For example, South Africa's apartheid ended more recently than American slavery or American segregation, and South African blacks are a political majority. South Africa's recent history of oppression therefore makes it surprising that the country's courts have been tough on affirmative action, requiring that those burdened receive procedural and other protections.[2] The U.S. Supreme Court's decisions in this area are also surprising in that acceptable American plans must support First Amendment values, not equalization.[3] The Supreme Court's recent rejection of public school racial assignments highlights this limitation.[4] Thus, the strong differences in social context do

---

[1] Ockert Dupper, "In Defense of Affirmative Action in South Africa," 121 S. Afr. L. J. 187, 194 n. 23 (2004) (arguing that affirmative action in South Africa is a "potentially inflammable issue").

[2] Pretoria City Council v. Walker, 1998 (2) SA 363 (CC) Par. 76.

[3] For an interesting discussion of the First Amendment implications of the U.S. Supreme Court's affirmative action decision in Grutter v. Bollinger, 539 U.S. 306 (2003), *see* Paul Horwitz, "Grutter's First Amendment," 46 B.C. L. Rev. 461 (2005).

[4] For an argument regarding the difficulty of comparing American affirmative action with foreign affirmative action, *see* Mark Tushnet, "Interpreting Constitutions Comparatively, Some Cautionary Notes, with Reference to Affirmative Action," 36 Conn. L. Rev. 649 (2004). Tushnet focuses on affirmative action in India and the "creamy layer"

not result in precisely the distinctions in constitutional doctrine that one might expect.

SOUTH AFRICAN JURISPRUDENCE

The Bill of Rights affirmative action provision, section 9(2), reads as follows:

> Equality includes the full and equal enjoyment of al rights and freedoms. To promote the achievement of equality, legislative and other measures designed to protect or advance persons, or categories of persons, disadvantaged by unfair discrimination may be taken.

As discussed in previous chapters, South African laws assisting the historically disadvantaged receive judicial deference because the Constitutional Court supports "substantive equality" as opposed to the American concept of "formal equality," in which everyone must be treated the same.[5] The fact that the South African Constitution distinguishes between unfair and fair discrimination shows that not all discrimination is banned. The South African cases also reject the U.S. Supreme Court's individualistic equality interpretation.

The Walker *Decision*

The 1998 decision in *Walker v. City of Pretoria*[6] was one of the Constitutional Court's first to address racial equality. But the Court's concern for white citizens was startling given the horrors of apartheid. The case was decided under the 1993 Interim Constitution.

The Pretoria city government required residents in predominantly white areas to pay metered electrical tariffs whereas residents in poor African areas were only charged a flat rate.[7] The African areas lacked electric meters and other infrastructure. Indeed many of the so-called

issue that is frequently raised there. The creamy layer concept suggests that affirmative action sometimes does not work well because its primary beneficiaries are those closer to the top of the vulnerable groups.

[5] President of the Republic of South Africa v. Hugo, 1997 (4) SA 1 (CC) Par. 41; Walker, *supra* n. 2 at Par. 62 ("I am unable to agree with this view which looks to formal rather than substantive equality."); Iain Currie, Johan de Waal, The Bill of Rights Handbook 232–34 (2005).

[6] 1998 (2) SA 363 (CC).   [7] Par. 5.

homes there did not receive electricity. Had there been meters, enforcement also would have been difficult because of social tensions.

In effect, the white areas were "cross-subsidizing" the black areas.[8] Some whites also raised a selective enforcement objection because the government only sought their overdue payments, not those of blacks.[9] White residents further alleged that the City Council failed to comply with proper procedures, aggravating the selective enforcement problem. For example, a town engineer allegedly decided in secret not to enforce the rates in black areas.[10]

Deputy Chief Justice Pius Langa ruled that the City Council could constitutionally charge differential rates[11] but that the selective enforcement was unconstitutional.[12] Interestingly, the majority was unwilling to treat Pretoria's approach with deference, as an affirmative action policy, because the City Council never used such a label.[13] It is worth mentioning that Langa, who is black and now the Chief Justice, rose from the ranks of a factory worker, unable to afford advanced schooling, to the apex of the judiciary. He was a a founding member of the National Association for Democratic Lawyers and was its president from 1988 to 1994.

Justice Albie Sachs wrote separately, asserting that the City Council approach was an example of affirmative action and therefore was entirely constitutional.[14] Thus, the *Walker* opinions show that South African courts are wrestling with what kind of government action on race even qualifies as affirmative action.

There were other disagreements. Langa found that there was "indirect evidence" of discrimination because the favored geographic areas were disproportionately African whereas other areas were mainly white.[15] The U.S. Supreme Court would call this a disparate effects case.[16]

This finding created a presumption of unfair discrimination. Langa, however, also found that Pretoria rebutted the presumption, as to differential rates, because the City Council was striving to integrate the disadvantaged areas into a new culture of rate paying and was also adding meters there.[17] But Langa said the City Council did not rebut the selective enforcement charge and could not meet the proportionality burden there.

[8] Par. 20.   [9] Par. 6.
[10] Par. 74.   [11] Par. 68.
[12] Par. 79.   [13] Par. 34-35.
[14] Par. 104.   [15] Par. 32-33.
[16] Par. 40.   [17] Pars. 49, 53, 55, 66-68.

Justice Sachs responded that there was no disparate racial impact, just geographic differentiation.[18] Sachs also argued that the Court should only find indirect discrimination if the burdened group was historically disadvantaged, which whites were not.[19] Moreover, Langa's approach could subject any law helping the disadvantaged to heightened scrutiny which the Constitution's framers never intended.[20]

Langa disagreed by reasoning that the Constitution was designed to protect vulnerable minority groups such as whites, even though they had been the historical oppressor.[21] It is striking to see an African Justice protecting whites and showing concern over the municipality's proce dures that disadvantaged them.[22] The "rule of law," however defined, seemingly trumped social transformation.

Who is right on the selective enforcement claim – Langa or Sachs? The answer is Sachs. Pretoria's imperfect enforcement techniques sought to derive revenues from the more advantaged to benefit the entire community, especially the victims of apartheid. Absent a more serious injury than having to pay ordinary tariffs for utility service,[23] minor procedural irregularities do not amount to a constitutional violation, even with the successful cross-subsidization. Justice Langa is right that whites are protected by the Bill of Rights but this is not a case in which that protection was needed.[24]

---

[18] Par. 105 ("In the present case, there is overwhelming evidence to show that the complainant has in fact benefited from accumulated discrimination and that he continues to enjoy structured advantage of a massive kind.") South Africa is therefore different from the United States where disparate impact alone creates no presumption of guilt. Discriminatory intent must be shown in constitutional cases, which is more difficult to prove. Washington v. Davis, 426 U.S. 229 (1976).

[19] Par. 115 ("The concept of indirect discrimination, as I understand it, was developed precisely to deal with situations where discrimination lay disguised behind apparently neutral criteria or where persons already hit by patterns of historic subordination had their disadvantage entrenched or intensified by the impact of measures not overtly intended to prejudice them. I am unaware of the concept being expanded so as to favour the beneficiaries of overt and systematic advantage.")

[20] Par. 111.   [21] Par. 48.

[22] A different argument for why the Court should not tolerate carelessly implemented affirmative action plans, which burden whites too easily, is that such approaches can injure the efficient operation of important businesses and government agencies if unqualified candidates are selected. Dupper, *supra* n. 1 at 210 n. 82. That's not the issue in *Walker*.

[23] *Walker*, Par. 65 (Even Langa acknowledges that the plaintiffs really suffered no material injury).

[24] Other scholars have critiqued the majority opinion. Saras Jagwanth, "What is the Difference? Group Categorisation in Pretoria City Council v. Walker," 15 S. Afr. J. on Hum. Rts. 200 (1999). *But see* Wesahl Agherdien, Hazel Shelton, "City Council

Indeed, Justice Langa employed an American-style process-based approach to equality that is incompatible with South African substantive equality principles. Langa's approach resembled the "representation reinforcement" view of equality propounded by John Hart Ely in *Democracy and Distrust*, which in turn draws from footnote 4 in *United States v. Carolene Products Co.*[25] American courts use stricter scrutiny whenever a political majority enacts laws that burden racial or other minorities because, in such circumstances, there is a suspicion that improper prejudicial motives might be involved. Yet, that suspicion did not make sense when applied to the efforts of a mainly white Pretoria City Council to help racial minorities.[26]

Justice Sachs's argument, however, was also flawed when he turned a blind eye to the fact that geographic differences were racial differences. In the end, however, the opinions were not far apart, as Justice Langa refused damages to the plaintiffs because they unreasonably engaged in "self help" by underpaying.[27]

The Van Heerden *Decision*

The 2004 case of *Minister of Finance v. Van Heerden*[28] was the first in which the Court formally examined affirmative action in detail. The issue

of Pretoria v. Walker," 15 S. Afr. J. on Hum. Rts. 248 (1999) (critiquing the Sachs opinion).

[25] 304 U.S. 144 (1937).

[26] To look from another angle, this part of the Langa opinion resembles, to some extent, the U.S. Supreme Court's decision in Richmond v. J.A. Croson Co., 488 U.S. 469 (1989), striking down a race-based set aside for contractors. One reason Justice O'Connor gave for using strict scrutiny was that the set-aside benefiting blacks was adopted by a majority black City Council. Thus, "racial politics" could have played a role rather than the more noble motive apparently evident when a white majority approves a preference for a black minority. In dissent, Justice Marshall said that it was certainly ironic that once the former Confederate capital achieved success in moving toward racial equality, the Court used that success to defeat further equality efforts. Similarly, Justice Langa was concerned that a transformation-oriented City Council was bringing about transformation for less than saintly political reasons. He should have been more deferential.

[27] Par. 96.

[28] 2004 (6) SA 121 (CC). The Constitutional Court touched on affirmative action in President of the Republic of South Africa v. Hugo, 1997 (4) SA 1 (CC) (in which the Court affirmed the constitutionality of the president's decision to pardon nonviolent female prisoners with children under age twelve, but not similar nonviolent male prisoners, in part by providing an affirmative action justification for assisting these women, given the pervasive gender discrimination under apartheid). *See generally* Mark S. Kende, "Gender Stereotypes in South African and American Constitutional Law: The Advantages of

was the constitutionality of a pension plan for parliamentarians that mostly favored members of traditionally disadvantaged groups.[29] The High Court had placed the burden on the government to justify the plan. The Constitutional Court reversed the High Court decision, upheld the plan, and adopted three principles for affirmative action. Justice Dikgang Moseneke authored the majority opinion and was joined by six other Justices, some of whom wrote concurrences.

Justice Moseneke, who is black, served on the technical committee that drafted the Interim Constitution. He is the Deputy Chief Justice and will likely become Chief Justice in 2009. He is considered a talented advocate and an adroit political figure who is perhaps to the left politically of Chief Justices Chaskalson and Langa. As described by Richard Calland:

> Dikgang Moseneke is a truly remarkable man. His life's journey is astounding; arrested and sentenced to ten years in prison when he was just 15, he then spent a decade on Robben Island. On release, he broke through into the legal profession and took silk after just ten years.... That Moseneke will push the same clear Africanist line as Gumbi and Mbeki should neither be doubted nor necessarily feared.... He will have considerable clout when he becomes chief justice, not least because his network of connections is so good, spanning the commanding heights of the economy to the presidency and the grand professions.[30]

While in prison, he obtained a BA degree in English and political science, as well as a bachelor of law degree. He also served for a period as chair of the country's first major empowerment corporation.[31]

In the first part of *Van Heerden*, Justice Moseneke wrote, "Absent a positive commitment progressively to eradicate socially constructed barriers to equality and to root out systematic or institutionalized under-privilege, the constitutional promise of equality before the law and its equal protection and benefit must, in the context of our country, ring hollow."[32] Therefore, affirmative action laws were presumptively fair in

---

a Pragmatic Approach to Equality and Transformation," 117 S. Afr. L. J. 745 (2000) (discussing *Hugo* in detail).

[29] Parliament established a graduated pension scheme that provided fewer benefits to former political figures who already had vested pensions, and greater benefits to newer officials.

[30] Richard Calland, Anatomy of South Africa 239–40 (2006). "Took silk" means that he moved from the position of attorney to the position of a specially recognized advocate under the traditions of the British Commonwealth.

[31] *Id.* at 223.   [32] *Supra* n. 28 Par. 31.

contrast to the ruling of the High Court.[33] He then outlined the three-part test:

> The first yardstick relates to whether the measure targets persons or categories of persons who have been disadvantaged by unfair discrimination; the second is whether the measure is designed to protect or advance such persons or categories of persons; and the third requirement is whether the measure promotes the achievement of equality.[34]

The first principle focuses on the *group* receiving the benefit. The second focuses on *purpose*, namely whether "the remedial measures are arbitrary, capricious or display naked preference."[35] The third looks at *results* such as whether the policy will bring about "reparations."[36] The Constitutional Court sought a "non-racial, non-sexist society" in which everyone was treated with "equal worth and respect." The touchstone is whether "the measure carries a reasonable likelihood of meeting the end."[37] This resembles the American principle of heightened rationality review, which is far different from the U.S. Supreme Court's strict scrutiny.

The Constitutional Court further said, "Central to this vision is the recognition that ours is a diverse society, comprised of people of different races, different language groups, different religions and both sexes. This diversity, and our equality as citizens within it, is something our Constitution celebrates and protects." It is hard to imagine the U.S. Supreme Court celebrating diversity as the rainbow nation does. Instead, in America, diversity facilitates the marketplace and the governing elites as discussed later in this chapter.

Justice Mokgoro concurred but disputed Moseneke's first principle about groups. She reasoned that the pension beneficiaries included some who were not historically oppressed. Thus, the measure must be more "carefully crafted" so that the wrong people do not receive a windfall.[38] Similarly, Justice Ngcobo wrote, "The beneficiaries of the measure included persons who were not disadvantaged by past discrimination."[39] Both he and Mokgoro nonetheless agreed with Moseneke's result but not because this was proper affirmative action. Instead, it was a remedial measure (short of affirmative action) that was discriminatory but not unfairly

---

[33] Par. 32.
[35] Par. 41.
[37] Par. 42.
[39] Par. 108.

[34] Par. 37.
[36] Par. 25.
[38] Par. 89, 93.

so.[40] These concurring opinions are more conservative than Moseneke's position though not by much.

Justice Sachs somehow agreed with all of these opinions! He said that the affirmative action provision was like a meta-principle embodying the equality section's transformative goals.[41] The section should be read substantively, not technically.[42] This reasoning resembled that of Moseneke. Sachs even relied on Justice Thurgood Marshall's dissent from the U.S. Supreme Court's *Richmond v. J.A. Croson Co.*[43] decision striking down an affirmative action plan for Richmond's municipal contracts.

Sachs, however, also agreed with Mokgoro and Ngcobo stating, "It is important to ensure that the process of achieving equity is conducted in such a way that the baby of non-racialism is not thrown out with the bath-water of remedial action."[44] He elaborated on this concept:

> If the measure at issue is manifestly overbalanced in ignoring or trampling on the interests of members of the advantaged section of the community, and gratuitously and flagrantly imposes disproportionate burdens on them, the courts have a duty to interfere.[45]

The Constitutional Court's willingness to protect whites is evident in these concurrences. Does Justice Moseneke's opinion upholding the plan nonetheless show the Court's commitment to social transformation? One could argue the answer is yes given the majority's broad language about reparations and about the state's obligation to move forward with affirmative action. The problem, though, is that the group receiving smaller pensions over a five-year period already had other vested pension benefits. That burdened group therefore hardly suffered much or needed significant judicial protection as the concurrences stated.

The Motala Decision

The South African affirmative action case most similar to U.S. decisions is *Motala v. University of Natal.*[46] In 1995, the Supreme Court of Durban upheld the university's medical faculty policy that limited to forty the number of Indian students who could be admitted. The Court noted,

---

[40] Par. 131.
[41] Par. 139.
[42] Par. 146.
[43] 488 U.S. 469 (1989).
[44] Van Heerden, Par. 137.
[45] Par. 152.
[46] 1995 (3) BCLR 374 (D); 1995 SACLR Lexis 256. For reference to some other lower court cases, *see* Saras Jagwanth, "Affirmative Action in a Transformative Context: The South African Experience," 36 Conn. L. Rev. 725 (2004).

"More black, coloured, and white students would be expected" and that "over the years many Indian doctors had qualified at the medical faculty of the University of Natal and relatively, not many blacks and coloureds had qualified. It was therefore the faculty policy to admit more blacks and coloured students."[47] Fathima Motala was rejected even though African students with poorer grades were admitted. The case was decided one year after apartheid's demise and under the Interim Constitution's affirmative action provision.[48]

Judge Hurt upheld the quota policy: "While there is no doubt whatsoever that the Indian group was decidedly disadvantaged by the apartheid system, the evidence before me establishes clearly that the degree of disadvantage to which African pupils were subjected under the system of education was significantly greater than that suffered by their Indian counterparts."[49]

This decision seems to support transformation more than those of the Constitutional Court. Judge Hurt's analysis, though brief, is sophisticated enough to account for the distinctive histories of two minority groups, rather than treating them the same.[50] However, the case's transformative potential is limited because it pitted one historically disadvantaged group against another, not the ideal solution to apartheid's legacy. Moreover, Judge Hurt failed to "focus on the second requirement of the affirmative action clause and satisfy itself that the programme is rational and carefully constructed so as to achieve equality."[51] Another scholar said the opinion did not sufficiently respect Ms. Motala's dignity interest.[52]

Statutory Provisions

South Africa's most important affirmative action provisions are contained in statutes as specified by section 9(4) of the Constitution: "National

---

[47] Motala, Lexis *14.

[48] Section 8(3)(a) of the 1994 Interim Constitution said, "This section shall not preclude measures designed to achieve the adequate protection and advancement of persons or groups or categories of persons disadvantaged by unfair discrimination, in order to enable their full and equal enjoyment of all rights and freedoms." The reference to "shall not preclude" is less affirmative than the 1996 Constitution's section 9(2) quoted previously in the text.

[49] Motala, Lexis *28.   [50] Jagwanth, *supra* n. 46 at 740.

[51] Currie *supra* n. 5 at 267.

[52] Karthy Govender, *Section 9:* "Response to the paper on the Right to Equality prepared by Professors Albertyn and Goldblatt " at the CLOSA conference on the 29th March 2006, <http://www.chr.up.ac.za/closa/> (last visited 6/20/2007).

legislation must be enacted to prevent or prohibit unfair discrimination." The preamble to the Promotion of Equality and Prevention of Unfair Discrimination Act of 2000 (Equality Act) holds that section 9 of the Constitution "implies the advancement, by special legal and other measures, of historically disadvantaged individuals, communities and social groups who were dispossessed of their land and resources, deprived of their human dignity and who continue to endure the consequences." Other Equality Act provisions require that the state remedy persistent inequality.

One relevant case testing these provisions is making its way through the courts[53]: *Katapodis and Forum of Black Journalists*.[54] In April 2008, the Forum of Black Journalists (FBJ) hosted an off-the-record speech given by ANC President Jacob Zuma from which whites were excluded. A complaint was lodged with the South African Human Rights Commission (SAHRC), which decided that the FBJ could not constitutionally exclude white journalists so long as those whites supported its goals. The SAHRC decided that overt racial exclusion policies had to meet a heavy burden. Even though the FBJ wanted to create a "safe space" for the historically oppressed black media, the SAHRC pointed out that the Black Lawyers Association still admitted sympathetic white members. Such a goal-sharing requirement would be a less restrictive alternative under the Equality Act than excluding by race.

Thus, the SAHRC ruled for the white complainants. This decision raises difficult questions on how to balance the right to associate, affirmative action, and prohibitions on discrimination. Nonetheless, it is consistent with the Court's concern for whites in affirmative action cases. Pierre de Vos thinks the SAHRC was right for important reasons.[55] Yet, the decision seems all too consistent with a surprisingly nontransformative approach to racial reparations. It is a bit reminiscent of the U.S. Supreme Court's decisions, to be discussed later, which reject racial quotas but allow race to be one among several factors to consider in university admissions. This kind of formalism seems ill suited for the South African model but the case is undoubtedly a hard one.

[53] PJM, "'Blacks Only' Briefing Splits South Africa Media," Reuters, April 20, 2008, http://www.reuterslink.org/news/Race.htm (last visited April 22, 2008).

[54] Case Reference No.: GP/2008/0161/L BIOS, http://www.sahrc.org.za/sahrc_cms/downloads/Katopodis_FBJ_finding.pdf (last visited April 16, 2008).

[55] Pierre de Vos, "Racial Exclusive Organizations Revisited...," Constitutionally Speaking (blog), April 10, 2008, http://constitutionallyspeaking.co.za/?p=518 (last visited April 16, 2008).

Further Thoughts

How should one best explain the South African Constitutional Court's cautiousness? Perhaps the Court believed it was simply adhering to the rule of law. When asked, most judges respond that they are doing the best they can in interpreting the Constitution, statutes, case law, and other available materials to render legally "correct" decisions.[56] Hopefully the decisions are also sensible and just, as demanded by the post-apartheid era.

Yet, academics are less sanguine about the ability of the courts to render sensible and just decisions. Gerald Rosenberg[57] and, more recently, Ran Hirschl argue that courts render decisions that protect "hegemonic interests."[58] Hirschl says that the South African Constitutional Court has been hesitant to allow dramatic change because it wants to ensure that affirmative action does not seriously injure the vested interests of wealthy whites. And David Benatar, a professor and chair of the Department of Philosophy at the University of Cape Town, gave his 2007 inaugural lecture on the topic, "Affirmative Action Not the Way to Tackle Injustice."[59]

How could the Court respond to this charge? Given apartheid's brutal history, perhaps the most radical thing the new Court has done was adhere to the rule of law even when affirmative remedies are sought. Etienne Mureinik famously said that the new Constitution was a bridge to a culture of justification, not to *ipse dixit.*[60]

Moreover, social reconciliation is among South Africa's major goals, rather than revenge or Nuremburg-style prosecutions. The Truth & Reconciliation Commission was the country's most internationally prominent

---

[56] *See generally* Jefferson Powell, Cotitutional Conscience: The Moral Dimension of Judicial Decisionmaking (2008). *But see* Richard Posner, How Judges Think (2008) (arguing that judicial decision making is largely political and that the best that judges can do is "constrained pragmatism").

[57] The Hollow Hope (1991).   [58] Toward Juristocracy 214 (2004).

[59] David Benatar, "Affirmative Action Not the Way to Tackle Injustice," ever-fasternews. com, <http://www.ever-fasternews.com/index.php?php_action=read_article&article_id=376> (last visited June 20, 2008) (referring to the "whole affirmative action enterprise" and asserting that "the architects of affirmative action in South Africa have done their best to insulate it from legal challenge").

[60] Etienne Mureinik, "A Bridge to Where? Introducing the Bill of Rights," 10 S. Afr. J. Hum. Rts. 31, 32: "If the new Constitution is a bridge away from a culture of authority, it is clear what it must be a bridge to. It must lead to a *culture of justification* – a culture in which every exercise of power is expected to be justified. . . . If the Constitution is to be a bridge in this direction, it is plain that the Bill of Rights must be its chief strut." (emphasis in original)

institution as the nation underwent transition. Its forgiveness theme had distinctly religious roots.[61]

The South African concept of *ubuntu*, discussed in Chapter 3 on the death penalty, promotes social harmony and inclusion, rather than punishment.[62] Certainly, the Court would be acting consistently with notions of reconciliation and the rule of law by ensuring that affirmative action does not amount to revenge against whites. The tragic history of vengeful actions in African politics is a cautionary lesson, especially with a neighbor like Zimbabwe. Thus, perhaps the most radical act the government and the Court could take was to include whites in the new nation.

Hirschl might then respond that such an approach promotes economic stability and judicialization.[63] It therefore serves the interests of the neoliberal institutions such as the International Monetary Fund and World Bank, as well as wealthy South Africans. Its effect is disappointing, not transformational.

One other interpretation is that the Court's decisions only reflect a narrow band of cases and that affirmative action is actually widespread throughout the nation and causing great discomfort to whites. Judge Edwin Cameron has indeed asserted that the legislature has been dominant in this area and fairly "wide-reaching."[64]

A recent development may support Judge Cameron's assertion. The Transvaal High Court entered an order in June 2008 declaring that South African Chinese people shall be defined as black people for the purposes of South Africa's affirmative action legislation, This order was entered once the government agreed to settle a lawsuit brought by the South African Chinese Association, which claimed that the apartheid regime had discriminated terribly against the Chinese. This extraordinary court order, which received international attention, reflects a nation that is serious about legislating affirmative remedies.[65]

---

[61] Desmond Tutu, No Future without Forgiveness (1999); Charles Villa-Valencio, A Theology of Reconstruction, Nation Building and Human Rights (1992). There have been, however, numerous criticisms of the truth and reconciliation process in South Africa.

[62] Tutu, *id.* at 54–55, Makwanyane, Par. 224 (Langa, concurring) (discussing the communitarian qualities of the *ubuntu* ethos). For an interesting critique of the *ubuntu* ideal as being "a romanticized version of an African traditional past," *see* Eleni Coundouriotis, "The Dignity of the "Unfittest": Victim's Stories in South Africa," 28 Hum. Rts. Q. 842, 867 (2006).

[63] Hirschl, *supra* n. 58 at 192.

[64] E-mail from Judge Cameron to Prof. Mark Kende, June 13, 2008 (on file with author).

[65] BBC News, "S Africa Chinese 'become black,'" June 18, 2008, http://news.bbc.co.uk/go/pr/fr/-/2/hi/africa/7461099 (last visited June 20, 2008).

U.S. SUPREME COURT JURISPRUDENCE

Affirmative action initially was implemented in the United States via the use of presidential executive orders designed to redress discrimination against blacks.[66] The U.S. Supreme Court, however, has generally prohibited affirmative action plans for broad social purposes. Surprisingly, promoting First Amendment values seems more important than supporting equality norms. Indeed, white women have been the primary beneficiaries of affirmative action, not racial minorities.[67]

Supreme Court Affirmative Action Rulings

The judicial debate began in 1978 with the Court's divided decision in *Regents of California v. Bakke*.[68] Justice Lewis Powell authored the controlling opinion stating that courts should use strict scrutiny for racial affirmative action because such plans could stigmatize their beneficiaries (minorities) and also injure innocent victims (whites). He then said that the racial quotas at the University of California at Davis undermined the supposedly individualistic premises of American equality jurisprudence.

He rejected the university's argument that affirmative action admission policies could remedy societal discrimination against minorities, because such an approach could have no stopping point. Moreover, there was no proof that minority doctors would work in underserved minority communities. Powell, though, wrote that the university could use a student's race as one of several personal qualities to promote student body diversity as long as applicants were considered individually.[69] He said universities had special First Amendment protection to develop such criteria given

---

[66] President Kennedy issued Executive Order 10925 in 1961, which established the Equal Employment Opportunity Committee and required that federally financed projects "take affirmative action" to ensure there is no bias. President Johnson in 1965 gave a celebrated speech at Howard University saying that affirmative action was needed to provide equal opportunity, given that society had held blacks in chains for years. He then sounded like a South African Constitutional Court Justice when he said, "We seek...not just equality as a right and a theory, but equality as a fact and as a result." That is substantive equality. In 1967, President Johnson issued the famous Executive Order 11246, which still requires affirmative action in federally funded contracts. Borgna Brunner, "Timeline of Affirmative Action Milestones," Infoplease, http://www.infoplease.com/spot/affirmativetimeline1.html (last visited July 11, 2007).

[67] African American Policy Forum, "Focus on Affirmative Action," http://www.aapf.org/focus/episodes/oct30.php (last visited April 22, 2008) (referring to the 1995 Department of Labor study drawing this conclusion).

[68] 438 U.S. 265 (1978).   [69] *Id.* at 311 & 315.

their role in the spreading of diverse ideas.[70] Interestingly, Justice Ginsburg pointed out that some of Justice Powell's key reasoning was based on South African research about education.[71]

In 2003, Justice Sandra Day O'Connor embaced this reasoning in *Grutter v. Bollinger*,[72] when she upheld the University of Michigan Law School's affirmative action plan for admitting students.[73] She supposedly applied strict scrutiny, found that diversity was a compelling justification, and concluded that the plan was tailored to permit individualistic consideration in which racial diversity is only a plus, not a quota. The law school looked beyond race to other student qualities and talents.

Justice O'Connor also wrote that the Court should "defer" to the law school's assessment of its educational mission.[74] She invoked the academic freedom and corresponding First Amendment rationales mentioned by Justice Powell to support this deference.[75] Moreover, she stated, "Narrow tailoring does not require exhaustion of every conceivable race-neutral alternative."[76]

She found that an admissions lottery was not feasible as that would abandon "all other educational values."[77] She acknowledged that a few states had adopted percentage plans for admitting undergraduates (for example, guaranteeing admission of the top 10 percent in each high-school class to a state university), but reasoned that it was unclear how

---

[70] *Id.* at 312.

[71] Justice Ruth Bader Ginsburg, "*Brown v. Board of Education* in International Context," 36 Colum. Hum. Rts. L. Rev. 493, 498 (Justice Powell quoted from an earlier opinion by former U.S. Supreme Court Justice Felix Frankfurter. Frankfurter drew from a 1957 "statement of a conference of senior scholars from the University of Cape Town and the University of Witswatersrand. The South African scholars were reacting to the then South African government's proposal to enforce racial apartheid in educational institutions.")

[72] 539 U.S. 306 (2003). On the same day, however, the Court struck down the University of Michigan's undergraduate admissions affirmative action plan as being too much like a quota in not providing sufficient individualized consideration of students. Gratz v. Bollinger, 539 U.S. 244 (2003).

[73] For a first-rate biography, *see* Joan Biskupic, Sandra Day O'Connor: How the First Woman on the Supreme Court Became its Most Influential Justice (2005).

[74] *Grutter*, 539 U.S. at 328.

[75] *Id.* at 329.   [76] *Id.* at 339.

[77] Id. at 340. Michigan Law School is known as one of the best schools in the country because of the quality of its faculty, resources, and entering student credentials (GPA and LSAT). Certainly this institutional reputation would be at risk if the law school could not take account of student academic caliber. Justice Clarence Thomas in dissent said that color blindness was more important than being an elite law school. Thus, Michigan cannot have it both ways.

that policy would translate to professional schools. Moreover neither lotteries nor 10 percent plans guranteed that the law school would assess applicants individually.[78]

She also explained the benefits of diversity in more detail than Powell. She agreed with the University of Michigan Law School that diversity required a "critical mass" of minorities in the classroom to be more than tokenistic[79] and that diversity would promote "cross-racial under-standing" by breaking down stereotypes. Classroom discussion would be "more enlightening" with students from various backgrounds.[80]

Justice O'Connor took special note of amicus briefs filed by separate coalitions of business and military leaders.[81] She elaborated that students are graduating into an "increasingly diverse workforce and society."[82] She wrote, "Major American businesses have made clear that the skills needed in today's increasingly global marketplace can only be developed through exposure to widely diverse people, cultures, ideas, and view-points."[83] To put it bluntly, affirmative action is good for business. This reflects a pragmatic approach.

She then relied on the military brief's argument that elite institu-tions, such as the service academies, must maintain race-based policies to ensure a diverse, highly qualified military.[84] Affirmative action is good for national defense. She also pointed out that "universities, and in par-ticular, law schools, represent the training ground for a large number of our nation's leaders."[85] Affirmative action is therefore also good for the nation's elites. She said that such plans should be temporary, subject to regular review, and, one would hope, be unnecessary after twenty-five years.[86]

There are also significant affirmative action cases in the government contracting area. Perhaps the most well known is *Adarand Construc-tors, Inc. v. Pena*,[87] in which the Supreme Court used strict scrutiny to strike down a congressional preference for minority construction contrac-tors. Justice O'Connor announced that three principles govern affirmative action cases: skepticism (strict scrutiny), consistency (no matter whether the burdened group is white or black), and congruence (federal affirma-tive action receives the same scrutiny as state affirmative action despite section 5 of the Fourteenth Amendment). These three principles are far more sceptical of affirmative action than Justice Moseneke's three factors.

[78] *Id.*
[80] *Id.* at 330.
[82] *Id.*
[84] *Id.* at 331.
[86] *Id.* at 343.

[79] *Id.* at 333.
[81] *Id.* at 330–31.
[83] *Id.* at 330.
[85] *Id.* at 332.
[87] 515 U.S. 200 (1995).

In *Richmond v. J.A. Croson Co.*,[88] the Court said that strict scrutiny could only be satisfied if the affirmative action plan was narrowly tailored to precisely remedy the city's prior discrimination against a group of contractors. Cities must say *mea culpa*. The plans also had to have a waiver, could not use quotas, and had to be temporary. This left open a tiny door for remedial affirmative action.

The U.S. Supreme Court's most recent affirmative action-type case, *Parents Involved v. Seattle School District*,[89] was decided in 2007. The Court issued a divided 5–4 ruling that voluntary race-based assignments of children in grades K–12 are unconstitutional. Chief Justice John Roberts said that *Brown v. Board of Education*[90] required districts to be color-blind absent *de jure* segregation. His opinion distinguished *Grutter* as involving universities.[91] Roberts also said that the Louisville and Seattle public school plans only took account of a student's race, not other personal qualities. This was impermissible racial balancing, not the promotion of real diversity.[92] Four Justices disagreed, with Justices Breyer and Stevens authoring dissenting opinions.

Justice Kennedy's separate opinion, however, is likely controlling in a strikingly similar way to Justice Powell's opinion in *Bakke*. Kennedy said that these plans unconstitutionally singled out race. However, the districts could achieve similar goals in other ways:

> School boards may pursue the goal of bringing together students of diverse backgrounds and races through other means, including strategic site selection of new schools, drawing attendance zones with general recognition of the demographics of neighborhoods; allocating resources for special programs; recruiting students and faculty in a targeted fashion; and tracking enrollments, performance, and other statistics by race. These mechanisms are race conscious but do not lead to different treatment based on a classification that tells each student he or she is to be defined by race, so it is unlikely any of them would demand strict scrutiny to be found permissible.[93]

---

[88] 488 U.S. 469 (1989).

[89] 2007 WL 1836531 (U.S. 2007).

[90] 347 U.S. 483 (1954).

[91] Parents Involved, *supra* n. 89 *14 ("This Court relied upon considerations unique to institutions of higher education, noting that in light of the expansive freedoms of speech and thought associated with the university environment, universities occupy a special niche in our constitutional tradition" and emphasizing "the unique context of higher education.")

[92] *Id.* *13 ("In the present cases, by contrast, race is not considered as part of a broader effort to achieve exposure to widely diverse people, culture, ideas, and viewpoints.... Race, for some students, is determinative standing alone.")

[93] *46.

There is much debate about how the lower courts will interpret these criteria because they require school districts to walk a tight rope between acceptable diversity and unacceptable balancing.

There are several problems with the Supreme Court's reasoning in these cases.

Symmetry

First, it is bizarre to see Justice O'Connor in *Grutter* invoke strict scrutiny to treat integration efforts the same as prejudicial acts excluding minorities.[94] Chief Justice Roberts elaborated in *Parents Involved* that motive should not influence the level of scrutiny,[95] yet he also said that "a politics of racial hostility" is not permitted.[96]

In his dissent, Justice Breyer criticized the Court's symmetry requirement by noting, "Law is not an exercise in mathematical logic."[97] Lesser scrutiny should be used in the integration context.[98] Moreover, Congress's creation of the Freedman's Bureau to help the newly freed slaves shows that the Fourteenth Amendment supports affirmative measures, substantive equality, and group rights.[99] Charles Black has also written about this subject.[100] The arguments in support of racial preferences are especially powerful in *Parents Involved* because even those students who "lose" still attend school and receive an education. Unlike affirmative action, there is no real injury here.

Moreover, it is Orwellian for the Court to read *Brown* as forbidding voluntary efforts by schools to achieve racial integration. Chief Justice Roberts nonetheless supported his position by quoting from the oral argument by *Brown* lawyer Robert Carter.[101] Yet, Carter is currently a

---

[94] Grutter, *supra* n. 72.

[95] Parents Involved, *supra* n. 89 *24.

[96] *Id.* *27. Roberts' echoing of Justice O'Connor's concerns about the Richmond City Council's racial makeup is odd because the Seattle and Louisville school districts were apparently not run by black majorities. Ironically, despite this formalism, Chief Justice Roberts actually says that "context" supports the analogy to *Croson.* *14.

[97] *72.

[98] *75 ("In my view, this contextual approach to scrutiny is altogether fitting. I believe that the law requires application here of a standard of review that is not strict in the traditional sense of that word.")

[99] *70.

[100] A New Birth of Freedom, Human Rights Named, and Unnamed (1997). *See also* George P. Fletcher, The Secret Constitution: How Lincoln Redefined American Democracy 183–87 (2001). Jack Balkin has taken similar positions.

[101] Parents Involved *27.

senior federal district judge who broke with judicial etiquette to announce that Roberts was incorrect.[102]

Inconsistency

In addition, the Court's supposed symmetrical use of strict scrutiny is a sham, raising other problems. Justice O'Connor actually employed reduced scrutiny in *Grutter* by deferring to the university and by stating that the law school did not need to use the least restrictive alternative. This was intermediate scrutiny.

Indeed, the Supreme Court is notorious for its plethora of scrutiny levels despite stating there are only three.[103] The situation is so bad that in *Lawrence v. Texas*,[104] the Court's famous gay rights decision, Justice Kennedy struck down a law banning homosexual sodomy without clarifying the level of scrutiny.[105] Thus, the U.S. Supreme Court ends up with the worst of both worlds compared to South Africa. Its inconsistent ad hoc approach promotes neither the rule of law nor social progress.

Moreover, Justice O'Connor's figure for the length of time that affirmative action would need to be in effect, twenty-five years. comes out of thin air.[106] The obstacle course the Court has now established for schools to voluntarily integrate is daunting. Instead, the Court entrenches white

[102] Opinion, "Post-desegregation: Supreme Court Ruling Sets a New Tone on Issues of Race, but It Will Take More Time and Cases to Clarify What It Means," Cleveland Plains Dealer, 2007 WLNR 12504712 (July 1, 2007) ("Yet Robert L. Carter, the attorney who actually spoke those words... insisted last week that the majority's interpretation of Brown amounted to a perversion of history.")

[103] *See e.g.* Suzanne Goldberg, "Equality without Tiers," 77 S. Cal. L. Rev. 481 (2004).

[104] 539 U.S. 558 (2003).

[105] Numerous scholars have debated what level of scrutiny was employed. *See e.g.* Mark Strasser, "Monogamy, Licentiousness, Desuetude and Mere Tolerance: The Multiple Misinterpretations of Lawrence v. Texas," 15 S. Cal Rev. L. & Women's Studies. 95 (2005).

[106] There are some interesting theories about this. Jeffrey Rosen apparently attended a meeting between some visiting Indian Supreme Court Justices and several U.S. Justices that included O'Connor. Rosen says that when the Indian Justices discussed how affirmative action worked in their country and said it had no time limit, Justice O'Connor made a face that seemed to show displeasure. Clark Cunningham, "After Grutter Things Get Interesting! The American Debate over Affirmative Action is Finally Ready for Some Fresh Ideas from Abroad," 36 Conn. L. Rev. 665, 667 n. 13 (2004). Moreover, given her view that the Court should utilize international and comparative materials, she could have known that the international conventions on affirmative action say such programs should be temporary.

privilege above all other considerations.[107] Justice O'Connor's emphasis on how affirmative action serves the business and military communities reflects this result. Indeed, the Roberts opinion's prominent discussion of the burden placed on two white children by the Seattle and Louisville plans contains no room for a similar narrative regarding black children affected by racial discrimination. This deference gives credence to Ran Hirschl's theory.[108]

The First Amendment

In the end, the U.S. Supreme Court's limited tolerance for affirmative action mainly promotes the First Amendment, not equality. Thus, according to *Grutter* and *People Involved*, affirmative action only receives deference when carried out by higher education institutions seeking to promote diversity and the exchange of ideas. Free speech is the Court's core value here.

This free speech emphasis is consistent with America's generally libertarian views about expression compared to the more restrictive approach taken by some other countries. But it is a surprising reading of what should have been a revolutionary Fourteenth Amendment.[109] One imagines Gerald Rosenberg saying, "I told you so."

One response to this thesis might be that the diversity rationale should be read as broadening civil democracy. Having people of different colors and backgrounds in elite positions promotes greater equality. This is

---

[107] *See* Daria Rothmayr, "Tacking Left: A Radical Critique of Grutter," 21 Const. Commen. 191, 207 (2004) ("Finally, the decision in Grutter appears to serve white interests more than it does the interests of communities of color. The diversity rationale symbolically reproduces racial inequality by prioritizing white interests. In addition, the Court's opinion endorses meritocracy as a compelling governmental interest, notwithstanding the fact that constitutional meritocratic standards privilege white applicants and exclude people of color. Diversity-oriented affirmative action also conceals the racially disparate impact of conventional admissions standards, and permits institutions to represent such a process as neutral and fair.") It is necessary to mention that scholars such as Michael Klarman and Mary Dudziak have shown how even the *Brown* decision served the interests of white elites in certain ways.

[108] *Id.* For a similar view from someone with a very different political perspective than Hirschl, *see* Robert Delahunty, "Constitutional Justice or Constitutional Peace: The Supreme Court and Affirmative Action" *forthcoming* Wash. & Lee L. Rev. (2007), http://papers.ssrn.com/abstract=993632 at 60 (last visited July 16, 2007).

[109] At least one noted scholar has argued that the primary function of *Brown* was expressive, to send a message that racial stigmatizing is not permitted. Charles Lawrence, "If He Hollers Let Him Go: Regulating Racist Speech on Campus," 1990 Duke L.J. 491. He argues that *Brown* was really about regulating racist speech.

certainly one explanation for why even the limited affirmative action in the United States is still worth supporting. But this justification ultimately promotes the efficient running of society rather than the redistribution of resources to the poor. It certainly does not suggest a great obligation on the part of white Americans to sacrifice for their historically oppressed fellow community members.

CONCLUSION

Comparing affirmative action in South Africa and the United States is difficult because fundamentally different purposes are being served. It is remedial in South Africa, whereas it facilitates free speech, meritocracy, and the marketplace in the United States.[110] Even the brief South African discussion of diversity celebrates the rainbow of humanity there, not stronger national defense as in the *Grutter* military brief. Perhaps South African remedial efforts in this area are actually most analogous to the American slave reparations cases, rather than American affirmative action policies, though the reparations cases have not been successful.

There is some similarity between the two juristocracies in that both have reined in affirmative action somewhat, with the U.S. Supreme Court to a greater degree. One glimmer of hope is that some Supreme Court Justices are influenced by international and comparative law in their cases, such as Justice Ginsburg's concurrence in *Grutter*. The U.S. Supreme Court's affirmative action approach is not consistent with various international human rights conventions,[111] but it will probably take many years for these international precedents to change the Supreme Court's approach, assuming there are also some favorable personnel changes. One hopes by then, in agreement with Justice O'Connor, that the underlying problem will be solved.

---

[110] It's worth pointing out that the Constitutional Court members seem to share many of the transformation values, unlike the seriously divided U.S. Supreme Court.

[111] *See generally* Stanley A. Halpin, "Looking over a Crowd and Picking Your Friends: Civil Rights and the Debate over the Influence of Foreign and International Human Rights Law on the Interpretation of the U.S. Constitution," 30 Hastings Int'l & Comp. L. Rev. 1, 22–39 (2006) (discussing how international conventions signed by the United States support temporary affirmative action policies that can be both backward and forward looking, which certainly covers remedial efforts, and these documents can also be interpreted to cover diversity-based affirmative action). Justice Ginsburg cites to these international sources in *Grutter* to support affirmative action going beyond diversity as the only compelling interest. 539 U.S. at 344.

This brings us back to the question bedeviling the South African Constitutional Court: What kinds of programs should be defined as affirmative action for purposes of their Constitution? My answer is that the Court should stay away from the U.S. Supreme Court's formalism. Affirmative action should be defined broadly and flexibly, as in the recent South African example involving the Chinese. Certainly, the apartheid victims deserve as much.

7

Freedom of Expression

The First Amendment to the U.S. Constitution is heralded domestically and abroad for protecting freedom of speech and thus promoting democracy, individual self-realization, and the search for truth. This assessment is well justified especially when the United States is compared to authoritarian regimes. One scholar, however, describes the U.S. Supreme Court's First Amendment doctrine as "arbitrary and unpersuasive."[1] Another writes that it "resemb[les] the Ptolemaic system of astronomy in its last days."[2]

In particular, the Court has divided speech into "protected" and "unprotected" categories.[3] The Court maintains that laws restricting protected expression, based on the speech's content, must be viewed with great skepticism.[4] Yet, the Court has actually ignored content discrimination in some cases. It has instead used a relaxed scrutiny level and then concluded that the speaker's interest is outweighed by the state's interest. The Court has also on other occasions ignored its usual categorical speech divisions.

In this chapter, I recommend that the U.S. Supreme Court stop the formalism and the inconsistencies. Actually, I go a step farther and argue that the Supreme Court should borrow a page from the way foreign

---

[1] Steven J. Heyman, "Spheres of Autonomy: Reforming the Content Neutrality Doctrine in First Amendment Jurisprudence, "10 Wm. & Mary Bill Rts. J. 647, 652 (2002).

[2] Eric M. Freedman, "A Lot More Comes into Focus When You Remove the Lens Cap: Why Proliferating New Communication Technologies Make It Particularly Urgent for the Supreme Court to Abandon Its Inside-Out Approach to Freedom of Speech and Bring Obscenity, Fighting Words, and Group Libel within the First Amendment," 81 Iowa L. Rev. 883, 885 (1996).

[3] Id.

[4] Police Dep't of the City of Chicago v. Mosley, 408 U.S. 92 (1972).

courts, such as the South African Constitutional Court, have explicitly weighed interests and values while also being minimalist when possible.

This chapter has four parts. The first part discusses key U.S. Supreme Court cases establishing the speech categories and the rule against content discrimination. The second part shows how the Supreme Court has been inconsistent in its treatment of unprotected speech and of content discrimination. The third section shows how the South African Constitutional Court has resolved its most important speech cases, and shows what the U.S. Supreme Court can learn from this approach.[5] This is not to say that South Africa has all the answers. The final part examines the problems that South African media freedom faces in the "real world" outside the Constitutional Court. For this purpose, it examines the controversy over a South African newspaper's republication of cartoon drawings of the Muslim prophet Muhammad, as well as several other disputes.

My conclusion is that American free speech doctrine has inconsistency and candor problems, but free speech in South Africa is more limited and fragile in various respects.

SUPREME COURT CATEGORIES OF SPEECH

The U.S. Supreme Court has a categorical approach to speech. Several kinds of expression are unprotected including obscenity, fighting words, incitement, threats, child pornography, and libel.[6] The Supreme Court decisions establishing these categories balanced the speaker's versus the state's interests and tried to provide clear rules for the future. This is categorical or definitional balancing, as opposed to ad hoc case-by-case balancing.[7]

---

[5] A noted Canadian scholar, David Beatty, wrote The Ultimate Rule of Law (2004), a book about proportionality analysis in a global context The book, however, does not focus on freedom of expression issues. *See also* William Funk, "Intimidation and the Internet," 110 Penn. St. L. Rev. 579 (2006) (arguing that balancing should have been used to resolve a noteworthy free speech case regarding an anti-abortion Web site that contained veiled threats against abortion providers, because traditional First Amendment categories did not easily apply). I should mention that I have used the terms "weighing" of interests and "balancing" of interests interchangeably throughout the book, even though weighing may be slightly more precise. A possible connotation of balancing is binary: one interest being compared with another. Weighing perhaps more clearly signals that multiple interests may be assessed. But at the end of the day, I do not share the binary interpretation of balancing so I use that term as well.

[6] Erwin Chemerinsky, Constitutional Law 1150 (2005).

[7] T. Alexander Aleinikoff, "Constitutional Law in the Age of Balancing," 96 Yale L. J. 943 (1987).

Thus, in *Miller v. California*,[8] the Court adopted a three-part obscenity test:

(a) whether the average person, applying contemporary community standards would find that the work, taken as a whole, appeals to the prurient interest

(a) whether the work depicts or describes, in a patently offensive way, sexual conduct specifically defined by the applicable state law

(b) whether the work taken as a whole lacks serious literary, artistic, political, or scientific value[9]

The Court made clear that this test only applied to "hard-core" sexual content.[10] The focus was on community morality.

In *Paris Adult Theaters v. Slaton*,[11] the Court determined that even consenting adults lacked a First Amendment right to view obscene material at an establishment when no children were present. The Court pointed to "the interest of the public in the quality of life, and the total community environment, the tone of commerce in the great city centers, and possibly, the public safety itself."[12]

In addition, the Court explained that the state legislature could assume that "commerce in obscene books, or public exhibitions focused on obscene conduct, [would] have a tendency to exert a corrupting and debasing impact leading to anti-social behavior," given the universal belief that exposure to classic works of art, literature, and theater ennobled the soul.[13] The Court also said it owed deference to the state legislature. Utimately, the Court's reasoning had a Puritan quality.

In *Chaplinsky v. New Hampshire*,[14] the Court upheld the conviction of a man for calling a police officer a fascist and a damned racketeer. The Court said this speech amounted to unprotected fighting words: "face to face words plainly likely to cause a breach of the peace by the addressee." Such words could cause concrete harms. Moreover, the Court reasoned that there was no exposition of ideas and that such words had little value in determining truth.

Another category of unprotected speech is incitement. In *Brandenburg v. Ohio*,[15] the Supreme Court addressed the constitutionality of a law that banned the advocacy of illegal activity. The case involved the prosecution

---

[8] 413 U.S. 15 (1973).

[9] *Id.* at 24.

[10] *Id.* at 27.

[11] 413 U.S. 49 (1973).

[12] *Id.* at 58.

[13] *Id.* at 63.

[14] 315 U.S. 568 (1942).

[15] 395 U.S. 444 (1969).

of those who led a small Ku Klux Klan gathering. The Court ruled that the law impermissibly permitted prosecution for abstract advocacy. The state could not "forbid or proscribe advocacy of the use of force or of law violation except where such advocacy is directed to inciting or producing imminent lawless action and is likely to incite or produce such action."

A law that bans protected speech, in contrast to obscenity, fighting words, or incitement, receives strict scrutiny.[16] The law must be narrowly tailored to promote a compelling governmental interest. No less restrictive alternatives should be available. Few laws satisfy strict scrutiny because government should not be able to pick and choose favored topics. The only thing worse than content discrimination is viewpoint discrimination in which the government actually outlaws one side of an argument. This kind of ideological bias is almost never permitted.

Some laws do not ban speech, but act as time, place, and manner restrictions. Because the speech still has an outlet, such laws do not get strict scrutiny. The laws must simply further an important governmental interest, must not be content discriminatory, and must provide real alternative avenues of communication.[17]

Interestingly, nonobscene sexually explicit speech supposedly receives the same protection as high-quality political speech. For example, in *Young v. American Mini Theaters*,[18] the Court examined the constitutionality of a law zoning adult establishments that provide sexually indecent entertainment. Justice Stevens favored relaxed scrutiny. He wrote in a plurality opinion that, "Few of us would march our sons and daughters off to war to watch unspecified sexual activities." Stevens could not obtain a majority.

Similarly, in *FCC v. Pacifica*,[19] Stevens reasoned that a radio broadcast of George Carlin's "Seven Dirty Words" comedy monologue was of low value because there was no exposition of ideas. Thus, the First Amendment interest was outweighed by the social interest in public order and morality, particularly because a child was exposed to the monologue while with his father in a car. Justice Powell agreed with the result but not with Stevens' low-value characterization. Powell wrote, "This is a judgment for each person to make, not one for the judges to impose upon him." Stevens therefore again could not secure a majority for strict scrutiny.

---

[16] Chemerinsky, *supra* note 6 at 1057 ("Content-based discrimination must meet strict scrutiny, and the Court has recently indicated that content-based distinctions within these categories must also meet strict scrutiny.")

[17] City of Erie v. Pap's A.M., 529 U.S. 277 (2000).

[18] 427 U.S. 50 (1976).   [19] 438 U.S. 726 (1978).

Thus, the Court has ostensibly been serious about the "protected" versus "unprotected" speech distinction and about using strict scrutiny when there is content discrimination even in cases where the interests of children are at stake like *Pacifica*.

THE OTHER FIRST AMENDMENT

There is another First Amendment in addition to the one just discussed. This other First Amendment does not stick with categories and rigid scrutiny levels[20] but is kept hidden by the Court.[21] This section discusses the cases embracing this other First Amendment.

The RAV *Decision*

In *RAV v. St. Paul*,[22] the U.S. Supreme Court struck down an ordinance designed to penalize hate speech, such as cross burning, even though the Minnesota Supreme Court had construed the law as only covering racist fighting words. The U.S. Supreme Court determined that the law was impermissibly content and viewpoint discriminatory because other fighting words were permitted.

The *RAV* decision throws a monkey wrench into the Court's speech dichotomy. Though fighting words are unprotected, racist fighting words are protected. *RAV* suggests that the crucial question is content discrimination and that the categories can be overridden.[23] Lower federal courts

---

[20] *Supra* note 7 (scholarship supporting balancing).

[21] The issue of the U.S. Supreme Court stating that it adheres to precedent or to a previously established standard, when it actually does not, resurfaced in 2007 on several occasions. For example, the Court's ruling against the use of race in school assignments in Parents Involved v. Seattle School District, 2007 WL 1836531 (U.S. 2007) is hard to reconcile with its ruling allowing affirmative action in Grutter v. Bollinger, 539 U.S. 306 (2003). And the Court's decision upholding a law against so-called partial birth abortions in Gonzales v. Carhart, 127 S.Ct. 1610 (2007) is hard to reconcile with its ruling striking down an almost identical law in Sternberg v. Carhart, 530 U.S. 914 (2000). Justice Scalia even accused Chief Justice Roberts of not being bold enough to admit that precedent was sometimes being overturned. Linda Greenhouse, "Supreme Court Memo: Even in Agreement, Scalia Puts Roberts to Lash," N.Y. Times, Sec. A Pg. 1 (June 28, 2007); Linda Greenhouse, "Supreme Court Memo: Precedents Begin Falling for Roberts Court," N.Y. Times, Sec. A Pg. 21 (June 21, 2007).

[22] 505 U.S. 377 (1992).

[23] Heyman, *supra* note 1 at 653 ("I argue that the courts' increasing reliance upon the content discrimination doctrine to resolve difficult First Amendment problems only obscures the crucial issues and leads to hypertechnical decisions that are inaccessible to the public."); Erwin Chemerinsky, "Content Neutrality as a Central Problem of Free Speech: Problems in the Supreme Court's Application," 74 S. Cal. L. Rev. 49, 51 (2000)

have used *RAV* to invalidate numerous hate speech codes at universities and elsewhere,[24] although some universities and other institutions have retained such codes.[25] Moreover the U.S. Supreme Court explicitly affirmed *RAV* in two more recent U.S. Supreme Court cases, but each seems to conflict with *RAV*.[26]

Justice Scalia also, had trouble reconciling his *RAV* analysis with several other First Amendment decisions. For example, federal law prohibits threatening the president of the United States. That law singles out only one type of threat, yet it has been found constitutional even though it seems to be viewpoint discriminatory.

Justice Scalia reasoned that the law can single out threats against the president because those are among the worst possible threats. The law was therefore not an example of impermissible discrimination, and it also preserved social stability. Yet this argument ignores that racist fighting words could cause urban riots and violence unlike other fighting words.

Then, Justice Scalia had to reconcile his approach with Title VII, the federal law prohibiting employment discrimination including workplace sexual harassment. Harassment can include offensive statements. Thus, Title VII can penalize workers or supervisors for making sexist statements but not other offensive comments. Justice Scalia reasoned that Title VII

("The principle of content neutrality has become the core of free speech analysis.") Heyman points out that this emphasis on content neutrality reflects the central tenets of the dominant liberal ideology. Heyman, *id.* at 657.

[24] *See, e.g.*, Robert M. O'Neill, "Bias, "Balance," and Beyond: New Threats to Academic Freedom," 77 U. Col. L. Rev. 985, 1006 (2006) (describing how virtually all university speech codes that have been challenged have been struck down as unconstitutional). *But see* Taunya Lovell Banks, "What is a Community? Group Rights and the Constitution: The Special Case of African Amricans," 1 Margins 51, 62 (2001) (suggesting some hate speech restrictions may survive *RAV*).

[25] There is a national organization that keeps track of remaining speech codes, and it often threatens to sue offending universities. *See, e.g.*, Samantha Harris, "Victory for Free Speech at Massachusetts College of Liberal Arts," http://www.the fire.org/index/php /article/7654.html/print Jan. 16, 2007 (last visited Jan. 21, 2007); Samantha Harris, "Speech Code of the Month: Fayetteville State University," http://www.thefire .org/index.php/article/7622.html/print Jan. 2, 2007 (last visited Jan. 21, 2007).

[26] Shortly after *RAV*, in Wisconsin v. Mitchell, 508 U.S. 476 (1993), the Supreme Court found it constitutional for a criminal penalty to be enhanced based on whether a racist motivation was involved. The Court said this was distinguishable because the underlying crime did not single out racist speech. Moreover, the Court said that the defendant's motive, or level of intent, often played a part in criminal sentencing. In Virginia v. Black, 538 U.S. 343 (2003), the Court ruled that it was constitutional to prohibit the burning of a cross with an intent to intimidate. The Court said the prohibition was analogous to a law against threats. No content discrimination was involved. Critics, however, have said both cases are inconsistent with *RAV*.

prohibited discriminatory conduct and that it only incidentally covered some speech. By contrast, the St. Paul hate speech law only prohibited disfavored expression. Yet courts have upheld harassment claims based largely on speech in several cases.[27] Finally, Justice Scalia said that the St. Paul law should have banned all fighting words to avoid content discrimination. It is a bit odd though that his solution to a difficult First Amendment problem is to ban more speech, not less.[28]

Indecent Adult Establishments

Another problematic area is sexually indecent speech. The Supreme Court has ruled that laws that create a zone of "adult" theaters,[29] and laws that restrict nude dancing,[30] are constitutional because they impose relatively benign time, place, and manner restrictions. Adult theaters are located in certain areas rather than others. Moreover, erotic dancing can still be done but not in the buff. Strict scrutiny is therefore unwarranted as the speech is "protected" and not banned. This speech was not technically obscene, as in *Miller* or *Paris Adult Theaters*.

Critics attack zoning laws as targeting sexually explicit speech because of its content, and thus, these laws deserve strict scrutiny. The Supreme Court has responded that such establishments are zoned because of their unpleasant secondary effects. Adult theaters often bring a criminal element with them and are bad for commercial and residential neighborhoods. The Court has likewise reasoned that nude dancing has detrimental secondary effects.

These laws, though, are content discriminatory on their face and in their impact. For example, banks generate crimes (bank robberies) yet banks are not pushed into the bad parts of town. Judge Posner has explained that the secondary effects doctrine:

---

[27] *See, generally,* Eugene Volokh, "What Speech Does: "Hostile Work Environment" Harassment Law Restrictions," 85 Geo. L. J. 627 (1997).

[28] The distinction between what is considered indisputably harmful (child pornography) versus what is considered worthy of protection (racist fighting words) is itself a social construction in which the notion of a truly objective and content- or viewpoint-neutral perspective is illusory. Cass Sunstein, "Pornography and the First Amendment," 1986 Duke L.J. 589, 615 (arguing that one does not see viewpoint bias where the law restricting speech aligns with the harms viewed as self-evident under the social consensus). An interesting treatment of similar jurisprudential issues can be found in Larry Alexander, Is There a Right to Freedom of Expression (2005).

[29] City of Renton v. Playtime Theaters, Inc., 475 U.S. 41 (1986).

[30] City of Erie v. PAP's A.M., 529 U.S. 277 (2000).

Cannot be taken completely seriously. Politically unpopular speech has secondary effects as well, in particular a heightened risk of public disorder; yet the Supreme Court has made clear that government cannot, by banning unpopular speakers in order to prevent disorder, allow a "heckler's veto."[31]

The Court in these cases even admits there is a content discriminatory element but answers that secondary effects are the major concern.[32] Yet this approach confuses one possible purpose of the law (reducing crime) with the law's indisputable content-based impact. Moreover, the sexual content of these establishments is intimately connected to their distasteful secondary effects.[33]

The secondary effects analysis is particularly weak regarding nude dancing. Whether a dancer is totally or partly naked will not change an establishment's effect on the neighborhood. The confusion in the Court's approach is augmented by the ideological divisions among the Justices and by the blurred line between what is obscene and what is indecent.

Other Problems

The U.S. Supreme Court's speech categories and its focus on content discrimination create numerous other problems. First, the protected and unprotected speech categories are insufficient for commercial speech, which has its own separate test.[34] What is bizarre, however, is that racist hate speech actually receives more constitutional protection than commercial speech. That is because laws restricting commercial speech receive a kind of intermediate scrutiny whereas *RAV* holds that laws against hate speech must undergo strict scrutiny. This is backward: Racist hate speech is more harmful.

Second, it is often unclear whether a law is content discriminatory,[35] particularly given relatively new technologies in which multiple interests and values may be at stake. Unfortunately, resolution of this very difficult

---

[31] Law, Pragmatism, and Democracy 366 (2003).

[32] City of Renton, 475 U.S. at 47.

[33] Some of the strongest free speech advocates acknowledge the bias problem. *See, e.g.,* Geoffrey Stone, "Content-Neutral Restrictions," 54 U. Chi. L. Rev. 46, 115-117 (1987).

[34] Central Hudson Gas & Electric Corp. v. Public Service Comm. New York, 447 U.S. 557 (1980).

[35] This issue was a focus of debate in the leading symbolic speech case involving a law prohibiting draft card mutilation. United States v. O'Brien, 391 U.S. 367 (1968).

question is frequently decisive. Winning or losing therefore artifically elevates a small distinction into a fundamental one.

For example, in *Turner Broadcasting System, Inc. v. FCC*,[36] the U.S. Supreme Court addressed whether it was constitutional to mandate that cable television systems provide access to local broadcasters, including those that are commercial and those that are acting in the public interest. Justice O'Connor thought the preference for the local entities revealed a bias for public interest programming. Other Justices reasoned that the law simply reduced the monopolistic control of the cable system and opened up speech channels. Similar internal divisions among the Justices exist in other cable television cases such as *Denver Area Educational Telecommunications, Consortium Inc. v. FCC*[37] and *United States v. Playboy Entm't Group, Inc.*[38] Indeed, the pro-speech result in this last case seems inconsistent with the pro-government result in a recent nude dancing case, though they were decided the same year.

Moreover in *Virginia v. Black*,[39] the Court was divided over whether a law that bans intimidating cross burning is content discriminatory. The majority held that the law was aimed at threats and was content neutral. The dissenters argued powerfully that cross burning, which is only done to intimidate, was racist in nature and thus involved content discrimination.

Third, the Court has applied its scrutiny levels inconsistently. For example, the Court has ruled that judicially imposed time, place, and manner restrictions deserve stricter scrutiny than similar legislatively mandated restrictions.[40] Specifically, in *Ward v. Rock Against Racism*,[41] the Supreme Court ruled that a law regulating the time, place, and manner of speech in a public forum must be narrowly tailored. But that did not mean the law must be the least restrictive possible regulation. Thus, the words "narrowly tailored" have multiple meanings in the Court's First Amendment cases.

The Court's decision in *Aschcroft v. ACLU II*[42] reveals other problems. The issue was the constitutionality of the Child On-Line Protection Act (COPA), which prohibited the transmission of indecent speech over the Internet to minors for commercial purposes. The Court found that the

---

[36] 512 U.S. 622 (1994).
[37] 518 U.S. 727 (1996).
[38] 529 U.S. 803 (2000).
[39] 538 U.S. 343 (2003).
[40] Madsen v. Women's Health Center, 512 U.S. 753 (1994); Eugene Volokh, The First Amendment and Related Statutes, Problems, Cases, and Policy Arguments 515 (2005). The Court in *Madsen* also split on whether the injunction was content based or not.
[41] 491 U.S. 781 (1989).
[42] 542 U.S. 656 (2004).

law violated the First Amendment, yet both Justice Kennedy's majority opinion and Justice Breyer's dissent claimed to be using strict scrutiny. Kennedy found that there were less restrictive alternatives to COPA such as filtering devices. Breyer reasoned that COPA's specificity and the importance of the state's interests in protecting minors outweighed any free speech interests. He also correctly said that filtering devices were already privately available and were not a statutory alternative. What is crucial though is that neither of the Justices really used strict scrutiny. Kennedy employed a kind of super strictness whereas Breyer's balancing approach resembled intermediate scrutiny.[43]

As this discussion shows, the Court should stop pretending that there are "fixed" speech categories and that the content discrimination principles solve all problems. Instead, it should openly acknowledge that there are gradations of speech and that sexually explicit speech is low on the list, certainly below political expression. That is why the zoning and nude dancing laws are treated with lesser scrutiny. As discussed earlier, Justice Stevens took that view in *Young* and *Pacifica*, and in 1993, he delivered an important address at Yale Law School highlighting the argument.[44] Yet, even he became inconsistent when he ruled in *Reno v. ACLU*[45] that a law banning indecent speech on the Internet for minors should receive the strictest scrutiny.

The idea of low-value speech is also recognized in public employment cases in which public interest matters receive more protection.[46] Fortunately, foreign courts can provide assistance here, as they have addressed difficult freedom of expression issues using a more nuanced analysis of competing interests and values.

SOUTH AFRICAN FREE SPEECH CASES

In contrast to the U.S. Supreme Court's categorical formalism, numerous other countries, like South Africa, openly weigh the burden on the individual against the government's justification, as well as other interests,

---

[43] *See also* Mark Kende, "Filtering out Children: The First Amendment and Internet Porn in the U.S. Supreme Court," 3 Mich. St. L. Rev. 843 (2005).

[44] The Honorable John Paul Stevens, "The Freedom of Speech," 102 Yale L.J. 1293, 1309–11 (1993).

[45] 521 U.S. 844 (1997).

[46] *See, e.g.,* Connick v. Meyers, 461 U.S. 138 (1983) (a public employee case that used balancing).

in deciding speech issues.[47] This section discusses several Constitutional Court cases and compares them to their American counterparts.

The central speech provision of the South African Constitution, in Chapter 2, section 16, is as follows:

(1) Everyone has the right to freedom of expression which includes –
  (a) freedom of the press and other media;
  (b) freedom to receive or impart information or ideas;
  (c) freedom of artistic creativity; and
  (d) academic freedom and freedom of scientific research.
(2) The right in subsection (1) does not extend to –
  (a) propaganda for war;
  (b) incitement of imminent violence; or
  (c) advocacy of hatred that is based on race, ethnicity, gender, or religion and that constitutes incitement to cause harm.

At first glance, the exclusion of hate speech, war propaganda, and inciting speech seems to make this provision less protective of speech than the U.S. Constitution's First Amendment which says, "Congress shall make no law . . . abridging the freedom of speech, or of the press, or of the right of the people peaceably to assemble, and to petition the Government for a redress of grievances." However, South Africa expressly protects academic freedom, artistic creativity, and other media in addition to the press.

Moreover, the hate speech provision reflects the South African Constitution's emphasis on protecting human dignity and transforming the country from its racist heritage. Interestingly, the drafters almost left out hate speech under the theory that it could be regulated by statute given the Constitution's strong equality and dignity protections.[48]

The Case Decision

The Court in *Case v. Minister of Safety and Security*[49] overruled the conviction of several men in a bench trial for possessing sexually explicit

---

[47] The former Chief Justice of the Israeli Supreme Court has discussed the essential nature of balancing in constitutional cases. Aharon Barak, The Judge in a Democracy 164 (2006). *But see* Richard Posner, Book Review, "Enlightened Despot, Barak, The Judge in a Democracy," New Republic 53, April 23, 2006.

[48] Lene Johannessen, "A Critical View of the Constitutional Hate Speech Provision," 13 S. Afr. J. Hum. Rts. 135, 141 (1997) ("Stated otherwise, s 16(2) is superfluous if it aims to provide the state with a right to introduce and enforce hate speech legislation.")

[49] 1996 (3) SA 617 (CC).

videotapes. The men violated the Indecent or Obscene Photogaphic Matter Act of 1967. Section 2(1) of the act says that possession of "any indecent or obscene photographic matter" is illegal. Section 1 defines indecent or obscene matter as including the following:

> Photographic matter or any part thereof depicting, displaying, exhibiting, manifesting, portraying or representing sexual intercourse, licentiousness, lust, homosexuality, lesbianism, masturbation, sexual assault, rape, sodomy, masochism, sadism, sexual bestiality or anything of a like nature.

The act reflects the apartheid era's Calvinist morality. Indeed, the Minister of Justice in 1967 said that the law prevented the moral undermining of a "Christian, civilized country such as the one in which we are living."[50]

In overruling the conviction, Justice John Didcott ruled that these individuals had a constitutional right to privacy that included possessing these videotapes in their homes. The Court's decision resembled the U.S. Supreme Court ruling in *Stanley v. Georgia*[51] that a man could not be prosecuted for possessing obscene films in his home. Interestingly, Didcott did not reference *Stanley* even though the Interim Constitution specified that the Court may look at foreign law.

Didcott also declined to decide whether the Interim Constitution's freedom of expression clause included a right to receive information because the 1967 act was likely to be revised.[52] He did, however, suggest that the law was overbroad, writing that "the trouble one now has with section 2(1) is that it hits the possession of other material too, material less obnoxious and sometimes quite innocuous which we cannot remove from its range."[53] He also wrote that the act contained a "preposterous definition" that "covers, for instance, reproductions of not a few famous works of art, ancient and modern that are publicly displayed and can readily be viewed in major galleries of the world."[54]

Justice Didcott was a long-time Durban-based lawyer who had served as a judge on the Natal Provincial Division of the South African Supreme

---

[50] Par. 12.

[51] 394 U.S. 557 (1969).

[52] Par. 92. Section 15 of the Interim Constitution said, "(1) Every person shall have the right to freedom of speech and expression, which shall include freedom of the press and other media, and the freedom of artistic creativity and scientific research. (2) All media financed by or under the control of the state shall be regulated in a manner which ensures impartiality and the expression of a diversity of opinion."

[53] Par. 93.   [54] Par. 91.

Court from 1975 to 1994 before joining the Constitutional Court. Did-cott, who was white, became famous at the Natal court for issuing numerous decisions questioning the bans imposed by the apartheid regime (on political parties, on travel in certain areas, on the right to association), as well as questioning the government's "idle and undesirable" legislation. Though frequently overturned on appeal, he continually strived to achieve justice. He died in 1998.

Justice Yvonne Mokgoro authored a separate opinion addressing the freedom of expression issues. She concluded there was a constitutional right to receive information. Because the later 1996 Constitution explicitly includes such a right, her concurring opinion sheds light on how that provision could be interpreted.

She initially explained that the 1967 Indecency Act's definition was based in part on a 1963 act that defined matters "harmful to public morals" as encompassing lust, passionate love scenes, night life, physical poses, inadequate dress, divorce, marital infidelity, "or any other similar related phenomenon."[55]

Mokgoro wrote that the apartheid authorities knew that the public morals test was even broad enough to include pinup calendars. The courts therefore also required that the material be "corrupting," defined from an objective perspective.[56] Despite that requirement, Mokgoro said that courts still engaged in "ad hoc" case-by-case analysis.[57] This resembles Justice Stewart's statement about obscenity that "I know it when I see it."[58]

Next, she addressed whether sexually explicit speech was protected by the Interim Constitution's free speech provision. She noted that the American First Amendment did not protect obscenity and that some scholars argued that political speech should be its centerpiece. Ultimately, she rejected the American categorical view regarding obscenity:

> The American bill of rights does not contain a limitations clause. Where, as in the case of our Constitution, the listing of rights is accompanied by a clause that provided for the limitation, on a principled and considered basis, of all enumerated rights, the better approach would seem to be to define the right generously, and to interpose any constitutionally justifiable limitations only at the second stage of the analysis.[59]

[55] Par. 10. [56] Par. 14.
[57] Par. 16.
[58] Jacobellis v. Ohio, 378 U.S. 184, 197 (1964) (Stewart J., concurring).
[59] *Case*, Par. 21.

Mokgoro further reasoned that limiting expression to the political realm would exclude areas like artistic speech.[60] She acknowledged the "marketplace of ideas" theory that free speech leads to truth, but she advocated the "self-realization" view by stating that freedom of expression is:

> A *sine qua non* for every person's right to realize her or his full potential as a human being, free of the imposition of eteronomous power. Viewed in that light, the right to receive others' expressions has more than mere instrumental utility, as a predicate for the addressee's meaningful exercise of her or his own rights of free expression. It is also foundational to each individual's empowerment to autonomous self-development.[61]

She then explained that the South African Constitution's provisions are "part of a web of mutually supporting rights" promoting human dignity and social transformation.[62] By contrast, the U.S. Constitution focuses more on individual liberty, and the clauses (such as the 14th Amendment's equal protection provision and the First Amendment's freedom of expression language) are not linked explicitly. The word "dignity" also does not appear in the U.S. Constitution, though dignity is at the heart of the post-World War II international human rights movement that so influenced South Africa.

Next, Mokgoro compared the U.S. and Canadian free speech jurisprudence. She described the U.S. Supreme Court's difficulties in deciding on an obscenity standard and explained how the Supreme Court focused on community morals.[63] She also found *Miller*'s three-part obscenity test to be vague, especially on whether a work has serious literary, artistic, political, or scientific value.[64] She then discussed Canada's focus on pornography's harms to women such as "the encouragement of violence, and the reinforcement of gender stereotypes."[65] Canada's statute is based on the novel anti-pornography law written by legal scholar Catherine MacKinnon and noted feminist Andrea Dworkin. This law has been

---

[60]Par. 23.   [61]Par. 26.
[62]Par. 27.   [63]Par. 42.
[64]Par. 41.
[65]Par. 45. The Canadian Supreme Court found problematic material that includes "explicit sex with violence" and "explicit sex without violence but which subjects people to treatment that is degrading or dehumanizing." The Court was concerned that such material predisposes "persons to act in an anti-social manner as, for example, the physical or mental mistreatment of women by men . . . The stronger the inference of a risk of harm the lesser the likelihood of tolerance."

rejected as content discriminatory by American jurisdictions but Canada upheld the law under its proportionality review.[66]

Mokgoro then argued that the harm approach "may offer a more promising route" than the American focus on morality, though the harm approach also has critics.[67] Her preference for Canada makes sense because the South African Bill of Rights borrowed more from the 1982 Canadian Charter of Rights and Freedoms, with its emphasis on human dignity, than from the U.S. Constitution.[68]

Justice Mokgoro, however, ultimately refused to select an approach. Instead, she said the government failed to show that the 1967 act was a justifiable rights limitation because it was overbroad[69] and therefore not "reasonable."[70] Interestingly, she relied on a Canadian case as the source of the overbreadth argument despite its frequent usage by American courts.[71] She noted that apartheid-era South African courts sometimes declared a statute to be *ultra vires*.[72] Mokgoro's pragmatic minimalism is characteristic of the South African Constitutional Court and is very different from the U.S. Supreme Court's convoluted and unnecessary discussion of speech categories in *RAV*.[73]

Next, Justice Mokgoro agreed with Justice Didcott that the conviction violated the right to privacy, but she did not join his opinion because she reasoned that the home was not impregnable from all state intrusion. Lastly, Justice Albie Sachs concurred with both Justice Didcott and Justice Mokgoro about the act's vagueness and overbreadth. Indeed, he noted that the privacy and expression analyses overlap.[74]

---

[66] *Compare* American Bookseller's Ass'n. v. Hudnut, 771 F.2d 323 (7th Cir. 1985), *aff'd mem.*, 475 U.S. 1001 (1986) (explicitly rejecting the MacKinnon/Dworkin approach) *with* Regina v. Butler, [1992] 1 S.C.R. 452.

[67] *Case*, Par. 47.

[68] Adam M. Dodek, "Canada as Constitutional Exporter: The Rise of the 'Canadian Model' of Constitutionalism," Supreme Court Law Review, Second Series, Vol. 36, 2007, *available at* SSRN: http://ssrn.com/abstract=1062361.

[69] *Case*, Par. 50 & 61.

[70] Section 33 of the Interim Constitution contained the Limitations Clause that specified, "The rights entrenched [in Chapter 3] may be limited by a law of general application, provided that such limitation – (a) shall be permissible only to the extent that it is – (i) reasonable; and (ii) justifiable in an open and democratic society based upon freedom and equality."

[71] Par. 49.   [72] Par. 51.

[73] *See, e.g.*, Mark S. Kende, "The Fifth Anniversary of the South African Constitutional Court: In Defense of Judicial Pragmatism," 26 Vermont L. Rev. 753 (2002); Iain Currie, "Judicious Avoidance," 15 S. Afr. J. Hum. Rts. 138 (1999).

[74] *Case*, Par. 112.

The Islamic Unity *Decision*

The Constitutional Court's decision in *Islamic Unity Convention v. Independent Broadcasting Authority*[75] involved hate speech. An Islamic community radio station speaker said on air that Israel was illegitimate, that Jews were not gassed during World War II, and that only one million Jews died during that war. The station was sanctioned under the following national regulation:

> Broadcasting licensees shall . . . not broadcast any material which is indecent or obscene or offensive to public morals or offensive to the religious convictions or feelings of any section of a population or likely to prejudice the safety of the State or the public order or relations between sections of the population.[76]

The constitutional question was whether speech could be restricted because it was "likely to prejudice relations between sections of the population."

The Court indicated that freedom of expression may be even more important in South Africa's new democracy than in the United States.[77] Then Deputy Chief Justice Langa reasoned that most speech restrictions should be rejected given the country's authoritarian past.[78] Thus, even offensive speech should be tolerated contrary to the regulation. Langa, however, explained that freedom of speech could not be absolute given other constitutional values such as equality, dignity,[79] and national reconciliation.

Langa next discussed how these other values were reflected in the hate speech provision. Langa noted that racist speech impinged on human dignity[80] and stereotyped people based on immutable characteristics. It "reinforces and perpetuates patterns of discrimination and inequality. Left unregulated, such expression has the potential to perpetuate the negative aspects of our past and further divide our society."[81]

The problem, though, was that the broadcasting regulation did not require that the racist expression take the form of advocacy or that it incite harm. Consequently, the regulation did not precisely prohibit hate speech

---

[75] 2002 (4) SA 294 (CC).
[76] Par. 22.   [77] Par. 26.
[78] Par. 27. Langa is now the Chief Justice.
[79] Par. 30. Indeed, section 10 of the Bill of Rights says, "Everyone has inherent dignity and the right to have their dignity respected and protected."
[80] Par. 33.   [81] Par. 45.

as defined by the South African Constitution. The regulation therefore outlawed protected speech, and a limitations analysis was required.

Justice Langa then used overbreadth doctrine:

> The prohibition is so widely-phrased and so far-reaching that it would be difficult to know beforehand what is really prohibited or permitted. No intelligible standard has been provided to assist in the determination of the scope of the prohibition. It would deny broadcasters and their audiences the right to hear, form, and freely express and disseminate their opinions and views on a wide range of subjects. The wide ambit of this prohibition may also impinge on other rights, such as the exercise and enjoyment of the right to freedom of religion, belief and opinion.[82]

The broadcasting authority, however, argued that the prohibition was acceptable for several reasons: It only governed broadcasters, there was no criminal sanction, and broadcasters could opt out. Langa disagreed. The regulation was not narrow as it affected all listeners. Moreover, the sanctions were serious as a license could be suspended. And the ability to opt out did not make the law itself constitutional. He also reasoned that less restrictive alternatives existed. The Court therefore struck down the regulation to the extent the broadcasting authority prohibited hate speech beyond the Constitution's definition.

This decision has several important dimensions. First, it shows that hate speech restrictions do not mean that everything racially offensive is outlawed. A well-drafted constitutional provision still permits controversial speech that does not incite. The slippery slope concerns of those opposed to hate speech restrictions may be exaggerated.

Second, the Court showed it would uphold speech restrictions aimed at real harms, not at speech that offends. This is similar to Justice Mokgoro's sympathy for the Canadian anti-pornography law in *Case*. This focus on harms also justifies protecting children from some speech.

Third, the Court's overbreadth emphasis, as in *Case*, prevented it from having to do a more complex categorical analysis as Justice Scalia did in *RAV*. The Constitutional Court, for example, did not resolve how the speech provision's internal limitations clause (where one finds the hate speech exception) related to the general South African limitations clause in section 36.

Fourth, the decision revealed that the Constitutional Court was granting ordinary protection to broadcast media speech, unlike U.S. Supreme

---

[82] Par. 44.

Court decisions that broadcasts' invasiveness and scarce frequencies justified less protection.

The case was not, however, flawless. The Court was mistaken in suggesting that freedom of speech is as important as human dignity under the South African Constitution.

The Khumalo *Decision*

In 2002, the Court not only decided *Islamic Unity* but it later ruled in a major defamation case, *Khumalo v. Holomisa*.[83] A politician claimed he was injured by a newspaper article that associated him with a gang. The legal question was whether freedom of speech was violated by the fact that a South African common law defamation claim could be brought without the plaintiff having to allege that the statement was false. The case therefore broached the "horizontality" issue of how the constitution applies regarding private actors.

The Court upheld the common law's constitutionality in an opinion authored by Justice Kate O'Regan. Early in her opinion, she evaluated various rights differently than Langa had in *Islamic Unity*. O'Regan wrote, "Although freedom of expression is fundamental to our democratic society, it is not a paramout value. It must be construed in the context of the other values enshrined in our Constitution. In particular, the values of human dignity, freedom, and equality."[84]

Later in the opinion, she wrote, "The protection of human dignity" is a "foundational constitutional value."[85] She elaborated that dignity involves the individual's self-worth and reputation.[86] She noted further that the mass media has a "constitutional duty to act with vigour, courage, integrity, and responsibility."[87] She said that defamation cases require balancing dignity interests and free speech interests.

The Court then explained that the fact that a South African defamation plaintiff need not allege falsity did not mean that veracity was irrelevant. A defendant, for example, could win a defamation suit by showing the truth of his or her statement.[88] Admittedly, placing the burden on the speaker, not on the alleged victim, protects less speech than in the United States. Moreover, public figure plaintiffs in the United States can only win a defamation case by showing actual malice, which is the "high-water mark of foreign jurisprudence" protecting the speaker.[89] But South Africa

---

[83] 2002 (5) SA 401 (CC).
[84] Par. 25.
[85] Par. 26.
[86] Par. 27.
[87] Par. 24.
[88] Par. 37.
[89] Par. 40.

values a person's dignitary interest more highly than a person's interest in speaking. O'Regan noted that determining the truth can also sometimes be tough; thus, the risk was placed on the speaker.

The burden on the speaker, however, was not to show truth in all cases. That would have a massive chilling effect on speech.[90] Instead, the accused need only show that the decision to publish was "reasonable" given all the circumstances, which could include the difficulty of proving the truth or falsity of certain assertions. Justice O'Regan concluded,

> In determining whether publication was reasonable, a court will have regard to the individual's interest in protecting his or her reputation in the context of the constitutional commitment to human dignity. It will also have regard to the individual's interest in privacy. In that regard, there can be no doubt that persons in public office have a diminished right to privacy, though of course their right to dignity persists. It will also have regard to the crucial role played by the press in fostering a transparent and open democracy. The defence of reasonable publication avoids therefore a winner-takes-all result and establishes a proper balance between freedom of expression and the value of human dignity. Moreover, the defense of reasonable publication will encourage editors and journalists to act with due care and respect for the individual interest in human dignity prior to publishing defamatory material, without precluding them from publishing such material when it is reasonable to do so.[91]

To summarize, Justice O'Regan found that dignity trumps free speech as a paramount value in South Africa, unlike in the United States. She also balanced competing interests as opposed to employing the U.S. Supreme Court's categorical framework. The major flaw in her approach, though, is that the reasonableness test is vague and could chill speech. The test does, however, provide an incentive for elevating societal discourse, something that the United States certainly could use.[92]

The South African Broadcasting *Decision*

The Constitutional Court's most recent speech case was its 2006 ruling in *South African Broadcasting Corp. v. National Director of Prosecutions*.[93] The issue was whether the courts could constitutionally refuse

---

[90] Par. 38. [91] Par. 44.

[92] Kevin Saunders writes about the "coarsening of [American] society." Saving Our Children from the First Amendment 57 & 202 (2003).

[93] 2006 ZACC 15 (Sep. 2006).

to broadcast some important criminal trials concerning national figures. The Court upheld the decision not to broadcast after balancing freedom of speech interests against the need for court proceedings to be fair. The Court relied heavily on the fact that no foreign jurisdiction had yet required televised court proceedings when the parties opposed it. Even the United States had not gone so far. A recent scholarly article criticizes the decision by contending that it reflected the erosion of press freedoms in South Africa.[94] While I disagree with this article, the overall erosion problem is discussed later and is serious, particularly regarding prior restraints.

It also deserves mention that South Africans have become concerned about the effect of the Internet on their children. Legislative action could be forthcoming following a governmental report on the problem.[95]

COMPARING THE APPROACHES IN CONTEXT

The previous sections highlighted the leading South African cases, showed some lessons that the U.S. Supreme Court could learn, such as the value of minimalism, and demonstrated that U.S. Supreme Court free speech doctrine has some inadequacies. This section, shows that free speech in South Africa is more fragile "on the ground" in certain respects than in the United States.

The most serious situation occurred in a case involving a South African newspaper's republication of a controversial Danish cartoon that contained a drawing of the prophet Muhammad. Other problems have arisen caused by overly broad speech codes, poorly drafted legislation, and political pressures. Indeed, the problems discussed in this section suggest that a Reporters without Borders Annual Press Freedom Index may be mistaken in ranking South Africa higher in press freedoms than the United States (44th vs. 53th).[96] One lesson is that South African civil society organizations have been crucial in protecting speech.

[94] Robert J. DaNay, Jacob Foster, "The Sins of the Media: The SABC Decision and the Erosion of Free Press Rights," 22 S. Afr. J. Hum. Rts. 563 (2006).

[95] Iyavar Chetty, Antoinette Basson, "Report on Internet Usage and the Exposure of Pornography to Learners in South African Schools," Film and Publication Board (Nov. 2006), http://www.info.gov.za/view/DownloadFileAction?id=81355 (last visited June 27, 2008).

[96] Reporters sans frontieres – "Annual Worldwide Press Freedom Index – 2006," http://www.rsf.org/article.php3?id_article=19390 (last visited Feb. 4, 2008).

Danish Cartoons: The South African Perspective

The South African *Cape and Guardian* newspaper published one of the Muhammad cartoons to highlight the Danish news story.[97] The newspaper's Muslim female editor made the publication decision, and her family later received threats.[98] Then, the Council of Muslim Theologians sought a prior restraint in the Johannesburg High Court to preclude publication of cartoons by the *Sunday Times* and other papers. The theologians argued that the cartoons were religious hate speech injurious to Muslim dignity and security: One of the Danish cartoons showed the Prophet Muhammad wearing a bomb-shaped turban with a lit fuse.[99] The South African media opposed the request based on free speech grounds. Moreover, there were precedents discouraging prior restraints.

Yet, the Court granted the injunction.[100] Judge M Jajhbhai of the High Court prohibited not only the cartoons but also caricatures or any other drawing of the prophet in the South African press. The judge relied on an affidavit from Moulana (priest) Ebrahim Bham of the Muslim Council stating that there was a clear and present danger that the rest of the media would publish these cartoons and that violence could occur as well as boycotts of South Africa. Bham wrote, "Islam does not know a depiction of Prophet Muhammad (Peace Be Upon Him) and it is a principle of Islam that a reproduction of the Holy Prophet (PBUH) in drawings, paintings, etc. is blasphemous."[101] The Council urged Muslims to protest peacefully.[102]

---

[97] Tribune Reporters, "Muslim Anger Hits SA," Feb. 5, 2006, http://www.sundaytribune.co.za/index.php?fSectionId=160&fArticleId=3097465 (last visited Feb. 19, 2008).

[98] BBC News, "SA Editor Threatened over Cartoon," Feb. 6, 2006, http://news.bbc.co.uk/2/hi/africa/4685040.stm (last visited Feb. 19, 2008).

[99] *Supra* note 97.

[100] Jamat-Ul-Ulama of Transvaal v. Johncom Media Investment, Ltd., High Court of South Africa (Wits Div.), Feb. 8, 2006, http://www.osall.org.za/docs/Hotdocs/Jamiat-Ul-Ulama_of_Transvaal_v_Johncom_Media_Prophet_cartoon_judgment.pdf (last visited Jan. 29, 2008).

[101] *Supra* note 97. A controversy has recently arisen over Wikipedia's article on Muhammad as the article displays an image taken from a medieval manuscript. Noam Cohen, "Online Petition Asks Wikipedia to Remove Pictures of Muhammad," International Herald Tribune, Feb. 5, 2008, http://www.iht.com/articles/2008/02/05/technology/wiki.php (last visited Feb. 19, 2008).

[102] UN Office for the Coordination of Humanitarian Affairs, Irin, "South Africa: Newspapers Barred from Publishing Prophet Muhammad Cartoons," Feb. 6, 2006, http://www.irinnews.org/report.aspx?reportid=58044 (last visited Jan. 29, 2008).

The *Cape Mail and Guardian* eventually apologized for publication of the cartoon.[103] Raymond Louw, of the Media Institute, however, argued that the injunction could have

> serious effects on the rights of freedom of press and expression contained in the constitution. This means that someone who feels a newspaper may publish something that harms his dignity or may damage him somehow, can go to the courts and get an interdict preventing them from publishing it.[104]

What was the High Court's reasoning? The court balanced freedom of expression with dignity and concluded:

> The critical need for our South African community is to promote and pro-tect human dignity, equality and freedom, the healing of the divisions of the past and the building of a united society. We are a diverse society. For many centuries, we have been bitterly divided through laws and prac-tices which encourage hatred and fear. Caricatures such as those depicting the Prophet Mohammed as a terrorist show a lack of human sensibility and in some cases constitute unacceptable provocation. These expressions advocate hatred and stereotyping of Muslims on the basis of immutable characteristics that is particularly harmful to the achievement of our core values as a nation, and reinforces and perpetuates patterns of discrimina-tion and inequality.[105]

This language is powerful but contains no clear constitutional analysis. For example, one does not know whether the Court viewed the cartoon as unprotected hate speech or as regulable because it violated Muslim dignity interests. South Africa's Constitution states that "advocacy of hatred that is based on race, ethnicity, gender or religion and that con-stitutes incitement to harm" is unprotected. The cartoon does not seem like advocacy, but like reporting. Moreover, if the cartoon is advocacy, does it promote hatred or just ridicule? The High Court mentions both but they are not the same.

Next, does the cartoon incite harm? That depends on whether it is likely to injure the psyche or spirit of Muslims or to cause others to harm Muslims. Another problem is determining what perspective should be

---

[103] Editorial, "The Constitution and the Qu'ran," Cape Mail & Guardian online, Feb. 10, 2006, http://www.mg.co.za/articlePage.aspx?articleid=263810&area=/insight/insight_editorials/ (last visited June 20, 2008).

[104] *Supra* note 102.   [105] *Supra* note 100 at 8.

used – that of a newspaper reader or a Muslim newspaper reader. The Court largely ignores these issues.

The Constitutional Court's ruling in *Islamic Unity* could have helped answer these questions. The Court interpreted narrowly the category of unprotected hate speech by noting that offensive statements were not sufficient. Therefore, the Constitutional Court would likely not see republication of a single cartoon, illustrating a newsworthy event, as advocacy or incitement amounting to hate speech. The Johannesburg High Court probably erred.

Can the High Court ruling nonetheless be justified as protecting dignitary interests? Section 36 specifies,

(1) The rights in the Bill of Rights may be limited only in terms of a law of general application to the extent that the limitation is reasonable and justifiable in an open and democratic society based on human dignity, equality and freedom, taking into account all relevant factors, including –
   (a) the nature of the right
   (b) the importance of the purpose of the limitation
   (c) the nature and extent of the limitation
   (d) the relation between the limitation and its purpose; and
   (e) less restrictive means to achieve the purpose.

The first problem is that no law of general application was involved. This was a judicial prior restraint entered in a particular case. Nonetheless, what would happen if one conducted the limitations analysis? Regarding the nature of the right, free expression is important. The limitations purpose here is also noble, though the prior restraint was troubling. Hate speech restrictions protect the dignity of Muslims. The restraint is broad as it covers all portrayals. Yet, some in the Muslim religion believe that any visual portrayal of Muhammed is blasphemy.

Lastly, are there less restrictive means? Yes, the Johannesburg Court could have just focused on cartoons and not on other depictions beyond the scope of the case. Moreover, the Court could have carefully tracked the Constitution and exempted any publications that were fundamentally newsworthy and that did not amount to incitement.

Danish Cartoons: The American Perspective

Although the Constitutional Court would probably have overturned the High Court's publication injunction, the U.S. Supreme Court would certainly have done so. Most American newspapers did not publish the Danish cartoons though journalists wrote about the issue.[106] The University of Illinois disciplined the student newspaper editor for publishing them.[107] No judicial cases about publication emerged because there actually was not much to litigate. Even hate speech is protected in American courts.

At first glance, the act of republishing one or several cartoons would seem to be a form of news about what happened in Denmark and across the world. One could also argue that the cartoons were protected political satire according to the U.S. Supreme Court ruling in *Hustler Magazine v. Falwell*.[108]

The cartoons were not obscene because they did not contain images of hard-core sex. The irony is that American obscenity doctrine originated in anti-blasphemy laws.[109] The cartoons also did not amount to defamation in American law because the images did not injure a living human's reputation and were neither true nor false. In addition, the cartoons did not meet the *Brandenburg* standard as they do not expressly advocate violence.

One could argue that the cartoons were a form of fighting words that might offend Muslims and create social disruption. The problem, however, is that fighting words must be directed by one person to another, which did not occur with newspaper publication. Notice that the above analysis is almost mechanical: Plug the situation into the categories and see if there is a fit.

What is striking is how disconnected this analysis is from Islam's rejection of a strictly secular realm distinct from the religious world. Treating these cartoons in a Western fashion, as mere offensive drawings, misses the point entirely from the Islamic perspective.

---

[106] The Editors Weblog, "Media Geopolitics of the Mohammed Cartoons," Feb. 15, 2006 ("How to define the position adopted by American, British, Canadian and Australian newspapers? Media responsibility, political correctness or self-censorship? The most surprising is not the position defined in many editorials (from the New York Times to The Guardian), but this strange impression of unanimity and consensus: only three regional newspapers of more than 1,400 newspapers in the States and zero newspapers, but a student daily, in the UK for taking the risk.") http://www.editorsweblog .org/newsrooms_and_journalism/2006/02/media_geopolitics_of_the_moham.php (last visited June 27, 2008); *See generally* Robert A. Kahn, "Why There Was No Cartoon Controversy in the United States," U of St. Thomas Legal Studies Research Paper No. 07-28 *available* at SSRN: http://ssrn.com/abstract=1008997.

[107] Kahn, *id.* at 11.   [108] 485 U.S. 46 (1988).

[109] Kevin Saunders, Violence as Obscenity 91 (1996).

Publication is sacrilegious. It is striking how the South African court can at least account for Muslim dignitary interest unlike the American categorical analysis. This makes sense because, like Islam, African religion does not neatly divide the secular from the spiritual world. American courts have dealt with hate speech issues involving swastikas and burning crosses but little like this.

Other South African Developments

Despite the above criticisms of the American approach, the Johannesburg High Court ruling shows that the South African balancing method can have a precarious effect on free speech. Yet, other South African "cases" have been more protective as shown below. Nonetheless, press freedom in South Africa is fragile in a variety of ways, especially given ANC threats.

The Press

The privately run Press Council of South Africa established a press ombudsman to hear complaints regarding newspapers. The decisions of the ombudsman do not have the force of court rulings, but the industry is supposed to follow them. The ombudsman applies the Council's Press Code, which was created to fend off government regulation. The Code, however, goes too far in regulating media expression.

For example, section 2.1 of the Press Code regarding "Discrimination and Hate Speech" prohibits derogatory religious references.[110] Section 2.2 holds that the press should not discuss a person's religion "in a prejudicial or pejorative context except where it is strictly relevant to readers' understanding of that matter." Both of these provisions appear to be constitutionally inadequate under *Islamic Unity* as they contain no incitement aspect.

Nonetheless, on February 1, 2007, the press ombudsman correctly decided that the South African *Sunday Times* did not violate Muslim rights by publishing a review of a book called *The Caged Virgin* by Ayaan Hirsi Ali.[111] Ms. Ali is an African-born member of the Dutch Parliament. Her book contended that Islam justified violence against women.

---

[110]The South African Press Code, 2007, http://www.presscouncil.org.za/pages/south-african-press-code.php (last visited Feb. 1, 2008).

[111]Press Ombudsman of South Africa Ruling, Muslim Lawyers, et al. v. Sunday Times, http://www.ombudsman.org.za/content/morenews.asp?id=16 (last visited Feb. 1, 2008).

The press ombudsman, E. H. Linington, found that free expression outweighed dignitary or religious interests given these facts and so approved publication of the book review:

> If it were not so, life in South Africa would be bleak indeed. No more of our traditionally robust politics; no criticizing of those in authority and power; no lampooning of public figures, no pricking the egos of the pretentious or hypocritical, no satire, no exposure of corrupt, lazy and inefficient officials. If we accept the complainant's view, would the press be able to publish, e.g. Minister Ronnie Kasril's views on Israel and Zionism, because they offend some local Jews? Would atheists be prevented from imparting their ideas, because they attack as false the very fundamentals of the beliefs of the adherents of all theistic religions, most of which are represented in South Africa?[112]

Linington also agreed with the newspaper's decision not to submit the review for prior approval. The newspaper had the right to avoid the prior restraint imposed in the Danish cartoons situation. It is fascinating to see this industry figure ignore the Johannesburg cartoon case as a precedent, with good reason.

Broadcast Media

Numerous other institutions regulate the media in addition to the Press Council. Section 192 of the Constitution authorizes parliamentary creation of the Independent Communications Authority of South Africa (ICASA). Parliament then mandated the creation of a Code of Conduct for Broadcasters. The Broadcasting Monitoring and Complaints Committee is part of ICASA and issues determinations akin to the press ombudsman. There is also an Independent Broadcasting Authority (IBA) and an Independent Communications Authority.

THE CODES. The revised ICASA Code of Conduct for broadcasters, which was supposed to correct the overbreadth discussed in *Islamic Unity*, still is problematic. Section 16.1 specifies, "Licensees shall not broadcast any material which, judged within context sanctions, promotes or glamorizes violence based on race, national or ethnic origin, colour, religion."[113] Section 17 specifies as follows:

---

[112] *Id.* at 2.
[113] http://www.journalism.co.za/index2.php?option=com_content&task=view&id+204 &Itemid . . . (last visited Feb. 2, 2008).

The aforementioned prohibitions shall not apply to –

(1) a bona fide scientific, documentary, dramatic, artistic, or religious broadcast, which judged within context, is of such nature;
(2) broadcasts which amount to discussion, argument or opinion on a matter pertaining to religion, belief, or conscience, or
(3) broadcasts which amount to a bona fide discussion, argumentor opinion on a matter of public interest.

Section 11, however, does not clearly define what is artistic, dramatic, or scientific. Despite these poorly drafted codes, industry adjudicators have protected free speech, perhaps because doing so coincides with their own interests.

THE CASES. The most noteworthy broadcasting tribunal case involved Mbongeni Ngema, the South African who wrote and directed the internationally acclaimed musical *Sarafina!* The case concerned a Zulu song he wrote and sang entitled *Amandiya* that criticized the Indian population.[114] Here are some of the translated lyrics:

> Oh men! Oh virulent men! We need a courageous man to delegate to the Indians. For this matter is complicated and now needs to be reported to men. Indians don't want to change, even Mandela has failed to convince them, it was better with whites we knew then it was a racial conflict... Indians are not interested to cast their vote but when do so they vote for whites... Being turned into clowns by Indians, Zulus do not have money and are squatting in shacks as chattels of Indians... I have never seen Dlamini relocating to India Yet here is Gurmede in Durban being homeless. We struggle so much here in Durban, as we, have been dispossessed by Indians who in turn are suppressing our people.

The South African Human Rights Commission brought a hate speech case against a radio station for playing the song.

The tribunal decision was controversial. It stated, "Our Constitution, is the result of an arduous and century-old struggle against the tyranny of the State and often, the Church." It offered examples of church censorship.

The tribunal also said that it would use an "objective" approach to determine whether a statement advocated hatred. It then said, "These demeaning accusations are likely to lead to the inference by most, if

---

[114] Case No: 2002/31 SABC "Ngema Song," http://www.bccsa.co.za/templates/judgement_template_37.asp (last visited Feb. 2, 2008).

not all, Indians in at least Kwa Zulu-Natal, that their safety is at stake and are, in any case, immensely degrading to Indians as a section of the population." Regarding harm, the human rights commission said that the issue was not whether Indians would be attacked but whether the song was reasonably likely to create fear, especially in a relatively young and fragile democracy. Despite finding that the song amounted to hate speech, the tribunal ruled for the station as the song was part of a "bona fide current affairs programme." In the end, this was a free speech victory though the tribunal's concerns about Muslim safety seem exaggerated.[115]

Another broadcasting tribunal case involved a radio station that played a club dance track that included the sacred Muslim call to prayer known as the *Azaam*.[116] The station apologized and said it did not know about this background track. The South African Broadcasting Corporation even acknowledged that the station needed a better music review process. Interestingly, the tribunal rejected any argument that an exemption protected the station because "the music cannot, as a result of its low value, be regarded as a bona fide work of art." This is a rather narrow definition of artistic. The tribunal, however, determined that the track at most amounted to "disrespect," not "advocacy of hatred." Thus, the station was not liable. These two tribunal decisions help make up for the Johannesburg High Court decision.

Note that American free speech rights are more limited in broadcast radio and television than in other media because of scarce frequencies and the supposedly invasive nature of broadcast. American media law, however, is beyond this book's scope.

Laws Relating to Free Speech
The Promotion of Equality and Prevention of Unfair Discrimination Act of 2000 implemented the Constitution's provisions related to nondiscrimination outside the employment context. Yet Shaun Teichner shows convincingly how the Equality Act's definitions of advocacy, hatred, and

---

[115] *But see* James L. Gibson & Amanda Gouws, Overcoming Intolerance in South Africa 72 (2003) ("Among the impediments to democratic consolidation is the high degree of subcultural pluralism within South Africa.... One important consequence of subcultural pluralism is political intolerance."). This study, however, has been criticized. Ineke van Kessel, "Review of James L. Gibson and Amanda Gouws, "Overcoming Intolerance in South Africa: Experiments in Democratic Persuasion," H-SAfrica, H-Net Reviews, June 2004, http://www.h- net.msu.edu/reviews/showrev.cgi?path=49031093440079 (last visited April 22, 2008).

[116] Case No: 2006/20 5FM – Mark Gillman Show, http://www.bccsa.co.za/templates /judgement_template_353.asp (last visited Feb. 2, 2008).

incitement are problematic.[117] Indeed, the Constitutional Court suggested the Act raised some questions, in the recent *Pillay* case involving a Hindu girl who wore a nose stud to her school.[118]

There have also been unsuccessful proposals to amend the Film and Publications Act of 1996 to require preapproval of all films by a board.[119] The existing act, however, already is problematic because it contains the same ambiguous exemptions as the broadcasting law described earlier.

Lastly the proposed Hate Crimes Bill of 2004 would have made it illegal for any person to advocate, in public, racial or religious hatred that could be hurtful or harmful. The International Freedom of Expression Institute correctly characterizes the bill's provisions as being "overly broad, extensive and inherently vague, [and they] have far reaching implications for freedom of expression in our country because whether or not an individual *intends* to propagate hate speech or incite hatred against another identifiable group of persons is, in the eyes of [these laws], immaterial."[120] Fortunately, the bill never passed.

Political Pressures on Free Speech

Another threat to free speech is the pressure placed on the media by leading ANC officials. Jacob Zuma, possible president in waiting, brought a multimillion dollar defamation lawsuit against the press.[121] It is virtually impossible to imagine an American president taking such inflammatory actions, though that may partly be due to the onerous burden faced by public figures in American defamation cases.

Moreover, Dr. Essap Pahad, Minister to former President Mbeki, decried the supposed inadequacy of press self-regulation to the Press Council on November 1, 2007.[122] Dr. Pahad said, "Recent accounts of

---

[117] Shaun Teichner, "The Hate Speech Provisions of the Promotion of Equality and Prevention of Unfair Discrimination Act 4 of 2000: The Good, The Bad, and The Ugly," 19 S. Afr. J. Hum. Rts. 349 (2003).

[118] Minister of Education v. Pillay, 2007 ZACC 21 (Oct. 2007).

[119] Wyndham Hartley, "Parts of Media Bill Are Still Unconstitutional, Say Editors," Business Day, Oct. 17, 2007, http://www.businessday.co.za/articles/national .aspx?ID=BD4A589039 (last visited Feb. 2, 2008).

[120] IFEX, "FXI Warns of Dangers in Proposed Hate Speech Bill," June 7, 2004, http:// www.ifex.org/en/layout/set/print/content/view/full/59374/ (last visited Feb. 2, 2008).

[121] SAPA, "Zuma Reduces Claims against Media," Mail & Guardian online, Feb. 1, 2008, http://www.mg.co.za/articlepage.aspx?area=/breaking_news/breaking_news_national /&articleid=331235&referrer=RSS (last visited Feb. 20, 2008).

[122] Dr. EG Pahad, "Address to the Press Council: Self Regulation or Government Regulation?," Nov. 1, 2007, http://www.presscouncil.org.za/modules/download_gallery /dl.php?file=5 (last visited Feb. 20, 2008).

President Mbeki in the press . . . have degenerated into the most ferocious, venomous malicious and unwarranted attacks on an incumbent Head of State in the World. The question is why? What does this tell us about standards of journalism and ethics?" He compared the current South African media to the American media's complicity in the McCarthy era's communist witch hunt. He also criticized the media's lack of diversity especially regarding languages. Dr. Pahad then argued that the government had the right to criticize the media. In effect, he threatened government intervention unless the press regulated itself more vigorously.

On December 3, 2007, Raymond Louw, chairman of the Press Council, responded by pointing out that even the ANC-dominated Parliament abides by self-regulatory mechanisms.[123] He said that the ombudsman was not supposed to serve a policing function because that was contrary to a free press. Moreover, he said that government threats to withdraw advertising from newspapers were illegal.

The ANC, however, has recently adopted a resolution entitled "Communication and the Battle of Ideas."[124] Paragraph 5 specifies, "The ANC is faced with a major ideological offensive, largely driven by the opposition and factions of the mainstream media, whose key objective is the promotion of market fundamentalism, control of the media and the image it creates of a new democratic dispensation in order to retain old apartheid economic and social functions."

Paragraph 10 then specifies, "With particular reference to the print media, the ANC notes that the current form of self-regulation as expressed in the form of the Press Ombudsman/Press Council is not adequate to sufficiently protect the rights of the individual citizens, community, and society as a whole." Thus, the resolution formally calls for Parliament to establish a Media Appeals Tribunal to "support" industry self-regulatory bodies.

The South African government therefore seeks to muzzle media criticisms. The ANC paints the press as colluding with the opposition yet these allegations confuse a critical press with a politicized press. Dr. Pahad's statements that President Mbeki has been subjected to unprecedented criticisms either show a stunning lack of awareness of the workings of the press in other countries or a cynical approach to free speech. Moreover,

---

[123] Raymond Louw, "Self Regulation The Only Way," Dec. 3, 2007, www.presscouncil .org.za/pages/documentation.php (last visited Feb. 2, 2008).

[124] Jan. 15, 2008 http://www.presscouncil.org.za/pages/posts/anc-resolution-on-communications-and-the-batt . . . (last visited Feb. 1, 2008).

there are pressures at work causing institutions to create overly broad hate speech restrictions. Yet, thanks to the Constitutional Court, media tribunals, and various civil society groups, the pressured media has remained vigorous and free.

CONCLUSION

This chapter argues that American free speech doctrine employs unworkable categories and tries to hide inconsistent approaches. Moreover, the U.S. Supreme Court frequently balances various interests despite its statements to the contrary. Though the South African Constitutional Court's decisions are far from perfect, the Court there openly acknowledges and weighs the real factors that are playing a role in its decisions. The South Africans also do a better job of avoiding unnecessarily broad rulings.

Outside the Constitutional Court arena, however, free speech in South Africa is fragile, given what amounts to a one-party state that is not above threats and a new democracy that needs a certain degree of social harmony. Moreover, hate speech restrictions and the balancing approach add to the fragility. Yet, civil society groups and leaders have, for the most part, kept the media as a thorn in the government's side, as it should be.

8

Freedom of Religion

We live in the age of international human rights.[1] We have witnessed the creation of an International Criminal Court, prosecutions of former heads of state, the globalization of legal norms, and an increased use of international peacekeeping forces. We have even seen the fall of the Berlin Wall, the emergence of many new nations, and the transformation of South Africa.

Freedom of religion is considered among the most important human rights.[2] This chapter analyzes how South Africa's judiciary has addressed religious liberty in comparison with U.S. Supreme Court decisions in the area.[3] My conclusion is that, despite a progressive Constitution informed by international human rights norms, the South African Constitutional Court has generally adopted a formalistic and narrow approach that treats religious minorities as second-class citizens based on Western assumptions. One goal of this chapter is to figure out why the Court has done poorly in this area when it has issued transformative decisions regarding the death penalty,[4] socioeconomic rights,[5] and equality.[6] The

---

[1] This is exemplified by the Universal Declaration of Human Rights. G.A. Res. 217 A (III) (Dec. 10, 1958).

[2] John Witte, Jr., "A Dickensian Era of Religious Rights: An Update on Religious Human Rights in Global Perspective," 42 Wm. & Mary L. Rev. 707, 717 (2001) (quoting George Jellinek as saying that religion is "the mother of many other rights").

[3] H. Kwasi Prempeh, Review essay, "African Judges in Their Own Cause: Reconstituting Independent Courts in Contemporary Africa," 4 Int'l. J. Con. L. 592–593 (2004) ("On the vast continent of Africa, South Africa's postapartheid Constitutional Court, known for its innovative jurisprudence in the area of rights has emerged as the undisputed favorite of comparative constitutional scholars and social scientists as well as a lodestar for jurists across the globe.").

[4] State v. Makwanyane, 1995 (3) SA 391 (CC).

[5] Republic of South Africa v. Grootboom, 2000 SACLR Lexis 126.

[6] President of the Republic of South Africa v. Hugo, 1997 SACLR Lexis 91.

answer to this question relates to religion's uniqueness as a human right. This chapter breaks new ground as few scholars have critically assessed the Constitutional Court's overall religion jurisprudence.[7]

The right to freedom of religion is unique because it has caused oppression as well as liberty. It can unleash blissful or deadly sentiments. The Romans slaughtered Christians for sport, Sunni and Shiia fight a civil war in Iraq, Catholics and Protestants battle in Northern Ireland, and Jews fight Muslims in Israel and the surrounding territories. In addition, religion can be used to promote less elevated ambitions such as political power or financial gain. Father Robert Drinan describes this history in a suitably titled book, *Can God and Caesar Coexist?*[8]

Moreover, there is no binding international covenant on religious freedom[9] because nations seek to maintain control over these combustible issues. This raises the question whether full religious freedom can coexist with other international human rights. Winnifred Sullivan, authored a book in 2005 fittingly called *The Impossibility of Religious Freedom*.[10]

This debate has two poles. Some scholars argue that international human rights norms reflect the Enlightenment's rejection of religion's hierarchy.[11] The liberal ideal is based on tolerance for differences not

---

[7] Perhaps the most detailed discussion of the Court's major religion cases can be found in Paul Farlam, "Freedom of Religion, Belief, and Opinion," in Stuart Woolman, et al. (Eds.), Constitutional Law of South Africa (Lansdowne: Juta 2004). Law journal articles generally only discuss one or two cases. *But see* Irma J. Kroeze, "God's Kingdom in the Law's Republic: Religious Freedom in South African Constitutional Jurisprudence," 19 S. Afr. J. Hum. Rts. 469 (2003) (short commentary on all the cases).

[8] Robert Drinan, S.J., Can God and Caesar Coexist?: Balancing Religious Freedom and International Law (New Haven: Yale University Press 2004).

[9] *Id.* at 8 ("The planet's 191 nations have not proposed, much less promulgated, a binding covenant on religious freedom, such as the several covenants on torture, freedom of the press, the rights of women, and the duties owed to refugees.").

[10] Winnifred Fallers Sullivan, The Impossibility of Religious Freedom (Princeton: Princeton Univ. Press 2005).

[11] Louis Henkin et al., Human Rights (New York: Foundation Press 1999) at 1 ("The idea of human rights grew in opposition to historic forms of authoritarianism such as the divine right of kings."); Johan D. van der Vyver, "Introduction," in Johan D. van der Vyver & John Witte, Jr. (Eds.), Religious Human Rights in Global Perspective: Legal Perspectives (The Hague: Martinus Nijhoff Publishers 1996) at xiii ("While Western traditions by and large founded the typical liberal perceptions of human rights on a secularized base, most Eastern proponents proponents of human rights seek to construct an intimate link of the values embodied in that ideology with decidedly religious presuppositions."); Steve Smith, "Recovering (from) Enlightenment," 41 San Diego L. Rev. 1263, 1289 (2004) ("Responses to this challenge vary, of course, but it seems that the characteristic stance of modern liberal theorists of an Enlightenment bent,

on everyone following the light.[12] This position supports church-state separation, as in France, the self-proclaimed center of Enlightenment thought.

Others respond that secular values without a God are problematic. Tolerance for everything can mean that anything goes. In extreme cases, it can lead to the godless worlds of communism or even Nazism. Western scholars such as Mary Ann Glendon[13] and John Witte Jr.[14] argue that the international human rights movement after World War II would not have succeeded without religious groups arguing for human dignity. It is no accident that the German Basic Law, written after the Holocaust, emphasized the inviolability of human dignity and rooted that principle in God.

As just implied, perhaps the best laboratory for measuring the reconcilability of freedom of religion with other human rights is the actual experiences of nations. France's separationism and Germany's cooperationism are two possible approaches, to borrow from Cole Durham's famous categorization. Durham developed a continuum of state approaches to religion from theocratic regimes, established churches, endorsed churches, cooperationist regimes, accommodationist regimes, separationist regimes, inadvertent insensitivity, and hostility.[15]

Iran is a theocracy in which the state and religion are supposed to function hand in hand. Iran, however, has repeatedly violated its

---

following the example of the architects of international human rights, is simply to spurn the demand for justifications and to base the central commitments to equality and rights on an ostensible consensus within the relevant constituency."); Witte, *supra* n. 2 at 720–21 ("The influential French jurist Karel Vasak pressed these [Enlightenment] sentiments into a full confession of the secular spirit of the modern human rights movement."). *See also* "Human Rights," Stanford Encyclopedia of Philosophy 6, http://plato.stanford.edu/entries/rights-human/ (July 29, 2006) (last visited Aug. 19, 2006) ("It appears that all human groups have moralities, that is, imperative norms of behavior backed by reasons and values.... One way in which human rights could exist apart from divine ... enactment is as norms accepted in all or almost all actual human moralities.").

[12] Henry Steiner, "Ideals and Counter-Ideals in the Struggle over Autonomy Regimes for Minority Rights," 66 Notre Dame L. Rev. 1522 (2001) ("That movement institutionalizes no one ideal of social order. To the contrary, it explicitly allows for many faiths and ideologies while denying to any one among them the power to impose itself by force.").

[13] A World Made New: Eleanor Roosevelt and the Universal Declaration of Human Rights (New York: Random House 2001).

[14] Witte, *supra* n. 2.

[15] Cole Durham, "Perspectives on Religious Liberty: A Comparative Perspective'" in van der Vyver, *supra* n. 11 at 19–23.

own citizens' human rights. Nonetheless, the Iranian theocracy appears here to stay. Separationist France bans conspicuous religious symbols in public schools under a policy known as *laicite*. This policy caused an uproar because of its disproportionate effect on Muslim girls who wear head scarves.[16] But the French overwhelmingly support *laicite*. Thus, both "extremes" along the continuum seem to raise human rights concerns. Clearly, Germany falls somewhere in between as does South Africa.

This chapter briefly describes South Africa's religious history. It then examines the Constitutional Court's four major religion decisions, with a special focus on the case of a Rastafarian man seeking to become an attorney. This part shows the problems that the Constitutional Court has had and makes comparisons with American religion cases. The last part then attempts to explain why the Constitutional Court has found it difficult to rule on religious freedom. The chapter's goal is to assess how a constitutional dispensation can best protect freedom of religion and other basic human rights.

COLONIAL OPPRESSION AND RELIGION IN SOUTH AFRICA

As discussed in Chapter 2, Europeans arrived in what is now South Africa in the seventeenth century.[17] White colonizers from the Dutch East Indies Company imposed themselves culturally, politically, and religiously on the indigenous peoples in the Western Cape.[18] They often acted brutally, leaving a legacy for apartheid.

The religions of the indigenous people in southern Africa, the Khosa and Zulu, both believe in one supreme being as well as in various ancestral spirits.[19] Attaining favor with the spirits depended on rituals involving "the use of dance and altered states of consciousness."[20] A *sangoma*, or healer, was responsible for the group's overall physical and spiritual well-being. Worshiping and spirituality were part of everyday life (even

---

[16] Adrien Wing, Monica Smith, "Critical Race Feminism Lifts the Veil?: Muslim Women, France, and the Headscarf Ban," 39 U.C. Davis L. Rev. 743 (2006).

[17] John Dugard, Human Rights and the South African Legal Order 4–5 (Princeton: Princeton Univ. Press 1978).

[18] George M. Frederickson, White Supremacy: A Comparative Study of South African and American History 3–5 (New York: Oxford Univ. Press 1981).

[19] "South Africa – Religion," Library of Congress, Country Studies at 2 http://countrystudies.us/south-africa/52.htm (last visited Aug. 10, 2006) .

[20] *Id.* at 1.

part of the beer drinking), not something segregated to a Sunday morning ceremony in a big building.[21]

Many Boers demonized Africans for not worshiping one god and for not having a single minister.[22] Missionaries used those indigenous practices to justify their attempts to convert the Africans to Christianity. The settlers also tried to change the values of indigenous peoples by imposing private property regimes and the like.[23] These Dutch descendants frequently fought with various African peoples.[24] European wealth and technological superiority often turned these battles into massacres.[25]

In the nineteenth and early twentieth centuries, the English dominated parts of the country and advocated conversion to Christianity and the elimination of *lobolo* – the tradition of an African man providing gifts of animals or other forms of wealth to his future wife's family.[26] However, the English generally opposed slavery.[27] Some prominent Africans converted to Christianity to gain opportunities with the elites.

After World War II, when apartheid became more formalized, most South African whites joined the Dutch Reformed Church. This Christian denomination became a pillar of apartheid, even supporting the idea that there was a master white race created by God.[28] The Dutch Reformed

---

[21] Steve Biko, "Black Consciousness and the Quest for a True Humanity," at 4 http://www.sahistory.org.za – People – Stephen (Steve) Bantu Biko (last visited Aug. 21, 2006) ("Worship was not a specialized function that found expression once a week in a secluded building, but rather it featured in our wars, our beer-drinking, our dances and our customs in general. Whenever Africans drank they would rotate to God by giving a portion of their beer away as a token of thanks.").

[22] *Supra* n. 19 at 4.   [23] *Supra* n. 18.

[24] Frank Berman, "South Africa: A Study of Apartheid Law and Its Enforcement," 2 Touro J. Transnat'l L. Rev. 1, 9 (1991) (Nine wars were fought between the frontiersman and the Khosas.).

[25] Makau Wa Mutua, "Limitations on Religious Rights," in van der Vyver, *supra* n. 11 at 430; George B. N. Ayittey, Africa Unchained 117 (New York: Palgrave MacMillan 2005).

[26] *Supra* n. 19 at 4. Ericka Curren, Elsje Bonthuys, "Customary Law and Domestic Violence in Rural South African Communities," 21 S. Afr. J. Hum. Rts. 607, 616 (2005) (discussing the evolving meaning of lobolo).

[27] Leonard Thompson, A History of South Africa 58 (Yale Univ. Press 1990). The British formally abolished slavery by the British Act of Parliament of 1834. But various forms of master-slave relations still remained. Berman, *supra* n. 24 at 6.

[28] *Supra* n. 19 at 2, "Religion and Apartheid," Gila Stopler, "Countenancing the Oppression of Women: How Liberals Tolerate Religious and Cultural Practices That Discriminate against Women," 12 Colum. J. Gender & L. 154 (2003).

Church established separate branches for blacks and Indians. It was not until the 1970s and 1980s that a few religious leaders, like the Reverend Beyers Naude, protested against their denomination's position.[29]

Naude was a white Afrikaaner Dutch Reformed cleric and at one time was a member of the Broederbond, "a secretive, elitist, highly influential club dedicated to promoting the interests of Afrikaaners by preserving Apartheid."[30] He believed that the Bible supported apartheid but abandoned that view after the 1960 Sharpeville massacres in which security forces killed a large group of black schoolchildren. Naude then started preaching that God did not want whites and blacks to worship separately or belong to distinct churches. He eventually joined the military wing of the ANC and began housing exiles and using his skills as a mechanic to refurbish cars for the ANC.[31] He established the interdemominational Christian Institute. The Dutch Reformed Church therefore stripped him of his clerical positions and the government banned him from 1977 to 1984. During that time he could neither speak out in public nor see associates and friends.[32]

In 1985, a group of theologians and lay people anonymously published the "Kairos Document" which argued that apartheid was a biblical abomination to be overcome. This document received international acclaim for its liberation theology.[33] It criticized those churches that argued for reconciliation in the absence of regime change:

> True justice, God's justice, demands a radical change of structures. This can only come from below, from the oppressed themselves. God will bring about change through the oppressed as he did through the oppressed Hebrew slaves in Egypt. God does not bring his justice through reforms introduced by the Pharaohs of this world.[34]

Numerous other South African churches eventually denounced apartheid.

---

[29] South Africa.info, "Beyers Naude: Man's Law Second," Sep. 8, 2004, www.southafrica.info/ess_info/sa_glance/history/beyers-naude.htm (last visited Jan. 19, 2008).

[30] *Id.*

[31] Farook Khan, "'Backyard Mechanic,' Naude Worked with MK," Independent Online, Sep. 14, 2004, http://www.int.iol.co.za/index.php?set_id=1&click_id=2975&art_id=vn20040917064007532C901033 (last visited Jan. 19, 2008).

[32] He was, however, accepted into the black branch of the Dutch Reformed Church. He was the only Afrikaaner on the ANC democracy negotiating committees. Before he died, he asked to have his ashes left in the Alexandria township.

[33] Bonganjalo Goba, "The Kairos Document and Its Implications for Liberation in South Africa," 5 J. Law and Rel. 313 (1987) (Goba was one of the signatories).

[34] *Id.* at 319.

Naude and the Anglican Archbishop Desmond Tutu, an African, eventually organized the South African Council of Churches (SACC) in 1968 to oppose apartheid.[35] Tutu won a Nobel Peace Prize for his long and dangerous struggle against apartheid. He has written eloquently about many of his experiences. Here is his description of the first free South African election:

> After breakfast, we drove out to Bishopscourt, the "official" residence of the Archbishop of Cape Town where Nelson Mandela had spent his first night of freedom after his release on February 11, 1990, and left the leafy upmarket suburb named after the Archbishop's residence to go and vote. I had decided that I would cast my vote in a ghetto township. The symbolism was powerful; the solidarity with those who for so long had been disenfranchised, living daily in the deprivation and squalor of apartheid's racially segregated ghetto townships. After all, I was one of them. When I became Archbishop in 1986, the Group Areas Act, which segregated residential areas racially was still in force. It was a criminal offence for me, a Nobel laureate without a vote and now Archbishop and Metropolitan of the Anglican Church in southern Africa, to occupy Bishopscourt with my family unless I had first obtained a special permit exempting me from the provisions of the Group Areas Act. I had, however, announced, after my election as Archbishop that I would not be applying for such a permit. I said I was Archbishop, would be occupying the Archbishop's official residence and that the apartheid government could act as it saw fit. No charges were ever preferred against me for contravening this obnoxious law.[36]

In 1992, SACC organized an important meeting of religious leaders, the National Inter-Faith Conference in Pretoria, that drafted proposed language for the Constitution's religion clauses.[37] The conference was also sponsored by the South African chapter of the World Conference on Religion and Peace (WCRP-SA). The conference issued a *Declaration of Rights and Responsibilities of Religious People*.[38] Professors Lourens du Plessis and Huge Corder acknowledge that the WCRP-SA proposed language assisted their work as Technical Committee members in drafting the religion part of the Interim Constitution.

---

[35] *Supra* n. 29.

[36] Desmond Tutu, No Future without Forgiveness 4–5 (1999).

[37] Lourens du Plessis, Hugh Corder, Understanding South Africa's Transitional Bill of Rights 155–56 (Kenwyn: Juta 1994).

[38] World Conference on Religion and Peace Media release, "Declaration on the Rights and Responsibilities of Religious People," http://70.84.171.10?~etools/newbrief/1992/news9211.13 (last visited Jan. 19, 2008).

DuPlessis and Corder have written that, "[d]uring the negotiations, it soon became clear that the negotiators had no intention whatsoever of using the Constitution and the Bill of Rights to erect walls to separate church and state."[39] Indeed, the Interim Constitution's Preamble stated, "In humble submission to Almighty God." Moreover, the Postamble to the final Constitution states, "May God protect our people."[40] It also references *ubuntu*, the quasi-religious South African concept of social harmony and inclusion.[41]

South Africa is about 80 percent Christian, but there are a wide variety of Christian denominations.[42] Many black South Africans believe in both Christianity and in parts of traditional African religion.[43] Moreover, "African traditionalists make up the second largest religious group, accounting for nearly fifteen percent of the South African population."[44]

The brutal means by which some whites forced blacks to become Christian, however, should not be forgotten. The noted anti-apartheid activist and Black Consciousness Movement leader Steven Biko wrote powerfully about religious colonization:

> There was no hell in our religion. We believed in the inherent goodness of man – hence we took it for granted that all people at death joined the community of saints and therefore merited our respect. It was the missionaries who confused people with their new religion. They scared our people with stories of hell. They painted their God as a demanding God who wanted worship "or else." People had to discard their clothes and their customs in order to be accepted in this new religion. Knowing how religious the African people were, the missionaries stepped up their terror campaign on the emotions of the people with their detailed accounts of eternal burning.[45]

Makau wa Mutua argues that African society should continue to discourage missionaries because proselytizing religions remain a threat to

---

[39] *Id.*

[40] Farlam, *supra* n. 7 at 41–46 n. 3.

[41] Christopher Roederer, "The Transformation of South African Private Law Ten Years after Democracy," 37 Colum. Hum. Rts. L. Rev. 447, 499 (2006).

[42] CIA – The World Factbook – South Africa, https://www.cia.gov/cia/publications/factbook/print/sf.html (last visited Aug. 21, 2006). *See also* Erin E. Goodsell, "Constitution, Custom, and Creed: Balancing Human Rights Concerns with Cultural and Religious Freedom in Today's South Africa," 21 BYU J. of Public L. 109, 115 (2006); *Supra* n. 19 at 1. The term "coloured" is not generally thought to be derogatory in South Africa as it might be in the United States. In South Africa, the term means someone of mixed race.

[43] *Supra* n. 19 at 1; Lourens du Plessis, "Religious Human Rights in South Africa," in van der Vyver, *supra* n. 11 at 442.

[44] Goodsell, *supra* n. 42 at 115.

[45] Biko, *supra* n. 21 at 4.

African indigenous cultures.[46] As is shown later in this chapter, one goal of the South African Constitution is to protect indigenous religions.

Through the efforts of Archbishop Tutu, various religious leaders, and other groups, South Africa established the Truth & Reconciliation Commission (TRC) in 1995. The TRC's emphasis on truth telling, forgiveness, and rebirth reveals its religious underpinnings. Nonetheless, the TRC remains controversial as discussed in an earlier chapter.

THE FORMALISTIC CASES

The South African Constitution has two major religion provisions. Section 15 states in part that

(1) Everyone has the right to freedom of conscience, religion, thought, belief and opinion.
(2) Religious observances may be conducted at state or state-aided institutions provided that –
    (a) those observances follow rules made by the appropriate public authorities;
    (b) they are conducted on an equitable basis; and
    (c) attendance at them is free and voluntary.

Section 15(3) explains that Parliament can pass legislation to recognize customary law, including traditional marriages. Such recognition, however, "must be consistent with this section and the other provisions of the Constitution."

Section 15 is noteworthy because it does not contain an establishment clause and therefore allows more religion in the public square than does the U.S. Constitution. Moreover, it authorizes religious observances in public institutions, with some restrictions. It also protects freedom of conscience and opinion.

Section 15's accommodationist nature raises the possibility of Christian dominance. Section 31, however, protects all religious communities:

---

[46] *Supra* n. 25. Specifically, Mutua asserts that proselytizing, as part of the right to freedom of religion, should be limited in Africa so that Christian and Islamic missionaries cannot use their superior wealth, resources, and technology to further subvert the right to self-determination of African cultures. This is interesting as it extends the self determination principle, which was used to justify creating sovereign nations, to protect domestic indigenous culture. By contrast, a European Court of Human Rights decision struck down a Greek law that restricted religious proselytizing. Kokkinakis v. Greece, 17 E.H.R.R. 397 (1993 ECHR).

(1) Persons belonging to a cultural, religious, or linguistic community may not be denied the right, with other members of that community –
    (a) to enjoy their culture, practice their religion and use their language...
(2) The rights in subsection (1) may not be exercised in a manner inconsistent with any provision of the Bill of Rights.

The South African religion provisions seek to facilitate pluralism but they are subject to the remaining Bill of Rights provisions. This tension, particularly between gender equality and traditionalism, has bubbled to the surface in South African debates over establishing customary law courts.[47] Commentators such as Ebrahim Moosa and Garth Abraham object that Section 31 subordinates religion to other rights.[48] By contrast, Charles Villa-Vicencio seemingly supports the section's approach.[49]

If there is a violation of either section 15 or section 31, the question becomes whether the government can justify its actions. The limitations clause plays a large role in the religion cases.[50]

The Sunday "Prohibition" Case

The Constitutional Court's first religion case, *S. v. Lawrence*,[51] which was decided in 1997, involved whether the state could ban grocery stores from selling liquor on Sundays. The Court correctly found there was no freedom of religion violation but used flawed reasoning to reach this conclusion. Chief Justice Arthur Chaskalson's plurality explained that

---

[47] Pearlie Joubert, "Back to the Dark Day, Mail & Guardian online," May 17, 2008, http://www.mg.co.za/articlePage.aspx?articleid=339389&area=/insight/insight_national/ (last visited May 18, 2008).

[48] Ebrahim Moosa, "Tensions in Legal and Religious Values in the 1996 South African Constitution," in Mahmood Mamdani, (Ed)., Beyond Rights Talk and Culture Talk 121–35 (2000) at 7 ("The 1993 Constitution did not explicitly require religious practices to be consistent with the overall constitutional values, but the final text was amended in order to make such a qualification explicit.") & 10 ("The partnership between religion and state in South Africa, as some would describe it, reduces religion to the 'junior partner.' There are no clauses which protect religion from the caprice of the state."); Garth Abraham, "Declaration on Religious Rights and Responsibilities: A Catholic Response," 111 S. Afr. L. J. 344 (1994).

[49] Charles Villa-Vicencio, A Theology of Reconstruction 264–68 (Cambridge Univ. Press 1992).

[50] To be a valid limitation, section 36 specifies that the law must also be "of general application to the extent that the limitation is reasonable and justifiable in an open and democratic society based on human dignity, equality and freedom."

[51] 1997 (4) SA 1176 (CC).

Sunday had become a secularized day of rest and that the law did not coerce people to make Sunday a holy day. Chaskalson added that South Africa's Interim Constitution allowed noncoercive public school prayer.[52]

Justice Chaskalson's reference to Sunday's secularization surprisingly echoes the U.S. Supreme Court as discussed later.[53] Yet Lourens du Plessis responds, "At any rate, had Sunday been a general day of rest, then wine and liquor should arguably be more freely available on this day than on normal days of work."[54] In addition, Chaskalson's coercion test does not protect religious minorities from subtle forms of indoctrination, which concerns scholars such as Mutua.

The Court's formalism is unexpected because Justice Chaskalson stressed its rejection of an American approach:

> Section 14 does not include an "establishment clause" and in my view we ought not to read into its provisions principles pertaining to the advance- ment or inhibition of religion by the state. To do so would have far reaching implications beyond the scope and purpose of section 14. If such obliga- tions on the part of the state are to be read into section 14, does this mean that Christmas Day and Easter Friday can no longer be public holidays, that "Family Day" is suspect because it falls on Easter Monday, that the SABC as public broadcaster cannot broadcast church services... These examples can be multiplied by reference to the extremely complex United States law which has developed around the "establishment clause."[55]

Moreover, Chaskalson had explicitly rejected American approaches in other areas such as the death penalty.

In her dissent, Justice Kate O'Regan argued that the purpose and effect of banning liquor sales specifically on Sunday were to benefit religion.[56] When the *national* government honors a Christian day of rest, it is not conducting religious observance on an "equitable basis."[57] In the pro- portionality analysis, she found the government's justification wanting

---

[52] This view of school prayer was supported by Nicholas Smith, "Freedom of Religion under the Final Constitution," 114 S. Afr. L. J. 217, 220 (1997). *Lawrence* was decided under the Interim Constitution's religion clause that resembles the final one so the result would remain the same.

[53] Justice Chaskalson mentions the U.S. Supreme Court cases but suggests he is not fol- lowing them. Par. 98 n. 81. However, his opinion's rejection of Sunday's religious dimension is similar.

[54] "Freedom of or Freedom from Religion? An Overview of Issues Pertinent to the Consti- tutional Protection of Religious Rights and Freedom in the 'New South Africa,'" 2001 BYU L. Rev. 439, 453 (also referencing the opinion's "secular sanitization").

[55] Lawrence, *supra* Par. 102.   [56] *Id.* Par. 127.

[57] *Id.* Par. 122.

because people could buy liquor elsewhere. O'Regan's approach is similar to the Canadian Supreme Court that had ruled unconstitutional a Sunday closing law, though that law had even more exceptions.[58]

Justice O'Regan's reasoning has at least three problems. First, the law's ineffectiveness means that it does not really burden those who seek liquor. Second, her approach reads like it was based on the Constitution's equality provision, not its religion sections.[59] The boundary between the provisions is unclear. Third she is actually more separationist than the U.S. Supreme Court because she finds that the law promotes religion too much, a view even rejected by the American Justices in Sunday closing cases. She reads a strict establishment clause into the South African Constitution.[60]

Justice Albie Sachs concurred with the Chaskalson plurality opinion but diverged from its reasoning. He agreed with O'Regan that the law violated freedom of religion but found the infringement *de minimis*.[61] For example, he noted that the plaintiff was actually not a religious person and suffered no offense. The plaintiff therefore had used the religion argument for commercial purposes. Unlike O'Regan, Sachs determined that the law served an important purpose by reducing drunken driving

---

[58] *Id.* Par. 126 n. 8. Interestingly, the Canadian case is cited even more prominently by Justice Chaskalson though he tries to distinguish its facts.

[59] Iain Currie, Johan de Waal, The Bill of Rights Handbook 273 (Kenwyn: 3d Ed. Juta 2000).

[60] Jerry Ismail, "South Africa's Sunday Law: Finding a Compromise," 12 Ind. Int'l & Comp. L. Rev. 1, 22 (2000) ("The dissent stated that there was no establishment clause in the Constitution, then proceeded to find one."); Christof Heyns, Danie Brand, "The Constitutional Protection of Religious Human Rights in South Africa," 14 Emory Int'l L. Rev. 699, 763 (2000) ("An implicit, general prohibition of the establishment of religion, insofar as this is done in an inequitable manner, should consequently be read into Section 14.") Section 15 of the final Constitution is quite similar to Section 14 of the Interim Constitution. *See also* Du Plessis, *supra* n. 43 at 450 (In discussing the South African Constitution, Du Plessis writes, "Tolerance of religious diversity goes beyond putting up with the free exercise of divergent religious beliefs and practices. It also entails the evenhanded treatment of diverse religions and of religious groups, communities, and institutions with potentially conflicting interests. A broadly conceived establishment clause can play a significant role in guaranteeing such treatment. The equality clause in the South African Constitution arguably caters to such expansively understood establishment concerns.").

[61] Other commentators find the views of Sachs and O'Regan more persuasive than that of Chaskalson. Paul Farlam, "The Ambit of the Right of Freedom of Religion," 14 S. Afr. J. Hum. Rts. 298, 303 (1998). Similarly, in *Jordan*, the prostitution case addressed in the Chapter 4, Justices Sachs and O'Regan dissented and rejected a government argument that the original moralistic purpose of some legislation had "shifted" over time and had become more acceptable. Par. 111.

accidents on weekends and holidays. Justice Sachs also sought to promote transformation and to protect religious minorities.

Sachs invented the government's drunk driving rationale *post hoc.* In addition, he adopted U.S. Supreme Court Justice Sandra Day O'Connor's "endorsement test" by asking whether a "reasonable non-sectarian South African" would find that this law favored Christians. This test, however, is vague, particularly for analyzing social attitudes toward the supernatural. Nonetheless, Sachs's emphasis on the need to carefully examine the factual context of the case (commercial plaintiffs and *de minimis* harms) and his focus on protecting religious minorities makes his opinion the strongest.[62]

How would this case be approached by the U.S. Supreme Court? The First Amendment's establishment clause (EC) states, "Congress shall make no law respecting an establishment of religion." The American framers designed the EC to prevent the government from promoting religion too much, whereas the clause – "prohibiting the free exercise thereof" – sought to prevent the government from suppressing religion. The South Africa framers left out an EC because they felt that it revealed hostility to religion. An EC also seemed unnecessary because laws promoting religion excessively would likely hurt other religions and thus could be challenged under free exercise grounds.

The South African framers also disliked U.S. Supreme Court EC decisions. For example, the Supreme Court adopted a three-part test for determining whether a law accorded with the EC in a 1971 decision, *Lemon v. Kurtzman*[63]: The law must have a secular purpose, its primary effect had to be neither to advance nor hinder religion, and it had to avoid excessive entanglement. Putting aside the ambiguity in these criteria and their separationist bias, the Supreme Court eventually replaced *Lemon sub silentio* with a neutrality test focusing on whether religious interests are being treated as well as secular interests.[64]

---

[62] *Lawrence, Id.* at Par. 141 ("We should be astute not to lay down sweeping interpretations at this stage but should allow doctrine to develop slowly and, hopefully, surely, on a case by case basis with special emphasis on the actual context in which each problem arose.").

[63] 403 U.S. 602 (1971).

[64] The Court has almost stopped looking at entanglement. The analysis was circular anyway as it turned on the question of whether the law would likely create social controversy, thus providing incentives for groups to foment conflict. Moreover, it is not clear why it would matter whether the law's primary effect is to hinder religion because that would seem to be a free exercise problem, not an EC problem. The leading "neutrality" case is perhaps Zelman v. Simmons-Harris, 536 U.S. 639 (2002) (the Court

The U.S. Supreme Court also upheld American Sunday closing laws, as preserving a day of rest, in the 1961 case of *McGowan v. Maryland.*[65] The Court decided the case a decade before *Lemon* so the ruling reflected a less separationist attitude, but it is still good law. The fact that Sunday happened to be the Christian day of worship did not constitute an EC violation any more than laws against murder were problematic because they correspond to the Ten Commandments. The American Court also reasoned that the plaintiffs were not religious and, as in the South African case, were only using the U.S. Constitution's religion provisions to promote commerce.

Spanking in the Schools

The Court's second major religion case, *Christian Education South Africa v. Minister of Education,*[66] involved a religious organization that asked for an exemption from a national law that banned corporal punishment in schools. This group took literally the biblical injunction, "Spare the rod and spoil the child." This case resembles a classic free exercise restriction under the U.S. Supreme Court's framework, unlike the Sunday liquor law case that involved the establishment of religion.

Justice Sachs authored a unanimous opinion finding no constitutional violation yet he bypassed the central question. He assumed *arguendo* that the law infringed on religious rights and then engaged in proportionality analysis. After recognizing corporal punishment's importance to the religious group, he concluded that the government's interest in protecting the dignity of children was stronger, given apartheid's brutality as well as international legal trends rejecting such punitive actions.

Sachs acknowledged that the Christian group had a protocol for how and when teachers could administer corporal punishment. It instructed the teacher to do the following: "Position the child, have them lean forward with feet spread apart. Put their hands on the desk. You want them to be stationery (sic). You don't want to hurt the child. Discipline is one thing, damage is another... Love the child, smile and tell them that you love them... Reaffirm your relationship with that child. When the child leaves they need to know that the slate is clean." Sachs, however, said there would be problems monitoring the use of corporal punishment

---

approved a tuition voucher plan because it permitted parents to spend state monies on tuition for all private schools, even though 96% of participating students went to religious private schools).

[65] 366 U.S. 420 (1961).   [66] 2000 SACLR Lexis 79.

in schools.[67] Most importantly, he stated that Christian parents could still use corporal punishment at home so the law did not burden them very much.[68]

Sachs wrote a minimalist opinion based on the limitations clause that did not fully resolve the conflict between the religious minority and the competing international human rights norms designed to protect children. One commentary argues, "This is an extremely artificial way of deciding a case. The balancing exercise required by the limitation clause cannot be accurately carried out with only a 'hypothetical' violation of rights on one side of the scale."[69] But any broader decision by Sachs could have had enormous ramifications for controversial issues such as the constitutionality of traditional religious practices like polygamy. Moreover, Justice Sachs assumed the gravity of the rights violation experienced by the Christian group, which takes care of the concern about the hypothetical nature of the violation.

Critics, however, are correct that this decision reflects a Court that is not ready to address the hardest religion questions. Patrick Lenta argues pragmatically that the group's request for a judicial exemption was hurt by the refusal of Parliament to grant one. This made the case look like the "rear guard strategy of a sore loser."[70]

How would this case have been decided by the U.S. Supreme Court? The key free exercise case is *Employment Division v. Smith*,[71] in which the Court ruled that the state did not violate the religious rights of two Native Americans by denying them unemployment compensation benefits, because they were fired for using an illegal drug called peyote. It also did not help their case that they had been drug counselors. The plaintiffs, however, argued that they adhered to a Native American religion in which peyote was as essential as wine is to the Catholic communion. Thus, they claimed that the firing unconstitutionally forced them to choose between their job and their religion.

---

[67] *Id.* at Par. 5 n. 4.

[68] Nicholas Smith, "Freedom of Religion in the Constitutional Court," 118 S. Afr. L. J. 1, 8 (2001) ("Banning corporal punishment in schools does not entail the suppression of the entire worldview of any religious grouping."). Patrick Lenta has said that the Sachs opinion means the dignity rights of children outweigh the religious group's need for an exemption. "Judicial Restraint and Overreach," 20 S. Afr. J. Hum. Rts. 544, 566 (2004).

[69] Ian Currie, Johan de Waal, The Bill of Rights Handbook 166 n. 11 (Wetton: 5th ed. Juta 2005).

[70] Lenta, *supra* n. 68. Lenta's phraseology is great for a case involving spanking.

[71] 494 U.S. 872 (1990).

Justice Antonin Scalia's majority opinion was controversial. He had to choose between two traditionally conservative positions: upholding a criminal law or upholding a freedom of religion claim. Ultimately, he favored the criminal law and refused the plaintiffs' exemption so as to avoid a slippery slope. His opinion established three freedom of exercise categories.

First, general laws that burden religion should only receive rationality review, creating a presumption against judicial exemptions. He placed *Smith* in this category because the state's antidrug laws were general. Second, ad hoc government decisions about whether to accommodate an individual's religion should receive strict scrutiny because there are greater chances of an arbitrary approach. Third, general laws that burdened religion and also impinged on some other fundamental right should receive strict scrutiny. This last category justified the Court in granting an exemption in *Wisconsin v. Yoder*[72] and allowed Scalia to distinguish that case from *Smith*. Most scholars, however, criticize *Smith* as hostile to religion and as not really being distinct from *Yoder*.

Even using the reasoning in *Smith*, the South African corporal punishment case would have been decided in the same way. The law against corporal punishment applies generally and thus deserves rationality. The law would be upheld because it protects children from abuse. Once again, the American result would be the same despite distinct constitutional provisions.

Smoking Weed and the Court

Perhaps the Constitutional Court's most important religion case was *Prince v. President of the Law Society of the Cape of Good Hope*.[73] The South African Law Society prohibited a Rastafarian law graduate, Garreth Prince, from becoming a lawyer, because he was twice convicted of cannabis possession and planned to continue using the drug as part of his religion. Prince claimed that the law was overbroad, given less restrictive alternatives,[74] and that he should be exempted because cannabis already enjoyed medical and research exemptions.[75] The Court, however, found

---

[72] 406 U.S. 205 (1972) (Court grants the Amish an exemption from state law requiring that children complete high school since Amish children complete ninth grade and the job of children is to work and learn at home after that point – religious and parental rights involved).

[73] 2002 (3) BCLR 231 (CC), 2002 SACLR Lexis 12.

[74] *Id.* Par. 114.   [75] *Id.* Par. 117.

that the Law Society did not violate Mr. Prince's rights. It is striking how similar these facts and the result are to the U.S. Supreme Court's *Smith* case involving peyote.

Prince was such a significant case that it merited two opinions. The Court had ruled previously that it needed a more complete evidentiary record regarding the Rastafarian religion. In addition, only nine of the eleven Justices voted in the second opinion; Justices Kate O'Regan and Pius Langa did not participate. This part of the chapter analyzes *Prince*'s strengths and weaknesses and explains why the dissenters made the better arguments, particularly Justice Sachs.

Chief Justice Chaskalson's Majority Opinion

Chief Justice Chaskalson's majority opinion was co-authored by Justices Ackermann and Kriegler, another indication of the case's importance. Chaskalson began by acknowledging that Rastafarianism is a religion[76] and that cannabis was central to its inspiration and vision. Cannabis use, however, often took place in an unstructured context. Nonetheless, the Court noted Mr. Prince's practice of ingesting "about 5 grams of cannabis daily for meditational purposes."[77] Mr. Prince claimed never to smoke cannabis more than twice a day and never before work. Mr. Prince admitted that some Rastafarians abused cannabis but others acted with restraint. He said that the religion disdained the abuses.

Then, the court explained that Rastafarian religious gatherings took place whenever two Rastafari gather in "Jah's" name. An official building was unnecessary for worship and rarely existed. Justice Chaskalson then said there was no organizational structure that could monitor cannabis distribution or usage and that there were too few members for such a structure. He acknowledged that this lack of structure also reflected the religion's world view.[78] Regarding cannabis, Justice Chaskalson wrote, "The use is extensive and takes different forms, including smoking it, burning it, using it as incense, in the preparation of food and drink, and in bathing."[79]

Interestingly, Chaskalson dismissed the value of this history to the case by declaring that "Sachs J refers to the history of the prohibition of the use of cannabis in South Africa. Whatever that history might have

---

[76] *Prince*. Par. 97.   [77] *Id*. Par. 100.
[78] *Id*. Par. 101.
[79] Par. 103. Later he describes the Rastafarian religion's disorganization. Par. 135–137.

been, it is not in our view relevant to the constitutionality of the present legislation."[80]

The majority determined that limitation was the crucial issue because the Law Society clearly infringed on Mr. Prince's religious freedom. Chaskalson then found, however, that the government's justification for doing so outweighed the burden on Mr. Prince because the state's goal was to cut off the supply of a potentially dangerous drug, even if certain cannabis uses might not be harmful.[81] Chaskalson suggested that any other decision would place South Africa in violation of international laws against drug trafficking.

Next, the majority discussed the U.S. Supreme Court's peyote decision, *Smith*.[82] Justice Chaskalson noted that the South African Constitutional Court would apply a stricter level of scrutiny, akin to Justice Blackmun's dissent in *Smith*, given the South African Constitution's goal of protecting minority religions. Under strict scrutiny, Blackmun had reasoned that the Native Americans should have prevailed because there was no evidence that granting an exemption would fuel an illegal peyote market. But Chaskalson argued that there is an illegal global trade in cannabis, unlike peyote.[83]

Chaskalson concluded that an exemption or permit system, as recommended by Justice Ngcobo, would have inherent administrative problems because a police officer could not determine whether particular cannabis stashes were illicit or religious.[84] Such a system would also rely too much on the cannabis user's self-discipline.

Justice Ngcobo's Dissent

Justice Ngcobo's dissent argued that the evidence showed that occasional cannabis smoking was harmless.[85] There was also no proof that using cannabis as incense, from a chalice, in a brownie, or bathing in it caused injury.[86] There was evidence, however, that long-term smoking of large amounts could create psychological dependence.[87] Ngcobo then stated there were strict protocols regarding how cannabis should be used.[88] He also described the Rastafarian religion's structure in South Africa.[89]

---

[80] Par. 105.
[81] Par. 116.
[82] 494 U.S. 872 (1990).
[83] *Prince* Par. 129.
[84] *Id.* Par. 129–130, 134.
[85] Par. 25.
[86] Par. 28.
[87] Pars. 24, 26, 53, 55.
[88] Pars. 40, 62.
[89] Pars. 16 & 70 (discussing the organization of the Rastafarian communities and the presence of seven priests in the country).

His characterization of the religion contrasts sharply with Chaskalson's portrait of disarray.

Justice Ngcobo agreed that the limitations clause was decisive. Ngcobo said that South Africa's religion provisions were designed to promote diversity and to promote the connection between religion and human dignity. He added that the case involved "a practice deeply rooted in African traditional worship,"[90] and that the law stigmatized Rastafari by turning them into criminals.[91] Thus, to support a total ban, the government had to show that virtually all uses were harmful.[92] Chaskalson by contrast focused on whether the law prevented distribution and essentially took harm for granted.

Justice Ngcobo concluded that a permit system was feasible, even if it might not work perfectly: "Such control and regulation may include restrictions on the individuals who may be authorized to possess cannabis; the source from which it may be obtained; the amount that can be kept in possession; and the purpose for which it may be used."[93] The state could establish a registration system in which the permit could be revoked upon misuse. Even the South African Narcotics Bureau Commander admitted that such systems could work.[94] Ngcobo gave the legislature one year to enact the permit system.[95] He gave the Law Society, however, discretion regarding how it should proceed with Mr. Prince.[96]

Justice Sachs's Dissent

The Sachs dissent emphasized the government's obligation to care for the historically disadvantaged. He explained that Ethiopian Emperor Haile Selassie I, once known as the Prince Regent Ras Tafari, was a venerated African king who smoked cannabis.[97] Sachs then described how smoking dagga (the "holy herb") was supposed to be the mystical instrument for healing the African diaspora's wounds.[98]

In a footnote, Sachs discussed Justice Blackmun's *Smith* dissent, in which Blackmun favored a peyote exemption but not a marijuana

---

[90] Par. 58.
[92] Par. 57.
[94] Par. 68.
[96] Par. 88.

[91] Par. 51.
[93] Par. 64.
[95] Pars. 65, 66, 86.

[97] Par. 145 n. 3. Sachs noted, "During argument it was submitted on behalf of the A-G that if a religious exemption in favour of the Rastafari were to be allowed this would lead to an influx of gangsters and other drug abusers into their community. The assumption which this submission makes demonstrates the vulnerability of this group." Par. 146.
[98] Par. 152. He described "dreadlocks" as an outward manifestation of the faith.

exemption. Sachs disagreed arguing that a limited dagga exemption would not injure the government's interdiction efforts.[99] He also critiqued a status quo approach which he characterized as:

> The tendency to somnambulistically sustain the existing system of administration of justice and the mind-set that goes with it, simply because, like Everest, it is there. . . . The hydraulic insistence on conformity could have a particularly negative impact on the Rastafari, who are easily identifiable, subject to prejudice and politically powerless, indeed, precisely the kind of discrete and insular minority whose interests courts abroad and in this country have come jealously to protect.[100]

This discrete and insular minority reference echoes the U.S. Supreme Court's *Carolene Products* footnote 4 as mentioned in earlier chapters.[101]

Sachs argued that the Constitutional Court should employ a transformative approach because South Africa had historically oppressed minority religious groups such as Mulsims and Hindus. He stated that the Court should balance the needs of the religious groups against law enforcement needs. He expressed disappointment that the attorney general had made no effort to work out an exemption with the Rastafarians.[102] He disputed Chaskalson's view that international law prohibitedcannabis exemptions.

Sachs also favorably discussed Germany's decriminalization approach.[103] He concluded, however, that Parliament should design any exemption, not the Constitutional Court.[104] He also recommended that the Law Society not maintain Mr. Prince's exclusion without a powerful justification.[105]

Analysis of the *Prince* Decision

Justice Sachs authored the most persuasive opinion for the reasons discussed in this section.

---

[99] Par. 152 n. 138.

[100] Par. 157. He added: "Rastafari are compelled to litigate to invoke their constitutional rights. They experience life as a marginalized group seen to dress and behave strangely, living on the outer reaches rather than in the mainstream of public life."

[101] 304 U.S. 144 (1938).   [102] *Prince* Par. 162.

[103] *Id.* Par. 166.   [104] Par. 148.

[105] Par. 170. Sachs also drew an analogy between Mr. Prince's exclusion and the exclusion from the legal profession faced by lawyers such as Bram Fischer and Ghandi. *See generally* Kenneth S. Broun, Black Lawyers, White Courts 18–19 & 162–63 (2000).

PROBLEMS WITH CHASKALSON'S OPINION. Chief Justice Chaskalson's opinion is flawed because of its formalism. First, Chaskalson dismissed the Rastafari history of oppression and stigma even though it showed that Mr. Prince was the kind of black South African that other black South Africans discriminated against. Yet Chaskalson wrote, "Whatever that history might have been, it is not in our view relevant to the constitutionality of the present legislation."[106] The Chief Justice showed further detachment when he said that the court cannot resolve the matter because "the Rastafarian Houses are not parties to the litigation."[107]

Second, Chaskalson showed little sympathy for the profound conflict between Mr. Princes's faith and his career. Chaskalson almost suggests that Prince's religion was a conduit to smoke weed recreationally.

Third, Chaskalson was overly concerned with the difficulties that law enforcement might face enforcing a permit system. This is backwards and hard to understand. As Patrick Lenta writes, "The majority in *Prince* did not appear to give sufficient protection to the appellant's right to freedom of religion.... The majority's decision appears to be excessively deferential in accepting that the state's interest in banning all consumption of cannabis outweighs the possibility of even a circumscribed exemption."[108]

Nonetheless, former Justice Richard Goldstone still maintains the decision was correct because "the exemption that [Prince] wanted was as wide as the prohibition. During argument, I asked whether an exemption of less than 24 hours a day, seven days a week use of cannabis would be acceptable and the response was that it was all or nothing. To have granted an exemption in those terms would have made the law impossible to administer."[109]

Fourth, Chaskalson's formalism actually resembles the U.S. Supreme Court's distressing ruling in *Gonzales v. Raich*.[110] The issue in that case was whether Congress's power to regulate commerce "among the states" could support prosecuting a woman, under federal law, for smoking locally grown marijuana that alleviated chronic pain. No other drug reduced her suffering. The Court showed little sympathy for the woman and far greater interest in the government's ability to fight the war on drugs. Several conservative Justices even ignored their federalist

---

[106] Par. 109. [107] Par. 142.
[108] Lenta, *supra* n. 68 at 565.
[109] E-mail from Justice Goldstone to Professor Kende, May 27, 2008 (on file with author).
[110] 125 S.Ct. 2195 (2005).

state-rights instincts to support this national intrusion into local self-administered medical care. The Supreme Court justified its ruling in part because of "the enforcement difficulties that attend distinguishing between marijuana cultivated locally and marijuana grown elsewhere, and concern about diversion into local channels." This sounds like the reasoning in *Prince*.

Moreover, Chaskalson could have reached the same result in a transformative way. He could have argued that a permit system would endanger Rastafarian religious liberty by requiring government "entanglement" with the group. Prince and the other Rastafarians, however, would probably prefer to use dagga even if that meant some regulatory entanglement.

PROBLEMS WITH NGCOBO'S DISSENT. Justice Ngcobo authored an impressive opinion sympathizing with Mr. Prince and other Rastafarians. He described the Rastafarian religion's "structure" in South Africa respectfully while admitting it was not like a traditional Christian church. He also discussed cannabis health effects in a sophisticated way by differentiating its various uses.

Ngcobo, did, however, write approvingly about the "war on drugs" even though evidence suggests the war has not been effective.[111] Moreover, Justice Ngcobo concluded in an unsatisfactory way by writing, "The validity of the decision of the Law Society depends upon whether possession or use of cannabis by persons in the position of the appellant is a criminal offence. As pointed out previously, it cannot be said at this stage whether Parliament will broaden the category of persons who may be authorized to possess and use cannabis for religious purposes to include non-priests such as the appellant."[112] Given Ngcobo's earlier analysis, he should have vigorously encouraged the Law Society to admit Mr. Prince, especially because Mr. Prince waited so long for the Court's two decisions.

WHY SACHS'S DISSENT IS THE MOST PERSUASIVE. Justice Sachs emphasized the transformative purpose of the Constitution's religion provision. For example, unlike Ngcobo, Sachs did not justify Rastafarianism by focusing on its structure and thus avoided buying into a Western concept of religion. Sachs also described the harsh reality of South African official bias toward the group. Moreover, he noted that restrictions on comparable Christian religious practices would not be tolerated.

---

[111] *Id.*, Prince, Pars. 52 & 154.   [112] *Id.* Par. 88.

Furthermore, Sachs was correct that a context-specific analysis is best able to resolve these difficult issues. For example, he revealed that there is a continuum of possible permit systems that raise differing problems. A system giving cannabis to priests for distribution to co-religionists could be more readily monitored than one in which Mr. Prince received it directly from government officials.[113] Finally, Justice Sachs was cautious about the unelected court's role, leaving the ultimate decisions to Parliament. Sachs's opinion, however, is flawed in that he romanticized Rastafarianism given that it historically had a violent racist streak embodied in the slogan, "beating down Babylon."[114]

To summarize, the Constitutional Court in *Prince* reached the same result as the U.S. Supreme Court in *Smith*. Moreover, both cases left vulnerable minorities, who engaged in religiously motivated drug use, unprotected from majoritarian sentiments. This consistency is odd, however, given the South African Constitution's more progressive provisions.

Nose Studs and the Court

In 2007, the Constitutional Court in *Kwa Zulu Minister of Education v. Pillay*[115] unanimously ruled that an elite private girl's high school could not prevent a student of South Indian ancestry from wearing a nose stud, despite school uniform policies. Chief Justice Langa said the school should have granted an exemption based on the freedom of religion and cultural protection provisions of the Prevention of Discrimination and Equality Protection Act of 2000 (PDEPA).[116] The Act implemented the corresponding constitutional provisions. Ironically, the school was an island of diversity among elite institutions.[117]

According to South Indian Hindu culture, families frequently honored young women who reached puberty by placing a gold stud in their nose.[118] The school, however, after consulting with experts, concluded it had no obligation to accommodate a mere cultural practice.[119] Langa disagreed by reasoning that the school policy against jewelry disadvantaged

---

[113] *Id.* Par. 148.

[114] *See generally* "Ennis Barrington Edmonds, Rastafari: From Outcasts to Culture Barriers; Edward Rothstein, Mystics and Militants: A Look at the Rastafari Kingdom," N.Y. Times, A16, May 10, 2008.

[115] CCT 51/06 (Oct. 5, 2007).   [116] *Id.* Par. 39.

[117] Par. 125.   [118] Par. 59.

[119] Par. 132.

minority cultures and religions though it appeared neutral.[120] For example, the policy allowed earrings but not a nose stud.[121]

Justice Langa then engaged in proportionality analysis under the PDEPA. He said that the Court should not question the family's sincerity.[122] He reasoned that the burden on the girl of denying permission for the nose stud far outweighed the school's interests in uniformity.[123] For example, there was no evidence that wearing a nose stud caused any disruptions.[124] Langa also rejected slippery slope concerns reasoning that this item had unique cultural and religious significance. The fact that the mother did not consult with the school initially and that the student never testified in the Equality Court proceedings did not nullify the claims.

Justice O'Regan concurred but disagreed with Langa's reasoning. She saw the case as being about a cultural practice, not a religious mandate, and said that an objective test should be used in weighing plaintiff's interest.[125] She also pointed out that culture is dynamic and therefore differed from dignity interests. Then, she argued that the school had inconsistently granted exemptions in less compelling circumstances.[126] Moreover, the school lacked formal procedures for evaluating exemption requests.[127]

What is fascinating is that the Court downplayed its earlier religion decisions in this case. For example, the Court presumed that the plaintiff had a strong accommodation case unlike the Rastafarian lawyer in *Prince*. The mother's testimony was enough in this case but Mr. Prince's testimony was treated with skepticism. Moreover, the Court in *Pillay* said that the school's case was not strengthened by the fact that the student could still wear the nose stud outside school. Yet, in *Christian Education*, the Court said that the parental religious interest was adequately accounted for because corporal punishment could be administered at home. At least, *Pillay* takes the Court in a pluralist direction.

It is important to note that the Canadian Supreme Court ruled similarly in a more difficult case involving a Sikh child who wore a ceremonial knife, known as a *kirpan*, to school.[128] A knife is potentially more harmful than a nose stud yet the Canadian Court did not doubt the religious and cultural motivations underlying the child's actions. Langa's approach is more consistent with this strong deference to the minority than is

---

[120] Par. 44.   [121] *Id.*

[122] Par. 52.   [123] Par. 90–102.

[124] Par. 101.   [125] Par. 143.

[126] Pars. 164 & 170.   [127] Par. 173.

[128] Multani v. Commission scolaire Marguerite-Bourgeoys, (2006) 1 S.C.R. 256.

O'Regan's quest for objectivity. Yet, both Langa and O'Regan are more tolerant than the U.S. Supreme Court, which would, almost certainly, have ruled against the student as American lower courts have in similar situations.[129] Perhaps the only Western institutions that would be more hostile than the American federal courts would be the courts in France, which has strict separationism as exemplified in the policy of *laicite* that is behind the head scarf ban.[130]

WHY THE FORMALISM?

The Constitutional Court's transformative decisions regarding the death penalty and socioeconomic rights have rightly received international acclaim. By contrast, the religion cases are generally formalistic. Indeed, *Prince* is even more incomprehensible because a ruling in his favor would have been consistent with the potentially competing constitutional goals of transformation and traditional culture. The Court will be asked in the future to resolve more difficult conflicts between traditional practices, such as male inheritance, and remedying gender discrimination.[131] Using Durham's categories, Chaskalson took an accomodationist constitution and made it unduly majoritarian in *Lawrence* and separationist in *Prince*.[132] What then explains the difficulty?

Pierre de Vos critiques the court's "grand narrative" version of apartheid's elimination. Justice Chaskalson opinion in *Lawrence* "did not mention the apartheid government's well documented history of favoring and endorsing the Christian religion and imposing its practices on all South Africans."[133] De Vos writes, "One judge [Chaskalson] stuck to a version of our past as an apartheid-inspired event, a narrative that

---

[129] People v. Singh, 516 N.Y.S.2d 412 (N.Y. Crim. Ct. 1987) (employment case involving a Sikh man who sought to wear a kirpan). This result is even more certain after the Supreme Court's famous free exercise decision, Employment Division, Department of Human Resources v. Smith, 494 U.S. 872 (1990) (laws of general applicability burdening religious practice generally do not require courts to create exemptions).

[130] *See generally* John R. Bowen, Why the French Don't like Headscarves: Islam, the State and Public Space (2007).

[131] The Constitutional Court recently issued a pro-gender equality decision in Shilubana and Others v. Nwamitwa, Case CCT 3/07 (ruling that the tribe could make a daughter the tribal chief, in light of the Constitution, rather than follow traditional customary law that limited chiefdom to son). The case is extraordinary because the tribe unilaterally changed its practices, to take account of the new national gender equality principles.

[132] Justice Sachs's dissent in *Prince* highlights the accommodationist goals of the religion provisions. Par. 146.

[133] Pierre de Vos, "South Africa's Constitutional Court: Starry-Eyed in the Face of History?," 26 Vermont L. Rev. 837, 853 (2002).

was developed in previous judgments, while the others revisited that narrative and discovered its silence regarding religious minorities. The former judgment had the effect of reinforcing the status quo regarding religious observance, while the latter attempted to challenge it."[134] I think de Vos is right but does not go far enough.

Prince downplays how African religions are fundamentally different from the messianic traditions. As Steven Biko, Makau wa Mutua, and Ebrahim Moosa explain, African religion is integrated into people's daily lives. This is *ubuntu* in action. Biko wrote that even drinking beer is religious, though consumption does not occur in a church building and no minister is present. It is striking that the *Prince* majority could not see that dagga is as important to Rastafarians as the communion wine is to Catholics.[135] A Zulu individual made a similar point:

> The ANC (government of South Africa) wants to transplant customs from other countries here, and that will destroy the Zulu nation and all that we value. We are poor but do you see any beggars in the streets like you do in the cities? The Inkhosi (traditional chief) make sure that we are all provided for. The municipality will make beggars of us. When I have a problem, I can go see the Inkhosi any time, day or night. I don't need an appointment. They can have their civilization, brother.[136]

In a similar vein, Winnifred Sullivan writes, "The anthropologist Talal Asad would add...that this colonialist invention of 'religion' as an autonomous cultural form can only be understood in the context of the invention of the nation-state. 'The separation of religion from power,' he says, 'is a modern Western norm, the product of a unique post-Reformation history.'"[137] She argues that the constitutionalizing of religion betrays religion's place in traditional African

---

[134] *Id.* at 855.

[135] As mentioned earlier in the text, Moosa says another example of insensitivity is that the Constitution explicitly made religion subordinate to other constitutional provisions. This subordination resembles an American approach. Scott Idelman, "Why the State Must Subordinate Religion," in Stephen M. Feldman, (Ed.), Law and Religion: A Critical Anthology (New York: NYU Press 2004).

[136] Ayittey, *supra* n. 25 at 93. Although this statement has many controversial elements, it certainly expresses a sentiment that traditional culture is being undermined by the "transformation."

[137] Winnifred Fallers Sullivan, Religious Freedom and the Rule of Law: Exporting Modernity in a Post-Modern World, 22 Miss. C. L. Rev. 173, 178 (2003).

culture.[138] Chaskalson's *Lawrence* and *Prince* opinions ignore this effect.[139]

Does *Pillay* change things? Not much. How could the Court have ruled against one girl wearing a nose stud to an elite diverse school? It was also technically a statutory case. The Court has simply not embraced transformation in tougher religion cases.

Prince also revealed a racial divide. The majority was all white except for one Indian. The black African justices dissented, joined by Justice Sachs. They were more sensitive to the plight of religious minorities. The African Justice, Sandile Ncgobo, bought into the Western framework, arguing that religion requires some structure, but at least he weighed Mr. Prince's burden as more troubling. Why was Justice Sachs the only white justice to dissent? One reason may be that most of the Justices were not that religious anyway.

Moreover, in his book, *The Free Diary of Albie Sachs*, Justice Sachs suggests that his upbringing and flirtation with communism played a role in his progressive approach. Though he ultimately failed his father "as a Bolshevik," he was still distressed to see many ex-communists lose their instincts for liberation.[140] Sachs wrote,

> My concern today with avoiding the imposition of orthodoxies of behavior or belief by the state influences the way I interpret our Constitution. I have gone further than any of my colleagues in emphasizing that the Constitution calls for the widest recognition of openness, difference and pluralism. Indeed, central to my preoccupation with the case of the Rastafarian lawyer is the question of tolerance and the right to be different. It is easy to tolerate beliefs and practices that are familiar and enjoy strong political support. The true test of tolerance comes when the practices exist

---

[138] *Id.*

[139] Elsje Bonthuys, "Accommodating Gender, Race, Culture, and Religion: Outside Legal Subjectivity," 18 S. Afr. J. Hum. Rts. 41, 55 (2002) ("Legal rules tend towards generality... It operates from the position of the 'reasonable man' – the ideal legal subject who, despite claims of neutrality is white, male, middle class, *Christian*.") & 56 ("We need a legal commitment to a political agenda. The eradication of gender, racial, *religious* and other forms of subordination. We need to remind ourselves constantly that the present context is structured and determined by past discrimination.") (italics added).

[140] Albie Sachs, The Free Diary of Albie Sachs 67 (Johannesburg: Random House, 2004). Sachs also discusses how much the Rastafarian case weighed on him at another point. *Id.* at 85. And he describes his difficulties with another religion case as well. *Id.* at 83–84. Though at times overly dramatic, and extraordinarily personal, the book provides a window into the mind of one of South Africa's most impressive jurists.

on the margins of society and appear bizarre, even threatening to the mainstream.[141]

In addition, because of threats from the regime, Justice Sachs lived in England and then Mozambique, where apartheid security forces still almost murdered him.[142] He was an outsider in England and Mozambique, and even in Afrikaaner-dominated South Africa. This may explain his appreciation for Rastafarianism's African roots and for the religion's marginalization.[143]

CONCLUSION

According to David Beatty,

> Judges in South Africa are just as divided on how one should analyse questions of church/state relations as their counterparts in Canada and the United States. Indeed, one can find similar divisions of opinion within almost every court that has ever been asked to protect someone's religious liberty from what they allege is arbitrary and discriminatory treatment by the state.[144]

Graeme McLean notes that the state cannot be neutral on religion; otherwise, religiously motivated child sacrifices might be permitted.[145] So what is the solution?

Justice Sachs's contextual accommodationism, along with his pluralist respect for disadvantaged religions, would reduce religious freedom

---

[141] *Id.* at 67–68.

[142] Albie Sachs, The Soft Vengeance of a Freedom Fighter (Cape Town: David Philip Publishers, 1990). The apartheid security forces blew up his car and Sachs almost died in the explosion. He ended up losing an arm.

[143] Bonthuys, *supra* n. 139 at 53 ("Since no-one has remained unaffected by apartheid in South Africa, there is no neutral ground from which to define the nature and effects of subordination. Neither does cultural neutrality exist. The ostensible neutrality of the legal system is merely western cultural domination rendered invisible. If, therefore, the choice is between the privileged and the subordinated, the law should afford the subordinated a decisive voice in this process.") & 57 ("Apart from the way in which the obvious approbation of Christian tradition implies that customary traditions are less desirable and 'unchristian,' the court's reluctance to apply customary norms is problematic.") The difficulties are also shown by the Constitutional Court's divided decision in Bhe v. Magistrate, Khayelitsha (CC 2004) (Court rules that the Black Administration Act's rule of male primogeniture is unconstitutional but divides over the remedy).

[144] The Ultimate Rule of Law 64 (Oxford: Oxford University Press, 2004).

[145] Graeme McClean, "Freedom of Religion and State Neutrality: A Philosophical Problem," 114 S. Afr. L. J. 174 (1997).

disputes. Making the South African judiciary less white would also help. But polygamy remains a contentious issue. To its credit, South Africa, has passed legislation regulating "traditional" relationships.[146] Such a use of nonjudicial avenues for promoting religious freedom can relieve pressures on the courts.

[146] One commentator explains that the strategy of using a variety of nonjudicial techniques to promote gender equality has been called critical pragmatism. She says it "overcomes dichotomization and enables proponents of gender equality to utilize and develop the opportunities presented by plural normative orders, while challenging and minimizing the impact of the setbacks presented by formal law, interpretations of custom, or the interaction between the two." Celestine Nyamu, "How Should Human Rights and Development Respond to Cultural Legitimization of Gender Hierarchy in Developing Countries," 41 Harv. Int'l L. J. 381, 410 (2000). South Africa's legislation is called the Recognition of Customary Marriages Act 120 of 1998. The law requires certain customary marriages to be registered with the government, in part to protect the women. There is general agreement, however, that noncompliance is massive.

9

Socioeconomic Rights

South Africa is internationally known for its bizarre official position on AIDS.[1] Apparently, former President Thabo Mbeki relied on Internet sites to conclude that HIV did not cause AIDS even though this view conflicts with the world's reputable scientific community.[2] Moreover, his Minister of Health, Dr. Manto Tshabalala-Msimang, arrived at a prestigious 2006 international AIDS conference in Toronto promoting lemon and garlic as an AIDS remedy.[3] These stories would be humorous if the government's slow response to the AIDS crisis had not led to so many deaths.

Among those at risk were the unborn babies of HIV-infected pregnant women. Fortunately, the Treatment Action Campaign (TAC), an AIDS advocacy organization, successfully brought suit claiming that the government must distribute the drug, nevirapine, to these women to block transmission of the virus. TAC relied on the South African Constitution's right to health care.

[1] BBC News, "Mbeki Digs in on AIDS," Sep. 20, 2000, http://news.bbc.co.uk/2/hi/africa /934435.stm (last visited June 21, 2008).
[2] Drew Forrest and Barry Streek, "Mbeki in Bizarre AIDS Outburst," Mail & Guardian (Johannesburg Oct. 26, 2001), http://www.aegis.com/news/DMG/2001 /MG011021.html (last visited June 21, 2008).
[3] Samantha Power, "The AIDS Rebel," New Yorker, May 2003, http://www.pbs.org /pov/pov2003/stateofdenial/special_rebel.html (last visited June 21, 2008). There is a new Minister of Health in place now, Barbara Hogan, and she has rejected her predecessor's odd positions while also promising to roll out anti-AIDS drugs frar more aggressively. AP, "South African Health Minister Strikes New Tone on AIDS," Int'l Herald Tribune, Oct. 13, 2008, http://www.iht.com/articles/ap/2008/10/13/africa /AF-South-Africa-AIDS.php (last visited Oct. 28, 2008). A recent study suggests that the South African governments delays in using effective anti-AIDS drugs may have cost 365,000 lives. Celia Dugger, "Study Cites Toll of AIDS Policy in South Africa," N.Y. Times A1 (Nov. 26, 2008).

By contrast, the U.S. Supreme Court has rejected arguments favoring socioeconomic rights though it has read others into the U.S. Constitution, including a right to privacy, marriage, and abortion.[4] The Supreme Court has questioned the feasibility of judicial enforcement of positive obligations[5] and raised separation of powers concerns.

The South African Constitutional Court's approach is generally consistent with the International Covenant on Economic, Social, and Cultural Rights (ICESCR), as well as the approaches taken by a few nations like India. The ICESCR requires governments to affirmatively provide socioeconomic necessities[6] on the theory that liberty presumes subsistence.

This chapter has two parts. The first critically examines the South African socioeconomic rights cases. It also evaluates some of the related South African and foreign scholarly commentary, as the socioeconomic rights provisions are one of the most innovative parts of the nation's Constitution. The second section briefly examines relevant American constitutional jurisprudence.

This chapter seeks to demonstrate that the South African Court has accomplished quite a feat: It has enforced socioeconomic rights, but has interpreted them in a pragmatic and minimalist way that limits separation of powers concerns. Moreover, this chapter asserts that the U.S. Supreme Court should reconsider its feasibility and separation of powers objections.

SOUTH AFRICA'S SOCIOECONOMIC RIGHTS JURISPRUDENCE

The South African Constitution's socioeconomic rights provisions have been celebrated internationally. Socioeconomic rights protected by the

---

[4] *See, e.g.*, San Antonio Indep. Sch. Dist. v. Rodriguez, 411 *U.S.* 1,35-36 (1973); Lindsey v. Normet, 405 *U.S.* 56, 74 (1972); Dandridge v. Williams, 397 *U.S.* 471, 487 (1970).

[5] Judge Richard Posner wrote, "[Our] Constitution is a charter of negative rather than positive liberties.... The men who wrote the Bill of Rights were not concerned that government might do too little for the people but that it might do too much to them. The Fourteenth Amendment, adopted in 1868 at the height of laissez-faire thinking, sought to protect Americans from oppression by state government, not to secure them basic governmental services." Jackson v. City of Joliet, 715 F.2d 1200, 1203 (7th Cir. 1983). Various scholars have questioned every part of Judge Posner's statement, including the dates he gives for the "height of laissez-faire." *See, e.g.*, Michael J. Gerhardt, "The Ripple Effects of Slaughter-House: A Critique of a Negative Rights View of the Constitution," 43 Vand. L. Rev. 409 (1990); David P. Currie, "Positive and Negative Constitutional Rights," 53 U. Chi. L. Rev. 864 (1986).

[6] *See, e.g.*, International Covenant on Economic, Social and Cultural Rights, Dec. 16, 1966, 993 U.N.T.S. 3; Vicki C. Jackson & Mark Tushnet, Comparative Constitutional Law 1436-40 (1999) (discussing Irish, Italian, and Indian Constitutions).

South African Constitution include rights to housing, health care, food, water, social security, and education, among others.[7] Several cases have interpreted these provisions.

Some argue that global communism's collapse contributed to their inclusion because the South African left sought to protect people from market excesses.[8] Yet, other South African scholars such as Dennis Davis argue that these rights are unenforceable.[9] These objections resemble the U.S Supreme Court's reasoning in several cases discussed later.

The Right to Housing

The seminal socioeconomic rights case is *Government of the Republic of South Africa v. Grootboom*,[10] which involved the right to housing. Irene Grootboom was one of several hundred poor people, half of whom were children, living in an informally organized squatter settlement. The settlement lacked running water, electricity, sewage, and garbage removal services. Millions of South Africans still live in such conditions as a legacy of apartheid's influx control policies and forcible relocations.[11]

Because of these conditions, the group of poor people moved onto vacant private land that was earmarked for low-income housing.[12] The group was trespassing so the owner obtained an eviction order. The situation worsened when the local government bulldozed the group's shanties and then burned the wreckage before the eviction date. This occurred during a cold, windy, and rainy Western Cape winter.[13]

The group then moved to a nearby municipal sports field where they erected flimsy temporary structures. Winter rains left them unprotected under plastic sheeting and the municipality declined to provide assistance. The group obtained legal counsel and brought suit charging that the government failed to comply with the right to housing.

---

[7] S. Afr. Const. ch. 2, §§ 26(1), 27(1), 29(1) (adopted May 8, 1996).

[8] Robert Gargarella, Pilar Domingo, Theunis Roux, "Courts, Rights and Social Transformation: Concluding Reflections" 255, 256 in Robert Gargarella et al. (Eds.), Courts and Social Transformation in New Democracies (2006).

[9] *See*, e.g., D. M. Davis, "The Case against the Inclusion of Socio-Economic Demands in a Bill of Rights Except as Directive Principles," 8 S. Afr. J. Hum. Rts. 475 (1992); Erika de Wet, The Constitutional Enforceability of Economic and Social Rights 92 (1996) (discussing future Constitutional Court Justice Ackermann's objections to the inclusion of enforceable socioeconomic rights). *But see* Etienne Mureinik, "Beyond a Charter of Luxuries: Economic Rights in the Constitution," 8 S. Afr. J. Hum. Rts. 464 (1992).

[10] 2000 (11) BCLR 1169 (CC), *available at* 2000 SACLR Lexis 126.

[11] *Id.* ¶ 7.   [12] *Id.* ¶ 8.

[13] *Id.* ¶ 10.

The Constitutional Court ruled for the settlers after applying chapter 2, section 26, of the South African Constitution, which states

Housing

26. (1) Everyone has the right to have access to adequate housing.

    (2) The state must take reasonable legislative and other measures, within its available resources, to achieve the progressive realization of this right.[14]

Initially, the Court quoted from its *First Certification Judgment*:

> [T]hese rights are, at least to some extent, justiciable. As we have stated in the previous paragraph, many of the civil and political rights entrenched in the [constitutional text before this Court for certification in this case] will give rise to similar budgetary implications without compromising their justiciability. The fact that socio-economic rights will almost inevitably give rise to such implications does not seem to us to be a bar to their justiciability. At the very minimum, socio-economic rights can be negatively protected from improper invasion."[15]

The Court then explained the importance of such rights:

> Our Constitution entrenches both civil and political rights and social and economic rights. All the rights in our Bill of Rights are inter-related and mutually supporting. There can be no doubt that human dignity, freedom and equality, the foundational values of our society, are denied those who have no, clothing or shelter. Affording socio-economic rights to all people therefore enables them to enjoy the other rights enshrined in Chapter 2 [The Bill of Rights]. The realisation of these rights is also key to the advancement of race and gender equality and the evolution of a society in which men and women are equally able to achieve their full potential.[16]

As Pierre de Vos writes, "Starving people may find it difficult to exercise their freedom of speech."[17]

The Court then examined international human rights law but refused to constitutionally mandate the government to provide a "minimum core"

---

[14] S. Afr. Const. ch. 2, § 26(1)-(2). *See also Grootboom*, 2000 (11) BCLR 1169 (CC)¶ 99.

[15] *Id.* ¶ 20 (quoting *Ex parte* Chairperson of the Constitutional Assembly: *In re* Certification of the Constitution of the Republic of South Africa, 1996 (10) BCLR 1253 (CC) ¶ 78).

[16] *Id.* ¶ 23.

[17] Pierre De Vos, "Pious Wishes or Directly Enforceable Human Rights? Social and Economic Rights in South Africa's 1996 Constitution," 13 S. Afr. J. Hum. Rts. 67, 71 (1997).

level of housing, health care, and the like.[18] The "minimum core" of rights lacked flexibility, and the text of South Africa's socioeconomic rights provisions differed slightly from international covenants.[19] The Court instead asserted that the key question was "whether the measures taken by the state to realise the right afforded by Section 26 are reasonable."[20]

The Court explained, "The measures must establish a coherent public housing programme directed towards the progressive realisation of the right of access to adequate housing within the State's available means."[21] This meant that the government had "an obligation to move as expeditiously and effectively as possible towards that goal."[22] The Court added that the program must be "reasonably implemented. An otherwise reasonable programme that is not implemented reasonably will not constitute compliance with the State's [positive] obligations."[23]

The Court then held:

> To be reasonable, measures cannot leave out of account the degree and extent of the denial of the right they endeavour to realise. Those whose needs are the most urgent and whose ability to enjoy all rights therefore is (sic) most in peril, must not be ignored by the measures aimed at achieving realisation of the right.... If the measures, though statistically successful, fail to respond to the needs of those most desperate, they may not pass the test.[24]

South Africa's construction of low-income housing therefore was admirable but it:

> Falls short of obligations imposed upon the national government to the extent that it fails to recognize that the State must provide relief for those in desperate need. They are not to be ignored in the interests of an overall programme focused on medium and long-term objectives [rather than

---

[18] *Grootboom*, 2000 (11) BCLR 1169 (CC) Par. 33.

[19] *Id. But see* David Bilchitz, "Giving Socio-Economic Rights Teeth: The Minimum Core and Its Importance," 117 S. Afr. L.J. 484 (2002). The Constitutional Court also rejected the argument that the government violated the rights of the children in the squatter camp. *Grootboom*, 2000 (11) BCLR 1169 (CC) ¶ 79. Section 28(1)(c) of the Bill of Rights provides that children have the right "to basic nutrition, shelter, basic health care services and social services." S. Afr. Const. ch. 2, § 28(1)(c). The Court construed this provision narrowly and held that the government only had an obligation to house the children when their parents failed to provide minimal shelter. *Grootboom*, 2000 (11) BCLR 1169 (CC) ¶¶ 77–79.

[20] *Grootboom*, 2000 (11) BCLR 1169 (CC) ¶ 33.

[21] *Id.* ¶ 41.

[22] *Id.* ¶ 45 (quoting United Nations Committee ESCR, ¶ 9 of general comment 3 (1990)).

[23] *Id.* ¶ 42.   [24] *Id.* ¶ 44.

short term objectives]. It is essential that a reasonable part of the national housing budget be devoted to this, but the precise allocation is for national government to decide in the first instance.[25]

This last sentence illustrates Justice Zac Yacoob's balancing act. Though the Court forced compliance with the Constitution, it gave the government discretion on how to comply. The Court rejected the supervisory remedy requested by the plaintiffs and instead ordered the Human Rights Commission to monitor progress. As an aside, Justice Yacoob is of Indian descent and blind. He had a long history of civil rights work against apartheid before being appointed to the Constitutional Court. The U.S. Supreme Court has never had a blind Justice.

Grootboom demonstrates that including socioeconomic rights in a Constitution does not mean that every individual is entitled to assistance on demand. Instead, the Court analyzed whether the overall government policy was reasonable. Cass Sunstein writes, "What the South African Constitutional Court has basically done is to adopt an *administrative law model of socioeconomic rights*."[26]

Grootboom evoked a mixed response. It has been hailed as "one of the most important examples of the judicial enforcement of socioeconomic rights known to comparative constitutional lawyers."[27] Some South African scholars, however, criticize the Court for rejecting the minimum core of rights.[28] Others disagree with Sunstein by arguing that the reasonableness test did not amount to deferential administrative law review.[29]

So did the plaintiffs' actual situation improve? Not really. South Africa's *Sunday Times* reported that officials erected a small building containing showers and toilets for the Grootboom community.[30] The

---

[25] *Id.* ¶ 66.

[26] Cass Sunstein, Designing Democracy 234 (emphasis in original) (2001).

[27] Rosalind Dixon, "Creating Dialogue about Socio-Economic Rights: Strong Form versus Weak-Form Judicial Review Revisited," 5 Int'l J. Const. L. 391 (2007).

[28] David Bilchitz, Poverty and Fundamental Rights (2007). Others said the case was about equality above all. Wesson, *infra* n. 29.

[29] *See e.g.* Carol Steinberg, "Can Reasonableness Protect the Poor? A Review of South Africa's Socio-Economic Rights Jurisprudence," 123 S. Afr. L. J. 264 (2006); Murray Wesson, "Grootboom and Reassessing the Socio-Economic Jurisprudence of the South African Constitutional Court," 20 S. Afr. J. Hum. Rts. 284, 289–93 (2004).

[30] Mia Stewart, "Left Out in the Cold," 21 S. Afr. J. Hum. Rts. 215–16 (also describing HRC report); Hirschl, "Constitutionalism, Judicial Review, and Progressive Change," 84 Tex. L. Rev. 471, 488 (2005).

government paid locals to clean the building but did not give them sufficient cleaning supplies or equipment. The amenities therefore stopped functioning, which created rubbish and smelly pools, even as the settlement grew. Moreover, as of 2003, the Cape Metropolitan Council had still not released new land for homeless families according to the High Court in *City of Cape Town v. Rudolph*.[31]

In *Rudolph*, the Cape High Court issued a structural interdict requiring the Council to report back in four months. The national government then enacted the "Housing Assistance in Emergency Circumstances Programme" in 2004 to satisfy the housing needs found in *Grootboom*. Pretoria, however, has not provided sufficient funding nor engaged in adequate capacity building.[32] Thus even *Rudolph's* structural interdict was no solution. According to one source,

> Cape Town's estimated housing backlog grew from 150,000 in 1995 to 240,000 in 2002, an increase of 60 percent. Johannesburg and Durban have even larger housing backlogs.... Corruption, incompetence and skills shortages contribute to the poor implementation of well intentioned policies and legislation.[33]

The *Sun Times* said part of the problem in *Grootboom* was that the Oostenberg locality and the Cape municipality disputed whether each had responsibility for providing housing. The Human Rights Commission also did not provide sufficient monitoring.[34] Tragically, Irene Grootboom died in 2008 while still living in a squatter settlement.

The Right to Health Care

The South African Constitutional Court has decided two major health care cases: *Soobramoney v. Minister of Health*[35] and *Minister of Health*

---

[31] 2003 (11) BCLR 1236 (C), 2003 SACLR Lexis 43.

[32] *See* Shadow Report to South Africa's First Periodic State Report to the African Commission on Human and People's Rights at 4, Nov. 21-Dec. 5, 2005, www.chr.up.ac.za/hr_docs/countries/docs/Shadow%20report.doc (last visited Dec. 13, 2007) ("While the Department of Housing in April 2004 adopted a policy on Housing Assistance in Emergency Circumstances, this policy has not been implemented reasonably. Millions of people in dire need for housing remain homeless and still live in appalling circumstances.").

[33] "South Africa: The Role of the Courts in Realizing the Rights to Health and Housing" at 6, http://siteresources.worldbank.org/EXTSOCIALDEV/Resources/3177394-1168615404141/3328201-1192042053459/South Africa.pdf?resourceurlname=South Africa.pdf (last visited Dec. 12, 2007).

[34] Wesson, *supra* n. 29 at 306 n. 79.

[35] 1997 (12) BCLR 1696 (CC), *available at* 1997 SACLR Lexis 41.

v. Treatment Action Campaign.[36] Chapter 2, section 27, "Health Care, Food, Water, and Social Security," of the Bill of Rights states:

27. (1) Everyone has the right to have access to
    (a) health care services, including reproductive health care;
    (b) sufficient food and water; and
    (c) social security, including, if they are unable to support themselves and their dependants, appropriate social assistance.
(2) The state must take reasonable legislative and other measures, within its available resources, to achieve the progressive realisation of each of these rights.
(3) No one may be refused emergency medical treatment.[37]

Soobramoney v. Minister of Health

The first socioeconomic rights case ever decided by the Constitutional Court was *Soobramoney*, not *Grootboom*, and commentators feared that *Soobramoney's* anti-claimant ruling in 1997 would render the rights provisions toothless.[38] The subsequent *Grootboom* and *Treatment Action Campaign* decisions have alleviated that worry.

Soobramoney addressed whether a public hospital unconstitutionally denied dialysis to a terminally ill man with diabetes, ischemic heart disease, and cerebrovascular disease. The hospital prioritized the provision of care to nonterminal patients because dialysis was a scarce resource. The terminally ill patient, Soobramoney, claimed that the hospital violated his right to health care and to emergency medical treatment under Chapter 2, section 27 of the Bill of Rights of the South African Constitution.[39]

Relying on a case from India, the Court held, "This is not an emergency which calls for immediate remedial treatment. It is an ongoing state of affairs resulting from a deterioration of the applicant's renal function which is incurable."[40] The Court also rejected the health care claim because the hospital had a rational policy for making a scarce resource available.[41] Indeed, the dialysis program would collapse and

---

[36] 2002 (10) BCI R 1033 (CC), *available at* 2002 SACLR Lexis 26.

[37] S. Afr. Const. ch. 2, § 27 (adopted May 8, 1996).

[38] Emily Bazelon, "After the Revolution," Legal Affairs 25, 28 (Jan./Feb. 2003), http://www.legalaffairs.org/issues/January-February-2003/feature_bazelon_janfeb2003.msp (last visited June 21, 2008).

[39] *Soobramoney*, 1997 (12) BCLR 1696 (CC) ¶¶ 5–7. The South African Constitution provides that "[e]veryone has the right to life" and that "[n]o one may be refused emergency medical treatment." S. Afr. Const. ch. 2, §§ 11, 27(3).

[40] *Id.*   [41] *Id.* ¶ 25.

"no one would benefit"[42] in the absence of a prioritization policy. Moreover, the Court stated, "These choices involve difficult decisions to be taken at the political level in fixing the health budget, and at the functional level in deciding upon the priorities to be met. A court will be slow to interfere with rational decisions taken in good faith by the political organs and medical authorities whose responsibility it is to deal with such matters."[43]

The ruling illustrates, once again, that a court can take socioeconomic rights seriously and yet respect legislative competence. Although the result was undeniably tragic, especially since Mr. Soobramoney collapsed upon being handed the ruling and died two days later, the Court could not pragmatically ignore the scarcity issue. Critics, however, argued that the Court rubber-stamped the government's position.[44]

Minister of Health v. Treatment Action Campaign

As previously mentioned, the 2001 case of *Treatment Action Campaign* (*TAC*) was among the Constitutional Court's most important decisions because it involved the South African government's unsatisfactory response to AIDS. The opinion was unanimous and jointly authored. Indeed, one in nine South Africans was infected with HIV when it was decided[45] and the number is higher now. In 2000, 2.4 million Africans died of HIV-related causes.[46] As of several years ago, 70,000 babies infected with HIV were born in South Africa each year as a result of mother-child transmission.[47]

As discussed earlier, for several years the South African government refused to distribute nevirapine at public health clinics.[48] In addition to

---

[42] *Id.* ¶ 26.   [43] *Id.* ¶ 29.

[44] Frank Michelman also mildly criticizes one part of the opinion, but it seems the Court resisted the temptation to make bad law in a hard case. *See* Frank Michelman, "The Constitution, Social Rights and Reason: A Tribute to Etienne Mureinik," 14 S. Afr. J. Hum. Rts. 499 (1998).

[45] "AIDS Drugs Battle Goes to Court," CNN.com (Nov. 26, 2001), at http://archives .cnn.com/2001/WORLD/africa/11/26/safrica.drugs/index.html (last visited June 21, 2008).

[46] "AIDS Drugs Court Battle Dropped," CNN.com (Apr. 19, 2001), at http://archives .cnn.com/2001/WORLD/africa/04/19/safrica.drugs/index.html (last visited June 21, 2008).

[47] Minister of Health v. Treatment Action Campaign, 2002 (10) BCLR 1033 (CC) ¶ 1 n. 1, 2002 SACLR Lexis 26. Richard Calland, "A Case of Power and Who Controls It: The Constitutional Court Faces Its Most Delicate Test Yet," Mail & Guardian online (Jan. 18, 2002), *at* http://www.mg.co.za/mg/za/features/calland/index.html.

[48] *TAC, id.* ¶ 10.

Mbeki's skepticism about whether HIV caused AIDS,[49] the government also claimed that nevirapine had troubling side effects.[50] For some reason, it cited cost concerns even though the manufacturer offered the pills for free.[51] The World Health Organization (WHO) ultimately dispelled these varied concerns.[52]

The national government eventually agreed to implement a pilot nevirapine distribution program at two public health centers in each province.[53] Government health officials contended that a broader program was not feasible because nevirapine only was effective when infected mothers used formula to feed their newborns,[54] and that practice could not be ensured.[55]

After years of unsuccessful lobbying, TAC brought suit to force nationwide distribution.[56] The group was led by AIDS activist Zachie Achmat who refused, for a while, to take his AIDS antiretroviral medications until the government made such drugs available to all. His refusal brought added international attention to the government's strange AIDS policies.[57] The government responded to the TAC lawsuit by contending that its pilot program was reasonable and that separation of powers concerns required the courts to stay out of the issue.

Nevertheless, the Constitutional Court ordered the government to provide the drug. Initially, the Court commented about the power of judicial review:

> Courts are ill-suited to adjudicate upon issues where court orders could have multiple social and economic consequences for the community. The Constitution contemplates rather a restrained and focused role for the courts, namely, to require the State to take measures to meet its constitutional obligations and to subject the reasonableness of these measures to evaluation. Such determinations of reasonableness may in fact have budgetary implications, but are not in themselves directed at rearranging budgets. In this way the judicial, legislative and executive functions achieve appropriate constitutional balance.[58]

---

[49] *See* Bazelon, *supra* n. 38 at *28 ("President Mbeki . . . attracted worldwide criticism for questioning whether HIV causes AIDS at all.").

[50] *TAC, Id.* ¶ 10.

[51] *TAC*, 2002 (10) BCLR 1033 (CC) ¶ 4 n.5.

[52] *Id.* ¶ 12.   [53] *Id.* ¶ 10.

[54] *Id.* ¶ 15.   [55] *Id.* ¶¶ 14–15.

[56] *Id.* ¶ 4.

[57] Tina Rosenberg, "Editorial Observer; In South Africa, a Hero Measured by the Advance of a Deadly Disease," N.Y. Times (Jan. 13, 2003) http://query.nytimes.com/gst/fullpage. html?res=940CEED71431F930A25752C0A9659C8B63 (last visited Dec. 19, 2007).

[58] *TAC, id.* ¶ 38.

The Court, nonetheless, defined the "progressive realization" obligation by noting, "The State is obliged to take reasonable measures progressively to eliminate or reduce the large areas of severe deprivation
that afflict our society."[59] The Court then decided that the government
"fail[ed] to address the needs of mothers and their newborn children who
do not have access to these [pilot] sites."[60] The government's goal of
maximizing nevirapine's effectiveness by limiting distribution to mothers
trained in baby formula use was unjustified[61] because too many babies
would become infected or die in the interim.[62]

The Court also rejected the government's separation of powers defense
by stating the following:

> There is... no merit in the argument advanced on behalf of government
> that a distinction should be drawn between declaratory and mandatory
> orders against government. Even simple declaratory orders against gov-
> ernment or organs of State can affect their policy and may well have bud-
> getary implications. Government is constitutionally bound to give effect
> to such orders whether or not they affect its policy and has to find the
> resources to do so. Thus, in the *Mpumalanga* case, this Court set aside a
> provincial government's policy decision to terminate the payment of sub-
> sidies to certain schools and ordered that payments should continue for
> several months. Also, in the case of *August* the Court, in order to afford
> prisoners the right to vote, directed the Electoral Commission to alter
> its election policy, planning and regulations, with manifest cost impli-
> cations.[63]

But the Court showed respect for separation of powers by asserting that it would be for the "government... to devise and implement a
more comprehensive policy that will give access to health care services to
HIV-positive mothers and their newborn children, and will include the
administration of Nevirapine where that is appropriate."[64] The Court
supported its remedial authority by citing cases from India, Germany,
Canada, and the United Kingdom.[65] The decision in *TAC* even relied on
the U.S. Supreme Court ruling in *Brown v. Board of Education II*.[66]

---

[59] *Id.* ¶¶ 35–36.
[60] *Id.* ¶ 67.
[61] *Id.* ¶ 80.
[62] *Id.* ¶ 72.
[63] *Id.* ¶ 99 (footnotes omitted). The Court added that it had a duty to grant "appropriate relief" when a violation of rights occurred. *Id.* ¶ 101. Section 172(1)(b) of the
Constitution states "a court may also 'make any order that is just and equitable." *Id.*
[64] *Id.* ¶ 122.
[65] *Id.* ¶¶ 108–12.
[66] *Id.* ¶ 107; 349 U.S. 294 (1955). It is hard to ignore the similarity between the U.S.
Supreme Court's efforts to eliminate segregation and the South African legal system's
attempt to eliminate the remnants of apartheid.

In sum, as Heinz Klug points out, *TAC's* particularized directive went beyond *Grootboom*.[67] What was the actual effect in the medical clinics? Though the government dragged its feet initially,[68] it eventually complied to a large extent, increasing distribution of neviparine and thereby saving many young lives.[69]

As with *Grootboom*, most scholars applauded the result but some preferred the minimum core. Moreover, the Treatment Action Campaign criticized the government in October 1, 2007 for administering single-dose nevirapine antiretroviral regimens to pregnant women, rather than multiple doses as recommended by the WHO. TAC maintained that dual therapy is affordable and could reduce transmission rates from 12 to 25 percent to 5 or 10 percent.[70]

Social Security

In *Khosa v. Minister of Social Development*,[71] the Constitutional Court in 2004 ruled that South African welfare statutes could not exclude permanent residents from benefits. The exclusion violated the constitutional provision specifying that "everyone" is entitled to social security. The law also violated equality guarantees. The plaintiffs were Mozambican citizens who escaped a civil war by migrating to South Africa in the 1980s. Several sought "old age" grants, and one sought welfare grants for her children.[72] *Khosa* differed from previous cases because the issue was *access* to the program, rather than whether the state had any such program at all.[73]

Justice Yvonne Mokgoro's majority decision ruled for the claimant, but did not include a limitations analysis. This omission is interesting because Justice Mokgoro reached the limitations issue quickly in previous

---

[67] Heinz Klug, "Five Years On: How Relevant Is the Constitution to the New South Africa?", 26 Vermont. L. Rev. 803, 808 (2002).

[68] Stewart, *supra* n. 30 at 224; Mark Heywood, "Preventing Mother to Child HIV Transmission in South Africa," 19 S. Afr. J. Hum. Rts. 278, 308 (2003); Bilchitz, Poverty and Fundamental Rights, *supra* n. 28 at 163 (The government initially did not roll out the protocol in two provinces even after the ruling.).

[69] "SA Govt Heeds Calls for Free Anti-Aids Drugs," Mail & Guardian online (Feb. 3, 2003), at http://www.mg.co.za/articledirect.aspx?area=%2fbreaking_news% 2fbreaking_news_national&articleid=15219 (last visited Dec. 30, 2007).

[70] "Improving Mother-to-child transmission Prevention," TAC Electronic Newsletter, Oct. 1, 2007, http://www.tac.org.za/nl20071001.html (last visited Dec. 13, 2007).

[71] 2004 (6) SA 505 (CC).   [72] *Id.* Par. 4.

[73] Kevin Iles, "Limiting Socio-Economic Rights: Beyond the Internal Limitations Clauses," 20 S. Afr. J. Hum. Rts. 448, 450 (2004).

cases, such as the gender discriminatory pardon in *Hugo*. Instead, the Court held that excluding permanent residents was not even reasonable under the social security provision's progressive realization clause.[74] First, the permanent residents did not pose a significant financial burden. Second, the community has the obligation to assist long-term residents.[75] Third, South Africa's "caring" society should not promote an "American self-sufficiency" ethos.[76] For a remedy, the Court "read in" language covering permanent residents. Justice Mokgoro's majority opinion is striking because she rigorously scrutinized the state's financial justifications, invoked egalitarian and communitarian values, and rejected the American model.

Justice Ngcobo disagreed. Reaching the proportionality issue, he emphasized that the law did not severely burden permanent residents because they could obtain benefits after some years, if naturalized, and sooner in exceptional cases.[77] Moreover, the government had limited resources. He added, "The legitimacy of a legislative goal of discouraging immigration that is motivated by the availability of the welfare benefits, cannot be gainsaid."[78]

South African legal scholars approve of Justice Mokgoro's aggressive scrutiny of the government positions while criticizing some of her reasoning.[79] For example, they assert that her discussion of the state's justifications was more appropriate for a section 36 limitations analysis than for a section 27 reasonableness determination.[80] Not surprisingly, these scholars support dissenting Justice Ngcobo's willingness to arrive speedily at the limitations question because this suggested an entitlement was at stake.[81] The scholars, however, uniformly oppose Ngcobo's pro-government result.

Moreover, according to David Bilchitz, Mokgoro curiously used "the reasonableness approach that had previously been applied to the question of the normative economic rights [and simply] applied [it] to the question

---

[74] *Khosa* Par. 43.
[75] *Id*. Par. 59.
[76] *Id*. Par. 65.
[77] *Id*. Par. 117.
[78] *Id*. Par. 121.
[79] Sandra Liebenberg, "Needs, Rights, and Transformation: Adjudicating Social Rights," NYU Law Center for Human Rights and Global Justice Working Paper, Economic and Social Rights Series 8, 2005, http://www.chrgj.org/publications/docs/wp/Liebenberg%20-%20Needs,%20Rights%20and%20Transformation.pdf (last visited June 21, 2008).
[80] Iles, *supra* n.73.
[81] Marius Pieterse, "Resuscitating Socio-Economic Rights: Constitutional Entitlements to Health Care Services," 22 S. Afr. J. Hum. Rts. 473, 493 (2006).

of who is entitled to such rights."[82] He argues that she was also wrong to suggest that temporary residents, unlike permanent residents, could never get benefits.[83] Yet, her definition of the political community is still praiseworthy because it extends beyond citizens unlike in many other countries. Dennis Davis claims that she relied so heavily on the equality issue that the social security provision became irrelevant.[84] Yet, the Court relied on the social security reference to "everyone."[85]

Interestingly, *Khosa* resembles some relatively progressive American cases. As previously stated, the U.S. Supreme Court has not supported affirmative rights. But it has ruled that the state usually cannot discriminate against the vulnerable once it grants a benefit. These American cases cover the right to vote, residency requirements for welfare benefits, and the right to marry. *Khosa* fits this framework neatly: The government could not exclude permanent residents once it awarded benefits to citizens.[86] This infringement shows that Justice Mokgoro should have reached the limitations analysis.[87]

Recent Housing Cases

The *Port Elizabeth* Decision

In *Port Elizabeth Municipality v. Various Occupiers*,[88] the Constitutional Court in 2004 ruled that a municipality could not evict sixty-eight impoverished people living in twenty-nine shacks located on unused residential property. The group refused the municipality's offer of another location

---

[82] Bilchitz, *supra* n. 28 at 172 (2007).

[83] *Id.* at 174. Bilchitz correctly argues, however, that temporary residents would be entitled to emergency medical assistance.

[84] Dennis Davis, "Adjudicating the Socio-Economic Rights in the South African Constitution: Towards 'Deference Lite'?," 22 S. Afr. J. Hum. Rts. 301, 309 (2006).

[85] Mokgoro also helped clarify what reasonableness meant by stating, "The differentiation, if it is to pass constitutional muster, must not be arbitrary or irrational nor must it manifest a naked preference. There must be a rational connection between the differentiating law and the legitimate government purpose it is designed to achieve." *Khosa* Par. 53.

[86] She said that reasonableness is a "higher standard than rationality." *Id.* Par. 67. This expands on *Grootboom* and *TAC* and explains why she did not easily allow the citizen vs. noncitizen distinction to be maintained.

[87] She quickly rejected the argument that the current law should be upheld, to create an incentive for people to become naturalized, by reasoning, "This argument, commonly found in American jurisprudence, is based on the social contract assumption that non-citizens are not entitled to the full benefits available to citizens." Par. 57. She suggested that South Africa had different assumptions.

[88] 2005 (1) SA 217 (CC).

because that site supposedly was unsafe. For the Court, Justice Sachs announced that he would break away from "a purely legalistic approach and hav[e] regard to extraneous factors such as morality, fairness, social values and implications ... which would necessitate bringing out an equitably principled judgment."[89]

The 1998 Prevention of Illegal and Unlawful Occupation of Land Act (PIE) also required flexibility. Sachs held that:

> PIE expressly requires the court to infuse elements of grace and compassion into the formal structures of the law. It is called upon to balance competing interests in a principled way and promote the constitutional vision of a caring society based on good neighbourliness and shared concern. The Constitution and PIE confirm that we are not islands unto ourselves. The spirit of *ubuntu*, part of the deep cultural heritage of the majority of the population, suffuses the whole constitutional order. It combines individual rights with a communitarian philosophy.[90]

This "grace and compassion" language is rare for a judicial opinion and shows the quasi-religious nature of the *ubuntu* ethos.

The Court then considered ordering mediation, but decided that doing so would be futile given the municipality's history of treating the squatters as anonymous and faceless.[91] Justice Sachs added that the parties could still resolve their conflict but that the municipality must assist the squatters[92] because of the "tenacity and ingenuity they show in making homes out of discarded material, in finding work and sending their children to school ... etc."[93] Scholars praise *Port Elizabeth* for creatively assisting the disadvantaged. Justice Sachs embraced idealism (the language on grace and compassion) and pragmatism (his realization that mediation woudn't work in this case) while rejecting legal formalism.[94]

The Jaftha Decision

In *Jaftha v. Schoenman*[95] the Constitutional Court nullified certain statutory debt collection procedures that allowed creditors to seize an entire house for a "trifling debt."[96] The Court held that the poorest homeowners "are a vulnerable group whose indigence and lack of knowledge prevents them from taking steps to stop the sales in execution, as is demonstrated

---

[89] *Id.* Par. 33.
[91] *Id.* Par. 59.
[93] *Id.* Par. 41.
[95] 2005 (2) SA 140 (CC).

[90] *Id.* Par. 37.
[92] *Id.* Par. 60.
[94] *Id.* Par. 43.
[96] *Id.* Par. 40.

by the facts of this case."[97] One woman even lost her house because she could not pay back a loan used to buy vegetables.

Justice Mokgoro concluded that a creditor must request execution against a debtor's immovable property from a court, rather than acting unilaterally.[98] The court should then examine the following: "the circumstances in which the debt was incurred; any attempts made by the debtor to pay off the debt; the financial situation of the parties; the amount of the debt; whether the debtor is employed or has a source of income to pay off the debt and any other factor relevant to the particular facts of the case before the court."[99]

Significantly, the case involved the negative aspects of socioeconomic rights (e.g., the ruling bans government from allowing a person's house to be taken), and the Court did not use a reasonableness test. Marius Pieterse describes this as a more "entitlement-based" approach[100] as do other scholars.

The Modderklip Decision

Over the last decade, Zimbabwe has deteriorated economically as President Robert Mugabe encouraged poor blacks to invade white-owned farms. Stripped of their independence, the Zimbabwe courts did not penalize the government for its actions. In 2005, the South African Constitutional Court in *President of the Republic of South Africa v. Modderklip Boerdery (Pty) Ltd*[101] dealt with 40,000 poor people occupying part of the Modderklip farm. The group erected shanties and even carved out roads on the farm.[102] The Court ruled that the group could stay but also found that the government had failed its constitutional obligations.

The *Modderklip* chronology is troubling. The farm owners had tried without success to persuade governmental institutions to remove the squatters, when they only numbered a few thousand. The sheriff did not act on an eviction order because she supposedly could not afford to pay the 18 million rand deposit needed to obtain assistance from a security

---

[97] *Id.* Par. 47.

[98] *Id.* Par. 54 (emphasis added). The statute did not require judicial involvement once there was a virtually automatic finding that an individual was in debt and had not paid.

[99] *Id.* Par. 60.

[100] "Resuscitating Socio-Economic Rights: Constitutional Entitlement to Health Care Services," 22 S. Afr. J. Hum. Rts. 473, 496 (2006).

[101] 2005 (8) BCLR 786 (CC).   [102]*Id.* Par. 8.

firm. Modderklip therefore filed an action with the Pretoria High Court arguing that the government failed to provide housing for the squatters and that its property rights were violated.

The court "imposed a structural interdict requiring the state to present a comprehensive plan to the Court and to the other parties indicating the steps it would take" to resolve the dispute.[103] The Supreme Court of Appeal, however, vacated the remedy and awarded compensatory damages to the farm. This avoided any need to evict such a large group.

Interestingly, the Constitutional Court's subsequent affirming of the Supreme Court's decision was not based on the right to housing or on property rights. The Court relied on section 1(c) of the Constitution, which makes reference to the "rule of law," and section 34 regarding access to the courts. This novel rule of law emphasis actually echoes how German courts might resolve such a case, and it has the potential to become a powerful tool in future cases. In his opinion, Justice Langa wrote:

> The obligation on the state goes further than the mere provision of the mechanisms referred to above. It is also obliged to take reasonable steps, where possible, to ensure that large-scale disruptions in the social fabric do not occur in the wake of the execution of court orders, thus undermining the rule of law.... I find that it was unreasonable of the state to stand by and do nothing in circumstances where it was impossible for Modderklip to evict the occupiers because of the sheer magnitude of the invasion and particular circumstances of the invaders.[104]

The Constitutional Court agreed with the damages remedy while leaving an expropriation option for the city.

Most commentators hail the decision as giving substance to socioeconomic rights. Dennis Davis disagrees, highlighting the Court's reliance on secondary provisions.[105] The Constitutional Court, however, recently ordered the parties to a major squatter dispute in Johannesburg to take part in mediation and "engagement," consistent with the competing rights to have access to housing and to own property. This endorsement of alternative dispute resolution is highly innovative.

---

[103] *Id.* Par. 16.

[104] *Id.* Pars. 43 & 48.

[105] Davis, *supra n.* 84 at 313.

Summary

The striking feature in these cases is the Court's pragmatic balancing of its transformative role and separation of powers concerns.[106] In *Soobramoney*, the Court suggested that other sick people would die if it did not defer to the hospital's rationing. In *Grootboom*, the Court left Parliament the job of crafting the national homeless policy. In *TAC*, the Court told the government what to do but rejected a broad supervisory remedy. The Court in *Khosa* said that permanent residents only caused a possible 2 percent increase in government spending so they should not falsely be portrayed as breaking the bank, especially because they also paid taxes.

The Court has been especially practical in the recent housing cases. In *Port Elizabeth*, the Court ruled for the squatters because of the municipality's refusal to negotiate in good faith. The Court also seriously considered mediation. The Court even said "equitable" and "pragmatic" grounds supported the result.

In *Jaftha*, the Court used common sense to nullify a law that would cost a person her house for buying vegetables. *Modderklip* is perhaps the most impressive example given a Zimbabwe-type situation in which 40,000 people occupied a farm. Removing the occupiers was not feasible. The Court therefore maintained the status quo and yet ordered the government to compensate the property owner, potentially averting a disaster.

All of the above cases flow from *Grootboom*'s reasonableness test. Moreover, as Rosalind Dixon argues and as the above examples show, the Court has implemented the test in such a way as to facilitate dialogue between the branches.[107] The test therefore opens up political participation.

A recent ruling from the Johannesburg High Court about the right to water shows that there is no limit to judicial progress in developing these rights. The court found that Pretoria discriminated on the basis of race and gender by allowing wealthier neighborhoods to pay water bills while installing capped prepaid water meters in the poorer areas. The court

---

[106] There is a distinct procedural due process component to the communitarianism in the cases. This is shown, for example, by Justice Sachs's concern in *Port Elizabeth* that the municipality ignored the squatters and treated them as faceless and anonymous. The voices of the squatters went unheard. *See also* Taunya Lovell Banks "Balancing Competing Individual Constitutional Rights: Raising Some Questions," http://ssrn.com/abstract=1292435 at 39 (2008) ("Perhaps the court is giving the state time to stabilize its economy and more completely actualize its plans for progressive realization of socio-economic rights like access to housing").

[107] Dixon, *supra* n. 27, at 407.

also said the allocated water amount in the poorer areas was inadequate especially because the municipality had the resources to provide more.

Criticisms of South African Jurisprudence in Socioeconomic Rights

Although the U.S. Supreme Court has opposed socioeconomic rights on diverse grounds, many South African scholars believe the Constitutional Court should go farther.[108] This section shows that most of these South African criticisms are incorrect except for the argument advocating stronger remedies.

The Minimum Core

David Bilchitz authored a *South African Law Journal* article and a subsequent impressive book arguing that *Grootboom* was wrong about the "minimum core."[109] Bilchitz asserts that every person has a right to toilets, running water, and protection from the elements.[110]

Moreover, he claims that the Court implicitly relied on a "minimum core" notion when it ruled for Irene Grootboom[111]: "In attempting to avoid recognizing a minimum core obligation, Yacoob J[.] ends up smuggling an obligation to meet short term needs into the very notion of reasonableness itself. It would certainly seem more transparent and theoretically coherent to recognize what he is actually doing outright."[112] He also asserts that the Court's weak remedy facilitated government intransigence.[113] Essentially, critics like Bilchitz argue that the Court was not fulfilling the new Constitution's promise of transformation.

Theunis Roux likewise writes that *Grootboom* failed[114] to clarify "the temporal order in which government chooses to meet competing social

---

[108] Other South African scholars approve of the Court's decision in these cases. *See, e.g.,* Pierre de Vos, "Grootboom, the Right of Access to Housing and Substantive Equality as Contextual Fairness," 17 S. Afr. J. Hum. Rts. 258 (2001).

[109] David Bilchitz, "Giving Socio-Economic Rights Teeth: The Minimum Core and Its Importance," 119 S. Afr. LJ. 484 (2002).

[110] *Id.* at 488.   [111] *Id.* at 498.

[112] *Id.* at 499.

[113] *See* David Bilchitz, Poverty and Fundamental Rights 150 & 163 (2007). *See also* Danielle E. Hirsch, "A Defense of Structural Injunctive Remedies in South African Law," Bepress Legal Series, Paper 1690 (2006), http://law.bepress.com/cgi/viewcontent.cgi?article=7940&context=expresso (last visited Dec. 30, 2007).

[114] Theunis Roux, "Understanding Grootboom – A Response to Cass R. Sunstein." 12 Const. Q. 41 (2002) (publication of the Canadian Centre for Constitutional Studies). *See also* Sandra Liebenberg, "South Africa's Evolving Jurisprudence on Socio-Economic Rights," Socio-Economic Rights Project, Community Law Centre, University of Western Cape 23 (2002) <http://www.communitylawcentre.org.za/Socio-Economic-Rights/research-project/2002-vol-6-law-democracy-and-development/liebenberg-12-march.pdf/> (last visited Dec. 30, 2007).

needs."[115] The Court put the homeless on the map, but provided no guidance regarding whether they trump the hungry or the sick if there are limited resources[116] Roux thinks the minimum core would help.

Though seemingly powerful, I believe these criticisms are mistaken for several reasons.

First, they lack perspective. South Africa is one of the only countries whose highest court treats socioeconomic rights with the same reverence as civil and political rights. This is a tremendous international advance, particularly in a country with virtually no judicial history in such matters.[117] Moreover, the United Nations Committee on Economic, Social and Cultural Rights as of 2004 had not even made clear whether it was "establishing a right that is vested in everyone, or as constituting a benchmark against which a state's progress in realizing socio-economic rights might be assessed."[118]

Second, the critics claim too much. Bilchitz argues, and Roux would agree, that the right "does not mean that some receive housing now, and others receive it later; *rather, it means that each* is *now entitled to a basic housing provision*, which the government is required to improve gradually over time."[119] This sounds like an individual right to demand immediate government assistance. Although I wish such a system were feasible, there are several problems with it.

Importantly, the South African Bill of Rights drafters never intended for the socioeconomic rights provisions to create an individual right.[120]

---

[115] Roux, *id.* at 46.   [116] *Id.* at 47.

[117] Roux grudgingly acknowledges the advancement in international human rights law that *Grootboom* represents. Roux, *supra* n. 114 at 44 (The Court in *Grootboom* "went further than any other court in the world has gone in giving effect to socio-economic rights."). Yet, he still maintains that the Court has failed to fulfill the South African Constitution's transformative vision. *Id.* I suspect the Constitutional Court would find this criticism to contain unrealistic assumptions and expectations.

[118] Murray Wesson, "Grooboom and Beyond: Reassessing the Socio-Economic Jurisprudence of the South African Constitutional Court," 20 S. Afr. J. Hum. Rts. 284, 298 (2004).

[119] Bilchitz, *supra* n. 109 at 493 (emphasis added). The author further says that the government should ensure the right is "partially realized immediately." *Id.* at 494. Roux likewise emphasizes the temporal priority that sheltering the homeless must take over other housing needs and presumably other social problems. Roux, *supra* n. 114 at 47.

[120] According to Sandra Liebenberg, the Technical Committee said that "the main duty on the state is to provide opportunities and remove constraints which prevent access to social and economic rights in South Africa." Sandra Liebenberg, "Socio-Economic Rights," *in* Mathew Chaskalson et al. (Eds.) Constitutional Law of South Africa 41–44 (rev. 1998).

One of the groups that played a central role in convincing the South African Constitutional Assembly (CA) to add such rights to the 1996 Constitution was the Ad Hoc Committee for the Campaign on Social and Economic Rights.[121] This advocacy group for the poor was so forceful that it felt the "progressive realization" standard was too slow. Yet, their CA submission rejected the Bilchitz argument:

> Social and economic rights do not have as their only or primary remedy the provision of a commodity on demand. Rather, they require the creation of an environment and processes which enable individuals and communities to realize these rights.... The experience of people working with poor communities, both here and in other jurisdictions, has been that these communities realize that the constitutional entrenchment of social and economic rights will not necessarily translate into the immediate provision of material goods.[122]

Moreover, government resources to provide basic health care, adequate education, food, and water would be exhausted if it had to provide housing on demand immediately. Thus, Marius Pieterse points out,

> To insist on a comprehensive, once-off definition of minimum core may be counter-transformative where such a definition over-essentialises the needs and experiences of a diverse populace, excludes the satisfaction of certain vital needs, inflexibly prescribes the state's response to such needs, or frustrates the satisfaction of legitimate needs that are regarded as falling outside of the minimum core. Insisting that the state adhere to acontextual minimum core standards in relation to a particular right, may further disrupt overarching transformation efforts by directing resources away from other pressing social needs.[123]

Such a system would also operate chaotically on a first come, first served basis. Even in health cases, Bilchitz acknowledges that the government could only meet a lesser and unclear "pragmatic minimum threshold."[124] Thus, he admits that the minimum core is not workable in some cases.

---

[121] Heinz Klug explains that ordinary people in various civil society groups, and within the ANC, convinced party elites to add socioeconomic rights to the South African Constitution of 1996, unlike the Interim Constitution of 1994. Heinz Klug, Constituting Democracy 115 (2000).

[122] Ad Hoc Committee for the Campaign on Social and Economic Rights Submission, May 16, 1995, at 4, at http://constitution.uctac.zalcgi-binlcatdoc/sh/cama/data/data/subs/4652.doc (last visited May 13, 2003).

[123] Marius Pieterse, "Resuscitating Socio-Economic Rights: Constitutional Entitlements to Health Care," 22 S. Afr. J. Hum. Rts. 473, 491 (2006).

[124] Bilchitz *supra* n. 113 at 223.

Third, Bilchitz is incorrect in arguing that Justice Yacoob in *Groot-boom* impliedly recognized a minimized core.[125] The minimum core *requires* government to provide basic necessities, yet Yacoob wrote that the government should *try* to provide them. Pierre de Vos says that *Groot-boom* was easy in retrospect.[126] The Court could rule for the plaintiffs without determining a minimum core.[127] The ruling, however, still sent a powerful message that government must act reasonably in assisting society's poorest.[128]

Fourth, the critics ignore that the Court may not agree on a minimum core or even on whether one is desirable. Cass Sunstein acknowledges the presence of incompletely theorized agreements.[129] Justice Kate O'Regan has said that the Court's members do not all have comprehensive philosophical views on each part of the Bill of Rights.[130] They decide actual cases, sometimes on narrow grounds.[131]

Fifth, it is not clear whether the government would have complied had the Court in *Grootboom* and other cases issued bolder rulings. Therefore, the Court's supposed cautiousness may not hinder social transformation.[132]

One final point. Marius Pieterse writes that the Court's rejection of the minimum core "has met with much derision in academic

---

[125] *Id.* at 148.

[126] Pierre de Vos, "Grootboom, The Right of Access to Housing and Substantive Equality as Contextual Fairness," 17 S. Afr. J. Hum. Rts. 258, 258 (2001).

[127] Bilchitz, *supra* n. 109 at 485 (Justice Yacoob said that it was not "necessary to decide whether it is appropriate for a court to determine in the first instance the minimum core content of a right.").

[128] *See* Mark S. Kende, "The Fifth Anniversary of the South African Constitutional Court: In Defense of Judicial Pragmatism," 26 Vermont. L. Rev. 753 (2002).

[129] Cass Sunstein, "The Supreme Court, 1995 Term: Foreward: Leaving Things Undecided," 110 Harv. L. Rev. 4 (1996). Bilchitz, *supra* n. 109 at 113–14. Carol Steinberg discusses this at length. *Supra* n. 29 at 123, 269 & 273.

[130] Kende, *supra* n. 128 at 765.

[131] *Id.* at 764. Emily Bazelon, "After the Revolution," Legal Affairs, Jan.-Feb. 2003, at 25-28. "On the South African court, a concurrence is usually the closest thing to a dissent. In 2000, 25 of the court's 28 decisions were unanimously decided." *Id.* The Court was unanimous in both *Grootboom* and *TAC*, with the Court in the latter case taking the dramatic step of jointly authoring the opinion, as in the famous U.S. Supreme Court desegregation remedy decision in Cooper v. Aaron. 358 U.S. 1 (1958). The Court's relative unity establishes clearer priorities than would be possible if the Court disagreed vigorously and in public over the minimum core.

[132] Indeed, even the critics of the remedies acknowledge that progress has occurred. *See* Bilchitz, *supra* n. 109. Perhaps the Court's hesitancy to strong-arm the elected branches of the South African government reflects the influence of *ubuntu* – a South African word that embodies the social goal of achieving harmony. Kende, *supra* n. 128 at 765–66 n. 80.

circles."[133] Indeed, prominent South African critics of the Court on this issue include David Bilchitz, Sandra Liebenberg, Theunis Roux, and Danie Brand. Jonathan Klaaren agrees with Theunis Roux that "local commentators were perhaps better placed to perceive weaknesses in the *Grootboom* approach."[134]

Yet, Pieterse is only partly correct. Another group of mostly South African commentators, including Pierre de Vos, Cora Hoexter, Murray Wesson, Rosalind Dixon, Caroline Steinberg, and Aarthi Belani, supports the Court. Dennis Davis, who is both a judge and former legal academic, labels some of the Court's South African academic critics "naïve or somewhat arrogant"[135] for arguing that the Court should have blindly followed the United Nations proposed approach.[136] Moreover, foreign scholars almost uniformly praise the Court's decisions.[137]

More Content

The currently fashionable view among South African scholars is that, even without the minimum core, the Court should require more of government in socioeconomic rights cases than reasonableness.[138]

Danie Brand criticizes the Constitutional Court for using legalisms to avoid wrestling with the difficult moral and political issues. He labels this approach as de-politicization and juridification,[139] asserting that the

---

[133] Pieterse, *supra* n. 123 at 486.   [134] Klaaren, *infra* n. 137.

[135] Dennis Davis, "Adjudicating the Socio-Economic Rights in the South African Constitution: Towards Deference 'Lite,'" 22 S. Afr. J. Hum. Rts. 301, 315 (2006).

[136] Davis said, "Examine most of the academic work in the area of socio-economic rights and you will find a detailed argument about the plain meaning of s.26(1) and 27(1) accompanied by a lengthy exposition of the implications of the International Covenant on Social and Economic rights in support of an argument for, at the least, a minimum core to these rights. What is not found is a new animating principle on which these rights can be developed." *Id.* at 318. It is worth mentioning that South Africa has not yet ratified the Covenant though they have signed it.

[137] Jonathan Klaaren, "A Remedial Interpretation of the Treatment Action Campaign Decision," 19 S. Afr. J Hum. Rts. 455, 459 (2003).

[138] Sandra Liebenberg, "Beyond Civil and Political Rights: Protecting Social, Economic and Cultural Rights under Bills of Rights – The South African Experience" 18 ("It is crucial that the courts ensure that reasonableness review receives a sufficiently substantive interpretation.") (Melbourne Law School Sep. 25, 2007) http://cccs.law.unimelb.edu.au/download.cfm?DownloadFile=8CE3B978-1422-207C-BAF80F413681F573 (last visited Dec. 30, 2007); Klaaren, *id.* n. 137 at 456 & 461. Pieterse, *supra* note 23 at 500 ("despite the dismissal of a minimum core approach").

[139] Danie Brand, "The Politics of 'Need Interpretation' and the Adjudication of Socio-Economic Rights Claims in South Africa" 17, in A.J. Van der Walt, (Ed.), Theories of Social and Economic Justice (2005).

Court is actually highly political and anti-transformative.[140] He adds, however, that the *Port Elizabeth* and *Modderklip* decisions were an improvement over earlier rulings because the Court took a "can do" approach and proposed participatory democratic solutions such as mediation.[141]

Brand ignores that the Court used the standard of administrative law reasonableness because that is the Constitution's language. Moreover, while accusing the Court of hiding its politics, Brand downplays the Court's deference to the elected branch. He also minimizes how the Court has facilitated political mobilization among the poor and people with HIV, as Sandra Liebenberg, Brian Ray and others point out.[142] This is participatory democracy. Indeed, the *Port Elizabeth* and *Modderklip* decisions show that *Grootboom* and *TAC* set a sound foundation.

Marius Pieterse argues that the minimum core's death is not fatal:

> The recognition and enforcement of socio-economic entitlements need not take the form of a once-off and comprehensive determination of need, coupled with a rigid insistence on adherence to acontextual standards. Nothing prohibits courts from incrementally awarding context-sensitive and need-specific, enforceable minimum content to S 27(1)(a) on a case by case basis. Indeed such a *pragmatic* approach would seem to be required if socio-economic rights disourse is to retain its vitality, adaptability, and transformative potential.[143]

The Pieterse acknowledgement of pragmatism's import is joined by Theunis Roux, who gave a speech about the Court titled "Pragmatism and Principle."[144]

---

[140]*Id.* at 23 ("Whilst juridification patently has an emancipatory intent (guaranteeing, for instance, access to basic social benefits to protect against the depredations of the market), it operates simultaneously in a repressive fashion in that it limits the potential for radical and critical political action.") & 29 (Justice Yacoob's unwillingness to acknowledge the absolute right that children have to housing, and his ruling that their rights exists only when the parent doesn't provide them are "profoundly depoliticizing. It allows Yacoob J simply to ignore the social fact that often children who are 'properly' with their parents or family are worse off than those who find themselves in some form of alternative care, because their parents or families are simply too poor 'properly' to take care of them.").

[141]*Id.* at 34–35.

[142]Liebenberg, *supra* n. 138 at 20 (discussing resulting political mobilization); Brian Ray, 2008. "Policentrism, Political Mobilization and the Promise of Socioeconomic Rights" ExpressO, Available at: http://works.bepress.com/brian_ray/1 (last visited June 23, 2008) (forthcoming in Stanford Journal of International Law).

[143]Pieterse, *supra* n. 123 at 491 (emphasis added).

[144]Theunis Roux, "Principle and Pragmatism on the Constitutional Court of South Africa," http://www.saifac.org.za/docs/2007/World%20Congress%20-%20Theunis%20Roux %20Abstract.pdf (last visited June 23, 2008).

Next, Pieterse argues that the Court can recognize an individual entitlement. For example, people have a right to emergency treatment, children have a right to health care, prisoners have a right to medical attention, and the government must provide reproductive health assistance.[145] He adds that the Court has supported socioeconomic entitlements when an equality issue is also present or when the state has impaired the "negative" aspect of such rights.[146] *Khosa* is an example. He acknowledges, however, that the Court has not found an entitlement unless some degree of access already existed.[147]

He then proposes an alternative to reasonableness:

> It is possible to recast this basis of the *TAC* finding as an entitlement to receive safe and efficacious medical treatment where such treatment has been medically indicated, as long as the treatment is affordable and where capacity to administer it exists.... It is also consistent with the progressive realization standard and with the principle of non-abandonment, in that it does not rule out direct relief for claims to more sophisticated forms of treatment where this is within the state's financial and human resource capacity.[148]

Indeed, *TAC* specified particular medical treatments as the remedy.[149] Klaaren also reads the early cases as not precluding a direct cause of action.[150] Pieterse acknowledges that his nonminimum core and nonreasonableness "test" is vague and that it does not require the Court to strictly scrutinize resource limitation assertions, but notes that it has promise.[151]

Unfortunately, Pieterse still underestimates separation of powers concerns in supporting an individual entitlement idea. For example, his test does not translate to areas such as housing or social security, where there are multiple possible remedies; for example, a sick person usually needs a specific treatment, whereas a homeless person could be helped by several possible outcomes (a shelter for a group, a temporary individual lodging for his or her family, etc.). These housing or social security situations will

---

[145] Pieterse, *supra* n. 123 at 492.
[146] *Id.* at 493. He adds that international law requires the state not disrupt existing health care and that it remove arbitrary access barriers. *Id.* at 494.
[147] *Id.* at 496.
[148] *Id.* at 498. He also says it avoids the rigidity of the minimum core.
[149] *Id.* at 499.
[150] Klaaren, *supra* n. 137 at 466. He says that TAC involved "hard look" reasonableness. *Id.* at 461.
[151] Pieterse, *supra* n. 123.

require the legislature to make choices from a menu of options precluding easy individual entitlements.

Resources

Another critique involves "available resources." Darrell Moellendorf writes,

> Available resources is...ambiguous, at it has both a narrow and broad sense. It may mean those resources that a ministry or department has been allocated and has budgeted for the protection of the right. Alternatively, it may mean any resource that the state can marshall to protect the right. These are the two extreme senses of the terms. To be sure, between the narrowest interpretation and the broadest lie other senses.[152]

David Bilchitz answers Moellendorf by saying the courts should divide the questions.[153] Initially, courts should determine whether there are enough department funds to solve the socioeconomic rights problem. If not, the courts must assess the government's overall budget, as well as appropriable private property such as capital obtainable from international lending institutions.[154]

Bilchitz is correct that courts should look beyond a single department in assessing available resources. That is consistent with its goal of transformation. Moreover, a narrow departmental views means that the government could avoid lawsuits by not allocating much money to specific departments. His argument, however, on expropriation and loans is flawed for several reasons.

First, it is inconsistent with the constitutional language about the resources being currently "available." Second, such an approach imposes no limit and therefore removes the scarcity presumed by the Constitution. Moreover, the Constitutional Court should not be given the discretion to order expropriations, thereby possibly destabilizing the economy.[155] The U.S. Supreme Court made economic policy in *Lochner v. New York*[156] to disastrous effect. Third it is probably not necessary to order expropriations. The South African Public Service Commission Report of 2008

---

[152]Darrel Moellendorf, "Reasoning about Resources: Soobramoney and the Future of Socio-Economic Rights Claims," 14 S. Afr. J. Hum. Rts. 327, 330 (1998).

[153]Bilchitz, *supra* n. 113 at 233–34.   [154]*Id.* at 229.

[155]Davis, *supra* n. 135.   [156]198 U.S. 45 (1905).

demonstrates that departments have often underutilized designated funding to meet socioeconomic needs.[157]

Another scholar, Cyrus Dugger, argues that *Khosa* took the "narrowest view when evaluating available resources," meaning that the Court only looked at one government department's resources.[158] Dugger also points out that the Constitution does not allocate the burden of proof.[159] He advocates placing the onus on the government because it possesses the financial data unlike ordinary plaintiffs.[160] Yet, the Constitutional Court has performed better than he expected. In a case involving the duty to protect rail commuters, the Constitutional Court said that it would require the government to reveal the funds available from an organ of state and how the funds were used.[161]

Stricter Scrutiny

Sandra Liebenberg argues for strict scrutiny in socioeconomic rights cases involving necessities.[162] She says the "reasonableness" test demands such scrutiny when so much is at stake. The government should therefore demonstrate compelling justifications, and "no less restrictive means" must be available. David Bilchitz is generally in accord.[163] However, this approach has several problems.

First, the constitutional text at most justifies heightened reasonableness. Courts must maintain the rule of law. Second, her approach would promote races to the courthouse by the destitute. Lastly, requiring the government to bear the entire burden of proof, as soon as any claimant

---

[157] *See e.g.* SAPA, "Gov't Depts. Still Underspend, Says New Report," Mail & Guardian online, April 17, 2008, http://www.mg.co.za/articlePage.aspx?articleid=337185& area=/breaking_news/breaking_news_national/# (last visited May 22, 2008); Monako Dibetle, "Fury over unspent millions," Mail & Guardian online, Mar. 28, 2008, http://www.mg.co.za/articlePage.aspx?articleid=335633&area=/insight/insight_ national/# (last visited May 22, 2008); South African Department of Labor, "Minister to Redirect Unspent SETA Funds," May 28, 2004, http://www.labour.gov.za /media/statement.jsp?statementdisplay_id=5397 (last visited May 22, 2008).

[158] Cyrus Dugger, "Rights Waiting for Change: Socio-Economic Rights in the New South Africa," 19 Fla. J. Int'l L. 195, 253 (2007).

[159] *Id.* at 261.   [160] *Id.* at 262.

[161] Rail Commuter Action Group v. Transnet Ltd., 2005 (2) SA 359 (CC) Par. 89.

[162] Sandra Liebenberg, "The Value of Human Dignity in Interpreting Socio-Economic Rights," 21 S. Afr. J. Hum. Rts. 1 (2005). *See also* Sandra Fredman, "Providing Equality: Substantive Equality and the Positive Duty to Provide," 21 S. Afr. J. Hum. Rts. 163 (2005) (advocating a heightened version of reasonableness review and placing the burden on the government to the extent possible).

[163] *Supra* n. 113 at 234.

files, mistakenly place the limitations analysis ahead of the infringement analysis.

Remedies

Several scholars criticize the Constitutional Court for adopting timid remedies.[164] In *Grootboom* and *TAC*, the Court refused to impose supervisory jurisdiction and problems arose. Moreover, Mark Heywood shows that politics has influenced the South African Human Rights Commission (SAHRC) while others demonstrate that the SAHRC has not engaged in aggressive monitoring.[165] Mia Stewart and others propose bolder remedies approaches.[166]

Stewart argues that constitutional damages, as in *Modderklip*, or structural interdicts are justified when lesser actions will not work.[167] Her focus is on cases in which government officials have failed to provide indisputably required social grants to poor citizens. She even advocates holding government officials in contempt so the courts are not rendered impotent. Murray Wesson recommends supervisory remedies for cases like *Grootboom* and *TAC*.[168]

Other countries support bolder approaches, including the United States, in which the Supreme Court authorized structural injunctions for illegally segregated school districts. Stewart then labels as outdated the argument that "constitutional remedies should be forward looking and community oriented rather than individualistic and corrective."[169] She writes, "If it is the function of constitutional remedies to help 'heal the divisions of the past' as the Preamble of the Constitution puts it, should the cure not be as individual as the ailment."[170]

---

[164] Roux *supra* n. 114.

[165] *See also* Dwight G. Newman, "Institutional Monitoring of Social and Economic Rights: A South African Case Study and a New Research Agenda," 19 S. Afr. J. Hum. Rts. 189 (2003). Others are in accord. Klaaren, *supra* n. 137 at 466 n. 54, Wesson, *supra* n. 118 at 306 n. 79.

[166] Mia Stewart, "Left Out in the Cold? Crafting Constitutional Remedies for the Poorest of the Poor," 21 S. Afr. J. Hum. Rts. 215 (2005). *See also* Mitra Ebadolahi, Note, "Using Structural Interdicts and the South African Human Rights Commission to Achieve Judicial Enforcement of Economic and Social Rights in South Africa," 83 N.Y.U. L. Rev. 1865 (2008).

[167] *Id.* at 225–28 & 233. Pieterse has similar views. Marius Pieterse, "Coming to Terms with Judicial Enforcement of Socio-Economic Rights," 20 S. Afr. J. Hum. Rts. 383, 414 (2004). *See also* Danielle Hirsch, *supra* n. 113.

[168] Murray Wesson, "*Grootboom* and Beyond: Reassessing the Socio-Economic Jurisprudence of the South African Constitutional Court," 20 S. Afr. J. Hum. Rts. 284 (2004).

[169] *Supra* n. 166. at 239–40.   [170] *Id.* at 240.

David Bilchitz, however, argues that stronger remedies cannot replace the need to provide content to the socioeconomic rights.[171] Vague "exhortations" are only likely to give the state excuses for non-compliance. These delays hurt the needy. Moreover, he says that "other branches of government may resent supervisory jurisdiction and see it as the Court's assuming final control over the performance of their duties."[172]

This last point is problematic as Bilchitz's minimum core would produce even greater interbranch resentment. It is more intrusive than a supervisory order, which simply ensures compliance with a court ruling. Bilchitz is correct that vague directives are problematic. Yet, *Grootboom* and *TAC* were not vague – the government just did not comply with the rulings to varying degrees. A supervisory order could have sped things up.

Another objection to the better remedy argument is that officials might not comply, which could bring about a crisis. Nonetheless, the alternative is to render constitutional provisions difficult to enforce from the start. That would certainly be a crisis, so it is better to know whether the courts can overcome the resistance rather than not try.

More on Pragmatism

There are other reasons why the Constitutional Court's pragmatic reasonableness approach, in socio-economic rights cases, made sense for South Africa.

The Hippocratic Oath Argument

In December 2000, I interviewed several Constitutional Court Justices.[173] Virtually all of them said that the Court in its early years was right to refrain from issuing unnecessarily broad rulings that could have been incorrect and that could have damaged its infant jurisprudence. In other words, the Court sought to avoid doing harm, much like the Hippocratic Oath instructs doctors.

For example, former Justice Richard Goldstone[174] said, "I . . . strongly believe that in the formative years it would be a serious mistake to craft

---

[171] *Supra* n. 113 at 164.   [172] *Id.* at 165.

[173] It is worth mentioning for completeness that I sought to interview several other Constitutional Court Justices, but was unsuccessful.

[174] Justice Goldstone is considered to be one of the greatest experts on international human rights law in South Africa and the world. For example, he was a chief prosecutor of the United Nations International Criminal Tribunals for former Yugoslavia and Rwanda. He has written a book about his noteworthy legal and judicial career. Richard Goldstone, For Humanity, Reflections of a War Crimes Investigator (2000).

wider opinions than necessary. It is far better to hasten slowly and be more certain of building a coherent jurisdiction. I have no doubt that principles should be clear but that is another matter."[175]

Justice Kate O'Regan[176] told me the following:

> The Court has been maximalist in some cases and minimalist in others. I'm a great defender of minimalism. It's very important that the Court after all avoid mistakes. It can't provide meaningful guidance to attorneys and clients and businesses if it's reversing itself. Of course the Court can't be perfect, but it should generally only issue broad rulings when it's pretty sure it's right.... Cautiousness is helpful because it promotes the rule of law.[177]

Former Chief Justice Chaskalson offered similar reasoning about the Court's early years in an interview with the *Green Bag*.[178]

The Argument from Democracy

The Constitutional Court's need to bolster the country's new and fragile democracy also supports pramatism.[179] For example, Parliament and the president must learn to act responsibly. Under apartheid, these institutions failed miserably so they can no longer be allowed to ignore their obligations to the people.[180] Judicial restraint also minimizes the counter-majoritarian dilemma.

---

[175] Mark S. Kende, "The Fifth Anniversary of the South African Constitutional Court: In Defense of Judicial Pragmatism," 26 Vermont L. Rev. 753, 761 (2002).

[176] Justice O'Regan was a Professor of Law at the University of Cape Town before being selected for the Constitutional Court. She had long been an advocate for abolishing apartheid and for adopting a Bill of Rights.

[177] *Supra* n. 175.

[178] Arthur Chaskalson, *Equality & Dignity in South Africa*, 5 Green Bag 2d 189 (2002).

[179] The fragility of democracy in South Africa should not be underestimated. Holding 266 of the National Assembly's 400 seats, the African National Congress is such a dominant party in Parliament that it can almost amend the Constitution unilaterally based on a straight party line vote. Official Web site of the Parliament of South Africa, The National Assembly, *at* http://www.parliament.gov.za/na/index.asp#parties%20in%20na (last visited Apr. 1, 2002). Amendments to section 1 of the Constitution require a 75 percent supporting vote in the National Assembly, while amendments to all other sections require two-thirds supporting vote (or 267 votes, close to what the African National Congress currently has). S. Afr. Const., ch. 4, § 74. Moreover, ANC party leaders have accused dissenters within the party of treason.

[180] Forcing the Parliament to make sensible decisions enforcing rights is one way to ensure that a culture does not develop, as in the United States, where the legislative branch does whatever it thinks is in its political interest and leaves the constitutional analysis up to the courts.

Former Justice Laurie Ackermann described how the Court walked a tightrope in the socioeconomic rights cases:

> The difficulty with this issue of course is where do you draw the line in the Court's involvement telling the legislature how to spend money or how to have an administrative structure to implement the rights. This raises separation of power problems as the Court can't rewrite the budget or declare the whole budget unconstitutional. In some ways, the Court's job is to prompt the elected representatives to act where necessary. Though the Court can't declare the budget unconstitutional, it can issue in real cases what amounts to advice that the budget is not in accord with the obligation on social rights and that it should be reassessed. The Court has done this by giving the legislature say six months to come up with some revised transparent budget and plan in this type of case like *Grootboom*. It's better that the legislature be given that chance.[181]

As Justice Ackermann summarized, "It's good to be modest, and leave much of the real equality action to the legislature."[182]

This view is consistent with the original intent of some of the Constitution's drafters, an issue not frequently examined in South African scholarship. In 1990, the year Nelson Mandela was released from prison and political opposition was no longer banned, the ANC Constitutional Committee issued "A Bill of Rights for a Democratic South Africa – Working Draft for Consultation."[183] The draft contained judicially enforceable socioeconomic rights provisions strikingly similar to those in the final draft of the 1996 Constitution.[184] Yet, the draft still said: "Parliament shall have a special responsibility for ensuring that the basic social, educational, economic, and welfare rights set out in this Bill of Rights are respected."[185]

In 1995, the ANC issued a document entitled "Building a Nation, ANC Proposals for the Final Constitution."[186] The document criticized the Interim Constitution and suggested improvements for the Final

---

[181] *Supra* n. 175 at 763.

[182] *Id.* at 762. The reference to Popper is to the famous philosopher of science Karl Popper.

[183] 18 Soc. Just. 49–65 (1991).

[184] *Id.* Article 10 (2) of the draft said, "The State shall, to the maximum of its available resources, undertake appropriate legislative and executive actions in order to achieve the progressive realization of basic social, educational, economic, and welfare rights for the whole population." *Id.* at 56.

[185] *Id.* at 63.

[186] Available at <http://www.anc.org.za/show.php?doc=ancdocs/policy/building.html> (last visited Dec. 30, 2007).

Constitution. Part two of the document is titled "Bill of Human Rights." That part had a section on "General Considerations," which said,

> Notwithstanding the need to address socioeconomic rights in the Constitution, it is also clear that such rights must be costed against an audit of available resources. It helps no-one to promise which cannot be granted, or which enables judges to set and prescribe government priorities. The task of allocating scarce resources to job-creation before health care, or vice versa, is *the government's job, not the courts.* This does not preclude a floor of basic economic rights, capable of expansion through legislation or the constitution.... The provisions on social and economic rights should be formulated in a way that does not hamper effective government.[187]

Institutional Legitimacy

The Court's cautiousness also preserves its reputation. The most empirically rigorous study of the South African Constitutional Court's public legitimacy showed that it lagged significantly lower than even the Russian Constitutional Court, though the study is not so recent.[188]

The legitimacy concern also meant that the Court's members had to avoid issuing too many conflicting opinions. As mentioned earlier in this book, Justice Goldstone told me the Court often had multiple meetings trying to reach consensus in cases. Justice O'Regan added that the Court "should keep its powder dry in cases and certainly avoid issuing numerous 6–5 decisions."[189] This is unlike the U.S. Supreme Court, which typically meets once after the oral argument to see how its members are voting and which has many divided opinions.

Justice O'Regan's consensus comments were not mere hypotheticals. During a trip to the United States, one of the Justices told me that the Court was badly divided over the *Grootboom* remedy. The Court, however, united behind Justice Zac Yacoob's opinion. This is essentially what the U.S. Supreme Court did in two of its most internationally renowned cases, *Brown* v. *Board of Education*[190] and *Cooper* v. *Aaron.*[191] Unified decisions in important cases promote institutional credibility.

---

[187] *Id.* (emphasis added).

[188] Gregory A. Caldeira & James L. Gibson. Defenders of Democracy? Legitimacy, Popular Acceptance, and the South African Constitutional Court, 65 J. Politics 1 (2000). For a brief discussion of the Gibson article's views, *see supra* n. 175 at 769 n. 116.

[189] *Supra* n. 175 at 762.

[190] Brown v. Bd. of Educ., 347 U.S. 483 (1954) (ruling unanimously that public school segregation in the South violated equal protection).

[191] Cooper v. Aaron, 358 U.S. 1, 19-20 (1958) (ruling unanimously that states must comply with *Brown*).

There are, however, counter-arguments. Several years ago, I was carrying out a rule of law project in Moldova, an independent nation that was once a Soviet Republic. I interviewed the Chief Justice of the relatively new Moldovan Constitutional Court. He had previously been a high-ranking Communist Party legal official before the fall of the Soviet Union. I asked him whether he thought it was wise for the South African Constitutional Court to make cautious decisions to preserve its institutional integrity. He seemed surprised. He said that such an approach sounded like a strategic and political one, not suitable for a court that must simply apply the law and let the chips fall where they may. Yet, applying the law in monumental cases is not so simple – there is plenty of judicial discretion.

UNITED STATES SOCIOECONOMIC RIGHTS JURISPRUDENCE

The U.S. Supreme Court's view of socioeconomic rights is evident in *Lindsey v. Normet,*[192] in which the Court held, "We do not denigrate the importance of decent, safe, and sanitary housing. But the Constitution does not provide judicial remedies for every social and economic ill." The first part of this section looks at various Supreme Court decisions. The second part relies on the South African cases described earlier to demonstrate the Supreme Court's unjustified doubts about the judiciary's competence to enforce such rights.

U.S. Supreme Court Cases

The Supreme Court has rejected socioeconomic rights claims in cases with varying facts. In *Dandridge v. Williams,*[193] the Court ruled that Maryland did not violate equal protection by imposing a $250 welfare cap regardless of family size.[194] The cap was rationally related to the state's interests in preserving scarce resources and in creating incentives for the poor to seek employment and to engage in family planning.[195] In *San Antonio Independent School District v. Rodriguez,*[196] the Court ruled that Texas's public education financing scheme was consistent with equal protection and substantive due process despite dramatic school district disparities in per student funding.[197] The law burdened neither a suspect class nor a fundamental right.[198] Additionally, in *Harris v.*

---

[192] 405 U.S. 56, 73–74 (1972).
[194] *Id.* at 474–75, 486.
[196] 411 U.S. 1 (1973).
[198] *Id.* at 28, 38.

[193] 397 U.S. 471 (1970).
[195] *Id.* at 483–84.
[197] *Id.* at 54–55.

McRae,[199] the Court ruled that a federal health care program that omitted coverage for abortions, even when the pregnancy endangered the woman's health, did not violate substantive due process.[200]

To be fair, strong dissents were issued in these cases. Moreover, the Court has upheld socioeconomic protections in a few circumstances. In *Shapiro v. Thompson*,[201] the Court ruled that a durational residency requirement for welfare recipients discriminated against a person's fundamental right to travel.[202] This was a hybrid case that implicated what has been called "equal protection fundamental interests."[203] In *Saenz v. Roe*,[204] the Court issued a similar ruling regarding welfare payments,[205] but held that the right to travel was based on the Fourteenth Amendment's privileges and immunities clause.[206] This travel issue was not present in *Dandridge*.

In *Plyler v. Doe*,[207] the Court ruled unconstitutional a Texas law that required illegal alien children to pay to attend public schools.[208] Though neither a suspect class nor fundamental right was implicated, the Court asserted that the law revealed an irrational animus toward a vulnerable group not responsible for its situation.[209] Children were not to blame for their parents' actions. This was a surprising result in light of *Rodriguez*. One distinction was that in *Rodriguez* the law provided students with a minimum education whereas certain students in *Plyler* were denied any education unless they paid for it.[210]

To sum up, the Supreme Court has rejected socioeconomic rights claims under both substantive due process and equal protection doctrines. The Court has generally not been willing to use the Ninth Amendment or the Fourteenth Amendment's privileges or immunities clause. The Court has been receptive to hybrid "equal protection fundamental interests" claims[211] but even then, the Court has tried to find another hook, such as the right to travel or the right to vote.[212]

---

[199] 448 U.S. 297 (1980).

[200] *Id.* at 326.

[201] 394 U.S. 618 (1969).

[202] *Id.* at 638.

[203] Erwin Chemerinsky, Constitutional Law 842 (2d ed. 2002) ("The right to vote is a fundamental right protected under equal protection. The right to vote is regarded as fundamental because it is essential in a democratic society.").

[204] 526 U.S. 489 (1999).

[205] *Id.* at 510–11.

[206] *Id.*

[207] 457 U.S. 202 (1982).

[208] *Id.* at 230.

[209] *Id.* at 223–24.

[210] San Antonio Indep. Sch. Dist. v. Rodriguez, 411 U.S. 1, 9-11 (1973); *Plyler*, 457 U.S. at 206.

[211] *See* Chemerinsky, *supra* n. 203.

[212] Harper v. Va. State Bd. of Elections, 383 U.S. 663, 670 (1966) (holding that poll taxes that affect the rights of the poor are unconstitutional because they discriminate regarding the right to vote).

Perhaps the Court's most infamous case is *De Shaney v. Winnebago County Department of Social Services*,[213] in which it refused to hold the government liable for returning an already abused child, Joshua DeShaney, to a father who subsequently beat the child into a coma. The Court said the private acts of the father were not the state's responsibility. In his dissent Justice Blackmun wrote these famous words: "Poor Joshua!" By contrast, the Constitutional Court has found that the government has a general affirmative duty to protect human life.[214]

Separation of Powers

The Supreme Court has raised separation of powers objections in socioeconomic rights cases. Of course, scholars such as Frank Michelman,[215] Peter Edelman,[216] Mark Tushnet,[217] Charles Black,[218] William Forbath, and Erwin Chemerinsky[219] challenge the Court's socioeconomic rights decisions based on their respective views of the Fourteenth Amendment. This chapter leaves the Fourteenth Amendment questions for a later day because the South African cases shed light on separation of powers issues, but not on the peculiarities of American substantive due process or the privileges and immunities clause. Moreover, Fourteenth Amendment theory becomes less important regarding socioeconomic rights if separation of powers objections cannot be overcome.

The Supreme Court has raised three separation of powers concerns. First, the legislature, not courts, should make socioeconomic funding allocations. Second, the judiciary lacks the competence to make such decisions. Third, separation of powers problems are minimized if the Constitution encompasses negative rights. The South African cases address these concerns.

---

[213] 489 U.S. 189 (1989).

[214] Carmichele v. Minister of Safety and Security, 2001 (4) SA 938 (CC).

[215] Frank I. Michelman, "Foreward: On Protecting the Poor through the Fourteenth Amendment," 83 Harv. L. Rev. 7, 26 (1969).

[216] Peter B. Edelman, "The Next Century of Our Constitution: Rethinking Our Duty to the Poor," 39 Hastings L.J. 1, 30–31 (1987).

[217] Mark Tushnet, "Civil Rights and Social Rights: The Future of the Reconstruction Amendments," 25 Loy. L.A. L. Rev. 1207 (1991).

[218] Charles L. Black, Jr., "Further Reflections on the Constitutional Justice of Livelihood," 86 Colum. L. Rev. 1103 (1986). George Fletcher's work makes similar arguments. *See* George P. Fletcher, Our Secret Constitution 152–63 (2001).

[219] Erwin Chemerinsky, "Making the Case for a Constitutional Right to Minimum Entitlements," 44 Mercer L. Rev. 525 (1992–1993).

The Legislature's Prerogative

The Supreme Court has made clear that the legislative and executive branches should resolve socioeconomic rights issues. In *Dandridge*, the Court said, "The Constitution does not empower this Court to second-guess state officials charged with the difficult responsibility of allocating limited public welfare funds among the myriad of potential recipients."[220] The Court added that the "problems presented by public welfare assistance programs are not the business of this Court."[221] In *Lindsey*,[222] the Court upheld Oregon's summary eviction procedures holding, "Absent constitutional mandate, the assurance of adequate housing and the definition of landlord tenant relationships are legislative, not judicial, functions."[223]

The majority in *Rodriguez* said that it lacked the "authority" to intervene regarding school financing decisions because it would then be a "super-legislature."[224] This objection resembles Justice Holmes's famous *Lochner* dissent.[225] *Rodriguez* also asserted that educational decisions should be left to government entities with local political and economic expertise.[226] Finally, in *Harris,* the Court said, "Whether freedom of choice [on abortion] that is constitutionally protected warrants federal subsidization is a question for Congress to answer, not a matter of constitutional entitlement."[227]

The South African cases, however, demonstrate that the judiciary can enforce socioeconomic rights without intruding into quintessentially legislative or executive functions. In *Soobramoney, Grootboom,* and *TAC,* the Constitutional Court asserted that it would uphold government socioeconomic policies so long as they were reasonable. This is a pro-government presumption. The government only lost in *Grootboom* and *TAC* because it had no plan for assisting people in difficult circumstances. Moreover, the Court's rejection of the "minimum core" in *Grootboom* and *TAC* provided the government with flexibility regarding other social problems. The 2008 Constitutional Court case directive requiring mediation and "engagement," involving Johannesburg squatters, further reveals the Court's pragmatic creativity.

Finally, *Grootboom* demonstrates that a court can issue a remedial order that still gives latitude to implementation by the legislature. Mark

---

[220]Dandridge v. Williams, 397 U.S. 471,487 (1970).
[221]*Id.*   [222]405 U.S. 56 (1972).
[223]*Id.* at 74.   [224]411 U.S. 1, 31 (1973).
[225]Lochner v. New York, 198 U.S. 45, 74–78 (1905) (Holmes, J., dissenting).
[226]411 U.S. at 40–41.
[227]Harris v. McRae, 448 U.S. 297, 318 (1980).

Tushnet called this an "action-forcing remed[y]."[228] In the context of employment rights, Tushnet writes, "Enforcement [of an order that the legislature offers plans for relief] could guarantee that legislatures make jobs policy a high or higher priority."[229] Frank Michelman argues that this remedy involved "a judicial mandate to legislative, executive, or administrative officers to prepare, submit, and carry out a corrective plan."[230] Michelman further confirms that *Grootboom* "does not as it stands seem shockingly pre-emptive of legislative and executive policy choice."[231] The Constitutional Court accomplished what the U.S. Supreme Court has said courts cannot do.[232] Indeed, the South African remedy should have gone a bit farther.

Competence

The Supreme Court has also questioned the judiciary's ability to make budgetary decisions. In *Dandridge,* the Court labeled such issues "intractable."[233] In *Rodriguez,* the Court said the judiciary lacked the "competence" to evaluate education funding levels.[234] *Rodriguez* also invoked "our federalism" by saying that the Court did not possess "the expertise and the familiarity with local problems so necessary to the making of wise decisions with respect to the raising and disposition of public revenues."[235] The Supreme Court added that its "lack of specialized knowledge and experience counsels against premature

---

[228] Mark Tushnet, "What is Constitutional about Progressive Constitutionalism?," 4 Widener L. Symp. J. 19, 31 (1999).

[229] William E. Forbath, "Constitutional Welfare Rights: A History, Critique and Reconstruction," 69 Fordham L. Rev. 1821, 1878 n. 261 (2001) (citing Mark Tushnet, *id.*)

[230] Frank I. Michelman, "In Pursuit of Constitutional Welfare Rights: One View of Rawls' Theory of Justice," 121 U. Pa. L. Rev. 962, 1006 (1973).

[231] Frank I. Michelman, "The Constitution, Social Rights, and Liberal Political Justification," 1 Int'l J. of Const. L. 13, 27 (2003).

[232] David Currie quoted a German critic of affirmative rights as saying that "notwithstanding the worldwide proliferation of constitutional provisions explicitly imposing affirmative social duties, '[n]o constitution recognizing the rule of law has yet actually succeeded in practice' in turning away from the classical negative understanding of fundamental rights." Currie, *supra* n. 5 at 889 (citing Forsthoff, "Begriff und Wesen des sozialen Rechtsstaates," *in* 12 VerOffentlichungen der Vereinigung der Deutschen Staatsrechtslehrer 20, 33 (1954)).

[233] Dandridge v. Williams, 397 U.S. 471, 487 (1970).

[234] San Antonio Indep. Sch. Dist. v. Rodriguez, 411 U.S. 1, 31 (1973).

[235] *Id.* at 41. It seems that the Supreme Court in *Rodriguez* was more concerned with separation of powers problems than with federalism problems. After all, the local entities that the Supreme Court assumed to be "competent" in making school budgetary decisions were school districts, not state or local courts. The basic theme is that the judiciary is ill equipped to handle such matters, no matter the level.

interference with the informed judgments made at the state and local levels."[236]

The Supreme Court's concerns are overstated. *Grootboom's* action-forcing remedy, along with a supervisory order, would allow the legislature or local entities to wrestle with implementation despite the court's intervention. Moreover, judicial intervention is justified when the other branches violate the Constitution.

Charles Black's 1997 book, *A New Birth of Freedom*, explains why lack of competency is not a valid defense against judicial action:

> About half our black children under six live in poverty, which very commonly entails malnutrition. Some helpless old people have been known to eat dog food when they could get it; it is not recorded that any Cabinet member has yet tried this out on elderly persons in his own extended family. Now you can bog down in a discussion about the exact perimeter of "decent livelihood," or you can cease for a moment from that commonly diversionary tactic and note that, wherever the penumbra may be, malnourished people are not enjoying a decent livelihood. In a constitutional universe admitting serious attention to the Declaration of Independence, a malnourished child is not enjoying a "right to the pursuit of happiness."[237]

Negative Rights

Another concern is that the American constitutional tradition presumes that courts can more easily enforce negative political and civil rights than positive socioeconomic rights.[238] It seems simpler to order the government to stop interfering than to determine how much funding is needed for secondary education.

This reasoning has two problems as previously suggested.[239] In the *First Certification Judgment*, as well as in *Grootboom* and *TAC*, the

---

[236] *Id.* at 42.

[237] Charles L. Black, Jr., A New Birth of Freedom (1997).

[238] Edelman, *supra* n. 216 at 30–31. *See also* Bernard H. Siegan, Economic Liberties and the Constitution 311–12 (1980) ("In a society that considers private incentives a primary means to economic progress, *affirmative* jurisprudence creates serious *pragmatic* problems.... The courts' traditional role in protecting individual rights [via a negative jurisprudence] remains the most promising judicial means *of* reducing the burdens of economic inequality.") (emphasis added).

[239] Commentators from diverse political spectrums question the stereotypical American view that only negative rights are constitutionally protected, including Philip Kurland, Laurence Tribe, David Currie, and Michael J. Gerhardt. See *generally* Gerhardt, *supra* n. 5, at 410 nn. 6–7, 438 n. 119 (1990). *See also* Cass Sunstein, The Partial Constitution 69–71 (1993).

Constitutional Court said that protecting socioeconomic rights sometimes requires the Court to negate government actions that interfere with
a right.[240] Thus, in *TAC*, as Frank Michelman points out, the Constitutional Court found that the government unconstitutionally interfered with
the right of public doctors to distribute nevirapine.[241] This "negative" role
regarding socioeconomic rights is little different from the "negative" role
that U.S. courts play when vindicating political rights.

Second, Mark Tushnet,[242] Cass Sunstein,[243] and others have established that enforcing negative rights also implicates budgetary matters.
Sunstein writes:

> Even conventional individual rights, like the right to free speech and pri-
> vate property, require governmental action. Private property cannot exist
> without a governmental apparatus, ready and able to secure people's hold-
> ings as such. So-called negative rights are emphatically positive rights. In
> fact all rights, even the most conventional, have costs. Rights of property
> and contract, as well as rights of free speech and religious liberty, need
> significant taxpayer support.[244]

Henry Shue writes that courts enforcing positive socioeconomic
rights are not performing a task "more difficult, more expensive, less
practicable, or harder to 'deliver'" than protecting negative rights.[245]
The U.S Supreme Court's intrusive efforts to implement a remedy against
segregation, in *Brown v. Board of Education II*, illustrate this point.[246]

---

[240] *In re Certification of the Constitution of the Republic of South Africa*, 1996 (10)
BCLR 1253 (CC) (First Certification Judgment), *available at* 1996 SACLR Lexis 79;
Government of the Republic of South Africa v. Grootboom, 2000 (11) BCLR 1169
(CC) ¶¶ 42–43, *available at* 2000 SACLR Lexis 126; Minister of Health v. Treatment
Action Campaign, 2002 (10) BCLR 1033 (CC) ¶¶ 30–32, *available at* 2002 SACLR
Lexis 26.

[241] *Treatment Action Campaign*, 2002 (10) BCLR 1033 (CC) ¶¶ 67–68; Frank I. Michelman, *supra* n. 229. *Grootboom* also discussed how the right to housing could involve
negative claims that the government is interfering with access to housing. *Grootboom*,
2000 (11) BCLR 1169 (CC) ¶ 34.

[242] Tushnet, *Civil Rights*, *supra* n. 217 at 1213–14.

[243] Cass Sunstein, Designing Democracy: What Constitutions Do 222–23, 234 (2001).

[244] *Id.* at 222–23 (endnote omitted).

[245] Henry Shue, Basic Rights: Subsistence, Affluence, and U.S. Foreign Policy 63 (1980).

[246] Stephen Holmes and Cass Sunstein critique the possibility of a libertarian low-tax minimalist state, which only protects negative liberties, by stating, "One piece of evidence to
the contrary is the amount we spend, as a nation, to protect private property by punishing and deterring acquisitive crimes. In 1992 ... direct expenditures in the United States
for police protection and criminal corrections ran to some $73 billion – an amount that
exceeds the entire GDP of more than half of the countries in the world. Much of this

New Approaches

The South African cases discussed earlier in the chapter suggest how the U.S. Supreme Court could have decided certain socioeconomic rights cases. The Supreme Court in *Dandridge* did not have to resolve "intractable" welfare budget questions. The Court could have ordered the government to develop a more equitable funding rule that took into account family size.

Similarly, in *Rodriguez*, the Court could have ruled against the Texas financing scheme, but left the state to devise an equitable alternative, subject to Court guidelines. Numerous state courts have invalidated school financing schemes.[247] The Supreme Court mistakenly assumed that it had to "direct the States either to alter drastically the present system or to throw out the property tax altogether in favor of some other form of taxation."[248]

Moreover, the Supreme Court could have ruled for the plaintiff in *Harris* by simply requiring the government to ensure that the health service was provided to these women, just as in *TAC*. It is also worth noting that the Supreme Court decisions in *Shapiro, Plyler,* and the "new property" entitlement case, *Goldberg v. Kelly*,[249] as well as the eloquent *Dandridge* and *Rodriguez* dissents,[250] demonstrate that the Court can address socioeconomic rights issues.[251]

The Reaction

One possible reaction to the arguments in this section is that the current Supreme Court will not be endorsing socioeconomic rights anytime soon. Indeed, Lawrence Lessig essentially suggested at a 1997 Fordham Law

---

public expenditure... was devoted to protecting private property." Stephen Holmes & Cass Sunstein, The Cost of Rights: Why Liberty Depends on Taxes 63–64 (1999).

[247] See Chemerinsky, *supra* n. 203 at 889 n. 14 for a list of these cases.

[248] San Antonio Indep. Sch. Dist. v. Rodriguez, 411 U.S. 1, 41 (1973).

[249] 397 U.S. 254 (1970).

[250] Justice Marshall's dissents in these cases are famous for criticizing the Supreme Court's levels of scrutiny. Marshall argued that the Court actually employed a sliding scale of scrutiny in equal protection and fundamental rights cases. *See, e.g.,* Dandridge v. Williams, 397 U.S. 471, 508-30 (1970) (Marshall, J., dissenting); *Rodriguez*, 411 U.S. at 70-137 (Marshall, J., dissenting). Suzanne Goldberg takes a similar view. *See* Suzanne B. Goldberg, "Equality without Tiers," 77 S. Cal. L. Rev. 481 (2004).

[251] Frank I. Michelman, "Welfare Rights in a Constitutional Democracy," 1979 Wash. U. L.Q. 659, 664 (1979) (noting that federal court decisions "show... how it is possible for courts to act on welfare-rights premises without having to... take on an unmanageable remedial task, or to arrogate legislative and executive functions").

School constitutional law conference that Frank Michelman's welfare rights theories made Michelman look like a dreamer, given the evolution of the Supreme Court's jurisprudence.[252]

Nevertheless, the South African cases illustrate that courts, acting cautiously, can enforce such rights without destroying separation of powers or taxing judicial competency.[253] Once these false concerns are eliminated, the more foundational issues about interpreting the Fourteenth Amendment,[254] and perhaps the Ninth Amendment,[255] can be addressed sensibly.

Moreover, there are several interesting American developments that suggest that Michelman-type arguments are not hopelessly outdated. First, most Americans think their children have both a right to a good education and to affordable quality health care. Indeed, there has been some successful state constitutional litigation regarding education rights. The health care issue was especially important during the 2008 presidential campaign because America is one of the few industrialized democracies that lacks national health coverage. The presidential candidates for the Democratic Party often told stories on the campaign trail about how specific families experienced unthinkable tragedies because they lacked health care. Moreover, health premiums have shot through the roof.

Second, there is a significant American historical pedigree for the view that the government should provide basic benefits as related in Cass Sunstein's book, *The Second Bill of Rights, FDR's Unfinished Revolution*

---

[252] This reference to dreaming was actually made in a colloquy between Lawrence Lessig and Frank Michelman at a 1997 conference that centered on Lessig's work concerning fidelity in constitutional interpretation. Lessig said, "It is to remark a change in the world to note that Professor Michelman can write one of the most influential articles of the 1960s [on the right to welfare] that now is so alien. It is an odd piece – beautiful, and wonderful and we can dream about it. But still it is a piece that none of us would write anymore." "Fidelity as Translation: Colloquy," 65 Fordham L. Rev. 1507, 1510 (1997).

[253] For more detailed discussions about the pragmatic elements of the South African Constitutional Court's progressive jurisprudence, see Mark S. Kende, "The Fifth Anniversary of the South African Constitutional Court: In Defense of Judicial Pragmatism," 26 Vermont L. Rev. 753 (2002); Mark S. Kende, "Gender Stereotypes in South African and American Constitutional Law: The Advantages of a Pragmatic Approach to Equality and Transformation," 117 S. Afr. L. J. 745 (2001).

[254] U.S. CONST. amend. XIV.

[255] U.S. CONST. amend. IX. The U.S. Supreme Court's recent gun control case seemed to indicate that the Ninth Amendment should be interpreted as generally protecting individual unenumerated rights, which means that it could one day be viewed as protecting an individual's socioeconomic rights. District of Columbia v. Heller, 2008 Westlaw 2520816 *4 (June 26, 2008).

and Why We Need it More than Ever. The book shows how President Franklin Roosevelt proposed such a second Bill of Rights in 1943. There is also a powerful constitutional pedigree for such a view, as detailed by Sotirios Barber in his book, *Welfare & The Constitution*, and by Charles Black. Many scholars disagree but they cannot reasonably argue that these positions have no foundation, especially if one takes the Civil War Reconstruction Amendments seriously.

Third, as already mentioned, there are Supreme Court cases upholding some positive obligations. For example, the government must provide funding for the police, and other services, to protect controversial speakers. Moreover, the Court has ordered the government to provide benefits in cases involving durational residency requirements and in the access to schools case dealing with the children of illegal aliens, as discussed earlier. Perhaps the strongest case in recent years, however, to support a duty of the government is *Romer v. Evans.*[256]

In that case, the Court ruled that Colorado violated the equal protection clause when its citizens enacted, by referendum, a state constitutional amendment removing all antidiscrimination protections for gay people.[257] The Court held that the amendment was based on animosity toward homosexuals and therefore failed rational basis review.[258]

The Court's analytical starting point was significant. The Court rejected the argument that Colorado had the legal right to repeal statutory protections it enacted. Instead, the Court assumed that Colorado had a positive constitutional obligation to continue protecting all of its citizens – including gay people. The South African Constitution embraces these positive constitutional obligation.

As Kimberlé Crenshaw and Gary Peller note, "The majority's construction of a baseline of general protection against discrimination for everyone is based on an outright reversal of the common law construction."[259] Louis Seidman writes, "*Romer* seems to impose an affirmative constitutional requirement on jurisdictions to protect gay people from private discrimination, at least so long as they maintain comprehensive protection for other groups."[260] He asserts that *Romer* would have "potentially

---

[256]517 U.S. 620 (1996).   [257]*Id.* at 635–36.

[258]*Id.* at 632.

[259]Kimberlé Crenshaw & Gary Peller, "The Contradictions of Mainstream Constitutional Theory," 45 UCLA L. Rev. 1683, 1709 (1998). *See also* "Leading Cases," 110 Harv. L. Rev. 155, 165 (1996).

[260]Louis Michael Seidman, "Romer's Radicalism: The Unexpected Revival of Warren Court Activism," 1996 Sup. Ct. Rev. 67, 82. He added, "The collapse of the ideal of

far-reaching consequences," particularly in its use of a heightened form of rational basis review.[261] Jefferson Powell argues that *Romer's* recognition that the government has affirmative duties to protect citizens is consistent with longstanding equal protection doctrine.[262]

Moreover, *Romer* is not unique. There is case law from the anti-*Lochner*, posteconomic substantive due process era, which assumed that government has affirmative obligations. For example, in *West Coast Hotel v. Parrish*,[263] the Court suggested that if the government lacked a minimum wage law, taxpayers would have to help more destitute people, which would essentially amount to a subsidy for low-wage-paying businesses.[264]

Romer's view that the government has an affirmative duty to aid subordinated groups sounds more like South African Constitutional Court decisions than like the U.S. Supreme Court's decisions in *Dandridge, Rodriguez,* and *Harris.*

Fourth, the Supreme Court's increasing reliance on foreign constitutional sources, discussed in Chapter 3 on the death penalty and Chapter 5 on gay rights, means that the Court could eventually follow the global trend in favor of second-generation rights. Lastly, various state supreme courts have upheld positive rights as judicially enforceable. Such rights are therefore not alien to our traditions. For example, the Montana Supreme Court ruled that Montanans have an actionable right to a clean and healthful environment under the Montana state constitution.[265]

---

constitutional neutrality is painfully obvious on even a superficial reading of *Romer*. Because government nonintervention is not a natural state of affairs, the Court, in good liberal activist fashion, takes the general regime of government-mandated antidiscrimination as a baseline. It claims that it is enforcing the neutrality requirement by insisting that gay people receive the same benefits from antidiscrimination policy accorded to other groups." *Id.* at 100–01.

[261] *Id.* at 84–85.

[262] H. Jefferson Powell, "The Lawfulness of Romer v. Evans," 77 N.C. L. Rev. 241, 243 (1998).

[263] 300 U.S. 379, 399 (1937) ("The community is not bound to provide what is in effect a subsidy for unconscionable employers.").

[264] *Id.*   [265] MEIC v. DEQ, 1999 MT 248.

10

Final Thoughts

In 1966, Senator Robert Kennedy travelled to the University of Cape Town in South Africa at the invitation of an anti-apartheid student group. He delivered a speech containing this famous passage:

> It is from numberless diverse acts of courage and belief that human history is shaped. Each time a man stands up for an ideal, or acts to improve the lot of others, or strikes out against injustice, he sends forth a tiny ripple of hope, and crossing each other from a million different centers of energy and daring those ripples build a current which can sweep down the mightiest walls of oppression and resistance.[1]

Senator Kennedy's various South African speeches inspired his audiences because he addressed their subordination.[2] Kennedy even alluded to South Africa one day teaching the world about social progress.

This book has compared one product of the post-apartheid era to which Senator Kennedy alluded, the South African Constitutional Court, with the U.S. Supreme Court. This chapter draws some conclusions regarding the South African cases, predicts what the future holds for the Constitutional Court, and briefly assesses recent U.S. Supreme Court developments.

SOUTH AFRICAN JURISPRUDENCE

The South African Constitutional Court's rulings regarding the death penalty, gay rights, and socioeconomic rights have been transformative.

---

[1] Robert F. Kennedy, Duty of Affirmation Address at University of Cape Town, June 6, 1966, http://www.americanrhetoric.com/speeches/rfkcapetown.htm (last visited June 13, 2008).

[2] Kennedy in Africa: A Sympathetic Chord, Newsweek Magazine, June 20, 1966, www.rfksa.org (last visited June 10, 2008).

The Court's gender discrimination and freedom of expression decisions are positive but not as significant. The religion and affirmative action cases have been disappointing. Nonetheless, this is a remarkable legacy for a Court that started from scratch. South Africa is unlike other African nations that Makau Wa Mutua describes as having constitutions without constitutionalism.

The disappointing South African rulings reflect lingering formalism. For example, in the Rastafarian bar admission case, the Court employed a Western notion of structured religion rather than South African values. What are these values? Lourens du Plessis contends that the South African Constitution embraces strands of libertarian and egalitarian liberalism, modernism, and three kinds of traditionalism: African communitarianism, religious conventionalism, and Afrikaaner nationalism.[3] The Constitutional Court in turn has developed a rights jurisprudence that is best characterized as *African transformative pragmatism*.[4] It combines a strong anti-subordination principle, the communitarian qualities of *ubuntu*, pluralism, and some caution. Think of *Makwayane's* focus on the real inadequacies of the death penalty system, *Hugo's* concern with real benefits to women *Fourie's* deferential one year delay, and the mutual engagement required in recent socio-economic rights cases.

The Court's pragmatism is not what Kroeze has called "complacent"[5]:

> Complacent pragmatism employs three techniques: immunizing value choices by obscuring these choices and the power relations they support; making coercion invisible by assuming a majority perspective on choices; and making an appeal to common-sense notions of (values).[6]

---

[3] Lourens du Plessis, "Constitutional Construction and the Contradictions of Social Transformation in South Africa," 72 Scriptura 31 (2000).

[4] *See* Karl Klare, "Legal Culture and Transformative Constitutionalism," S. Afr. J. Human Rts. 146 (1998) (emphasizing the transformational principles embodied in the Constitution); Richard Calland, Anatomy of South Africa 220 (2006) (agreeing with the Constitutional Court's "politically pragmatic yet humane" approach). Some scholars use the phrase "African liberalism" to describe South African constitutionalism, rather than my transformative pragmatism concept. Yet, the Western liberal typology, with its artificial value neutrality in place, seems inadequate to describe what is really occurring. *See e.g.* Nelson Tebbe, "Witchcraft and Statecraft: Liberal Democracy in Africa," 96 Geo L. J. 183, 209–10 (2007) (discussing Will Kymlicka's critique of using the liberal paradigm in this context).

[5] Irma J. Kroeze, "Doing Things with Values II," 13 Stellenbosch L. Rev. 252, 261 (2002).

[6] *Id.* at 263, *quoting*, Andre van der Walt, "Tradition on Trial: A Critical Analysis of the Civil-Law Tradition in South African Property Law," 1995 S. Afr. J. Hum,. Rts. 169, 193.

Kroeze says the Court should instead employ "critical pragmatism,"[7] which has been discussed in feminist legal scholarship and elsewhere.[8] Here is one African-based definition of critical pragmatism:

> In a plural setting, proponents of gender equality must balance idealistic aspirations with a pragmatic realization that different contexts may call for diverse sets of tools to challenge unequal power relations. The term critical pragmatism is borrowed from scholarship exploring the critical potential of pragmatism as a legal framework that can be used to articulate the interests of less powerful groups. In one situation, an effective strategy may require insistence upon the recognition of customary obligations owed to women. In another context, an insightful critique may question the validity of of specific assertions of culture. Human rights principles embodied in constitutions and international instruments may provide a basis for such questioning, but concrete engagement with the politics of culture creates a much more productive challenge.[9]

The Constitutional Court's socioeconomic rights reasonableness approach and its context-based remedies (such as mediation and engagement) exemplify this brand of pragmatism, with its transformative yet realistic possibilities.

Having characterized the Constitutional Court's methodology in its strongest cases, this section now examines two major criticisms of the Court's rulings. The first is that the Court has actually not been transformational. The second is that the proportionality method is problematic, not pragmatic. This section then discusses the Court's future.

The Juristocracy Objection

Ran Hirschl argues in *Towards Juristocracy* that courts in democracies often decide the most important issues, not the elected branches. Moreover, judicial "rights talk" protects the hegemonic elites rather than supporting distributive equality. Hirschl focused in his 2004 book on New Zealand, Canada, Israel, and South Africa. He echoes American judicial review skeptics like Gerald Rosenberg and Mark Tushnet. His book has received international praise because it is well argued and his empirical

---

[7] *Supra* n. 5 at 263 n. 7.

[8] *See e.g.* Margaret Jane Radin, "The Pragmatist and the Feminist," 63 S. Cal. L. Rev. 1699 (1990).

[9] Celeste I. Nyamu, "How Should Human Rights and Development Respond to Cultural Legitimization of Gender Hierarchy in Developing Countries," 41 Harv. Int'l L. J. 381, 409–10 (2000).

analyses are useful. Nonetheless, his South African analysis does not hold up.

First, there is the straw man problem. Of course, the Constitutional Court cannot solve South Africa's wealth gap or stop the spread of AIDS. Hirshl has to be careful about unrealistic expectations.

Second, his frequent disclaimers in the South African context show that his analysis is in trouble. For example, he admits, "The widely celebrated South African constitutional revolution meanwhile represents a most difficult case to scholars skeptical of the conventional views concerning the progressive driving forces behind bills of rights and the overwhelming positive effects of such bills."[10] Moreover, he says that implementation of South Africa's Constitution "is still in the formative stages," which "prevents us from reaching any definitive conclusions regarding the impact of constitutionalization on this country's political sphere."[11]

Hirschl also says of the Court's gay rights cases that "these landmark judgments have been crucial in enhancing the everyday lives of millions of historically discriminated-against people."[12] Hirschl even acknowledges that the South African Constitutional Court "is taking workers' rights more seriously than its counterparts in" other nations.[13]

Third, his empirical evidence is not so clear. Hirschl writes,

> This systematic analysis of the four countries' complete record of constitutional rights jurisprudence reveals a clear common tendency to adopt a narrow conception of rights, emphasizing Lockean individualism and the dyadic and antistatist aspects of rights.[14]

According to Mark Graber, "Ran Hirschl observes how judges throughout the world are typically allied with secular elites who promote libertarian agendas."[15] Yet, several of the South African Justices were former political prisoners and revolutionaries. Moreover, Lisa Hilbrink writes, "Scarcely present in the judicial ranks in 1994, by 2003, Blacks filled 34 percent and women 12 percent of all judicial offices, and the majority of the judges on the Constitutional Court are now black."[16] In addition, the Constitutional Court has emphasized group and communal interests

---

[10] Ran Hirschl, Towards Juristocracy 10 (2004).
[11] *Id.* at 28. [12] *Id.* at 125.
[13] *Id.* at 143. [14] *Id.* at 14.
[15] Mark Graber, "Does It Really Matter? Conservative Courts in a Conservative Era," 75 Fordham L. Rev. 675 (2006).
[16] Lisa Hilbink, "Assessing the New Constitutionalism," 40:2 Comparative Politics 227, 231 (Jan. 2008).

as discussed in the earlier chapters, not Lockean individualism. Indeed, South Africa stands out in Hirschl's Table 4.2 for having a higher percentage of positive rights cases and a higher success rate for plaintiffs than other countries.[17]

The findings of Tracy Higgins' empirical study on gender equality in South Africa call into question Hirschl's evidence. During a two-week period, she interviewed one hundred South African men and women from subcultures that generally reject gender equality. The men complained about their status change, and the women understood that they should be treated differently. Higgins concludes:

> This evidence stands as a counterexample to Hirschl's suggestion that translating political goals into legal rights may frustrate their realization. On the contrary, it suggests that the South African Constitution's guarantee of gender equality has begun to inform the intimate relationships even of individuals living with little formal attachments to courts or legal culture. In the end, though, this may be an exception that proves the rule in that the significance of the constitutionalization of gender equality emerges not from the potential for its judicial enforcement but from the (sometimes grudging) acceptance of the norm as an aspect of South Africa's political culture.[18]

The Higgins conclusions received affirmation when the Constitutional Court issued its 2008 ruling in *Shilubana and Others v. Nwamitwa*.[19] In that decision, the Court affirmed a tribe's right to replace its chief with his daughter, rather than his son, even though this violated customary law and tradition. The Court said the tribe was following the new Constitution's gender equality mandate at its own behest contrary to what Hirschl would expect.

Moreover, Emily Zackin authored a sophisticated empirical study showing that popular constitutionalism is not feasible for controversial groups such as the American Civil Liberties Union (ACLU), which is why the group initially turned to the courts.[20] Though her study focused on the group in the 1920s, its logic applies today. South African groups like the Treatment Action Campaign need the courts.

Fourth, even without empirical evidence, Hirschl is incorrect when he states, "Channeling pressures for social justice to courts has a

---

[17] Hirschl at 105 (The positive rights claim success rate in South Africa is 45% compared to 28% in Canada, 21% in Israel, and 18% in New Zealand.).

[18] Tracy E. Higgins, "Constitutional Chicken Soup," 75 Fordham L. Rev. 709, 719 (2006).

[19] 2008 ZACC 9 (2008).

[20] Emily Zackin, "Popular Constitutionalism's Hard When You're Not Very Popular," 42 Law & Society Rev. 367 (2008).

considerable potential to harm reformist social movements by pacifying activists with the illusion of change and by luring resources away from political processes and lobbying strategies through which more substantial change might be achieved."[21] The American law firm with which I served as a civil rights attorney always assumed that reform was best achieved by pursuing all avenues including the judiciary, the legislature, and popular mobilization.[22] Securing social justice is not a zero-sum game and three weapons are better than one. Moreover, prevailing civil rights attorneys in South Africa and the United States receive attorney fees.

In addition, the main beneficiaries of the Constitutional Court's death penalty ruling were poor people and black prisoners, most of whom were convicted under apartheid. Hirschl could argue that Western-dominated institutions and intelligentsia are against the death penalty, but that does not change who benefited from the ruling. In a related argument, Lisa Hilbink contends, "Because... courts have no autonomous agenda-setting power, that is because they must and (in most cases) can only respond to petitions brought before them, they may thus serve as a welcome forum in which average citizens can stake claims dismissed or ignored by elected politicians."[23] Judge Edwin Cameron likewise stated,

> Perhaps "popular constitutionalism" would have produced more widely disseminated and internalized activism, but my observation is that the Constitution has nonetheless been widely appropriated as a source of rights in people's thinking. My view is that despite the elite role rightly observed, most South Africans (including non-citizen residents) regard themselves as bearers of constitutional rights, not just legal subjects.[24]

In addition, the Court's gay equality and socioeconomic judgments have mobilized the public. Samantha Power describes the Treatment Action Campaign (TAC) as the most significant dissident group in the nation.[25] For example, hundreds of their members protested outside a South African court to stop a lawsuit brought by international pharmaceutical companies. The companies sought to maintain rigorous

---

[21] Hirschl at 198.

[22] Jane Schacter, "Sexual Orientation, Social Change, and the Courts," 54 Drake L. Rev. 861, 881 (2006).

[23] Hilbink, *supra* n. 16 at 20.

[24] E-mail from Judge Cameron to Professor Mark Kende, June 13, 2008 (on file with author).

[25] Samantha Power, "The AIDS Rebel," The New Yorker (May 2003), http://www.pbs .org/pov/pov2003/stateofdenial/special_rebel.html (last visited June 13, 2008).

intellectual property rights and higher prices for anti-AIDS drugs. The companies dropped their suit after the protests.[26]

Moreover, the University of the Western Cape's Community Resource Centre has educated the poor regarding socioeconomic rights, and the Legal Resource Centre has brought to court many of the resulting cases. Numerous "squatter" groups have challenged their treatment by municipalities through the courts. And of course, the Court saved thousands of lives by requiring the government to distribute nevirapine. Scholars such as Sandra Liebenberg, Brian Ray and others agree that these rights and cases have been social "catalysts." Their views are confirmed by scholars, such as Michael McCann and Susan Sturm, who go beyond the South African context. Ironically, Hirschl's critique that courts are "out of touch" ignores these realities.

Fifth, Hirschl imprecisely argues that the ANC only accepted a Bill of Rights when economic elites abroad insisted on property rights and protections.[27] Even if this pressure motivated the ANC, it does not mean that it is what motivates the Constitutional Court. Indeed, the Court has pushed the envelope to the point that ANC leaders have threatened its independence.

Sixth, Hirschl's case summaries are inaccurate. He dismisses the gay rights decisions as demonstrating "a negative-liberty, small-government worldview" because the rulings are "simply . . . redefining an individual's sexual preference as an extention of his or her private sphere."[28] This characterization is incorrect for two reasons. First, the South African cases are based on equality, not privacy. Second, the South African gay marriage decision provides an affirmative benefit, namely a marriage license, not a negative liberty.

Hirschl then incorrectly describes the *TAC* ruling by saying that in it the Court

> drew primarily on equal protection reasoning; it remains to be seen whether this potentially revolutionary judgment is interpreted in future court rulings as an ordinary equal protection ruling (the drug was available in several sites across the country, but not in others) or as having wider implications on the provision of health care and other subsistence social and economic rights as legally enforceable rights.[29]

Yet, *TAC* was about the government's failure to provide cheap, life-saving health care, not equal protection.

[26] *Id.*
[28] *Id.* at 125.

[27] Hirschl at 96.
[29] *Id.* at 134.

Regarding the Truth & Reconciliation Commission (TRC) and the Constitutional Court's accompanying *AZAPO* decision, Hirschl writes, "This case clearly illustrates how moral and political quandaries pertaining to restorative justice in the wake of large-scale human rights abuses can be turned into judicial questions."[30] The TRC, however, removed these matters from the judicial process and placed them in a quasi-religious forum.

It is true that the Constitutional Court has been overly cautious regarding affirmative action and religion. Yet, the affirmative action cases reflect a Court that refuses to be vindictive toward whites. Hirschl ignores the connection between reconciliation and transformation. Moreover, on socioeconomic rights, the Court must follow the Constitution's text which speaks of reasonableness and available resources, not radical upheaval.

Hirschl concludes by criticizing "the degree of parochialism among many scholars of constitutional politics," the overemphasis on the United States, and "the dearth of genuinely comparative research in the field."[31] Yet, Hirschl's South African research and predictions were flawed. Indeed, his position is contradictory because he criticizes the Constitutional Court for resolving major issues while also questioning it for not ordering "revolutionary distributive measures."[32] Courts could not order such measures unless they took on major issues.

A better summary of how the Constitutional Court has performed comes from two South Africans, Jackie Dugard and Theunis Roux:

> In short, the lesson to be learned from the South African experience over the last ten years is that pro-poor judges and a pro-poor constitution are necessary but not sufficient conditions for courts in new democracies to function as an institutional voice for the poor. At least in the early part of their life, these courts need to accept that the inherent limits on their powers will prevent them from becoming a forum in which the poor are able to win concrete benefits that they are unable to win in the ordinary political process. This does not mean, of course that courts cannot function as important sites for communicating the concerns of the poor. It simply means that the use of courts by the poor must be part of a broader political strategy.[33]

---

[30] *Id.* at 192.   [31] *Id.* at 223.

[32] *Id.* at 150 & 162.

[33] Jackie Dugard, Theunis Roux, "The Record of the South African Constitutional Court in Providing an Institutional Voice for the Poor: 1995–2004," in Roberto Gargarella et al. (Eds.), Courts and Social Transformation in New Democracies 120 (2006).

Proportionality

Proportionality is one of the most important components of transformative pragmatism because it facilitates context-based determinations. David Beatty's book, *The Ultimate Rule of Law*, advocates the test globally whereas Stephen Gardbaum argues that American constitutional doctrine already embraces an implied version.[34] Justice Breyer authored a 2008 dissent, joined by three colleagues, arguing for the balancing of interests in a significant U.S. Supreme Court case about the Second Amendment and gun restrictions.[35] Recently, however, scholars have criticized balancing.

Against the Two Stages

Bradley Miller contends that the two-stage rights analysis ultimately breaks down. Focusing on Canada, Miller expresses dismay that losing claimants still can misleadingly assert that their "rights" were violated even if they lose at the second stage.[36] He relies on Ronald Dworkin's famous distinction between principles and policies to "rehabilitate" the two stages. Principles are fixed moral values, whereas policies are discretionary choices among alternatives on how to address specific issues.[37] Miller says the first stage could be about whether a principle has been violated, whereas the second stage could examine whether there are overriding policy justifications.[38]

Yet Miller notes that John Finnis and others have shown that legislatures can enact policies based on moral principles.[39] Thus, Miller says the rights analysis should be one unified stage of moral calculation. Miller supports this argument by describing a recent Canadian Supreme Court ruling, in which it held that Newfoundland's delay in paying a gender equity verdict had a moral dimension:

> In order to determine whether what has been described as a fiscal decision is justified, one must attend to the *moral evaluations* motivating the fiscal decision. This point was well understood by the Supreme Court of Canada, which rejected the characterization of the government's purpose

[34] Stephen Gardbaum, "Limiting Constitutional Rights," 54 UCLA. L. Rev. 789 (2007).

[35] D.C. v. Heller, 2008 Westlaw 252081 6*64 (U.S.S.Ct. June 26, 2008).

[36] Bradley W. Miller, "Justifications and Rights Limitations." at 4 & 7 http://ssrn.com/abstract=1084468 (last visited May 1, 2008).

[37] Ronald Dworkin, Taking Rights Seriously 22 (1978).

[38] *Id.* at 12.

[39] John Finnis, Natural Law and Natural Rights (1980).

as majoritarian self-interest, and instead characterized it as having been undertaken in service of the common good.[40]

Miller acknowledges that the Canadian Supreme Court would not abandon the two-stage approach but argues:

> Bills of rights are in the service of the entire political community. To the extent that a constitutional interpretation works injustice on that community, it should not be followed. Those courts that are not willing to abandon the two-stage structure can, and should, relax the demand that the analysis conducted at each stage be kept distinct. A court that draws watertight distinctions between definition and limitations can only do so artificially – there are only so many reasons to go around.[41]

Miller's argument is powerful because the South African Constitutional Court has struggled to separate the two stages of rights analysis, particularly when there is an internal limitations qualifier in the rights provision. Kevin Iles argues that the external South African limitations clause cannot be applied to the socioeconomic rights and equality provisions.[42] In terms of equality provisions, Iles contends that an unfair discrimination finding really cannot be overcome. Justice Mokgoro's concurrence in *Hugo* is one of the few counter-examples.[43]

One problem is that Miller does not explain why disciplined courts cannot separate first-stage factors from second. Moreover, having separate stages gives the contextualization greater precision. In addition, American rights are not absolute, so it is not clear why a Canadian "prima facie" right is so problematic.

Undervaluing Rights
Denise Meyerson argues:

> Instead of balancing rights against the public interest, courts should "over-enforce" rights, and downgrade the public interest arguments. In effect, this approach would give rights and the public interest different weights from the weight that they would attract on a balancing approach.[44]

[40] *Id.* at 27 (italics added).   [41] *Id.* at 31.

[42] Kevin Iles, "A Fresh Look at Limitations: Unpacking Section 36," 23 S. Afr. J. Hum. Rts. 68 (2007).

[43] *Id.* at 89.

[44] Denise Meyerson, "Why Courts Should Not Balance Rights against the Public Interest," 31 Melbourne L. Rev. 801, 806 (2007).

She objects that standard balancing "assumes that there is a single scale on which the value of protected rights and that of protecting the public interest can be measured, compared and balanced."[45] She writes, "Dworkin, Habermas and Schauer, by contrast assert that it can be justifiable to protect rights *even when the consequences are, on balance, detrimental.*"[46] She defends her viewpoint on several grounds. Interestingly, her views echo Justice Scalia's majority opinion, in the U.S. Supreme Court's 2008 gun regulation case, criticizing Justice Breyer's proposed balancing.[47]

First, Meyerson says that monists wrongly believe that rights and the good are commensurate. She instead adopts the pluralist view held by scholars such as Thomas Nagel and Charles Taylor:

> That there is a a fundamental and qualitative difference between "the right" (the realm of justice) and "the good" (the realm of *consequences*). On this view, rights and the public interest are incommensurable – the wrongness of violating rights is not measured in the same terms as the social gains that might be brought from violating them.[48]

The reference to consequences is important.

Her second argument is that judges are likely

> to go *systematically* wrong in attempting to assess the relative costs and benefits of infringing rights. Bills of rights exist to protect individuals from the political pressures of the moment, but judges are not archangels, immune to popular sentiment and fear.[49]

This argument resembles American First Amendment cases in which courts overprotect controversial speech on the theory that public sentiment will otherwise influence judges.

Third, like Scalia, she seeks to minimize judicial subjectivity:

> Although bills of rights require judges to engage in moral and political reasoning – and perhaps particularly when making choices between rights and the public interest – the reweighting approach puts a break on this reasoning. It prohibits judges from engaging in finely-tuned, practical enquiries as to the relative merits of the considerations on both sides – enquiries which would inevitably involve speculative and subjective reasoning.... The result will be that courts will allow infringements only when the need to do so is very obvious, substantially diminishing the subjectivity in the process.[50]

---

[45] *Id.* at 809.   [46] *Id.* at 814 (emphasis in original).
[47] *Supra* n. 35 *27.
[48] Meyerson, *supra* n. 44 at 815 (emphasis added).
[49] *Id.* at 817.   [50] *Id.* at 818.

Her reasoning has several flaws. For example, concepts of justice can be measured against notions of the common good, especially if the latter notions are not limited to consequentialism. Indeed, economists and statisticians handle complex comparisons like that all the time. In addition, her concerns about popular sentiment may be overstated. The South African Constitutional Court rejected public opinion when issuing gay marriage and death penalty decisions. Even in the United States, a group of southern federal court judges became famous for their decisions against segregation.

Regarding her judicial subjectivity questions, legal reasoning is constrained because decisions are reviewable. Meyerson's distrust of "finely tuned" analysis by judges also opens the door to a formalism that ignores factual differences in cases. Moreover, under her approach, courts might interpret rights narrowly because the judges know that the government justifications will rarely prevail. Her approach could cause a backlash. Indeed, her Scalia-type rights absolutism vitiates the limitations clause.

Vagueness Problems

T. Jeremy Gunn does not reject proportionality, but argues, "It is a peculiar characteristic of legal systems to advocate single words, e.g., 'proportionality,' 'subsidiarity,' and 'Rechstaat' (rule of law), to encapsulate core values with broad implications but whose actual meanings can be maddeningly vague and even incoherent."[51] He elaborates, "The most severe criticism of the application of the doctrine is that the terms are so vaguely and inconsistently applied that it ultimately serves as a fog that obscures what ultimately may be a results-oriented analysis."[52]

For example, proportionality does not clarify how strictly a court should examine the state's justifications or the burden on individual rights.[53] Another problem is determining how the court should perceive the institutional competencies of other branches. Interestingly, these problems suggest that one cannot completely escape the American level of scrutiny issue. Gunn says that it is also unclear who bears the burden of proof, what evidence should count, how courts should treat the legislature's motives, how courts should assess the effects of a statute, and the like.

---

[51] T. Jeremy Gunn, "The Permissible Scope of Legal Limitations on the Freedom of Religion or Belief," 19 Emory Int'l L. Rev. 465, 468 (2005).

[52] *Id.* at 470–71.   [53] *Id.* at 477–78.

Gunn then makes two strong normative arguments. First, "courts ought to be candid" about what they are doing in these areas.[54] Second, "the court should, therefore, be prepared to scrutinize the extent to which the right is infringed with the same degree of specificity that it directs towards scrutinizing the legislative objective and actual effect of the statute."[55] This equalization of scrutiny is a clever idea. He then describes which balancing techniques favor the complainant and which favor the government.[56] Gunn's article superbly addresses issues faced by all constitutional courts.[57] One hopes that the South African Court will follow his suggestions.

The Future

The Constitutional Court's future may be difficult. The first Justices have led extraordinary lives and possess incomparable legal skills.[58] Yet, in 2009, five of the Court's eleven Justices will complete their terms.[59] The Court's early opinions were philosophical and comparative treatises, such as Justice Laurie Ackermann's discussion of freedom in *Ferreira v. Levin*.[60] Today, the opinions are shorter and rely more on the Court's own precedents. The Court also began as mostly white and male, but now is predominantly black with more females. The Court's credibility and that of the legal system generally depend on this demographic transformation.

Moreover, the Court will address increasingly difficult issues, such as reconciling customary law with the Constitution's gender discrimination provisions in cases like *Bhe v. Magistrate, Khayelitsha*[61] and *Shilubana*.

---

[54] *Id.* at 479.   [55] *Id.* at 492.

[56] *Id.* at 495–498.

[57] *See e.g.* Iles, *supra* n. 42. Similar to Gunn, Iles suggests that even internal limitations clauses in South Africa's Bill of Rights should be interpreted in a manner consistent with the general limitations clause in Section 36. *Id.* at 88.

[58] Richard Calland and many others viewed the Court's quality as "excellent." Anatomy of South Africa 238 (2006). *See also* Sello S Alcock, "Judging the Class of 1994," Mail & Guardian On-line, Oct. 14, 2008, http://www.mg.co.za/article/2008-10-14-judging-the-class-of-1994 (last visited Oct. 29, 2008).

[59] Calland *Id.* at 241. Ordinarily, the Justices serve twelve-year terms but they can serve fifteen-year terms in certain situations. *Id.* at 216. *See also* Pierre de Vos, "What Happens when 5 judges retire," Constitutionally Speaking, June 24, 2008, http://constitutionallyspeaking.co.za/?p=594 (last visited Oct. 29, 2008).

[60] 1996 (1) SA 994 (CC).   [61] 2005 (1) SA 580 (CC).

The Court will also have to clarify the Constitution's horizontality provisions. There will be additional socioeconomic rights cases given the nation's wealth gap. Justice Richard Goldstone maintains that affirmative action will become even more of a question: "Until now all black South Africans were prejudiced by Apartheid. In the coming years more and more black South Africans will not have been prejudiced and the question of 'tailoring' will become important. There will undoubtedly be some thorny issues."[62]

Lastly, the Constitutional Court will face challenges to its independence and to maintaining the rule of law. The *Modderklip* ruling relied on the rule of law principle to resolve a socioeconomic rights case. In a related vein, Judge Edwin Cameron contends that "separation of powers cases" will be among the Court's most important upcoming matters.[63] There is indeed concern that the five new Justices may be overly sympathetic to the government that appointed them. The Court will also lose the progressivism of Sachs and O'Regan, though Moseneke is no shrinking violet.

Most significantly, South Africa essentially remains a one-party state in which the ANC has severely criticized the Court and does not readily brook dissent, as shown in Chapter 7 on freedom of expression. The government even proposed constitutional amendments that would have reduced judicial independence but they did not pass.[64] Then there is the widespread crime problem. Unfortunately, former President Mbeki recently disbanded the Scorpions, an elite police unit that investigated high-level corruption.[65]

Moreover, the apparent president-in-waiting, Jacob Zuma, was acquitted of rape in a trial where he admitted sexual misconduct with a much younger female relative.[66] Zuma has also been indicted for corruption which may explain the disbanding of the Scorpions. Recently, a major conflict arose because the Constitutional Court accused a High

---

[62] E-mail from Justice Goldstone to Professor Mark Kende, May 27, 2008 (on file with author).

[63] *Supra* n. 24.   [64] Calland, *supra* n. 58 at 237.

[65] Reuters, Sapa, "Mbeki's Govt Sounds Death Knell for Scorpions," Mail & Guardian online (May 4, 2008), http://www.mg.co.za/articlepage.aspx?area=/breaking_news/breaking_news_national/&articleid=338387&referrer=RSS (last visited June 14, 2008).

[66] Sapa, "Zuma Rape Accuser Gets Asylum in Netherlands," Mail & Guardian online (July 3, 2007), http://www.mg.co.za/articlePage.aspx?articleid=312965&area=/breaking_news/breaking_news_national/ (last visited June 14, 2008).

Court judge, John Hlope, of making veiled threats against two Constitutional Court Justices in an effort to improperly influence the Zuma proceedings.[67] Furthermore, it is troubling that Zuma may end up appointing the five new Justices who could assess his guilt or innocence.

Given the corruption, numerous land seizures by squatters, the crime problem, xenophobia,[68] the continuing poverty, and the impending death of the nation's elder statesmen, the rule of law and judicial independence could be at risk. One hopes that the Court can survive and bolster its legacy.

SUPREME COURT JURISPRUDENCE

The American cases discussed in this book differ dramatically from their South African counterparts. First, the American rulings are more conservative in all areas except freedom of expression. For example, the U.S. Supreme Court sometimes relies on originalist methodology. Justice Scalia's recent Second Amendment decision reached the apex of originalism though the Court often uses other modalities.[69] The U.S. Constitution's absence of interpretive directions leads to this unpredictability.

The Court's emphasis on individualism and on political and civil rights only confirms its relative conservatism. The Supreme Court is also more categorical and formalistic, as shown by the Court's hostility to most balancing tests and by rulings like *RAV* (hate speech is a protected subcategory of unprotected fighting words) and *McCleskey* (sophisticated statistical proof of a racially discriminatory system does not show individualized discrimination). Many scholars agree that even the Supreme Court's boldest rights decisions actually followed public opinion changes, not the reverse.[70]

Second, the U.S. Supreme Court has higher institutional legitimacy ratings according to public opinion polls. This is understandable as it has been around for more than 200 years, and the Justices have life tenure, reducing public pressures. The federal government's other branches and

---

[67] Editorial, "Stand up for the Constitution," Mail & Guardian online, June 20, 2008, <www.mg.co.za/article/2008-06-20-stand-up-for-the-constitution> (last visited June 29, 2008).

[68] Barry Bearak, Celia Dugger, "South Africans Take Out Rage on Immigrants," N.Y. Times, May 20, 2008, http://www.nytimes.com/2008/05/20/world/africa/20safrica.html?_r=1&oref=slogin (last visited June 14, 2008).

[69] Phillip Bobbitt, Constitutional Fate: Theory of the Constitution (1982).

[70] Gerald Rosenberg, The Hollow Hope (1991).

the states have usually complied with Court decisions. By contrast, it is too early to know whether the Constitutional Court will last, will command obedience, and will continue to perform at a high level.

Third, the Supreme Court is more polarized personally and politically than the Constitutional Court with its division between liberals (Breyer, Ginsburg, Stevens, Souter) and conservatives (Alito, Roberts, Scalia, Thomas). Mark Tushnet also shows that the conservatives are divided between the "movement" variety and the more traditional type.[71] Chief Justice Roberts is seeking more consensus but is having limited success.[72] Justice Kennedy has become the swing Justice. Thus, many experts call it the Kennedy Court though Roberts is the Chief Justice.[73]

Even the rhetoric can be hyperbolic. The Supreme Court recently struck down a federal law that prohibited Guantanamo enemy combatants from filing habeas corpus petitions.[74] Justice Scalia's dissent held that the majority opinion "will almost certainly cause more Americans to be killed."[75] Interestingly, the liberals did not make the same accusation when Justice Scalia struck down gun control laws in Washington, D.C. Conservatives and liberal commentators have traded accusations that their least favorite Justices are unprincipled activists.

Some scholars suggest that the Court's polarization on issues, such as foreign law, reflects their lack of experience with the give and take of politics, though Justices Thomas and Breyer held political positions. Nonetheless, former Chief Justice Warren brought the Court together by using the skills he had developed as Governor of California. The current Justices do not have that acumen.[76] Moreover, the American judicial confirmation process has become ugly enough that it is hard to imagine colorful political figures making it through.

Fourth, the Supreme Court decisions have more doctrinal disarray than those of the Constitutional Court. Indeed, Laurence Tribe refused to continue writing his famous constitutional law treatise because he said

---

[71] Mark Tushnet, A Court Divided: The Rehnquist Court and the Future of Constitutional Law (2005).

[72] Linda Greenhouse, "Kennedy Made the Boldest Mark on a Court That Defied Labeling," A1, N.Y. Times (June 29, 2008).

[73] *Id.*

[74] Boumedienne v. Bush, 2008 Westlaw 2369628 (U.S.S.Ct. June 12, 2008).

[75] *Id.**65.

[76] Scott Gerber, "Harriet Miers and the Myth that Great Supreme Court Justices Must be Former Justices from Elite Law Schools," Findlaw, Oct. 5, 2005, <http://writ.news.findlaw.com/commentary/20051005_gerber.html> (last visited June 30, 2008).

the doctrine was in too much flux.[77] Such a problem is inevitable, even with an extraordinary document, that is old and vague, especially where there are so many cases to reconcile. Yet, the disarray also relates to the polarization mentioned earlier and to the dispute over interpretive method.

Here are some examples of doctrinal inconsistencies. Regarding substantive due process, the U.S. Supreme Court was conservative in rejecting a right to die, *Washington v. Glucksberg*,[78] but relatively liberal regarding gay sex, *Lawrence v. Texas*.[79] Moreover, *Lawrence* never clarified its scrutiny level. This raises a separate problem – the Court's lack of transparency as compared to South Africa's candid weighing of interests. As a result, the federal appellate courts are now divided on whether *Lawrence* recognized a fundamental right.[80] In addition, two similar partial abortion cases reached opposite results.[81]

On equality, the Court states that it has three levels of scrutiny but it actually uses seven.[82] This is another example of the formalistic candor problem and the need for balancing. Regarding affirmative action, the Court in *Grutter v. Bollinger*[83] was deferential in upholding a law school admissions plan, though the Court said it was strict. Then, there is the Court's infamous *Bush v. Gore*[84] case in which the conservative members refused to allow any remedy for the supposed equality violation other than ending the election counts. The Court's hate speech decision, *RAV v.*

---

[77] Laurence Tribe, The Treatise Power," 8 Green Bag 2d 191 (2005).
[78] 521 U.S. 707 (1997).   [79] 539 U.S. 558 (2003).
[80] *See e.g.* Reliable Consultants, Inc. v. Earle, 517 F.3d 738, 745 n. 32 (5th Cir. 2008) (*Lawrence* did not recognize a fundamental right); Cook v. Gates, Nos. 6-02313 (1st Cir. 2008) (*Lawrence* recognized a liberty right that requires court to balance interests); Witt v. Air Force, No. 06-35644 (9th Cir. 2008) (the court ruled that the military policy of "don't ask, don't tell" for gay members is unconstitutional as *Lawrence* requires intermediate scrutiny).
[81] Gonzales v. Carhart, 550 U.S. __ (2007) (upholding a federal partial birth abortion ban); Stenberg v. Carhart, 530 U.S. 914 (2000) (striking down a state partial birth abortion ban).
[82] R. Randall Kelso, "Standards of Review under the Equal Protection Clause and Related Constitutional Doctrines Protecting Individual Rights: The 'Base Plus Six' Model and Modern Supreme Court Practice," 4 U. Pa. J. Const. L. 225 (2002). In addition to Kelso, other scholars have highlighted the breakdown of the three tiers of scrutiny. Suzanne Goldberg, "Equality without Tiers," 77 S. Cal. L. Rev. 481 (2004); Calvin Massey, "The New Formalism: Requiem for Tiered Scrutiny," 6 U. Pa. J. Const. L. 945 (2004); Jeffrey Shaman, "Cracks in the Structure: The Coming Breakdown of the Levels of Scrutiny," 45 Ohio State L. J. 161 (1984).
[83] 539 U.S. 306 (2003).   [84] 531 U.S. 98 (2000) (per curiam).

City of St. Paul,[85] ruled that previously unprotected speech could receive protection. On the establishment clause, the *Lemon*[86] test still exists on paper but the Court employs a neutrality principle. The Court's free exercise approach is opposed both by religious groups and progressive groups like the ACLU.

Other examples abound. The Court's decisions in favor of the Guantanamo "enemy combatants" have received praise from international allies, but they have been closely divided and left many unanswered questions. These conflicts make it difficult for lower court judges, lawyers, and the public to know how the Court will decide certain questions.

This is not to downplay the extraordinary stability of the American polity created by the U.S. Constitution and maintained by the Supreme Court. Fortunately, American culture embraces constitutionalism, for reasons other scholars have discussed. Moreover, South African constitutionalism has doctrinal tensions in areas such as indirect discrimination, the relation between equality and dignity, the use of the limitations clause (and the significance of internal limitations qualifiers), deference to the government, the use of foreign law, and the battle between real transformation and lingering formalism. The Constitutional Court's short history, however, and the South African Constitution's level of detail provide less opportunity for inconsistency.

The U.S. Supreme Court's future depends on the outcome of the 2008 presidential election and on the relative youth of the Court's conservatives. The Obama victory probably means that there will not be many changes, as the older liberal Justices (perhaps Stevens and Ginsburg) could retire and be replaced by younger liberals. Thus, the Court would still render frequent conservative decisions, like that in *Baze v. Rees*,[87] upholding a lethal injection death penalty protocol that has proven to be cruel in some cases. McCain, however, would have replaced the liberal Justices with younger conservatives.[88] That could have endangered the Court's rulings on abortion, affirmative action, executive power, federalism, and several other areas.

It is hard to predict the U.S. Supreme Court's likely constitutional rights cases. The Court may address gay marriage (or related questions

---

[85] 505 U.S. 377 (1992).
[86] Lemon v. Kurtzman, 403 U.S. 602 (1971).
[87] 553 U.S. __ (2008).
[88] Robert Barnes, "A Win by McCain Could Push a Split Court to Right," Washington Post A01, June 29, 2008, http://www.washingtonpost.com/wp-dyn/content/article /2008/06/28/AR2008062802078_pf.html (last visited June 30, 2008).

about state defense of marriage acts, full faith and credit, the federal Defense of Marriage Act), privacy questions involving genetic mapping, computers, and the Internet, issues regarding preemptive law enforcement, the balance between the war on terror and civil liberties, as well as conflicts over immigration, gun control regulations, religion, and the relevance of foreign human rights law. Certainly, the lower courts and the political culture are debating these questions. It is noteworthy that poverty and racial discrimination do not make the list, in contrast to South Africa.

What is extraordinary is how far the U.S. Supreme Court has traveled in the past few decades. In the late 1960s, the Court almost ruled that Americans had a right to welfare, similar to the Constitutional Court of South Africa. The Supreme Court used to embrace the plight of minorities and other vulnerable people in cases like *Brown* and *Miranda v. Arizona*.[89] The Court even endorsed busing as part of a structural remedy for segregation. Now it is known for frequent pro-business activism and racial blindness in constitutional matters.[90] For example, it has backed away from structural and inter-district remedies in the segregation area, and has ruled that discriminatory effects do not trigger a presumption of illegality.

Cass Sunstein and others debate whether this shift was caused by changes in the Court's composition (Sunstein's legal realist assessment), the American public's supposed conservatism,[91] the energetic right wing of the Republican party, or the related activism of groups like the Federalist Society and the Institute for Justice.[92] Certainly, progressive efforts to counter these developments have not been successful. What is surprising is that the Court's liberals have not used obvious textual tools, such

---

[89] 384 U.S. 436 (1966).

[90] Jeffrey Rosen, "Supreme Court, Inc.," N.Y. Times, Mar. 16, 2008, http://www.nytimes.com/2008/03/16/magazine/16supreme-t.html?fta=y (June 14, 2008); Taunya Lovell Banks "Exploring White Resistance to Racial Reconciliation in the United States," 55 Rutgers L. Rev. 903, 904 (2003).

[91] *See e.g.* Gregory Alexander, "Socio-Economic Rights in American Perspective: The Tradition of Anti-Paternalism in American Constitutional Thought," in A.J. van der Walt (Ed.), Theories of Social and Economic Justice 6, 12 (2005) (discussing Sunstein's arguments and rejecting them); David M. Kennedy, Sunday Book Review, Sep. 19, 2004, N.Y. Times, http://www.nytimes.com/2004/09/19/books/review/19KENNEDY.html (last visited June 14, 2008) ("Roosevelt's unfinished revolution may be destined to stay unfinished, for reasons embedded in our history and values.").

[92] *See generally* Steven Teles, The Rise of the Conservative Legal Movement (2008).

as the Ninth Amendment or the Fourteenth Amendment's privileges or immunities clause, to counter these conservative trends.

Even today, it would make a huge difference if the Supreme Court adopted a transformative pragmatic approach to rights issues. Here are a few examples to begin the discussion. The Court would strike down the death penalty because the legal system makes too many mistakes and is affected by racial bias, as well as by wealth disparities. Affirmative action would receive lesser scrutiny because a context-based examination would not permit treating benign discrimination the same as malicious discrimination.

In assessing any proposed future abortion restrictions, the Court would acknowledge that women will still get abortions either by travelling abroad or from potentially unscrupulous black-market physicians. Even some notable American Catholic conservatives such as Doug Kmiec have said the chances of making abortion illegal are limited. Indeed, Germany's Constitutional Court initially required a legislative ban on abortion but has since relented because the penalties were essentially unenforceable. Moreover, the authorities are never likely to search out and vigorously prosecute women who have made the difficult abortion decision. Of course, there are profound moral arguments on both sides but the pragmatic realities should receive more attention.

Not all the results would be liberal. The Court would be less separationist on religion given the reality that religion and the public square cannot be kept apart. The fiction of "ceremonial deism" regarding Sunday closing laws, legislative chaplains, and friezes on the Supreme Court's walls would be jettisoned. Indeed, the Court has already moved in a direction that is more tolerant of religion. The contorted *RAV* decision would be reversed. Some issues, however, would be tough, such as socioeconomic rights. The Court would nonetheless reject the artificial distinction between positive and negative rights.

Thus, the South African Constitutional Court is important because it highlights a new and relatively successful progressive approach. It is therefore no accident that Justice Ginsburg spoke about foreign law's significance on her visit to the Constitutional Court. It is also no accident that a man with African roots, Barack Obama, has become president of the United States given his transformative, inclusive (bringing red and blue states together), and pragmatic message akin to *ubuntu*. Perhaps, the Supreme Court's new willingness to look at foreign law will lead it to more fully embrace human rights again one day. Though

South Africans welcomed Senator Robert Kennedy's visit, he spoke of the powerful impact that South Africa had on him.[93] I hope this book strengthens South Africa's impact on the United States.

[93] Robert F. Kennedy, "Suppose God is Black," Look Magazine, Aug. 23, 1966 ("With all of the difficulties and suffering I had seen, still I left tremendously moved by the intelligence, determination, the cool courage of the young people, and their allies scattered throughout the land.").

Index

Breinigsville, PA USA
23 June 2010
240441BV00002B/3/P